Dangerous Strait

Dangerous Strait

THE U.S. – TAIWAN – CHINA CRISIS

NANCY BERNKOPF TUCKER, EDITOR

COLUMBIA UNIVERSITY PRESS   NEW YORK

COLUMBIA UNIVERSITY PRESS
Publishers Since 1893
New York, Chichester, West Sussex
Copyright © 2005 Columbia University Press
All rights Reserved

Library of Congress Cataloging-in-Publication Data

Dangerous strait : the U.S.—Taiwan—China crisis /
    Nancy Bernkopf Tucker, editor.
    p.   cm.
    Includes bibliographical references and index.
    ISBN 0-231-13564-5 (cloth : alk. paper)—ISBN 0-231-50963-4
    (electronic)
        1. United States—Foreign relations—China. 2. China—
    Foreign relations—United States. 3. United States—Foreign
    relations—Taiwan. 4. Taiwan—Foreign relations—United States.
    5. China—Foreign relations—Taiwan. 6. Taiwan—Foreign
    relations—China. 7. Taiwan Strait—Strategic aspects. I. Tucker,
    Nancy Bernkopf.

    E183.8.C5D26 2005
    327.73051'09'045—dc22
                                                    2004059373

Columbia University Press books are printed on
permanent and durable acid-free paper

Designed by Lisa Hamm
Printed in the United States of America
c 10 9 8 7 6 5 4 3 2

Contents

Acknowlegments

ALL THE AUTHORS who contributed to this book owe debts of grati-
tude to organizations that supported their research, employers
who provided nurturing environments for inquiry and exploration, as well as families willing to endure separation and irritability during research travel and late night writing. We all hope that their investments in our effort have proven worthwhile.

Two sponsors in particular must be singled out. The Smith Richardson
Foundation has made dozens of projects on the international relations of
East Asia possible in recent years when most foundations have turned their
attention to other parts of the world or to entirely different categories of
problems. SRF has thereby performed a great service to the country and
provided much needed aid to scholars. This volume, among others, would
not have been undertaken without SRF support and encouragement, particularly the continuing patience and goodwill of the Foundation's senior
vice president Marin Strmecki.

The book also benefited from the interest of individuals in the Intelligence and Research Bureau of the Department of State and especially the
Assistant Secretary Thomas Fingar who saw our inquiry as a contribution
to the deliberations of policy makers in the US government. To this end, he
invited the authors to present their research in a workshop during the summer of 2003 where the ideas and the substance could be discussed and debated. The event stimulated a day of rich exchange among several dozen at-

tendees, posing new ways of looking at old dilemmas and sparking serious inquiry into both the future of Taiwan and where the triangular US-Taiwan-China relationship might be headed. The authors of these essays anticipate that the resulting volume will do no less.

A NOTE ON ROMANIZATION

It is difficult to select one romanization system that will satisfy scholars and activists in the United States, Taiwan, and China. The following rules guided the authors of this volume:

1. All political figures on Taiwan are romanized as they spell their names, or under the old Wade-Giles system. (The rule also extends to the large political party known as the Kuomintang.)

2. For reasons of uniformity, and in recognition of the fact that electronic databases and card catalogs increasingly utilize *pinyin* romanization, academic authors and footnote contents appear in *pinyin*.

3. All other terms and individuals have been romanized using *pinyin*.

Contributors

RICHARD BUSH is director of the Center for Northeast Asian Policy Studies (CNAPS) and a senior fellow in Foreign Policy Studies at the Brookings Institution in Washington DC. He previously served as chairman of the board and managing director of the American Institute in Taiwan and as National Intelligence Officer for East Asia. From 1983 to 1995, he was a staff member of the House Committee on International Relations (formerly the Committee on Foreign Affairs). He is the author of *At Cross Purposes: U.S.-Taiwan Relations Since 1942* (2004).

MICHAEL S. CHASE is an associate international policy analyst at the RAND Corporation in Arlington, Virginia. He holds an MA in International Relations, with concentrations in China Studies and International Economics, from the Johns Hopkins University School of Advanced International Studies (SAIS) in Washington, DC, and has studied at the Hopkins-Nanjing Center in Nanjing, China. He coauthored *You've Got Dissent! Chinese Dissident Use of the Internet and Beijing's Counter-Strategies* (2002)

T. J. CHENG is professor of government and chair of the East Asian Studies Committee at the College of William and Mary in Virginia. Educated at the University of California at Berkeley, he has taught at the University of California, San Diego and, as a visiting associate professor of political science, at the University of Michigan, Ann Arbor. He has written extensively in the area of the political economy of East Asia. His publications include co-edited books with Chi Huang and Samuel S. G. Wu, *Inherited Rivalry: Conflict Across the Taiwan Straits* (1995); and, with Stephan Haggard, *Newly Industrializing Asia in Transition: Policy Reform and American Response* (1987).

STEVEN PHILLIPS is associate professor of history, Towson University. From 1997 to 1999 he served as a historian in the U.S. Department of State, where he located, compiled, and annotated materials for a volume of the Foreign Relations of the United States series examining Sino-American relations during the first Nixon Administration (1969–1972). He is author of *Between Assimilation and Independence: The Taiwanese Encounter Nationalist China, 1945–1950* (2003).

SHELLEY RIGGER is Brown Associate Professor of East Asian Politics at Davidson College, North Carolina, and earned her PhD at Harvard University. Her publications include *From Opposition to Power: Taiwan's Democratic Progressive Party* (2001) and *Politics in Taiwan: Voting for Reform* (1999).

MICHAEL D. SWAINE is senior associate and codirector of the China Program at the Carnegie Endowment for International Peace. He came to the Carnegie Endowment after twelve years at the RAND Corporation. He specializes in Chinese security and foreign policy, U.S.-China relations, and East Asian international relations and is the author of more than ten monographs on security policy in the region, including *Taiwan's National Security, Defense Policy, and Weapons Procurement Processes* (2000), *The Role of the Chinese Military in National Security Policymaking* (1998) and with Ashley Tellis, *Interpreting China's Grand Strategy* (2000).

NANCY BERNKOPF TUCKER is professor of history at Georgetown University and at the Georgetown School of Foreign Service. She is an American diplomatic historian who specializes in United States relations with China, Taiwan and Hong Kong. She served in the Office of Chinese Affairs, Department of State and at the U.S. Embassy in Beijing in the mid-1980s. She is the author of *Uncertain Friendships: Taiwan, Hong Kong and the United States, 1945–1992* (1994)—winner of a 1996 Bernath Book Prize of the Society for Historians of American Foreign Relations, *Patterns in the Dust: Chinese-American Relations and the Recognition Controversy* (1983), co-edited *Lyndon Johnson Confronts the World* (1994) and edited and annotated *China Confidential: American Diplomats and Sino-American Relations* (2001).

Abbreviations

AIT	American Institute in Taiwan
AMCHAM	American Chamber of Commerce
ASD	Assistant Secretary of Defense
C4ISR	command and control, communication, computers, intelligence, surveillance, and reconnaissance
CGS	Chief of the General Staff
DPP	Democratic Progressive Party
DRAM	dynamic random access memory
DSP	digital-signal processors
EW	early warning
fab	chip manufacturing facility
FAPA	Formosan Association for Public Affairs
FDI	foreign direct investment
FRUS	Foreign Relations of the United States
GSH	General Staff Headquarters
IAO	Integrated Assessment Office
IC	integrated circuits
IIT	intra-industry trade
KMT	Kuomintang
LY	Legislative Yuan
MAC	Mainland Affairs Council
MNC	multinational corporation

MND	Ministry of National Defense
MOFA	Ministry of Foreign Affairs
NUC	National Unification Council
NUG	National Unification Guidelines
PLA	People's Liberation Army
PRC	People's Republic of China
ROC	Republic of China
SME	small- and medium-sized enterprise
SNTV	single, non-transferable voting in multi-member districts
SPD	Strategic Planning Department
SRAM	static random access memory
SRBM	short range ballistic missile
Taidu	Taiwan independence
TFT-LCD	thin-film-transistor, liquid crystal display
TIM	Taiwanese independence movement
TSMC	Taiwan Semiconductor Manufacturing Corporation
TSU	Taiwan Solidarity Union
UMC	United Microelectronics Corp
WTO	World Trade Organization
WUFI	World United Formosans for Independence

Dangerous Strait

CHAPTER 1

Dangerous Strait

NANCY BERNKOPF TUCKER

AT THE BEGINNING of this new century, nowhere is the danger for Americans as great as in the Taiwan Strait where the potential for a war with China, a nuclear armed great power, could erupt out of miscalculation, misunderstanding, or accident. Skeptics might argue that other threats are more volatile or more certain—conflict in the Middle East, terrorism at home and abroad, clashes with angry and chaotic rogue or failed states. But although the United States risks losing lives and reputation in these encounters none but a collision with China would be as massive and devastating.

War with China over Taiwan may or may not be inevitable. The prospect, nevertheless, shapes the course of U.S.-Taiwan relations and significantly influences the texture of Taiwan's domestic affairs. Similarly, though the level of tension between Washington and Beijing fluctuates, depending on security, proliferation, trade, and human rights concerns, the dilemma of Taiwan's future remains a constant and can become incendiary with little warning. Optimists believe that, with time, ground for reconciliation between China and Taiwan can be found and the two sides will be able to arrive at a mutually acceptable solution despite an impasse that has produced repeated military skirmishes and political upheaval for more than fifty years. Pessimists argue that the road to war has been laid, and nothing that anyone does, short of realizing the immediate unification demanded by Beijing, will deter combat. Indeed some feel that progress toward such a calamity has speeded up, making Washington's struggle to keep the rivals at peace, and the United States out of war, much more difficult.

It is not surprising, therefore, that those who write on the interactions among the United States, Taiwan, and the PRC inevitably are drawn to, and quickly become preoccupied with, the situation in the Taiwan Strait. The tendency to focus on the clash of interests surrounding Taiwan's status and future follows naturally from the hazards inherent in the existing situation. For decades the contending parties have struggled toward largely incompatible objectives. China insists upon recovery of the island of Taiwan which it asserts is a part of China's sovereign territory, severed from the mainland first by imperialists and then by the losing side in a civil war. Taiwan's rulers initially believed as adamantly as those of the PRC in the unity of China, but declared that Taipei not Beijing was the legitimate capital. More recently, Taiwan has sought increasing autonomy and international space despite Beijing's objections, with the majority of the population favoring a status quo that shuns both independence and Chinese control. For the United States also, the status quo is desirable since Washington has acknowledged, without accepting, the one-China principle asserted by Beijing. At the same time, the United States has legally obligated itself, in a way some see as a contradiction, to help provide for Taiwan's defense and has asserted its preference for a solution to the problem that will meet with the assent of the people of Taiwan.

The authors whose thoughts are captured in the pages of this book, although centrally concerned with the explosive nature of the Taiwan Strait conundrum, are equally troubled by the misunderstanding that most people—whether specialists or casual observers, whether in the United States, Taiwan, or China, whether inadvertently or intentionally—bring to it. Their purpose in writing these essays, therefore, has been to clarify the history of developments in the Strait and among these entities, to examine myths about past and present policies, and to assess the state of play as well as the trajectory for future decisionmaking. In undertaking this inquiry, they have, above all, rejected conventional wisdom and have tried to rethink the dynamics of the triangular relationship. Not satisfied with generally accepted interpretations or answers to common questions, they have approached the political, economic and strategic aspects of the cross-Strait situation anew. Indeed, they have discarded the usual terms of inquiry, challenging assumptions and structuring different ways of exploring old ground to provide fresh insights into an exceedingly complex problem.

Thus the book shares new thinking, new research, and new interpretations of an old and daunting predicament, and places these inquiries in the context of reform and change in the participant societies. The durability of the Taiwan Strait dilemma suggests to some observers that the components of the problem are as immutable as the confrontation itself. In reality, almost everything has been in flux and the authors assembled here take the fluidity of the situation as the core of their effort. This volume, then, is not simply a collection of disparate views of Taiwan, U.S.-Taiwan interaction or triangular relations, but rather a joint inquiry into a tortuous, perilous, and unstable arena of continuing debate and potential war.

Finally, the authors have undertaken broad inquiries into the underlying issues that repeatedly roil relations among the United States, Taiwan and China. Each contributor has considered the larger context within which the policymaker operates, hoping to add perspective. Toward this end, early drafts of the papers were presented at a workshop held in conjunction with the Department of State to air conclusions and exchange ideas. The essays presented here, therefore, are both the product of extended scholarly inquiry and have been sharpened by the insights of the policy community.

The place to begin the study is in the political transformation that has reoriented the environment for everything else in this triangular relationship. Having started in the 1980s with the coalescence of a strong political opposition newly tolerated by then president Chiang Ching-kuo, democratization accelerated in the 1990s with the election of a Taiwanese, Lee Teng-hui, as his successor. This split the ruling party between a mainstream wing inclined toward reform and a non-mainstream faction determined to preserve existing institutions and mainlander control. Lee, accordingly, took a somewhat erratic path to overcome Kuomintang (KMT) resistance and to respond to the young Democratic Progress Party's (DPP) growing popularity. He declared an end to the civil war, forced aged legislators to retire, introduced direct election of the president, and abolished the provincial government at the same time as he pursued pragmatic diplomacy and engaged in talks with Beijing. During his twelve years in office, his administration repeatedly amended the constitution of the Republic of China to eliminate outmoded practices and, above all, to strengthen the hand of the executive.

Nevertheless, the political terrain in Taiwan remained complex, characterized by partisanship, corruption, and weak governing structures. The hold of the past upon the present was obvious everywhere. Although oppressive wartime emergency regulations had been lifted, lines of authority still largely accommodated the requirements of a one-party state.

After the KMT lost control in 2000 with passage of the presidency to the DPP, the burden of this legacy became fully apparent for the first time. On the one hand, the KMT refused to accept the role or responsibilities of a loyal opposition and sought at all costs to prevent the success of the new ruling authorities. In part, this reflected bitterness, outrage, and shock at the loss of a half century monopoly. It accorded with simple electoral politics as the party scrambled to protect seats in the Legislative Yuan and to improve prospects for subsequent presidential campaigns. Certain members of the KMT also worried about retribution from DPP officials who had been imprisoned by the KMT regime. Special concern arose because the DPP had campaigned strongly for eliminating black-gold (i.e. corruption) from society and pledged to investigate the holdings of the KMT, the single richest political party in the world.

At the same time, the DPP's ascendancy brought a group to power that quickly demonstrated inexperience and lack of knowledge about governing. The members of the party had become proficient at protesting and campaigning, but knew nothing about operating large, complex organizations, about reconciling priorities across institutional boundaries, about providing abundant and effective staff work for officials and legislators, or about dealing with cross-Strait relations and international affairs. Furthermore, as a minority party, the DPP had to fight for every plan and project while the leadership simultaneously struggled to keep hardcore supporters committed.

Shelley Rigger addresses the frustrating stalemate in Taiwan's political journey in her essay "The Unfinished Business of Taiwan's Democratization." Having studied Taiwan's political system and particularly the DPP for many years, she astutely surveys not just the rivalries and personal idiosyncrasies that shape politics, but delves beneath the surface to pinpoint the fundamental restructuring that must be pursued if the new democratic system in Taiwan is to work. The weaknesses quickly become apparent as she examines in turn a series of ugly disputes over the construction of a fourth nuclear power plant, President Chen Shui-bian's declaration in August 2002 of "one country on each side of the Strait," (yibian yiguo) and the use of referenda. As she concludes, "although each one demonstrates the difficulties Chen has experienced in office, they also each reveal aspects of Taiwan's political system that make governing difficult—perhaps more difficult than it needs to be. It is easy to blame individual leaders and political parties for the government's failings; however, replacing the incumbents will not produce better outcomes, unless political institutions are adjusted to allow for effective government." The problem, of course, is to decide which changes are necessary and find a way to achieve them. Rigger's analysis shows that the effort will not be easy.

Some reforms appear obvious. Rigger suggests that advocates hope "reducing the number of legislators will weed out the opportunists and hacks, leaving behind the most professional law-makers . . . reducing the size of the legislature will help it run more efficiently and improve the quality of staff . . . [and] synchroniz[ing] presidential and legislative elections . . . [will allow] the two branches . . . [to] be brought to account in a single election." If new election laws can also be crafted to sharpen competition, recruit better candidates, and imbue greater party discipline, she opines, then perhaps democracy will be consolidated and Taiwan's future will look more promising. These clearly are alterations that will take time to implement even if opposition should disappear. They are just a beginning. Certainly, they are needed regardless of which party wins any particular election. To outside observers, the truly perplexing question is how long Taiwan can enjoy the luxury of its political disarray given the pressing security problems that it faces.

One reason that reconciling conflicting viewpoints has been so difficult since the emergence of the DPP as a serious political force has been its uncertain, and perhaps changing, commitment to Taiwan's independence. Steven Phillips takes on the question of the Taiwan independence movement in his historical and contemporary examination of the most controversial of political impulses on the island. Discussions of the past often point to Japan's occupation of the island as having changed the local dynamic, making of its residents people who sometimes seem more comfortably Japanese in their outlook and customs than Chinese. Beijing has blamed this amalgamated heritage for Lee Teng-hui's allegedly unpatriotic, separatist behavior. Phillips, however, points out that, "as important as what islanders experienced was what they missed: the key events that shaped the national consciousness of the Chinese." Moreover, when the KMT fled the mainland, not only did it fail to bring along a transferable nationalism, it forced a struggle for political rights that alienated those already in Taiwan.[1] Nevertheless, as Phillips clearly shows, the independence movement did not overwhelm Taiwan politics, remaining more notable for its disarray than its accomplishments during much of its existence.

As the inheritor of that legacy, today's DPP wrestles with a formidable political mission and burden. Phillips observes that the party "made independence only one of many issues in its platform, and its leadership fiercely debated how to prioritize the quest for international recognition, democratization, rule of law, economic development, environmental protection, and a host of other domestic problems." Because the threat of war loomed over any declaration of independence, the DPP had little chance for electoral success unless it evinced a moderate profile and emphasized other popular and safer goals. To everyone's astonishment, triumph quickly followed the DPP's readjustment, helped along by factional and personal disputes in the KMT.

Election of the DPP to national office, however, changed the political landscape. Not only did it reveal the fundamental flaws in governance detailed by Shelley Rigger, it also highlighted and exacerbated strains within the DPP. Rigger makes clear that, having first shifted the KMT agenda and then seized the presidency, the DPP "all but accomplished" core principles of "democratization and ethnic justice," leaving "the party . . . hard-pressed to articulate positions that command universal support from its members." Confronted with serious questions about economic performance and political competence, DPP leaders find themselves beholden again, argues Phillips, to "the Separatists [who] played pivotal roles in establishing the DPP and provided some of its most adamant support." Party leaders must cultivate this core constituency which continues to be more radical than the broad electorate.

But it is debatable whether courting the fundamentalists accounts for dangerous moves or if assertive behavior results when the true views of leaders who have attained high office finally emerge. As Rigger shows, Chen's frustration with China's unresponsiveness, and his own domestic political requirements led to, "the statement on July 21, 2002 that Taiwan was prepared to 'go its own way' [and that] laid the ground for Chen's August 3 [2002] speech, in which he told an audience at a meeting of the World Federation of Taiwanese Associations that Taiwan and the PRC were two countries, one on either side of the Strait."[2] In the hard fought presidential campaign of 2004, Chen stressed that Taiwan must act in its own interests, being neither a province nor a state of any country, thereby simultaneously disparaging Beijing and Washington for trying to manipulate Taipei. Chen declared his intention to craft a new constitution for Taiwan by 2006, one that would make Taiwan a "normal, complete, great state." This draft constitution would then be approved by the people through referendum and enacted in 2008, simplifying and improving Taiwan's governing structure, but perhaps also redefining geographical boundaries or changing the name of the state.

Indeed, in Taiwan today although the Taiwan independence movement continues to be a "disorderly, faction-ridden nationalist coalition lacking international support," according to Phillips, it may be true that it "is nevertheless stumbling toward success." Phillips is quick to say that this does not mean a declaration of independence any time soon. The consequences would be too bleak. But it does involve a quickening of Taiwanization—language, history, culture, symbols—to distinguish the island from China. Although the progress toward differentiation frightens Beijing, China's choices are severely limited and unpleasantly stark while Washington remains divided over what to do.

How this accelerated de-Sinification proceeds and with what implications for the political future of the island is likely to be the most incendiary issue challenging the security of Taiwan, China, the United States and the region in the years ahead. Although there is no unanimity even in Taiwan about moving in this direction, the real resistance to it comes from the PRC where an emphasis on Taiwan's identity is seen as indisputable evidence of separatist ambitions. This is not just provincialism run amuck, although Beijing insists that Taiwan remains a province of China, but an assertion of something more. If it stops short of independence, it is deemed almost as provocative. And, whereas the Chinese leadership hopes the trend will be reversed, expecting the voters at some point to strip the DPP of power and bring back more sober rulers from the KMT or its offshoots, Beijing also blames the last KMT president Lee Teng-hui for stimulating the drive to Taiwanize.

Lee Teng-hui, in fact, emerged as a villain for Beijing during the later years of his presidency as he struggled to raise Taiwan's status internationally and reform its politics domestically. Even in Taiwan, Lee became a focus of mistrust and anger among those who felt that he baited the PRC unnecessarily, and disregarded the parameters of security and who could not find a way to cope with Lee's unorthodox, but successful, political style. The Republic of China, of course, has had a succession of colorful leaders and Lee followed in the tradition of authoritarian paternalism, guiding the people's political, security and personal choices through a difficult and contentious period. Ironically, although largely a practitioner of one-man decisionmaking, he cultivated and implanted democracy in Taiwan society and, although he divided the people through calls to ethnic and factional competition, he also unified the population behind the idea of gaining greater respect for Taiwan in the world community. Above all, as PRC leaders contend, he sought to elevate the status of Taiwanese in Taiwan, educating them about the island's history, legitimizing the use of the local language, and promoting an awareness of a distinctive Taiwan culture.

Lee's trajectory in office also led many U.S. policymakers to condemn him as a troublemaker. Americans sympathized with, indeed nurtured, the democratization of Taiwan. They respected the desire of the public to preserve the status quo rather than seek either independence or unification, emphasizing only the centrality of peace to some future resolution of the Straits issue. On the other hand, Lee Teng-hui's energetic "pragmatic" or "flexible" diplomacy, in which he sought to enter international organizations and establish relations of varying kinds with a wider networks of countries, as well as his desire to travel to the United States, appeared to destabilize a fragile calm. Of course, Beijing and Washington had clashed over human rights abuses, trade barriers, and weapons proliferation in the 1990s even as China's bitterness over George H.W. Bush's 1992 sale of F-16 advanced fighter aircraft to Taiwan and annoyance with the Clinton administration's 1994 Taiwan Policy Review had not abated. Thus the crisis occasioned by Lee's trip to Cornell University in 1995 came in the context of Sino-American friction. Nevertheless, the aftermath of Lee's trip easily surpassed other developments for drama, notoriety, and lasting repercussions.

Lee Teng-hui's visit to the United States constituted a striking reversal of U.S. policy, which had precluded trips by the highest officials from Taiwan, and violated U.S. promises, since officials such as the secretary of state had reassured Beijing that it would not materialize. That it occurred at all reflected changes in U.S.-Taiwan relations and world politics between 1979 and 1995. Not only had the cold war ended and China's strategic significance dissipated, but the Tiananmen Massacre of 1989 had undermined the U.S. national consensus supporting relations with China which even in the mid-1990s had yet to be fully reconstituted. At the same time, Taiwan's democratization, its adept use of lobbying, its prosperity and cultural diplomacy all facilitated approval of Lee's visa.

The actual trip, discussed briefly by several authors in this volume, may have added to the provocation, given Lee's rhetoric and behavior, but the fact of the event and the Chinese reaction proved decisive. It cost Lee the confidence of many of his American friends and the forbearance, however minimal, of his Beijing interlocutors. It led to a temporary breach in U.S.-China relations, repeated PRC missile firings in the Taiwan Strait, deployment of two U.S. aircraft carrier battle groups and the rupture of a nascent cross-Strait dialogue.

Although Washington rallied to protect Taiwan and the peace of the region from misjudgment and error during China's provocative missile tests, estimates of Lee after Cornell, both inside and outside the U.S. government, increasingly saw him as a man seeking independence for his people. This conventional view of Lee's motives helped shape the way Taiwan's leader was treated in the last years of the Clinton administration and, more recently, have begun to influence the way his presidential legacy will be evaluated. Richard Bush, however, contends that this interpretation of Lee's behavior was, and is, simplistic. In fact, Lee had a far more complex agenda that varied somewhat over time, but aimed fundamentally at a stronger, reformed Taiwan able to work with, not bend to, China in seeking an answer in the Taiwan Strait.

Richard Bush, as chairman of the board and managing director of the American Institute in Taiwan (the unofficial organization that has carried out the rough equivalent of diplomatic institutional links after 1979), met with Lee often, explored his thinking, delivered bad news, and endured his outrage. Bush came to know Lee Teng-hui in ways that very few Americans did. Bush's meticulous investigation of the record, therefore, is deepened and broadened by a unique personal insight in his analysis of the question of Lee's alleged separatist solution for Taiwan.

Bush argues that Lee as president was not opposed to unification, but rather that "all of his statements can be read as an objection to the specific kind of unification that Beijing was proposing." His examination of Lee's career suggests that, "A China in which Taiwan was a subordinate unit with little or no role in the international community was not the kind of China Lee wanted Taiwan and the ROC to be a part of. Because [China's leader] Jiang [Zemin] had ignored Taiwan's proposals and gestures, Lee saw the need to place more emphasis on the Taipei government's fundamental equivalence to Beijing, to define what Taiwan was, and to pursue a more aggressive international agenda." Whereas early in his presidency he had been content to use democratization to "strengthen his leverage vis-à-vis Beijing by releasing populist forces on Taiwan," subsequently he came to believe that more was demanded of him, his government and, perhaps, of his foreign friends.

As Bush contends, the dispute over Lee's intentions needs to be clarified and settled because it has real world consequences. Beijing's determination to define Lee's views as "splittist" and accordingly as grounds for war made and makes the Strait more dangerous because the voters of Taiwan not only found Lee an attractive figure, but also elected a DPP president who claimed to adhere to the same principles. The presidential Lee, Bush suggests, had a vision for the future that should have been given a more benign interpretation than Beijing permitted. Had China done so, progress toward a mutually beneficial settlement might have been possible, more so than it appeared subsequently. Instead, China treated Lee with mounting contempt and hatred, perhaps helping to create or unloose the man it feared.

Lee's actions after leaving office have been more militant and overtly dedicated to establishing a separate Taiwan identity. In 2001, he publicly identified himself with Chen Shui-bian and became a critical moving force behind a new political party, the Taiwan Solidarity Union (TSU), whose agenda emphasized "Taiwan first" and ethnicity issues. When he openly backed TSU candidates, the KMT expelled him despite his twelve-year tenure as head of the party. By 2003, Lee was demanding a rectification of names, declaring that the Republic of China no longer existed and that the island ought to be called Taiwan. Only then could, "the people of Taiwan . . . muster the determination to be their own masters . . . shoulder the responsibilities they alone ought to bear . . . [and] deliberate on the nation's future goals."[3] This, and nothing less, would make Taiwan a normal country.

On the economic front, during his presidency, Lee had at first cautiously welcomed economic engagement across the Strait, but he shifted in 1996 to a "go slow, be patient" policy, fearful that Taiwan would become too dependent upon China. Taiwan appeared on the verge of jeopardizing its security and compromising its political autonomy. As a result, he lost interest in speeding the three links of communication, transportation, and commerce with China even as the business community became more and more eager. Despite regulations, taxes, and the use of personal suasion, however, Lee failed to keep Taiwan's entrepreneurs from the opportunities that the mainland had to offer, including trade and investment which grew greatly in size and significance during his tenure.

Controversy over the dual nature of economic integration has become a central part of the cross-Strait standoff in recent years. To some observers, particularly those in Beijing, economic entanglement has clear and immediate political benefits. As Taiwan's industrial manufacturing and commercial sales become increasingly intertwined with Chinese production platforms, Beijing believes that Taiwan's businessmen will not only resist interruption of ties, but also pressure Taipei for closer political relations to gain benefits and protections. Large colonies of Taiwanese already live and work in China where they are subject to Beijing's influence. China looks forward to creating a business alliance with Taiwan commercial interests as it did with Hong Kong entrepreneurs. In Hong Kong this arrangement proved important in facilitating reversion of the British colony to Chinese control and to the subsequent implementation of Beijing's model of "one country, two systems." Thus China views these connections as a logical mechanism for peacefully resolving the existing cross-Strait impasse.

There are those in the United States who share this vision of profitable economic interaction which eventually leads to a political solution. Burgeoning cross-Strait linkages expedite triangular business deals at lower costs and eliminate political risks for multinational companies that seek to operate in both China and Taiwan. The gradual but steady multiplication of economic ties are believed to make political association all but inevitable and almost assuredly peaceful.

T. J. Cheng examines the complex issue of economic integration, and from the outset overturns conventional wisdom by declaring that the process is misnamed. Integration, he contends, assumes "a goal-driven process that nation-states legally commit to and consciously promote." That condition, he asserts, does not exist between Taiwan and China. Furthermore, Cheng maintains, contrary to accepted views of this phenomenon "asymmetric economic interdependence does not seem to give Beijing leverage to coerce Taipei, nor does it necessarily turn Taiwan businessmen . . . into a pro-unification force." Even as he concedes that Taiwan has lost control of the lopsided economic flow, Cheng asserts that, "the high costs of replacing Taiwan's investment and suspending trade with Taiwan" buffers the island from China's manipulation and creates mutual dependency. Action on the part of the Taiwan business community to bring pressure in Taipei for concessions to Beijing, he argues, is no more vociferous than business lobbyists appealing to any other government. Finally, the feared "hollowing out" of Taiwan's economy has, he believes, been avoided through careful management so far, but there are signs that danger looms.

Taiwan, then, faces long-term structural problems in its political and economic makeup that its successes in both arenas may not be able to disguise or compensate for as pressure upon it intensifies. That reality puts ever greater weight on its security establishment and relationships, but these too are under increasing strain. In the final section of the volume three essays examine Taipei's defenses from different perspectives, pointing out the strengths, the weaknesses, and suggesting remedies for the future.

Michael Swaine's analysis of Taiwan's military reform and modernization program closely scrutinizes the objectives, achievements, and obstacles encountered. Taipei's determination to revolutionize its defense capabilities, remedy the shortfalls, and cope with Beijing's accelerating military transformation are the focus of his detailed and sometimes painful review of the enormous task Taipei has embarked upon. Swaine's inquiry shows that the Taiwan military establishment has confronted the demands of converting a party army into a national defense force and of accepting civilian control and the oversight of the Legislative Yuan. He also demonstrates that the enthusiasm for change varies by reform, by service and by individual as well as by price tag.

On the positive side, Swaine believes that "the quality of the ROC armed forces has increased in recent years. In the view of knowledgeable observers within the U.S. government, individual ROC front-line military units are generally well-respected, their operators reasonably well-trained and in some notable cases (e.g., air force units) functioning at a higher level of readiness, and the equipment on major weapons platforms such as surface ships is well-maintained." Although harder to achieve, there have also been advances in "creating joint warfighting capabilities among the services."

"On the negative side," Swaine warns, "serious problems remain in coordination, communication, integration, and planning among Taiwan's fighting units—all absolutely critical areas for creating the kind of force that can more effectively deal with the growing Chinese threat. Although concerted efforts are being undertaken by Taiwan with U.S. assistance to improve performance in each realm, progress remains relatively slow and internal debates in Taiwan (as well as differences with Washington) continue over the proper concept and configuration that should guide each area of modernization." Of course, it ought to be noted, that military reform moved slowly in the United States as well when mandated by Congress. Dr. David Finkelstein, Lieutenant Colonel, U.S. Army, Ret., in commenting on hesitation in Taiwan's military establishment remarked that, "those of us in the U.S. Armed Forces who lived through Goldwater-Nichols [the Department of Defense Reorganization Act of 1986] understand how profoundly dislocating it can be when all of the rules of the road and the paths to success are changed in midstream in one stroke. . . . The reform of the Taiwan Armed Forces will take years, just as it took years to change the nature of the U.S. Armed Forces."[4]

Transformation also must overcome the mutual suspicions entertained by a government under the leadership of the Democratic Progressive Party and the armed forces traditionally used by the ruling KMT authorities to suppress the DPP and its precursors. Given the concentration of mainlanders in the upper reaches of the officer corps, one of the central questions raised as the DPP's popularity grew in the 1990s was whether the military would take orders from a non-KMT president. That issue has been resolved, and the military has proven to be compliant, but its compliance remains cautious. Fears continue to be voiced that the DPP will seek independence, leaving the Taiwan military to fight a war it does not support.

Most disturbing for Swaine, however, "is the fact that much of the momentum behind Taiwan's effort to carry out improvements in both hardware capabilities and supporting "software" infrastructure and C4ISR [command and control, communication, computers, intelligence, surveillance, and reconnaissance] systems is still largely provided by the U.S. government." Swaine, therefore, raises the issue of urgency, questioning how serious Taipei is about its own defense. Outspoken in his criticism, Swaine concludes that, "it will remain very difficult to push forward with defense reform under conditions in which the president, much of the military, and the Legislative Yuan regard one another with intense suspicion, when force modernization remains highly dependent on the vagaries of U.S. support and assistance, and when the public is left largely uninformed about the potentially lethal nature of the threat posed by the Chinese military."

Michael Chase approaches the defense problem by looking at U.S.-Taiwan security cooperation, exploring the evolution of that relationship and the advantages and problems it has entailed for both participants. In the context of the disruption of diplomatic relations and renunciation of the Mutual Defense Treaty, which left little more than arms sales behind, developments in recent years have been extraordinary. Chase details the large number of projects and dialogues and training ventures that engage Taiwan with the U.S. in improving the island's "software" capabilities. The common view of a largely isolated Taiwan military, a picture shared by all but the innermost circle of specialists, is greatly outdated as Chase's essay makes clear. Not only are Taiwan military officers being educated at U.S. military academies and war colleges, there are regular U.S.-Taiwan Defense Review Talks and annual discussions at Monterey, California which encompass Taiwan's civilian as well as military security establishment and range broadly over bilateral and regional issues. High-level defense officials travel to the United States, call at the Pentagon, and attend conferences. Probably, of greater moment, the U.S. military sends representatives to Taiwan to observe military exercises and gauge capabilities. At the same time, new arms sales procedures have eliminated special Taiwan-only requirements and allowed for transactions when needed rather than on a preset schedule. In the view of the Pentagon, the new order has made a significant contribution both to Taiwan's preparedness and to the potential effectiveness of joint action were that to prove necessary.

Cooperation has not always proceeded smoothly, however, and Chase points to "emerging differences between Washington and Taipei over weapons procurement and threat perceptions." Various constituencies in the United States have voiced frustration at not being able to make the sales of potent and expensive weapons systems to Taiwan long sought by Taipei and approved by the George W. Bush administration. In part these difficulties have arisen from the greater democratization of the procurement process in which the Legislative Yuan has unprecedented leverage over acquisitions and from financial constraints. Delay also appears to be a product of conflicting assessments of the performance and appropriateness of specific weapons and pricing policies as well as disparate estimates of whether Beijing will attack Taiwan. Thus, Chase points out that officials in Taiwan resent what they characterize as the overbearing and patronizing behavior of their American interlocutors and the Americans believe that Taipei is too indecisive and unrealistic.

It is, of course, striking and deeply troubling to find, as both Swaine and Chase do, that in spite of growing military interaction between Washington and Taipei, and a rapidly escalating missile buildup on the coast of southern China, the United States and Taiwan differ increasingly as to the degree of jeopardy that Taiwan is in. Indications are that in Taipei officials actually believe that Washington exaggerates the danger to the island. Some appear to think that China's stake in cross-Strait economic interaction and global markets provide Taiwan an invulnerable shield. At the same time, Taiwan authorities may fear the unpopularity of military expenditures or simply want to shift the defense burden to the United States. Under any of these circumstances, security cooperation, newly revived, may be doomed. If Washington and Taipei are truly so far apart on their readings of Beijing's intentions, Taipei could undertake policies that the United States might deem provocative and would refuse to support or defend. Taipei's confidence in its understanding of China's intentions and its possession of a U.S. deterrent could comprise two huge miscalculations.

A final aspect of the security dilemma in the Taiwan Strait, to be discussed here, is the role of the United States. Although there is no formal alliance between Washington and Taipei, the United States under the terms of the Taiwan Relations Act of 1979 is obliged to sell weapons to Taiwan to allow it to provide for its own defense and to view any assault upon the island by China with "grave concern." At the same time, the United States wants no war with China and values growing economic and strategic ties with Beijing. Whether Washington would go beyond lamentation and do something in the event of a violent confrontation in the Strait remains uncertain although increasingly some anticipate that the United States would react while others insist that Washington must clarify its position to avoid a dangerous crisis.

In the volume's final essay, I examine the debate regarding Washington's traditional policy of strategic ambiguity. After tracing the origins of the approach and the challenges that developed to it over the years, I contend that the conditions under which the policy was devised still pertain and that it would be a costly mistake to jettison it. I make this argument in the face of a growing chorus of those who insist that the hazards inherent in the Strait situation demand greater clarity regarding the U.S. position and its intentions. To these people in the government and the think tank world, it appears wise to set out markers so that both Taipei and Beijing will know what not to do lest they provoke a U.S. reprisal or sacrifice Washington's support. Essentially they wish to impose strategic clarity upon a heretofore ambiguous policy.

I counter this popular view by showing why it is misguided, laying out and analyzing its flaws and disadvantages. Among the most important problems with strategic clarity is that no one can predict all possible contingencies, and that by attempting to define what the United States will do under specific circumstances, policymakers will encourage probing, not eradicate it. Furthermore, having announced policies and made bargains, the government will have undertaken prior commitments that limit its options, tossing aside the very flexibility that strategic ambiguity was designed to impart to the complex problem of cross-Strait relations. Since American domestic politics will determine Washington's reaction to developments between China and Taiwan as much, or more, than circumstances in the Strait, no president will want to be constrained by decisions made in the past—his own or, even less, those of a predecessor. Indeed, in times of potential war, the president, his cabinet, and his advisers will want to be able to determine policy independently and the commander-in-chief and his military establishment will want to be free to utilize force in the national interest.

Each of these essays has in one way or another challenged existing views of the alarming confrontation in the Taiwan Strait and sought fresh understandings of the dynamics in Taiwan or among Taiwan, China, and the United States that make the impasse there endure from year to year and decade to decade. Conditions obviously are too fraught with peril for decisionmakers, public intellectuals, or the U.S. citizenry to ignore the situation or accept flawed conventional knowledge. In the coming months and years, flexibility and change will be at the heart of successful policies that prevent disaster. The only truly immutable facts are that Taiwan will remain 100 miles from the Chinese mainland, hostage to China's power and politics, but also a threat to China's development and relations with the United States. Beyond these verities, interpretation and debate take over.

Sometimes war appears to come closer than at other times. At these moments, patience has worn thin, innovation dried up, and political challenges seem about to prevail over sober thought. When the confrontations have receded, as they have so far, all participants congratulate themselves for having weathered the storm. One side or another feels satisfied at having exerted sufficient coercion or resisted the temptation to wield force or rallied the people to stand firm or sold the right weapons. None are sufficiently appreciative of the fact that some mishap did not engulf them or irresponsibility overwhelm rational decisionmaking. Whether the precariousness of the confrontation in the Strait will permit this unstable situation to continue long enough for a peaceful denouement is today unclear. For now, nevertheless, the United States has no good alternatives to participation in an unnerving confrontation fraught with uncertainty and danger.

CHAPTER TWO:

The Unfinished Business of Taiwan's Democratization

SHELLEY RIGGER

MOST OBSERVERS agree that Taiwan's democratic transition was complete when, in spring 2000, Chen Shui-bian, the candidate of the island's oldest opposition party, was elected president of the Republic of China on Taiwan. Chen's inauguration marked a critical moment in the island's political development: the first transfer of national governing authority to a representative of a political party other than the long-time ruling party, the Kuomintang (KMT). Even as they celebrated the achievement of party alternation in Taiwan, however, political observers on and off the island saw profound challenges facing the new administration. As one of Chen's top advisers said a few days after the election, "I was euphoric for the first three hours or so. Then I got really scared, thinking about what was ahead."

In the early months of Chen's presidency, there was a widespread feeling that stumbles and missteps were inevitable, but that Chen and his party would soon find their footing. The setbacks of those early months seemed an acceptable price to pay for a breakthrough on the road to democracy. By the midpoint of Chen's presidency, however, the mood had turned gloomy. A column from the *Economic Daily News* published in December 2002 conveyed the growing sense of frustration and anxiety emanating from Taipei:

During the more than two years in which the DPP [Democratic Progressive Party] has been in power, national affairs have been chaotic and the economy has declined; despite the various rationalizations it resorts to, the ruling group cannot escape responsibility. The high-sounding excuse that was used in the initial period of the administration was that with new hands on the job it was difficult to avoid an inadequacy of experience, and that constant sharpening and refining was needed. But half of the administration's term of office has already passed, and it is hard to exercise that excuse any more; nevertheless, today's administration can still be described as having an inadequacy of experience and the need for constant sharpening and refining. Besides the fundamental reason that the DPP is lacking in talented people, an even more important factor is that those in power do not know to use people properly; they frequently appoint the wrong people to the wrong post, even viewing important national officials as mere decorations or playthings, or as people given positions as a reward for services rendered. They treat the administration of the country as a children's game, trampling down the dignity of government officials and completely destroying the government's most important base of support.[1]

Foreign observers have tended to be more circumspect in their criticism; it is hard to find such a direct assault on Chen in the English-language press. However, a toned-down (and more even-handed) version of the *Economic Daily News* editorialist's exasperation can be read in the 2001 *White Paper* of the American Chamber of Commerce in Taiwan:

Overall government performance has suffered as well from the new Administration's lack of governmental experience and shortage of technocrats. This inexperience coupled with disputes between various DPP factions and between the President's Office and party members in the executive branch and the Legislature often results in inconsistent expressions of government policy. It has also led to two Cabinet reshuffles, including the change in premier. The separation of power issue among the President's Office, the Cabinet, and the Legislature poses a pressing task for the new government. This has had a continuing impact on the Chen Administration's ability to achieve policy consistency and administrative efficiency. In short, as many analysts point out, "The ruling party hasn't learned how to rule, and the opposition party hasn't learned how not to rule." Critics have labeled the DPP as incompetent, and the KMT as obstructionist.[2]

AMCHAM's anxious assessment—emphasizing DPP inexperience and KMT obstructionism—captures the tone of much of the discourse abroad about Taiwan's politics during Chen Shui-bian's first term. The events surrounding his reelection in March 2004 only deepened foreign observers' concern.

Chen's critics point to a number of events as examples of his administration's poor performance. Especially prominent are the (mis)handling of the fourth nuclear power plant construction project (which led Chen's first premier, former defense minister Tang Fei, to resign in October 2000), Chen's August 2002 description of Taiwan and the PRC as "one country on each side of the Strait," and the administration's determination to carry out a referendum vote alongside the presidential balloting in March 2004. These incidents each illuminate weaknesses plaguing Chen's administration.

The fourth nuclear power plant has been under construction—and under attack—for more than a decade, and Chen's party, the DPP, has helped lead the charge against it from the beginning.[3] One of Chen's most important campaign promises to his party's core supporters was to roll back policies promoting nuclear power as a solution to Taiwan's growing energy needs. Thus, less than a year into his presidency, Chen's administration announced that it would not release funds that the Legislative Yuan had allocated for completing construction of the island's fourth nuclear power plant. The decision to halt construction came after an extended debate, one that many observers thought would end in compromise. Instead, just hours after a closed-door meeting with Lien Chan, the leader of the parliamentary opposition (a coalition of the KMT and People First Party [PFP] controlled a narrow majority of seats in the legislature), Chen's administration announced that the plant's funding would be cancelled. KMT and PFP leaders were outraged, and some KMT and PFP legislators launched a recall against Chen, hoping to remove him from office.

The recall idea was not popular with voters, however, and Chen's opponents eventually thought better of it and called it off. Nonetheless, the incident spooked foreign investors, and relations between the presidential office and the opposition caucus in the legislature reached their nadir.[4] In particular, many observers viewed the incident as proof that Chen was more interested in ideological purity than economic pragmatism. Also, many observers believed that Chen's decision to release the information just after meeting with Lien meant that he either intended to provoke the opposition or else was appallingly ham fisted in his politicking—either way, the result was discouraging.

Chen's approach to cross-Strait relations—while falling short of foreign policymakers' worst fears—reinforces the suspicion that he is ready to put ideology ahead of practical considerations. In the first two years of his presidency, Chen took what his party saw as a conciliatory line toward Beijing.

He knew that his biggest political liability domestically was voters' fear that electing him would lead to conflict with the PRC. He also was aware that his greatest challenge on the international front was the perception that Chen and his party were "closet independence supporters" whose retreat from a strong pro-independence stance was purely tactical. To address these fears, Chen spent the first two years of his presidency distancing himself from the independence camp. His inaugural address paid homage to the "Republic of China," and he pledged that, "during my term in office, I will not declare independence, I will not change the national title, I will not push forth the inclusion of the so-called 'state-to-state' description in the Constitution, and I will not promote a referendum to change the status quo in regard to the question of independence or unification. Furthermore, there is no question of abolishing the Guidelines for National Unification and the National Unification Council."[5] This formulation has come to be called the "Five Nos." Chen also paid lip service, at least, to economic policies aimed at promoting cross-Strait trade and investment, and rolled back some of his predecessor's restrictions on cross-Strait economic ties. He offered to meet with PRC leaders, and later even set forth "political integration" with the Mainland as a goal.[6]

This policy was effective, in that it stabilized Taiwan's relations with the PRC and prevented the precipitous downturn that many had expected would follow a DPP victory in national elections. However, the policy failed to persuade Chen's domestic opponents and PRC interlocutors that he was sincere about pursuing better relations across the Strait. Political attacks from his domestic opponents—including the Sino-phobic wing of his own party—raged on. Beijing continued to stonewall Chen's overtures, demanding that Taiwan accept its One China principle before negotiations could begin.[7] After two years without a response to what the Chen team saw as genuine concessions, Chen withdrew toward the comfort of his party base. The statement on July 21, 2002 that Taiwan was prepared to "go its own way" laid the ground for Chen's August 3 speech, in which he told an audience at a meeting of the World Federation of Taiwanese Associations that Taiwan and the PRC were two countries, one on either side of the Strait.[8]

Beijing greeted the "one country on either side" statement as confirmation that Chen's true intention was to create an independent Taiwan. Many in the United States, too, reacted with dismay. As the French scholar François Godement put it, "In Washington, there is nothing that any U.S. administration, even the 'whatever it takes' George W. Bush variety, dislikes more than being led by the nose from Taipei: even more so if it creates difficulties for an already tense relationship with China."[9]

In the year following his August 2002 statement, Chen did not retreat from his stance. Although denying that the statement was a gesture toward independence, Chen repeated the phrase, even suggesting that it would be the "central theme" of his reelection campaign in 2004.[10] Whether or not the incident revealed Chen as a "closet independence advocate" (as PRC commentators asserted), it left little doubt that the lack of cooperation from Beijing had left Chen extremely vulnerable to pressure from fundamentalists in his party. Clearly, Chen's ability to reshape his party's position on cross-Strait relations was limited.

A third issue arising in Chen's first term, the referendum debate, adds to the suspicion stimulated by the nuclear power plant controversy and cross-Strait debates that Chen is willing to put aside policy prudence in order to gain a short-term political advantage.[11] The notion of using referendums to resolve key policy dilemmas facing the island is not new, but it gained unprecedented momentum in the spring and summer of 2003, when Chen and his party threw their weight behind the idea. One reason for the burst of enthusiasm was political: party strategists hoped that conducting a referendum on an issue of great importance to Chen's core supporters would increase turnout by those groups for the presidential election, and might even mobilize undecided voters behind the president. Three issues, in particular, were frequently suggested as potential topics of popular votes: Taiwan's participation in the World Health Organization (WHO), the cancellation of the fourth nuclear power plant, and reforms to the legislature.

The idea that Taiwan might hold national referendums was intensely troubling to PRC leaders for two reasons. First, the notion of referendum is linked to independence historically; the first referendum advocates were motivated by a desire to hold a plebiscite on independence. Even more worrisome to Beijing is the possibility—raised in late September 2003—that Taiwan might hold a referendum to ratify a new constitution, which could easily slip into to an overt statement of independence. Even if referendums are limited to domestic policy issues, the concept of a referendum—in which the people of Taiwan directly determine their fate—suggests a level of sovereignty that Chinese leaders are reluctant to concede. The implications of referendum for cross-Strait relations were so troubling that the United States signaled its concern to Taiwan's leaders in private and public forums.

KMT and PFP legislators calling themselves the "Pan-Blue" alliance seemed to have stopped the referendum juggernaut in November 2003, when they passed legislation to enable national referendums, but under conditions that were impossible for Chen to meet in time for a March 2004 vote. The only exception to the time-consuming procedure established in the new law was a clause allowing a referendum in the event Taiwan's sovereignty was threatened—what came to be called the "defensive referendum." Within days of the bill's passage, Chen declared that the precondition had been met—PRC missile deployments targeting Taiwan constituted a threat to sovereignty—and a defensive referendum was therefore justified. He announced that he would proceed with plans for a such a vote on March 20, 2004, presidential election day.

Chen's decision to push forward despite the legislature's action, foreign criticism, and unfavorable reports from public opinion surveys underscored his determination to carry out a referendum concurrent with the presidential election. The newly passed Referendum Law stipulated a narrow range of topics for a defensive referendum, and in the end the two questions put before the voters proved anodyne.[12] Still, the measures failed. Responding to a Pan-Blue call to boycott the referendum, many voters declined to ask for the ballots, so that the tally failed to reach the level of 50 percent participation by eligible voters, as required in the Referendum Law. But although Chen had insisted that succeeding in the referendum was more important to him than his own reelection, the failed referendum actually represented a significant victory for Chen: he forced the Pan-Blues to drop their opposition to referendums in general, he pushed through enabling legislation and he established a precedent for future votes—which is precisely the aspect that is most troubling to Beijing.

Each of these incidents—the fourth nuclear power plant, the "one country on either side" statement, and the decision to pursue a referendum—can be viewed as evidence of inexperience or demagoguery on the Chen Administration's part. However, these events can also be interpreted in another way. Although each one demonstrates the difficulties Chen has experienced in office, each also reveals aspects of Taiwan's political system that make governing difficult—perhaps more difficult than it needs to be. It is easy to blame individual leaders and political parties for the government's failings; however, replacing the incumbents will not produce better outcomes, unless political institutions are adjusted to allow for effective government. Indeed, a key reason for the political traction of proposals like the referendum—and Chen's announcement that Taiwan needs a new constitution—is the inability of existing institutions to balance and resolve the competing pressures that have emerged over the course of the island's democratization. In political science terms, each of these incidents highlights the degree to which Taiwan's democratic consolidation still is incomplete.

DEMOCRATIC CONSOLIDATION

As the "third wave" of democratic transitions subsided, democratization theorists turned their attention to the question of consolidation; they began to study how nations that had recently made the transition to democracy would solidify and secure their new political regimes. The most widely used definition of consolidation is provided by Juan Linz and Alfred Stepan, who write, "by a 'consolidated democracy' we mean a political regime in which democracy as a complex system of institutions, rules, and patterned incentives and disincentives has become, in a phrase, *the only game in town.*'"[13] Larry Diamond, a political scientist specializing in the study of democratization, expands and specifies this definition in his book, *Developing Democracy*. A consolidated democracy, in Diamond's view, is one in which elites, political organizations and the mass public all embrace democratic norms and beliefs and eschew anti-democratic behavior in the political realm.[14]

In *Developing Democracy*, Diamond pursues the concept of consolidation beyond definitional issues. A particularly useful starting point for looking at Taiwan's performance in consolidation is Diamond's elaboration of the tasks a regime must complete in order successfully to consolidate a new democracy: democratic deepening, political institutionalization, and regime performance. Where these tasks are performed successfully, democratic systems take root and grow, until nondemocratic alternatives become unthinkable. Where these tasks are not performed, deconsolidation can occur; the institutions that were created during the transition from authoritarianism can lose their democratic character. Some states revert to authoritarianism, while others retain the formal trappings of democracy (elections, political parties, etc.) but lose the ability to hold elected officials accountable for their actions, provide genuine representation for the public, and guarantee the rights of citizens.

Diamond describes the three tasks of consolidating democracies in detail. By *democratic deepening*, he means the efforts of a new democracy to become more liberal: more respectful of citizens' rights, more accountable and more representative of public preferences and interests. Political *institutionalization* refers to the introduction of "routinized, recurrent and predictable patterns of political behavior."[15] This is important not least because "[b]y defining clear, workable rules of the game to which contending political forces can credibly commit themselves, and by establishing more authoritative, proficient, and dependable structures for mediating political conflicts and interactions, institutionalization enhances trust and cooperation among political actors. . . . [It also will] facilitate trust, tolerance, moderation, civility and loyalty to the democratic system."[16] *Regime performance* refers to the young democracy's ability to provide the public policy outcomes, both economic and political, that citizens desire. If regime performance is very poor, citizens may begin to look nostalgically at the predemocratic period, and may even begin to welcome appeals from politicians who promise to roll back democratic reforms.

THE STATUS OF TAIWAN'S DEMOCRATIC CONSOLIDATION

In June 2003, DPP legislator and party official Bi-khim Hsiao (Hsiao Mei-chin) spoke at the Center for Northeast Asian Policy Studies at the Brookings Institution.[17] While calling attention to the progress Taiwan has made in replacing an authoritarian, single-party regime with a multi-party democracy, Hsiao listed areas the DPP has identified as in need of continued reform. She discussed her party's efforts to improve the functioning of the judicial system and terminate political corruption, reform the financial sector, rationalize the Legislative Yuan and electoral system, increase administrative efficiency and revitalize Taiwan's educational system. She also pointed to weaknesses in the mass media as a shortcoming of Taiwan's democratization.

Viewed through the lens of Diamond's three tasks of consolidation, Hsiao's comments highlight both strengths and weaknesses in Taiwan's young democracy. The eagerness of a Taiwanese legislator to discuss her party's agenda for continued reform underscores the degree to which elites in Taiwan recognize the need to push forward democratic consolidation; the broad range of sectors Legislator Hsiao identified as in need of reform reflects the difficulty of this task.

DEMOCRATIC DEEPENING

Taiwan's democracy has performed best on the first of Diamond's three tasks, democratic deepening. From 1949 to 1987, Taiwan was under martial law, which imposed severe restrictions on civil rights and liberties. Although the ROC government loosened its enforcement of some martial law provisions in the 1970s and '80s, it continued to prohibit the formation of new political parties, tightly controlled newspaper and broadcast licenses, and selectively prosecuted dissident speech. The political opposition was effectively silenced in the 1950s and '60s; it was only in the '70s, when Taiwan's flagging international status began to erode the ruling party's legitimacy, that the movement for democratization began to gain visibility.

Liberalization preceded democratization by many years in Taiwan, in large part because the KMT authorities hoped to retain their status as the leaders of "Free China," the only currency they possessed in a world increasingly willing to engage with the PRC. In the 1970s, dissident editors and writers played a cat and mouse game with the authorities that gradually expanded the space available for political speech and opposition organizations. After a heavy-handed attempt to suppress the opposition in 1979 failed, the 1980s brought a period of diminishing controls and heightened activism. Even before martial law was lifted, the regime declined to prosecute opposition politicians who founded the Democratic Progressive Party. Once martial law was gone, the number of political publications and organizations skyrocketed, and in the early 1990s, illicit cable television and radio stations forced a partial opening in the broadcast media.

In sum, political and civil rights are respected in Taiwan, and the island's government also performs well on the two other measures of democratic deepening: accountability and representation. Political leaders are increasingly accountable to the law, to one another, and to the people. Politicians who venture too far from the preferences of the electorate find it difficult to gain reelection: the Chinese New Party, founded in 1993 to represent the pro-unification current in Taiwan society, saw its share of votes and seats decline steadily, as the party's views fell out of synch with the electorate. Meanwhile, those who violate the law—including high officials—are increasingly likely to face prosecution. Although political corruption remains a problem, substantial progress has been made toward forcing public officials to bear the consequences of their actions. For example, in 2003 Taiwan's judicial authorities launched a far-reaching investigation of Liu Tai-ying, the long-time boss of KMT enterprises, and other high ranking members responsible for their party's vast—and shady—financial empire. Scrutinizing party holdings and candidates' personal financial assets was a favorite campaign tactic and media pastime during the 2004 presidential campaign, and numerous politicians have been found guilty of corruption, ranging from vote buying to abuse of power.

Accountability among government institutions is also strong—sometimes exasperatingly so. With a closely divided legislature and divided government, no one branch or individual leader can exercise decisive authority. The resulting gridlock is often frustrating; however, it reveals the effectiveness of the checks and balances built into the ROC constitution. On the other hand, accountability to the electorate has not always succeeded in Taiwan. Even proposals that enjoy wide popular support rarely sail smoothly through the legislative process, and citizens' complaints about political inefficiency have not resulted in significant power shifts. One obstacle to accountability is the island's electoral system—discussed in detail below—which favors politicians with small, but enthusiastic, support bases. This can make it difficult for voters to turn out politicians who have put their own interests or those of their core supporters ahead of the public welfare. Also, as we shall see, semi-presidentialism, the party system, and the electoral system all work against the enforcement of party accountability through the electoral process.

Diamond's third indicator of democratic deepening is a new democracy's representativeness. Improvement in this area is measured by shrinking barriers to political participation, an increasingly active civil society, and the decentralization of power. On these measures Taiwan's democracy performs well. Twenty years ago, Taiwan was an authoritarian, single-party state, and seemed likely to remain so. But since the DPP was founded in 1986, new political parties have appeared regularly. Some, like the Taiwan Independence Party, the Worker's Party, and the Greens represent ideological positions with limited popular appeal. Others, like the Social Democratic Party, are vehicles for individual politicians' ambitions. The New Party and the People First Party (both of which split off from the KMT), have played important roles in Taiwan's political development. A proliferation of interest groups and other popular organizations has accompanied the pluralization of political party options, giving Taiwanese yet another way to participate in public affairs. The decentralization of power is evident throughout Taiwan's political system. No longer is decisionmaking concentrated in the hands of a president who also serves as chair of the ruling party; instead, it is spread among officials in the executive and legislative branches, while the central government no longer dictates the actions of local governments.

POLITICAL INSTITUTIONALIZATION

Taiwan's consolidation stands up well on Diamond's democratic deepening dimension, but its progress toward institutionalization is less advanced. As Diamond explains, institutionalization occurs in two distinct, but mutually reinforcing, ways. First, institutionalization has an attitudinal component; it is "the settled convergence around (and internalization of) common rules and procedures of political competition and action."[18] Second, institutionalization requires "strengthening the formal representative and governmental structures of democracy so that they become more coherent, complex, autonomous, and adaptable and thus more capable, effective, valued and binding."[19] On both counts, Taiwan's democracy falls short of full consolidation.

To begin with, politicians of all ideological stripes have tried to use extra-legal means to achieve their political objectives—a clear sign that they have not internalized a common notion of the boundaries of political competition. After the Central Election Commission announced the presidential election result on March 20, 2004, Chen's challenger, KMT party head Lien Chan, appeared on television. Many viewers expected a concession speech, as the final count put him 30,000 votes behind Chen. Instead, Lien called the election invalid, and demanded that it be annulled. For a week, supporters of the "Pan-Blue" movement, which had backed Lien and his running mate, People's First Party head James Soong (Soong Chu-yu), occupied a block of Ketagalan Boulevard, a main street in Taiwan's government district. Blue camp politicians filed several complaints and lawsuits aimed at forcing a recount or overturning the election, leveling accusations ranging from minor electoral irregularities to staging an assassination attempt to win sympathy votes. Overturning Chen's victory was unlikely from the start, but by challenging the election the Pan-Blue camp raised doubts about Chen's legitimacy and laid a foundation for four more years of acrimony and deadlock. Overall, the Blue candidates' refusal to accept a democratically rendered verdict revealed the fragility of some political elites' commitment to democratic procedures and norms.

The Lien-Soong team's antics after the 2004 election were egregious, but the Blue team is not unique in succumbing to the temptation to use extra-systemic methods to achieve its goals. The DPP's determination to draft a new constitution, and to implement it through a popular referendum, if necessary, reveals a similar impatience with Taiwan's democratic institutions.

The DPP's effort to dissolve the legislative-executive stalemate and push forward political reform headlined political debates for much of 2003 and 2004. Party leaders first attempted to use direct democracy—referendum—to overhaul the political system. But referendum, too, has its limitations, and these became evident in the fall of 2003, when a number of local communities conducted referendums on specific proposals, including one that demanded the central government add a highway exit to serve an out-of-the-way village. The results highlighted the dangers of putting complex policy issues before poorly informed and self-interested voters. An editorial in the *Taipei Times* on October 6 took the Chen administration to task for promoting referendums on political grounds:

> The problem with these mini-referendums is that they threaten to bring the whole idea of referendums to decide highly controversial issues into

disrepute. People will soon begin to see referendums both large and small as a money-wasting way of telling us what we already knew. . . . The mess that the whole referendum issue is in is, of course, the result of the ineptness of the government's policy. For it was the central government, in fact President Chen Shui-bian himself, who encouraged people to think of the referendum not as a way of deciding between what may only be the lesser of two evils, but as a way of expressing a wish for something out of reach—not an "advisory" referendum but an "aspirational" referendum. [20]

It is against this background of frustration over his inability to accomplish his goals within the framework of the ROC constitution and diminishing confidence in referendum as the solution to Taiwan's institutional problems that President Chen's September 28, 2003 call for a new constitution can best be understood. Clearly, other factors contributed to this initiative as well; electoral strategy and the DPP's long-standing desire for a new constitution are foremost among them. But whether it is a genuine justification or a convenient excuse, DPP leaders consistently cite the failure of existing institutions as the reason a new constitution is needed. Joseph Wu (Wu Jau-hsieh), then the president's deputy secretary-general, expressed this argument succinctly, writing:

As Taiwan's democratization gained momentum in the late 1980s, the fallacies and problems inhering in the Constitution were brought to the attention of liberal intellectuals. . . . While some argued that Taiwan had to write a new Constitution to straighten out all the problems and allow the Constitution to be based on a single philosophy, many thought that a slight revision would suffice. The KMT, which had the majority in both the National Assembly and the Legislative Yuan, ignored the voices calling for the drafting of a new Constitution. Subsequently, six rounds of revisions were made. . . . However, the problems continue to arise and issues are as confusing as ever. . . . The KMT government had its chance to revise the Constitution in installments, but failed miserably. It is time for Taiwan to think of a suitable package that will properly represent our modern society. . . . At the threshold of Taiwan's democratic consolidation, the DPP—as a responsible government and a responsible political party—believes that the public ought to think about adopting a new Constitution.[21]

Many outside observers, including many in Washington and Beijing, view Chen's calls for a new constitution with alarm. U.S. officials have reminded Chen of his pledge not to seek independence for Taiwan, or to change the constitution in a way that would formally incorporate the idea that Taiwan and the PRC are separate states. These responses are rooted in anxiety about the potential consequences for cross-Strait relations of Taiwan's pursuit of a new constitution. But from the standpoint of democratic consolidation, the implications of scrapping and replacing the ROC constitution in an effort to avoid the painstaking consensus-building necessary to change the constitution through existing legal mechanisms are even more ominous. It is understandable that some Taiwanese leaders believe democratization has reached a bottleneck; however, using extraconstitutional—or even unconstitutional—means to break through that impasse could profoundly damage Taiwan's democracy in the long run.

Diamond's notion of institutionalization as a necessary element of democratic consolidation includes the idea that a consensus among political elites and ordinary citizens about the rules of the democratic game is important because it allows political actors to trust one another, and to cooperate. In Taiwan, however, political trust and cooperation are in very short supply. Taiwan politics is hyper competitive; political elites constantly view for position and advantage in ways that undermine their ability to cooperate and compromise on policy issues and promote rational solutions to policy dilemmas. The legislative maneuvering behind the Referendum Law provides an apt, but by no means unique, illustration.

In a special legislative session held in July 2003, DPP legislator Trong Chai (Tsai Tong-rong) and the DPP legislative caucus both offered enabling legislation aimed at establishing the legal basis for referendums. Unlike the DPP caucus version, Chai's bill would have permitted votes on such fundamental issues as Taiwan independence, making his bill especially provocative to Beijing. KMT legislators—who did not a want a referendum bill at all, but were under pressure from constituents to support some kind of referendum measure—should have preferred the DPP caucus version, as it more closely reflected their own caution in dealing with the PRC. However, during the special session, KMT legislators announced their support not for the moderate DPP proposal, but for Chai's more radical version. Their goal was to embarrass the DPP by forcing its legislators to vote against a referendum bill. (They also planned to amend Chai's bill to remove its most offensive provisions.) In other words, the KMT caucus was more interested in gaining a political advantage than in advancing its public policy goals.

Taiwan politics' hyper competitiveness has both historical and institutional roots. The pattern of political conflict during the Lee Teng-hui era habituated politicians to a winner-take-all mode of political combat. Those who rose through the ranks of local politics discovered that losing an election cut them off from the state resources that were the lifeblood of their patronage-based political factions. At the national level, as the Taiwanese political scientist Kuo Cheng-tian writes, "Cabinet ministers and potential ministers became more absorbed in the political struggle than in their governmental responsibilities. Exacerbating the matter was the emergence of a hideous competitive norm among top leaders. . . . The winner takes all, and the loser loses all—forever. This norm of jungle survival has enlarged the costs and risks of democratization. It also greatly undermines interpersonal trust, long-term compromise and political stability, all of which a new democracy urgently needs."[22] Even within the DPP, there is little room for politicians who are not moving up. Three of the DPP's former chairs, Lin Yi-hsiung, Shih Ming-te and Hsu Hsin-liang, have become outspoken critics of the party in their retirement.

Hyper competition makes political trust and compromise difficult, and Taiwan's political institutions reinforce this contentiousness. To begin with, the ROC constitution does not articulate a clear division of power between the executive and legislative branches. In some respects, the constitution leans toward presidentialism (the president is directly elected; his choice of premier does not require legislative confirmation), while in others, it defines a parliamentary system (the president's powers in the domestic sphere are limited; the legislature can use a vote of no confidence to remove the premier).[23] Because the power, responsibilities, and democratic mandates of the two branches are still under debate, neither is willing to yield to other. The result is gridlock.

The fourth nuclear power plant debate sharply demonstrated this unresolved tension between the parliamentary and presidential models of government. The legislature passed a budget that included money for continuing the plant's construction, and KMT and PFP legislators considered the matter closed. President Chen, in contrast, believed it was within his power to defund the plant by refusing to release the allocated money. In a fully presidential system, the president could have used his veto power to impose his preference; the legislature then would have had the opportunity to override the veto if it wished.

In Taiwan, however, these legal mechanisms were unavailable, and the issue became a contest of wills between the president and the legislative majority. Technically, the decision to cancel the power plant's funding came from the cabinet, led by the premier. Chen's first premier, a former KMT defense minister, quit over the issue, leaving it to his successor, a DPP insider, to announce the cancellation. To many observers, Chen's domination of the premier violated the constitutional principle that places president and premier on an equal footing in domestic policy matters. For his part, Chen insisted on his prerogative, arguing that the mandate conferred upon him by his election in March 2000 gave him the power to alter legislative decisions and guide cabinet deliberations. If the members of the legislature were unhappy with the premier, they could pass a vote of no confidence.

KMT and PFP legislators knew of this constitutional measure, but they believed it was ineffective, and they chose not to employ it.[24] They were reluctant to use a no confidence vote for two reasons. First, they viewed the idea of early elections with dread; Chen had just won a presidential election that had split the KMT in two, and many legislators were afraid to face the voters so soon. Second, legislators knew that removing the premier would not solve their problem, because the presidential office, not the cabinet, was behind the decision. Instead of a vote of no confidence, then, politicians opposed to Chen's policy attempted to recall him from office. Recall requires a supermajority vote in the legislature, followed by a popular vote. The KMT and PFP had the votes in the legislature to put the recall before the voters, but with polls running heavily against the idea, they decided to drop the recall effort.

The nuclear plant issue was finally resolved, not by elected officials, but by the Council of Grand Justices. On January 15, 2001, the Justices released a tepid decision in which they said the executive branch's actions included "procedural flaws," and threw the issue back to the legislature. In the end, Chen's government decided to cut its losses on the issue and move on, and construction of the plant resumed.

The battle over the fourth nuclear power plant had profound—mostly negative—consequences. First, it consumed almost half of Chen's first year in office, diverting attention from other important issues and priorities, including a flagging economy. Second, it eliminated any chance of bipartisan cooperation between the chief executive and the legislative majority. Both sides felt deeply betrayed. KMT and PFP supporters were appalled at Chen's determination to assert his power over the legislature, while DPP supporters were furious that the conservative parties would contemplate overturning Taiwan's first fully democratic presidential election to maintain their grip on power. The nuclear issue also damaged Taiwan's reputation among international investors, who worried that with the DPP in control, the island was no longer friendly to business.

The nuclear power plant debate illustrates a number of limitations of Taiwan's democratic consolidation. Most importantly, it shows how a hastily amended constitution (the ROC constitution was substantially altered six times in the twelve years of Lee Teng-hui's presidency) could leave the country without a stable institutional framework in which to resolve controversial issues and could spark, as we have seen, a destabilizing campaign for a new constitution. Even the Council of Grand Justices, to whom the executive and legislative branches turned for a solution to the crisis, was unable to provide a decisive response. The incident also highlights the difficulty of assigning responsibility in the ROC system. The vote of no confidence proved an ineffective tool for holding the executive branch accountable to the legislature. But the proposal to recall the president over a policy difference violated core democratic principles, including popular sovereignty and separation of power. The ROC state needs mechanisms for resolving intergovernmental conflicts that are both effective and democratic.

The nuclear power plant crisis also underscores the lack of incentives for compromise in the political system. An ambiguous constitutional framework need not result in absolute stalemate, even when a country is under divided government. Politicians have the option of compromising to bring such a conflict under control before it can do lasting damage to political stability and economic confidence. In Taiwan, however, politicians have not chosen this path. In addition to the reasons highlighted above—hyper competition and a winner-take-all tradition—political combat is heightened still further by the frequency and expense of electoral campaigns.

Taiwanese politicians never really stop campaigning. Very few years pass without elections; it is not uncommon for national elections to occur in December with local elections following four or five weeks later. The 2004 presidential election is to be followed barely nine months later by a legislative contest. Unlike most parliamentary systems, in which the prime minister schedules elections a few weeks in advance, Taiwan's many elections are all conducted on a regular schedule, which means politicians can (and therefore must) begin their campaigns very early.[25] (Presidential terms last four years, legislative terms, three.) Lengthy campaigns are expensive, and Taiwan's candidate-driven electoral system adds to their cost. The electoral system also reduces the number of "safe" seats. Over time, politicians have learned to maximize the return on their pricey campaigns by cultivating tight networks of core supporters. Pleasing one's committed base (which, given Taiwan's multi-member districts, need not be very large) is more important than appealing to centrist voters, a calculus which further diminishes incentives to cooperate and compromise. To make matters worse, legislative and presidential elections are staggered, increasing the chances of divided government.

Taiwanese leaders' tendency to view politics in adversarial terms is reinforced by the behavior of voters and the mass media. The island's historical experience of electing local officials who lacked policymaking authority created an ethic in which constituent service and local pork barrel projects play a central role in proving a candidate's worth to voters. National policy issues often get short shrift, as politicians cannot afford to focus so much effort on them that they become distracted from the local issues that matter most to voters. Of course, Taiwanese legislators are not alone in their susceptibility to pork barreling and local favoritism. But in most parliamentary systems, the emphasis on partisan competition and party discipline reduces individual legislators' flexibility and directs attention to national platforms. However, Taiwan's electoral system—like its pre-1994 Japanese counterpart—undermines the role of party identification in the electoral process. Taiwanese voters do not use party cues to choose candidates; instead, they look at the personal qualities and past performance of the individual candidates.[26] For this reason, a candidate's record of constituent service and pork barrel spending in the district play a key role.[27] Throughout the five decades of single-party dominance in Taiwan, the KMT was happy to assist its candidates by channeling resources to their districts.

Legislators' tendency to put local concerns ahead of national policy debates is reinforced by the structure of the ROC legislature. For example, the Legislative Yuan lacks expert staff members (including committee staffers) who can perform research and bill-writing for the members. At the same time, cash-strapped legislators maintain large staffs in Taipei and in their districts for whom satisfying constituent requests is a full-time job. Nor do Taiwan's voters have a very good record of holding politicians responsible for their behavior. Loyal local supporters have handed reelection victories to political candidates under indictment for corruption and other crimes— even at a time when opinion polls found a large majority of Taiwanese deeply concerned about political corruption.

The mass media, too, bears a measure of responsibility for the shortage of political civility, trust, and cooperation in Taiwan. Taiwanese journalists have a tendency to shoot from the hip, and they do not always follow up on stories to correct distorted first impressions. For example, during the referendum debate, the unofficial U.S. representative in Taiwan, AIT head Douglas Paal, offered his assessment of the issue in a conversation with President Chen Shui-bian. According to early reports in the Taiwan press, Paal told Chen the United States did not want Taiwan to pursue referendum. Many Taiwanese were furious at what they saw as a U.S. effort to interfere with the island's democracy. Denials of this story, which came from top officials in Chen's office, the Executive Yuan, and the legislature, had a harder time finding an audience.[28] Journalists also tend to reward outrageous acts—from goofy campaign stunts to abusive interpellations in the legislature—with airtime. For politicians competing in multimember contests in which name recognition is an important factor, any publicity is good publicity. Taiwanese have invented a term for the behavior that results: *zuo xiu* (put on a show).

In addition to these behavioral aspects, political institutionalization also has a formal component. As Diamond puts it, the essence of institutionalization is "strengthening the formal representative and governmental structures of democracy so that they become more coherent, complex, autonomous, and adaptable and thus more capable, effective, valued and binding."[29] Here, too, Taiwan's democracy is a work in progress; there are defects in the design of the legislature, the relationship between the executive and legislative branches, and the political party system. In each case, the underlying cause of trouble is historical.

As discussed above, constitutional design and historical practice are out of synch when it comes to balancing the power of the legislature, the presidential office and the cabinet (Executive Yuan). During the Chiang Kai-shek, Chiang Ching-kuo, and Lee Teng-hui presidencies, Taiwan's government functioned as a presidential system. Because those presidents served concurrently as chairmen of the Kuomintang—which controlled the legislature, the military, local politics, and even the mass media—no individual or institution could match or challenge those presidents' authority. The premier served at the president's pleasure, and was responsible for implementing his initiatives in the legislative and executive branches. As a result, politicians and citizens alike became accustomed to strong presidents. Although few people noticed this at the time, the power of the first three postwar presidents was rooted in KMT domination, not the ROC constitution. Thus, a widespread expectation developed that the president would play the leading role in the government—an expectation that was based on practice, not constitutional principle. After 1996, this assumption was reinforced: the president, unlike any other political figure in Taiwan, was chosen in a nationwide election, and thus bore a unique mandate.

In May 2000, Chen Shui-bian was inaugurated as president, and the problematic relationships among the president, premier, and legislature suddenly became starkly evident. When Chen took office the KMT still held a legislative majority, so one of his first challenges was to select a premier who would be able to move his agenda through a KMT-dominated legislature. Chen understood that he would not be able to ram through his ideas as his predecessors had done; however, KMT legislators wanted even more. In view of the ROC constitution's parliamentary leanings, the majority party expected that Chen would consult with their party leadership before selecting his premier.

Chen refused to surrender this important presidential prerogative, although he chose a premier he thought would be acceptable to KMT and

PFP legislators, senior KMT figure Tang Fei. This was not enough to satisfy the legislative majority. But in the absence of a constitutional requirement for legislative confirmation, Tang assumed the post anyway, in
essence taking office as a lame duck. From the beginning, Tang was under
constant attack from KMT and PFP legislators, some of whom demanded
his resignation before he ever reported for work. During the fourth nuclear
power plant debate, Tang's position became untenable (he did not support
the president's position), and he resigned. At that point, Chen folded the
premiership into the presidential wing. Henceforth he would appoint-
members of his own party to the post. The result was a more unified front
on the executive side, but continuing stalemate between the executive and
legislative branches.

Of course, checks and balances are not necessarily a bad idea. They can
act as a valuable restraint on political leaders. The problem in Taiwan is that
gridlock all too often stiffens into paralysis. In part, this tendency results
from the disinclination of Taiwanese politicians to engage in compromise
and negotiation, although their skills in this area have improved since the
wretched autumn of 2000. To a significant extent, however, the halting performance of Taiwan's political system is rooted in poor institutional design.

A disinterested observer could be forgiven for finding Taiwan's constitutional reforms rather haphazard. In fact, many of them were implemented for political reasons, without much regard for their long-term implications. The ROC constitution originally established a parliamentary system,
but by strengthening the presidency, President Lee Teng-hui both reinforced his own power and won the support of the DPP (whose leaders believed their best chance for winning power lay in capturing the presidency).
As he worked to enhance the power of the presidency, however, Lee failed
to pursue complementary changes in the legislature that might have helped
the system run more smoothly.

This model of constitutional revision is not unique to Taiwan. On the
contrary, it is typical of democratizing states. Taiwan is an apt example of
the phenomenon British political scientist Sarah Birch described in an article on the Ukrainian elections of 1994:

> In democratizing countries, institutional design is more often decided
> by political bargaining than by considerations of democratic ideal. This
> approach tends to lead to compromise solutions: semi-presidential sys-
> tems (as in Ukraine) or semi-proportional electoral laws. In either case,
> a situation is created in which one group of elite actors rises to power
> according to one set of institutional constraints, and another group ac-
> cording to another set. The consequence is a displacement of competi-

tion from that between parties representing sectors of society to that between institutional structures. This often means that the public at large
feels marginalized from politics and disillusioned with democracy.[30]

The interactions among the presidential office, premier, and legislature
are only one example of Taiwan's weakness in political institutionalization.
Other such challenges abound within the legislature. For half a century, the
Legislative Yuan served as a rubber stamp for decisions taken by the KMT
leadership. It had no policymaking role, and even as a debating forum it
was weak.[31] Its role changed significantly in 1992, when legislators frozen in
office since the 1940s were forcibly retired and replaced by popularly elected members. In the decade since, the body's independence and clout have
increased; however, it has not fully matured into the authoritative deliber-
ative and decisionmaking body Taiwan's citizens expect. As sociologist
Chiu Hei-yuan, put it, "The legislature is now the biggest obstacle in the
nation's politics, economy and even social development. During the recent
session, the legislature ended up becoming a battlefield for partisan strug-
gles and the seeking of personal gain."[32] Public opinion polls reveal deep
dissatisfaction with the politicians in general, and with the legislature in
particular, which many Taiwanese perceive as unwieldy, inefficient, obstructionist, and of questionable competence.[33]

Some of the shortcomings of Taiwan's legislature can be blamed on
politicians whose motivations for entering the legislature have less to do
with policymaking or public service than with lining their own pockets and
inflating their reputations, for despite the low opinion many voters hold of
the legislature as an institution, the material and status rewards to individual legislators are substantial. However, legislators' weak qualifications and
bad motivations are only part of the problem. Structural factors also contribute to the legislature's poor performance. To begin with, the rubber-
stamp legislature the KMT regime created in the 1940s had no policymaking role, so it was not equipped with the resources to perform such a
function. Today, the ROC legislature is starved of research expertise and
professional staff. Few individual members can spare staff for in-depth policy research and bill-writing, and there are no staffed committees to perform those tasks, either. Legislators recognize these liabilities, but beefing
up legislative budgets at a time of austerity in public spending is not a popular move, and few legislators have the leisure to devote themselves to such
an arcane crusade.

Another institution that compromises the legislature's effectiveness is
the electoral system. Taiwan uses single, nontransferable voting in multi-
member districts (SNTV), with the number of seats in each district ranging

from one to more than ten, but averaging around six. This electoral formula influences the behavior of parties, candidates, and voters, not to mention the outcome of elections. In order for a party to win a legislative majority, it must win multiple seats in most districts, so all of the major parties have multiple nominees in each district. Getting those nominees elected requires careful coordination: candidates must be willing (and able) to divide the party's votes evenly. If not, some nominees will be elected with more votes than they need, while others will lose.

Candidates, meanwhile, face a different challenge. If they base their campaigns on party, ideology or issues, they will not be able to differentiate themselves from their party brethren. Over time, Taiwanese politicians have learned that the most effective campaign strategy is to build a network of loyal supporters that can mobilize their friends and neighbors at election time.[34] The number of supporters need not be very large, since the multi-member system ensures that one can be elected with a relatively small vote share. For voters, the challenge is to choose from among a long list of candidates, many of whom represent the same two or three parties. Under these circumstances, party identification is useful only for narrowing the list of candidates; the final decision must be made on other grounds. For many voters, a personal relationship is the deciding factor.

Taiwan has held SNTV elections for more than half a century. Over the years, parties, candidates and voters have crafted electoral practices suited to this system. One way to win in these elections is to position oneself at an extreme on the political spectrum. Since some district seats can be won with less than 5 percent of the vote, taking a position—in favor of Taiwan independence, for example—that has fervent support from a small, motivated cadre of voters is a good strategy. As a result, Taiwan's legislature has more than its share of ideologues. For moderate candidates, the strategy of choice is to exploit the voters' dilemma and encourage personalistic, candidate-oriented voting. By offering clientelistic rewards, ranging from pork barrel projects for a whole community to cash payments to individual voters, a candidate can carve out a support base that allows him to defeat opponents from within his own party.

The incentives built into the SNTV electoral system are not conducive to political institutionalization or democratic consolidation. Candidates and voters whose political behavior centers on personal relationships and instrumental loyalties cannot provide or demand ideological coherence or political accountability. Party discipline is weak in Taiwan, in large part because politicians know they owe their seats to loyal constituents, not party identity. When asked to choose between the preferences of constituents (who may represent only a small percentage of the electorate) and the demands of the party leadership, most incentives push politicians to ignore their parties and pacify their core supporters. The lack of party discipline undermines accountability and renders the legislative process unpredictable by weakening parties' and politicians' attachments to coherent ideologies and programs.

As we have said before, prior to the democratization process, the Legislative Yuan was a rubber stamp; a single party held the overwhelming majority of seats. At that time, the SNTV system served the KMT's purposes well. It allowed for competitive elections, which relieved social tension, allowed ambitious Taiwanese to rise in politics and supported the ROC's democratic image abroad, but it confined the realm of competition to local issues and personalities. SNTV also served the DPP's purposes in the party's early years, because it allowed DPP candidates to be elected at a time when support for the party was relatively limited. If 10 percent of the voters in a district were willing to choose a DPP candidate, SNTV elections meant the DPP could capture a seat. Winning representation did not require majority support in any district. As a result, the DPP gained access to local and national elected offices earlier than it otherwise would have done, so it accepted SNTV as part of the democratic pact.

Over time, however, the shortcomings of SNTV elections have become starkly evident. Elections driven by personality and clientelism contribute to the overall poor quality of legislators, and worse. Confessed gangsters have been elected to the legislature, thanks to their small, but well-oiled, political machines. Once there, they have interfered with criminal investigations. The grip of clientelistic politics is especially strong in municipal and submunicipal elections. And since "delivering the goods" is expensive, corruption is rife. For most of 2003, 34 of the Kaohsiung City Council's 44 members were wanted in court in connection with a vote buying scandal.

The DPP has come to view the problems in the legislature and the electoral system as items on an unfinished reform agenda. The specific reforms proposed by the president's party include halving the number of legislators, abandoning the SNTV electoral system, lengthening legislators' terms from three years to four, and abolishing completely the National Assembly, an ad hoc body charged with debating constitutional revisions. Proponents of these reforms believe that reducing the number of legislators will weed out the opportunists and hacks, leaving behind the most professional lawmakers. Reform advocates also expect that reducing the size of the legislature will help it run more efficiently and improve the quality of staff. The Democratic Progressives also want to synchronize presidential and legislative elections, so that the two branches can be brought to account in a single election and the likelihood of divided government reduced.

The logic of the pro-reform arguments is compelling, but reducing the size of the legislature could produce a smaller body that is just as incompetent or unsavory as the current one. Hence, the DPP also advocates reforming the electoral system to replace SNTV with a German-style two-vote system. Under the DPP's proposal, each voter would cast his first vote for a candidate in one of 90 single-member legislative districts, and his second for a party. Sixty at-large seats would be distributed proportionally, according to the party vote.[35] The goals of this reform are to sharpen party competition and party discipline, raise the bar for legislative candidates (in terms of competence and professionalism), and promote moderation by making it harder for extremist candidates to win seats. As a December 2001 editorial posted on Taiwan News.com put it, the two-vote system "will change the relationship between candidate and party, strengthen the role of the party in elections and encourage the parties to adopt a policy position, making policy substance more apparent. As a result, it can be anticipated that policy debate and the stance of the parties will become the election focus, space for the emergence of new parties will be diminished and the current turbulent composition of the political parties will tend to stabilize."[36]

The reforms DPP leaders are proposing are extremely popular, but they have made little concrete progress toward implementing them. During the 2000 presidential campaigns, all three major candidates expressed support for electoral reform, and the major party caucuses signed an agreement to pursue electoral reforms just before the 2001 legislative elections. However, no progress followed. An op-ed column by sociologist Ku Chung-hwa captured the mood of the public on the slow pace of reform. Wrote Ku, "The biggest obstacle to legislative reform is the legislature itself. Our elected representatives were willing to make all kinds of promises before they were elected. Most legislative candidates and political parties signed the pledge of legislative reform. But after the lawmakers were elected, they only showed concern for their own interests and shirked their responsibilities."[37] As DPP Legislator Yeh Yi-jin put it, "The stalled program proves that it is impossible for legislators to do something that would deprive them of their power and interests even though so many of them pledged to carry out the reforms in 2001."[38]

It is hardly surprising that legislators would hesitate to vote themselves out of a job, or that politicians who have mastered the art of winning SNTV elections would be reluctant to change the rules. Nonetheless, the slow pace of reform is profoundly frustrating for its advocates and has led, ironically, to a search for reform mechanisms that can circumvent Taiwan's existing institutional framework. Their search for a way around the legislature's obstinacy led them to referendum. A binding referendum would allow the public to bypass elected officials altogether, but some referendum advocates have a more modest goal: using popular votes to pressure elected officials into passing legislation mirroring a referendum question. DPP legislator Julian Kuo (Kuo Cheng-liang) explained this logic in a *Taipei Times* article in July 2003, pointing out that referendum is a tool for getting reform bills through the legislature. Said Kuo, "Pressure from the people is the only way to drive lawmakers to cope with issues such as halving the number of legislature seats, since it is understandable that lawmakers will try to avoid harming their interests by delaying discussion of these bills."[39]

Weaknesses in the legislature and the electoral system are compounded by Taiwan's political party system. According to Diamond, the measure of consolidation in the party system is its coherence, stability, and adaptability. On each of these counts, Taiwan's parties fall short. First, Taiwan's major parties lack ideological and programmatic coherence. The party system is rooted in the movement for democratization; thus, the political arena is divided into the old ruling camp—the KMT and its spinoffs—and its opponents. Most KMT members were attracted to the party not by ideology, but by opportunities for career advancement and by a sense that the KMT was doing a good job. There are few common interests or preferences among these members, and since the party leadership can no longer dictate party policies, the positions taken by politicians in the KMT and its spinoff parties are increasingly contested and inconsistent. Each of Taiwan's political parties contains internal factions, groups of politicians with similar vote bases that band together in the legislature and party congresses to ensure that their constituencies are protected, with little regard to overall ideological or programmatic coherence.

The DPP is similar; with its founding objectives (democratization and ethnic justice) all but accomplished, the party is hard-pressed to articulate positions that command universal support from its members. This is one reason why the issue of cross-Strait relations—on which none of Taiwan's leaders have much room to maneuver—continues to play an important role in Taiwan politics: there is simply no other issue on which the parties can draw a clear line. In the absence of class-based politics, party leaders are very reluctant to take strong stands on social and economic issues, because they can anticipate that doing so will alienate some of their supporters.

Stability and adaptability also present problems for Taiwan's political parties. Obviously, these are somewhat contradictory requirements. If the party system is too stable, it will not be adaptable. Diamond's definition of consolidation requires a balance between these qualities, a balance I would argue Taiwan has not achieved. The island's party system is clearly unstable. The two main tendencies in the political system, which have come to be called "Pan-Blue" and "Pan-Green" camps, represent the pre-transition cleavage between the KMT and its opponents. However, within those tendencies, instability reigns.

The DPP is Taiwan's most stable party, having split only once, and then losing only a handful of members. It also is relatively adaptable; DPP positions have changed markedly over the years in response to electoral pressures and changes in the political environment. This is most evident in the party's rapidly changing position on relations with Mainland China: in 1991 the party explicitly endorsed Taiwan independence, but less than nine years later, the first DPP president pledged to eschew independence so long as Taiwan was not under military attack. However, when that approach failed to extract concessions from the PRC, Chen moved back toward his party's original position. Despite these strengths, the DPP is not without weaknesses. The party's stability comes at the expense of unity of purpose; it rests on an agreement to allow disagreement within the party. When there are differences of opinion that cannot be resolved, the Democratic Progressive often choose not to take a position, rather than risk an internal schism.[40]

The KMT, on the other hand, has split repeatedly. In 1993 the New Party broke off, playing an important part in politics for a few years before fading into obscurity after 1996. The People First Party was formed after former-KMT superstar Soong Chu-yu (James Soong) left the party to run an independent presidential campaign. The PFP's issue positions are vague; its differences with the KMT are primarily political. Soong, the PFP leader, agreed in early 2003 to take the vice presidential position on a KMT-led ticket for the 2004 election, suggesting that the parties' differences are manageable. Many observers have speculated that the KMT and PFP may eventually recombine; however, mutual suspicion and animosity seem quite strong among rank-and-file KMT and PFP politicians. Even after their joint effort to win back the presidency, support for a "remarriage" was weak.[41]

The third KMT schism sent part of the Pan-Blue camp over to the Pan-Green side. Former president Lee Teng-hui founded the Taiwan Solidarity Union to assist candidates in the 2001 legislative election, and the party has since become an important player in the legislature. The TSU is allied with the DPP, but its views are the most extreme of the major parties. Its anti-China agitation has caused problems for its erstwhile ally, which generally prefers the political center. (On the other hand, TSU voters were an important factor in increasing Chen's vote share from the 39 percent he won in 2000, when TSU godfather Lee Teng-hui supported KMT candidate Lien Chan, to the 50.1 percent he captured in 2004, with Lee's endorsement.[42])

The volatility of Taiwan's party system could indicate progress toward consolidation, if it were in the service of useful adaptation. However, the parties' shifts to date have shown little sign of improving the party system's ability to respond to the needs and preferences of the electorate. On the contrary, all three of the KMT's splits reflect power conflicts among faction leaders and their followers within the KMT. Although ideological and programmatic differences played a role in two of the three ruptures (the New Party and the TSU), personal rivalries were a decisive factor in all three. Meanwhile, the persistent failure of Taiwan's parties to present clear policy alternatives on a full spectrum of national policy issues suggests that healthy adaptation is not occurring.

In addition to the weaknesses in executive-legislative relations, the legislature, the electoral system, and the political parties, critics of Taiwan's democratic consolidation point to problems in the judiciary and in civil-military relations. The judicial system is making gradual progress toward meeting Diamond's standards of coherence, competence, and autonomy, but the public is still dissatisfied with the pace of anti-corruption efforts and the judiciary's responses to other challenges. After years of politicization, Taiwan's courts have only slowly embraced the power bestowed upon them in the democratization process. A number of decisions on fundamental political issues are worded weakly, leaving them open to interpretation. Perhaps the best example is the top court's decision on the fourth nuclear power plant, which did not resolve the issue, but tossed it back to the legislature. The weakness of the judiciary is due in large part to legislative inaction; in 2001, the Council of Grand Justices gave the Legislative Yuan two years to revise the laws governing the judiciary. The revisions promptly stalled. Meanwhile, although Taiwan's military clearly is loyal to the democratic system, the distrust between the officer corps and top civilian leaders is evident, and the behavior of the military under extreme circumstances is hard to predict.

REGIME PERFORMANCE

The third task for democratic consolidation is regime performance; the new democracy's political performance and policy outputs need to be successful enough to ward off pressures for a return to authoritarian or semi-authoritarian rule. On this front, Taiwan faces challenges, but there is little evidence of a desire to abandon democracy. According to a 2002 survey, more than 85 percent of Taiwanese agreed with the statement, "Democracy may have problems, but it is still the best system."[43]

The presidential election in 2000 marked the first turnover of power from the KMT to the opposition. In that same year, Taiwan entered a period of severe economic difficulty. Although the economy began to improve in 2002 and 2003, growth was weak, and unemployment high. Many factors contributed to Taiwan's recession, and the most important of these was probably the world-wide economic downturn that accompanied the bursting of the high-tech bubble. Nonetheless, the recession coincided with President Chen's election, which left many Taiwanese convinced that Chen's election was a significant factor. *Taipei Times* president Lee Chang-kuei conveyed this outlook in an editorial published in December 2000. He wrote, "Under President Chen's leadership during the past eight months, the political situation at home became chaotic, the island's economic development began to regress, and the political struggle between ruling and opposition parties climaxed. People's faith in the government became shaky, and their suffering index hit the roof. Taiwan is experiencing a political, economical, social, and cultural crisis that is essentially a complication from a transfer of power."[44]

The search for domestic political explanations for Taiwan's economic misery in the past few years yields plenty of blame for all sides. As Kuo Cheng-tian convincingly argues, during the 1990s the KMT allowed crony capitalism, "a system in which those close to the political authorities who make and enforce policies receive favors that have large economic value,"[45] to develop in order to maintain its dominance in the political realm. The result was a diminished state capacity to manage the economy effectively.[46] Companies in state-protected industries ran up huge debt-to-equity ratios, income inequality increased rapidly, and anti-trust legislation was not enforced.[47] Nor have policymakers managed to turn the economy around since 2000. Although the inexperience of the DPP administrative team plays a part, legislative obstructionism, which has created a bottleneck in economic reform, bears much of the blame.

If the post-transition regime's economic policy performance is perceived as poor, its political performance is not viewed much more favorably. Taiwanese hold the legislature—and politicians in general—in very low regard. Lee Chang-kuei's editorial reserved particular contempt for the Legislative Yuan: "the legislature is often the source of social disorder and chaos. The legislators have the right to make interpellation, legislate, approve budgets, execute treaties and declare wars. However, with respect to the execution of their most important and professional powers—budget approval and lawmaking—the legislators have been incapable and [uninterested]. Instead, they irresponsibly abuse their right to make interpellation, paralyzing governmental functions, and making government operation virtually impossible."[48] Lee's assessment echoes that of other journalists; in a 2000 survey, 79 reporters who covered the Legislative Yuan gave the legislature's overall performance a failing grade.[49]

Taiwan's sluggish consolidation holds lessons for those seeking to build democracy in other nations. Democratic consolidation faltered because in the early stages of the transition, reforms were distorted to ensure the continued dominance of pre-reform elites. As the hegemonic party, the KMT was able to manipulate reforms in ways that prolonged the party's influence at the expense of efficient, effective democratic institutions. Thus, the presidency was strengthened, but without regard for maintaining a workable relationship between executive and legislature, while the rubber-stamp legislature was given power without the resources to wield that power effectively.

The opposition DPP acquiesced in many of these flawed reforms, because at one time they seemed to offer a shortcut to power. But now that DPP politicians have gained a significant share of political power, they suddenly want to "fix" those aspects of the system that work against them, even to the point of replacing the ROC constitution through a popular vote.

Despite its shortcomings, there is little evidence that Taiwanese are about to give up on their democracy and bring back authoritarian institutions. Nonetheless, there is deep frustration with the poor performance of politicians and political institutions, and many Taiwanese believe additional reforms are necessary to complete and consolidate the island's democratic transition.

Whether or not a new constitution is the cure, the evidence suggests that advocates of a constitutional overhaul are correct in their diagnosis of Taiwan's problems. Taiwan's democracy is not consolidated, because fundamental structural problems stand in the way of political institutionalization and improved regime performance. Until the exchange of political power between parties becomes routine and ordinary, until elections become contests over platforms and competence rather than clientelistic payoffs, and until mechanisms are in place to prevent political stalemate from paralyzing Taiwan's government, consolidation will be deferred.

Clearly, divided government and inexperienced leadership have exacerbated Taiwan's problems since 2000. However, the structural problems in the island's political system predate Chen Shui-bian's presidency. Under different circumstances these shortcomings might have manifested themselves differently. But so long as they are not resolved, anyone who accedes to the presidency will be plagued by these same institutional challenges.

CHAPTER THREE:

Building a Taiwanese Republic:

THE INDEPENDENCE MOVEMENT, 1945–PRESENT

STEVEN PHILLIPS

THE POSSIBILITY of Taiwan's formal and permanent independence from China is a source of international tensions in East Asia, the cause of Sino-American discord, and a heated issue in the island's domestic politics. The Taiwanese independence movement, however, can take only partial credit for these developments.[1] To date, changes to the island's relationship with China have resulted from conflicts having little to do with Taiwanese aspirations or loyalties: two Sino-Japanese wars, World War II, civil war between Communists and Nationalists, and the cold war.

For more than a century, control of Taiwan has reflected the balance of power among Beijing, Tokyo and, eventually, Washington. After a series of military defeats, the ailing Qing Dynasty ceded Taiwan to Japan in the 1895 Treaty of Shimonoseki. For the next fifty years, as China endured a myriad of political, military, and social conflicts, Japanese colonial rule brought economic modernization and stability to Taiwan, albeit at the price of institutionalized discrimination and a brutal police state. America's entrance into another Sino-Japanese conflict raised Chinese hopes of recovering the island. With the establishment of Nationalist Chinese control in late 1945, the issue of Taiwan's status seemed to have reached a resolution.[2]

Thanks as always go to my wife Barbara Cavanaugh Phillips for reading my drafts and also to Nancy Bernkopf Tucker who commented on different versions of this paper.

The Chinese Communists agreed, in part. They applauded the restoration of Chinese sovereignty, but called for the island's liberation from Nationalist rule. During the cold war, the Nationalists, Communists, and Americans dominated discourse over Taiwan through the one China policy, which stated that there existed one China and that Taiwan was a province of that China awaiting reunification with the mainland. Today, Beijing continues to insist on acknowledgement of its one China principle from any nation desiring trade ties or diplomatic relations with the People's Republic of China (PRC)—a requirement that the vast majority of nations, including the United States and Japan, willingly meet.

Less noticed until recently were the individuals who built the Taiwanese independence movement (TIM). The movement grew in the context of the Nationalists' authoritarian rule and, until the 1990s, focused on overthrowing Chiang Kai shek and his son Chiang Ching-kuo as the first step toward changing the island's international status. Japan was the first center of Taiwan independence (*Taidu*) sentiment but, as more Taiwanese came to the United States to study or to avoid oppression, the movement's center of gravity shifted. Besides widespread acceptance of the one China principle in the international community, personal rivalries, Nationalist brutality and threats, apathy in the host countries, dispersion across several continents, and disputes over issues such as socialism or the necessity of violence all stymied the efforts of exiled Taiwanese. However, the collapse of the Republic of China's (ROC) international position, the gradual attrition of mainland-born leaders, and the first stirrings of political change on Taiwan in the 1970s heartened activists. The TIM's expansion on the island was due to democratization and Taiwanization, so that by the 1990s it was possible to advocate independence on the streets of Taipei. Elements of the movement's agenda have shaped the platform, if not always the actual policies, of the Democratic Progressive Party (DPP), now the ruling party. The island enjoys de facto independence, even though the mainland's threats of military action prevent Taiwanese from making a formal declaration. Further, Taidu advocates have proved unable to convince the majority of the island's population or the international community that announcing permanent independence from the mainland is feasible.[3]

During the final years of Japanese colonial rule, some Taiwanese called their island Asia's Orphan (*Ya xi ya de gu'er*), a place cast off by China and accorded second class status by Japan. The island was also an orphan of the cold war, as it remained trapped in the one China framework that precluded serious discussion of independence. This "bled over" into scholarship, and the island has not become a significant part of the academic literature on nationalism.[4] For example, Benedict Anderson, a prolific scholar of nationalism best known for his discussion of the nation as an "imagined community," does not address Taiwan in his work. Despite this lack of attention, the history of the TIM offers case studies of nation-building and politics in exile communities. The oft-quoted observation of the famous nineteenth-century historian Lord Acton that "exile is the nursery of nationality" fits perfectly with Taiwan's experience.[5] Anderson notes that exile communities are often among the most adamant, vocal, and well-funded.[6] This, too, describes the TIM's history. Anderson also points out the role of higher education in sparking and spreading nationalist sentiment.[7] The Taiwanese movement was filled with overseas students and was often led by scholars until the 1980s.

Ironically, the TIM experience resembled Chinese exile movements. Ian Buruma's *Bad Elements: Chinese Rebels from Los Angeles to Beijing* examines the fate of post-Tiananmen dissidents in the United States. He wrestles with the problem of whether personal rivalries and the lack of unity among these intelligent exiles represented an aspect of Chinese culture, the nature of all exile communities, or the specific personalities of individual activists. Buruma details how countless dissidents were unable to speak kindly about one another, much less cooperate: "Denunciation is the common poison within any dictatorship based on dogma. And paranoia is not a uniquely Chinese vice. Political exiles fight among themselves wherever they come from: Cut off from a common enemy, they tear into each other."[8] This, too, could describe the Taiwanese experience.

NATIONALIST MISRULE AND THE RISE OF THE TIM

The growth of the TIM illustrates the complex relationship between history and the nation. The events of Taiwan's recent past spurred some Taiwanese to seek independence from China. At the same time, activists consciously sought to shape a version of history that "proved" an inexorable march toward nation-hood, and attempted to place the rise of a national consciousness as far into the past as possible.[9] For example, independence activists at times point to Zheng Chenggong as proof of Taiwanese nationalism hundreds of years ago. In reality Zheng, a regional strongman and pirate during the Ming-Qing transition of the seventeenth century, used the island as a base to attack the mainland in the name of restoring a fallen dynasty. To him, Taiwan was less a homeland than a temporary refuge.[10] Activists have hailed the short-lived 1895 Republic of Taiwan as a manifestation of the Taiwanese national consciousness, even though the Republic had little popular support.[11] The Taiwanese Communist Party (TCP), founded in 1928, also has been placed in the context of independence.[12] Although some individual Party members did support independence, Taiwanese, Japanese, and Chinese factions all fought for influence, and the TCP proved one of the least successful communist parties in the region. Certainly, a sense of Taiwanese identity, an island-wide consciousness, grew under Japanese colonial rule, in no small measure due to the regime's labeling of islanders—which ignored the ethnic and linguistic diversity of the population. This does not, however, prove the existence of nationalism. Only during the late 1940s did a true movement, with organizations dedicated to independence, espousing a coherent ideology and vision for the island's future, appear.

Fifty years of Japanese rule laid the base for much of the conflict between the Taiwanese and the Nationalists. The Taiwanese endured the dual nature of colonialism: law and order in a brutal police state, economic development and exploitation, education and forced cultural assimilation. As important as what islanders experienced was what they missed: the key events that shaped the national consciousness of the Chinese, including the collapse of the Qing, Sun Yat-sen's revolutionary efforts, warlord depredations, the literary revolution of the May 4th Movement, the glory of the Northern Expedition, the epic suffering of the Long March, and the myth of national unity during the War of Resistance. Most Taiwanese were happy to see the end of colonial rule in October 1945, but there existed vast differences in political cultures and expectations on both sides of the Strait. In the latter half of the 1940s, Taiwanese views of their relationship with the Chinese nation and Nationalist state fell along a continuum. Some completely accepted and supported Nationalist rule, others called for greater local self-government, and a few advocated that federalism define Taiwan's relationship with China. Independence, not communism, became the strongest manifestation of discontent with Nationalist rule on Taiwan.

More than any other event, the February 28 Incident of 1947 both created and justified independence sentiment. Taiwanese concerns over inflation, unemployment, corruption, and lack of political participation exploded in early 1947. Unemployed youth, workers, students, peddlers, and small-businessmen briefly wrested control of Taiwan from the provincial administration. Prominent Taiwanese moved initially to limit violence and to restore law and order, then used the opportunity to press for reforms under the broad rubric of local self-government. During negotiations with the provincial administration, islanders enlarged their demands to the extent that they threatened to weaken drastically Taiwan's ties with the Nanjing government. After a week of increasing tensions, mainland reinforcements arrived and massacred thousands—those integrally involved in the Incident, those who had made enemies among the Nationalists, and others unfortunate enough to be on the streets. This brutal retribution changed the face of the island's politics by killing many of the Japanese-era elite, cowing others into silence, and spurring a few to oppose the regime from exile. The memories of many Taiwanese would distill the Incident into proof of Nationalist brutality and illegitimacy, and evidence of the islanders' long-term drive for self-determination.

Even as the Nationalists consolidated control over Taiwan in the late 1940s, their government lurched toward collapse on the mainland. In the wake of defeat, in 1949 and 1950 the island faced an influx of approximately 2 million refugees who carried with them history, political goals, and ideology that grew out of their mainland experiences. As a result, the issues, organizations, and personalities of politics in Republican China came to dominate Taiwan. Chiang Kai-shek created a highly centralized political structure—a goal of the Nationalists on the mainland for almost half a century. The anti-communist paranoia that came with defeat accentuated his authoritarian tendencies. In December 1949, the island was placed under martial law. That, and the 1948 Provisional Amendments for the Period of Mobilization, which essentially set aside parts of the constitution and gave the president dictatorial powers, facilitated the regime's arrest and harassment of dissidents of all stripes. Based on control of political, educational, and cultural institutions, mainlanders dominated discourse over the history of the Chinese nation and Taiwan province for almost forty years. It became dangerous to discuss, much less question, the island's relationship with the mainland, as Taiwan had become the last bastion of the real, "free," China against the alien rule of Mao Zedong's Communists.

A complex combination of altruism and self-aggrandizement, a sincere belief in what was best for the island's people and frustration with a lack of personal success under Nationalist rule, drove many activists. Liao Wen-i (Liao Wenyi, 1910–1986), who often used the name Thomas when dealing with Americans, became the first prominent leader of an organized independence movement. He toiled in exile, attempted to highlight ambiguities in Taiwan's international status, combined calls for nationalism with promises of democratic reform, dealt with Nationalist threats to friends and family, struggled against a general lack of interest in his cause, and engaged in personal rivalries with other Taiwanese. Like many Taiwanese dissidents or Taidu leaders, Thomas Liao came from a Presbyterian family, in his case, landlords in southern Taiwan.[13] He was one of the few Taiwanese before the 1950s to visit the United States, as he studied in Michigan and Ohio. He then moved to China to teach before returning to the island after his father's death in 1939. No friend of the colonial regime, he came under suspicion by the Japanese for alleged ties to the United States. Liao, like many Taiwanese, did not immediately favor independence, but a combination of Nationalist misrule, the regime's brutal reaction to February 28, disappointment due to his failure to win an election, and his inability to shape the ties between the island and China (Liao favored a federal system) pushed him toward a more radical position. Liao was in Shanghai during the events of February 28, but his criticism of the regime led the highest-ranking Nationalist official on the island, Chen Yi, to brand him a rebel.

In late 1947, Thomas Liao formed the Formosan League for Re-emancipation (*Taiwan zai jiefang lianmeng*) , the first Taiwan independence organization.[14] Based in Hong Kong, the League lobbied for a United Nations' trusteeship for Taiwan, followed by a plebiscite. The first years of the League proved difficult. The attempt to create a Taiwan branch in 1949 led to the arrest of one of Liao's brothers and the League's secretary. Liao vied with the Taiwan Democratic Self-Government League (*Taiwan minzhu zizhi lianmeng*), led by Hsieh Hsueh-hung (Xie Xuchong). Hsieh, a Taiwanese communist, had fled to Hong Kong after leading a short-lived resistance to the Nationalists during the February 28 Incident. Her group strongly opposed trusteeship or independence, and had close ties to the Chinese Communists. Hsieh's League offered limited autonomy as a formula to win Taiwanese support. Neither group had much success. Hong Kong did not prove conducive to independence activists, as the Chinese community was divided between supporters of the Nationalists or Communists, and the British had little interest in antagonizing either Chinese faction with independence activity. Hsieh moved to China and Liao went to Japan, which had a sizable Taiwanese population. Taiwanese in the People's Republic found they had to accept completely the Communists' approach to the island, which emphasized the need for class struggle and liberation, not autonomy.[15] The Anti-Rightist Campaign and the Cultural Revolution on the mainland destroyed the careers of Taiwanese communists, who discovered that Beijing could not tolerate their relative moderation and focus on "local" issues. In Japan, Liao quickly found that there existed little sympathy for his efforts. He was imprisoned for seven months for entering the country illegally.

Liao and the Formosan League for Re-emancipation helped create the ideology of independence that later activists would follow. Self-determination formed one pillar of the new movement, and League members would frequently evoke article 1 of United Nations charter of 1945: "The Purposes of the United Nations are . . . to develop friendly relations among nations based on respect for the principle of equal rights and self-determination of peoples, and to take other appropriate measures to strengthen universal peace." They also pointed to ambiguity in statements on postwar Taiwan's fate to bolster their case. The problem was that, for every declaration suggesting the island's status remained undecided, there existed another that indicated the island was irrevocably China's. The Cairo Declaration of November 1943, where Franklin Roosevelt, Chiang, and Winston Churchill agreed that the Nationalists were to take control of the island at war's end, would seem to preclude debate:

> It is their [the Allies] purpose that Japan shall be stripped of all the is-lands of the Pacific which she has seized or occupied since the beginning of the First World War in 1914, and that all territories Japan has stolen from the Chinese, such as Manchuria, Formosa, and the Pescadores, shall be restored to the Republic of China.[16]

Statements by President Harry S Truman in June 1950 and the peace treaties formally concluding World War II in the Pacific in 1951, however, suggested that the island's status awaited final resolution.[17] Nevertheless, other than a short period of time when the survival of the Nationalist regime on Taiwan was in doubt, the Americans *acted* as though they accepted Chiang's control over the island, and that his government represented China.

The early champions of independence discovered that America's oc-casional ambiguity never translated into steady support. The nascent Taidu movement stood on the sidelines even as instability again threat-ened to weaken the island's ties with the mainland. In the late 1940s, ru-mors abounded about possible foreign intervention on the island or the overthrow of Chiang by other Nationalists.[18] Other gossip suggested that the island would enjoy independence with United States support, a Unit-ed Nations trusteeship, or even the return of the Japanese—none of which the Americans considered seriously.[19] As early at August 1947, Spe-cial Envoy to China General Albert Wedemeyer reported to the Secretary of State:

> There were indications that Formosans would be receptive toward the United States guardianship and United Nations trusteeship. They fear that the Central Government contemplates bleeding their island to sup-port the tottering and corrupt Nanking machine and I think their fears are well founded.[20]

Yet, the possibility of independence depended upon events across the Strait, not on the island itself, much less the wishes of a few Taiwanese. In December 1947, American officials considered the possibility of an independent Taiwan only if the Nationalist government collapsed on the mainland and could not control the island.[21]

Three interrelated factors prevented Taiwanese separatists and American diplomats from cooperating. First, many Americans saw Chiang Kai-shek as the only figure with any chance of preserving a unified, noncommunist China. In effect, they accepted and approved of the Nationalists' political agenda for China both before and after the regime's mainland defeat. For example, in mid-1948, an American official in Nanjing wrote

> It may conceivably get so bad that the Gimo may, by one means or another, be removed from the scene. Yet the Gimo seems to be the only element holding this vast country together, and should he go there would be a very strong chance that we would see a return to regionalism, making the pickings much more easy for the Communists.[22]

Even as the Nationalists collapsed on the mainland, they continued to enjoy the support of staunchly anti-communist politicians and publicists in the United States. Most Americans accepted, or simply did not address, the Nationalists' political agenda as it related to the Taiwanese. Second, the United States felt publicly obliged to uphold the status of Taiwan as a territory returned to its rightful ruler after World War II.[23] For example, the Central Intelligence Agency stated that although technically Taiwan's fate was not final until a peace treaty was signed with Japan, the Cairo and Potsdam declarations made independence unlikely.[24] The United States was not eager to become embroiled in an issue of China's territorial integrity—a problem that could only invite comparisons to the era of unequal treaties.[25]

Third, the Americans described the Taiwanese as "politically immature" and unlikely to overthrow the Nationalists.[26] Further, Taiwanese and Americans had little contact prior to 1945. Islanders usually spoke Japanese or one of several local dialects, not Mandarin (*Guoyu*), and thus had a difficult time communicating with America's China experts. In Tokyo, few Americans were interested in Taiwanese affairs or the machinations of a few exiles. Islanders had more specific "defects." American military intelligence officials in Tokyo revealed that many Taiwanese in Japan had entered that country illegally and that "the activities of the League [Formosan League for Re-emancipation] in Japan are financed by large-scale penicillin smuggling."[27] For the next five decades, American officials monitored the Taidu movement's activities and met with its leaders, but refused to make any commitments of support.[28]

TIM IN JAPAN AND THE UNITED STATES

Other activists would follow Liao's example as they struggled to organize while avoiding Nationalist pressure upon friends or relatives on the island, and to publicize their efforts in the face of apathy among non-Taiwanese. In 1950, Liao established the Taiwan Democratic Independence Party (*Taiwan minzhu dulidang*) in Kyoto. Most of his backing came from Taiwanese who had been educated during the colonial era, many of whom had hoped that retrocession would enable them to enjoy greater rights and influence than they had experienced under Japanese rule. Personal rivalries and issues of funding were constant problems.[29] In order to invigorate their efforts, Liao and his supporters formed a provisional assembly in 1955 and a Provisional Government for the Republic of Taiwan (*Taiwan gongheguo linshi zhengfu*) in 1956.[30] Liao would submit dozens of petitions to the United Nations or to American diplomats, all seeking support in the name of national self-determination. Reflecting a key aspect of separatist thought, he used history in the service of nation building.[31] Liao, as president of the provisional government, declared that his was the third attempt at creating a Taiwanese nation and that his efforts built upon Zheng Chenggong's removal of the Dutch in the 1660s and the short-lived 1895 republic. In short, Taiwan was already a nation, the problem was recognition. Expanding upon ideas first expressed in Hong Kong, Liao often evoked America's independence struggle and Wilsonianism.[32] However, it is impossible to know whether this was done out of sincere belief that Taiwan's experience was that similar to that of the United States, or out of more cynical motives. To the Americans, he took every opportunity to claim that Taiwan's status was "undecided" and that the people of the island would enthusiastically support independence: "We Formosans maintain that [the] independence movement for Formosa is absolutely not treason or criminal. It is a patriotic action." Liao recognized the cold war priorities of the United States, and he worked hard to convince the Americans that his anti-Nationalist efforts were in no way pro-Communist.[33] In light of President Truman's movement of the 7th Fleet to the Taiwan Strait and President Eisenhower's mutual security treaty with the ROC, activists realized that America's relationship with the Generalissimo was growing stronger, not weaker, after the retreat to Taiwan.

Liao was attacked by the Nationalists as an American or Japanese puppet and by younger Taiwanese émigrés as one of the older gentlemen who came of age under Japanese rule—relics (*yiwu*) as one author calls them.[34] In fact, most independence leaders had to contend with charges that they were pawns of foreign powers dedicated to containing or humiliating China. That these activists were often foreign educated and courted Japanese and American support only served as fodder for anti-independence propaganda. By the 1960s, Liao's movement seemed "tired" as new leaders with ties to students in Japan became more prominent. Contact between his government and supporters on Taiwan proved difficult, and Liao's relatives on the island were under constant surveillance or imprisoned repeatedly.[35] The president in exile was encouraged to return by Taiwanese supporters of the Nationalists, and was promised employment in the provincial administration and the release of family members.[36] In 1965, he agreed to come home.[37] The provisional government would continue for decades, but would slide into obscurity. Pro-independence historians have written that although Liao's endeavor failed, he created a legacy of resistance, and his surrender opened the door to the next generation of activists.[38]

New voices in the Taiwanese community in Japan added social and economic concerns to the independence agenda. In Tokyo, Wang Yü-te (Wang Yude, 1924–1985) shifted the movement's focus from the Japanese era elite to a younger generation. He helped form the Formosan Youth Society (*Taiwan qingnianshe, Taiwan seinensha* in Japanese) in 1960, and began one of the important early independence publications, *Taiwan Seinen* (*Taiwan qingnian* in Chinese, translated as *Formosan Youth*).[39] His goal was to work among Taiwanese students in Japan and to influence international public opinion. The society, like all Taidu groups, sought to build its presence on Taiwan with little success.[40] By the mid-1960s, this organization demonstrated publicly as the Formosan Youth Independence League (*Taiwan qingnian duli lianmeng*).[41] Shih Ming (Shi Ming) and other activists in Japan made socialism one facet of the independence agenda, a development that would provide an ideological framework for some Taidu supporters, but would drive others away. Like Liao's works, Shih Ming's *Four Hundred Year History of the Formosan People* (*Taiwanren sibainian shi*), first published in Japan in 1962, became an inspiration to many separatists (and was banned on the island itself). This book combined Marxist-Leninist analysis with nationalism. He explicitly connected Nationalist rule to capitalist exploitation, suggesting that national liberation and class struggle went hand in hand.[42] Shih and other leftists encountered two problems with this approach. First, the Japanese Socialist Party and the Japanese Communist Party were eager to see their nation cut diplomatic ties to Chiang's regime, which meant party members had little reason to support an agenda that was sure to enrage Beijing. Second, land reform and other Nationalist policies brought economic development and a relatively equitable distribution of wealth to the island. Most Taiwanese had little interest in class struggle or revolutionary violence.

During the 1950s, influence over the TIM shifted toward the United States as more Taiwanese studied or immigrated there. In 1955, Taiwanese students, including prolific Taidu author Loo Tsu-yi (Lu Zhuyi, pen name: Li Tianfu), organized America's first independence organization, Free Formosans' Formosa (*Taiwanren de ziyou Taiwan*). This group became the United Formosans for Independence (UFI, *Taiwan duli lianmeng*) in 1958 under chairman Ch'en I-te (Chen Yide). Membership in these and similar organizations was secret during the early years due to fears of Nationalist reprisals against family members on Taiwan, or possible arrest when members returned to the island. In 1961, because UFI activists saw the need to court support from the American media and public, and determined that returning home was impossible, they went public with their efforts. Ch'en organized United Formosans in America for Independence (UFAI, *QuanMei Taiwan duli lianmeng*) in 1965 in order to unify the growing number of groups, particularly Taiwanese student associations at major research universities.

Academia became a battleground for Taidu advocates. Universities were vital for the recruitment of supporters, offered a forum for meetings and employment for activists, and presented an opportunity to promote study of the island by American scholars. UFI began holding conferences at universities in 1961 and the University of Wisconsin became home to the Taiwan Studies Association (*Taiwan yanjiuhui*) in 1965. There existed constant conflict on campuses between Taiwanese and the better funded pro-Nationalist student groups.(By the 1980s, growing numbers of mainland-born students would join the fray.) Among the students and émigrés were Taiwanese who supported the Nationalists as well as Nationalist intelligence agents who monitored political activity. This led to the arrest of some Taiwanese upon their return to the island, limited the effectiveness of the groups on Taiwan, and deterred many from participating in the movement. The Nationalists constantly monitored overseas critics of the regime, preparing blacklists of dissidents banned from returning.[43]

By the 1960s, the pursuit of independence expanded from organizing among Taiwanese to seeking support from the American press and public. In 1961, the first public protest occurred in the United States, as a handful of activists demonstrated during Vice President Chen Cheng's visit.[44] UFI led a series of protests at the ROC embassy in Washington on the anniversary of the February 28 Incident. Independence groups also began to demonstrate against the PRC and its claim to Taiwan in the 1970s. Publications represented another key aspect of separatist efforts. *The Independent Formosa*, a joint publication of Japan's Formosan Youth Independence

League, the Union for Formosa's Independence in Europe, and United Formosans in America for Independence, was indicative of the genre. This journal, and its successors, became one of the best ways to obtain information on the arrests of dissidents on Taiwan.[45] Independence publications reprinted any article or letter they could find that suggested backing for their cause.[46] Although a few Japanese or Americans, such as State Department official turned scholar George Kerr, voiced support for independence, most people knew little of Taiwanese aspirations for national self-determination.[47] Much of the American criticism of the Nationalists focused less on self-determination for islanders than on the authoritarian nature of the regime. As was the case in Japan, American leftists had more interest in building relations with the People's Republic than in supporting a small and struggling movement led by the Taiwanese.

Almost every significant independence group labored to establish an underground organization on Taiwan.[48] It is impossible to know to what extent Taiwanese favored independence during the martial law era, and organized activity was extremely dangerous. The Military Police, Military Intelligence Bureau, Taiwan Garrison Command, Investigation Bureau, and National Security Bureau searched for any sign of dissent and sent thousands to jail. Even possession of works by overseas activists such as Liao Wen-i or Shih Ming could lead to lengthy prison sentences. Next to allegations of communist conspiracies, independence plots were the main justification for arrests during the White Terror that began in the late 1940s. On a few occasions, however, Taiwanese took extraordinary risks by promoting Taidu on the island.[49] It is difficult, however, to connect the efforts of exiles to independence activity on the island during the martial law era. For example, in 1964, Peng Ming-min became one of the most famous leaders of the TIM. His life and writings offer an excellent example of the separatists' understanding of the island's history, and the difficulties encountered in their quest.[50] Like many independence leaders, he was born into a Christian family and educated in Japan.[51] Under Nationalist rule, Peng transformed from politically apathetic professional to opposition activist. He became swept up in February 28, then went into political hibernation after the Nationalist troops reestablished their control. Peng enjoyed success under Nationalist rule, and became the youngest professor at National Taiwan University.

Peng's general impression of misrule and specific events like the arrest and harassment of intellectuals coaxed him back into politics. In 1964, he and two associates drafted the "Declaration of the Taiwanese Self-Salvation Movement" (*Taiwan zijiu yundong xuanyan*), a damning indictment of Nationalist oppression and a demand for national self-determination. They were arrested before the statement could be disseminated widely on the island. Taiwanese groups in the United States and Japan published Peng's statement, which seemed to inspire the activists for a brief time. His relatively prominent position enabled him to avoid execution or a long jail sentence, and he was released in 1965 under a special pardon. Constant harassment and surveillance, however, spurred him to flee Taiwan in 1970. Peng ended up in the United States, where he published the best-known English-language work on the TIM, *A Taste of Freedom*.[52] In exile, Peng would prove one of the most media savvy advocates of Taidu by highlighting Nationalist brutality and the Taiwanese peoples' hopes for self-determination. At times, he overshadowed more established organizations and sparked jealousy from other activists.

Although open opposition to the Nationalists was impossible, one organization proved difficult for the government to control. The Presbyterian Church played a key role in Taiwan's politics by fostering many of the island's native-born elite, offering an avenue for dissemination of Western political as well as religious ideas, and providing a noncommunist framework for dissent against ruling regimes (whether Japanese or Nationalist).[53] The Church focused on the needs of the Taiwanese after the Japanese forced foreign missionaries to leave in 1940. Native-born Church members promoted—and thus helped to define—Taiwanese culture and language in the face of Japanese, then Nationalist Chinese, attempts to inculcate their own national culture on the island. The Church never formally allied itself with any Taidu organization, but a disproportionate share of its members became supporters of independence, including Thomas Liao, Peng Ming-min, many opposition leaders who remained on the island, and future President Lee Teng-hui.

The Presbyterian Church consistently supported greater political rights for those who advocated democratization or independence, but never endorsed violence. Three key statements by the Church illustrated this institution's dangerous dance under Nationalist rule. The December 1971 declaration, "Public Statement on Our National Fate" (*Guoshi shengming*) rejected the possibility of Communist rule and demanded that the island's fate be determined by its inhabitants. In 1975, these themes appeared again in "On Appeal," which called for freedom of religion and human rights. Finally, the 1977 "Declaration on Human Rights" called upon the United States to preserve the independence and security of Taiwan.[54] These statements, and the presence of so many dissidents in the Church, led to growing police surveillance and pressure in the 1970s. At times, the Presbyterian Church became more directly involved in opposition activities. Several Church members were arrested for their role in protecting Shih Ming-te

(Shi Mingde), a prominent opposition leader and general manager of *Formosa* magazine, who was sought by police after the Kaohsiung Incident of 1979.[55] Silencing the Presbyterian Church proved problematic for the Nationalists, as the arrest of Christians was certain to spark criticism in the United States.

Lack of unity, as much as Nationalist oppression, prevented progress. Activists could agree upon two broad goals: to overthrow Nationalist rule and to prevent the Chinese Communists from taking possession of the island. The question of means, however, sparked constant conflict. In an attempt to unify the movement, in 1970, representatives from the United States, Japan, Taiwan, Canada, and Europe established the World United Formosans for Independence (WUFI, *Taiwan duli lianmeng*), which became the most famous organization.[56] Independence advocates also worked in other places where Taiwanese students or immigrants lived, including the Philippines and South Korea, and established a South American branch of WUFI. Chang Ts'an-hung (Zhang Canhong) became the face of WUFI for almost two decades, as chairman from 1973 to 1987 and 1991 to 1995.[57] Chang, like many champions of independence, was born in southern Taiwan in 1936. After earning an engineering degree from National Taiwan University, Chang studied at Rice University, where he became active in the movement. His support of socialism during the 1970s (although by no means ardent) and his long tenure sparked controversy among other activists who wished to lead WUFI. WUFI's ability to bring discipline was limited as national chapters often went their own way, and many of the top leaders served as chairmen of their own organizations. Untangling personal egos from policy differences proved difficult. For example, Peng Ming-min led WUFI in 1972, and then tended to work in other, smaller, organizations, or independently. His relationship with WUFI would be difficult for decades.

Terrorism proved one of the most controversial issues in the history of the TIM. In the 1970s and early 1980s, many of those connected to WUFI called for revolution—usually defined as the overthrow of the Nationalist government.[58] The most infamous event of the TIM's violent period was the April 1970 attempt on the life of Chiang Ching-kuo during his visit to New York City. Shooter and WUFI member Huang Wen-hsiung (Huang Wenxiong) and an accomplice were quickly arrested. Both jumped bail, but were found guilty in absentia.[59] Officially, WUFI condemned the attack:

> The incident connected with Chiang Ching-kuo, Chiang Kai-shek's son and heir apparent, on April 24, 1970, at the Hotel Plaza in New York is

unfortunate and deplorable. As we made clear immediately after the incident, the World United Formosans for Independence is in no way associated with or responsible for the vigorous and dramatic act.[60]

However, WUFI also defended the two, claiming that Huang did not actually fire at Chiang Ching-kuo and that he and his accomplice were "assaulted by the N.Y. Police and Chiang's personal security guard."[61] Criticism of the movement increased in 1973 when another independence supporter murdered a Nationalist official in Paris. Taidu leaders found themselves trapped between the respectability that came with rejecting violence and the legitimacy brought by militancy.

Independence publications illustrate the radicalism of the early 1970s. WUFI's *Taidu yuekan,* first published in March 1972, printed speeches by Peng Ming-min, manifestos, and reports on activities as its predecessor, *The Independent Formosan,* had done. It also included items such as a self-quiz on guerilla warfare on Taiwan.[62] WUFI's "Taiwan People's Independence Salvation Handbook" printed in *Taidu* in 1972, made clear that terrorism was acceptable. The handbook included instructions on bomb making and arson.[63] *Taidu* printed alleged reports from activists on the island itself, detailing attempts to assassinate Nationalist officials or Taiwanese who supported the regime, and to destroy property and infrastructure.[64] In 1976, WUFI's Taiwan branch claimed responsibility for bombing a power line near Kaohsiung, and seriously wounding Taiwan Provincial Chairman Hsieh Tung-min (Xie Dongmin) with a letter bomb. In 1979, independence activists briefly took over the Nationalists' diplomatic office in Los Angeles. There followed a series of small arsons and bombings on Taiwan in 1980, for which WUFI's Taiwan branch claimed credit.

To what extent did WUFI control violence on Taiwan? Certainly, WUFI members and other independence supporters were involved in terrorism, but it is difficult to prove that leading figures in the movement initiated any attacks. WUFI was not a highly centralized or disciplined organization—at times it acted more as an umbrella for other groups around the world.[65] These acts did nothing to advance the cause of independence, frightened away potential Taiwanese supporters, and reduced Japanese and American support. The Nationalists saw bombings and attempted assassinations as justification for continued political oppression on the island. By 1982, WUFI had firmly renounced violence.[66] As had been the case with socialism, the attempt to use violence in the service of nationalism would accomplish little for the Taiwanese.

CONFRONTING POLITICAL CHANGE ON TAIWAN

Taiwanese independence activists would benefit from a series of political trends they neither caused nor controlled. First, the ROC's growing international isolation raised questions about the regime's legitimacy and the island's future. Richard Nixon announced the secret talks with Beijing in July 1971, the ROC left the United Nations in October 1971, Japan switched recognition to the PRC in September 1972, and the United States formally switched recognition and announced the termination of the mutual security pact in January 1979.[67] Second, Chiang Kai-shek's death in 1975 symbolized the decline of the mainland-born Nationalists and the waning of the ideology of the Three Principles of the People, staunch anti-communism, and promises of restoring Taiwan to China. Third, Taiwan's "economic miracle" created a social base for political change as a growing middle class demanded increased attention to its concerns.[68] The terms of political debate shifted, as these prosperous Taiwanese had less interest in "saving" China, promoting anti-communism, or achieving unification with the mainland, a place few of them had ever been. Democratization, quality of life, corruption, and Taiwan's international status became the principal political issues.[69]

These developments emboldened the opposition on the island. Since the late 1940s, some Taiwanese who did not join the Nationalist Party (Kuomintang) did compete in elections and attempted to influence state policies (or at least limit their harmful effects upon islanders). They made up a small portion of those elected to the county, provincial, or national assemblies. These politicians, who struggled against corrupt elections and a lack of resources, dared not discuss independence in public. Through the 1950s and 1960s, they were careful critics of the regime who attempted to obtain more resources for their constituents or to attack malfeasance by low-level Nationalist officials. The term *dangwai* ("outside the [Nationalist] party") became popular in the 1970s to describe these Taiwanese, who were forbidden from forming their own political party.

In the late 1970s, some *dangwai* activists started to suggest publicly what had been safe to discuss only from exile. For example, articles in *Meilidao* (Formosa), a magazine by dissidents that began publication in 1979, tested the limits of Nationalist tolerance by demanding immediate democratic reform and by discussing Taiwan's international status. Hsu Hsin-liang (Xu Xinliang), Lin I-hsiung (Lin Yixiong), and other future Democratic Progressive Party leaders who ran *Meilidao* magazine sought publicity for their cause by organizing a demonstration on Human Rights Day, December 10, in Kaohsiung, a city on Taiwan's southwest coast. The rally focused on the need for democratic reform and the protection of human rights, but many of the speakers, including future Vice President Lu Hsiu-lien (Lu Xiulian, "Annette"), came very close to calling for independence by claiming that Taiwan's status had not been determined with finality. She suggested that mainlanders were outsiders, stating that only a "small minority" did not "regard Taiwan as their homeland."[70] In what became known as the Kaohsiung or Meilidao Incident, hostility between protestors and police soon degenerated into a riot, which the Nationalists claimed injured almost 200 police officers. In reaction, the Nationalists arrested leaders of the opposition movement and gave many lengthy prison sentences.[71] This short-term victory for the government became a rallying cry for the opposition and sparked international criticism of the regime. With few exceptions, for the next two decades resistance to the Nationalists would be dominated by those involved in the events of December 1979.

As had been the case with Peng Ming-min's 1964 declaration, the Incident briefly united the far-flung branches of the pro-independence community. The major groups issued a joint statement denouncing the arrests and claiming that the Nationalists were perpetrating another February 28 "tragedy": Japan's Independent Taiwan Society led by Shih Ming; the remnants of Liao Wen-i's provisional government; the Overseas Alliance for Democratic Rule in Taiwan led by Kuo Yü-hsin (Guo Yuxin); Hsu Hsin-liang, who had recently come to the United States; WUFI chaired by Chang Ts'an-hung, and the Taiwan-American Society led by Peng Ming-min.[72] The number of groups joining in the declaration of solidarity, however, indicated the fractured nature of the movement, where each major leader tended to have his own organization. Membership in many of the groups within this constantly shifting coalition was small. Personality, rather than policy, continued to shape the TIM.

Tensions persisted between those who focused on Taidu in exile, and those who had remained on the island and participated in electoral politics under the watchful eye of the Nationalist police or were arrested after the Incident.[73] For example, Kuo Yü-hsin and Hsu Hsin-liang, two well-known politicians turned exiles, had difficult relations with WUFI.[74] Both sought to link the movement in exile with the realities of electoral politics under martial law on Taiwan. They possessed strong credentials as dissidents but could not translate their legitimacy into effective organizations.[75] In 1974, Kuo, an independent politician and Presbyterian Church member, lost a close election to a Nationalist candidate. The protests over voting irregularities in this contest brought more pressure on Kuo from Nationalist officials, and he moved to the United States in 1977. His experiences initially gave him some credibility in the diaspora community. He formed the Overseas Alliance for Democratic Rule in Taiwan (*Taiwan minzhu yundong haiwai tongmeng*) in January 1979, but soon found himself criticized for his relative moderation and focus on democratic reform instead of immediate independence. Kuo announced that because the United States and the People's Republic normalized relations, Taiwan merited recognition as a political unit—a statement as close to advocating independence as he was willing to make.[76] One biographer claimed later that Kuo's organization had no mass base, but was a vital conduit for information about events on Taiwan.[77] Hsu took a more hardline stance on independence. He had been a successful Taiwanese politician within the Nationalist Party. In 1977, he ran for office and won without the party's endorsement, and thus moved into the ranks of the opposition. When the Nationalists made clear that they viewed Hsu as a trouble-maker and independence advocate, he fled to the United States in 1979. There, he would establish a plethora of groups while awaiting the opportunity to return to the island.[78]

At a 1983 meeting at the University of Delaware, leading independence advocates demonstrated the conflicts endemic to the movement. Besides personal rivalries and personality clashes, the role of socialism and democracy were contentious issues. Hsu Hsin-liang, who focused on his future political career on Taiwan, emphasized that his goal was to advance the revolutionary resistance movement on the island itself.[79] He assured participants that the current stage of revolution was democratic, not socialist.[80] Longtime activist Shih Ming noted that the class conflict normally predicted in socialist theory was different on Taiwan, as it was a colony under Nationalist rule. The primary contradiction was the national (*minzu*) problem, not class conflict.[81] Nevertheless, Shih was accused of supporting communism.[82] The WUFI representative claimed that his organizations' main goal was "comprehensive warfare" (*zongtizhan*). Although not rejecting the possibility of armed struggle, he encouraged activists to engage in a legal, democratic, and foreign affairs struggle in order to promote the cause.[83] Hsu was subtly portrayed as an interloper. One WUFI leader claimed that officers in their organization were elected based on their ability, not their age or reputation.[84] He noted that Hsu advocated democracy, but that organizations with internal democracy, such as WUFI, provided the best example and guarantee of successful political change on the island.[85] WUFI participants also called attention to their long-standing dedication to the cause and systematic efforts to build up the organization on the island itself. As evidenced by the 1984 elections, however, WUFI was not democratic enough for some of its members. The organization split as some of those who lost resigned, attacking Chang Ts'an-hung and other leaders as undemocratic and ineffective.[86]

WUFI survived these conflicts to remain the largest and most prominent Taidu organization, and to expand its efforts. The "foreign affairs" struggle referenced by Li became a key aspect of the TIM even as Americans became slightly more receptive to Taiwanese dissidents. The end of official ties to Taipei in 1979 caused a few more Americans to acknowledge the possibility of the island's permanent separation from China. The arrests after the Kaohsiung Incident, the brutal murder of opposition leader Lin I-hsiung's family, and the Chiang Nan murder also sparked more criticism of the Nationalists and advocacy of democratic reform on the island.[87] In 1982, the Formosan Association for Public Affairs (FAPA, *Taiwanren gonggong shiwu xiehui*) was established in the United States as an offshoot of WUFI. This group focused on lobbying American politicians to support democracy and self-determination for Taiwan.

The Association's activities would highlight another shift in the TIM. The decline of the ROC's international position and the PRC's increasing power made Beijing's claim to Taiwan a growing problem. FAPA's goal, one spokesman noted, was to prevent the Chinese Communists from invading the island.[88] In 1983, one FAPA representative decried America's acceptance of Beijing's claim to the island while ignoring the desires of the Taiwanese people.[89] Whatever the logic of FAPA's arguments, the island's fate remained hostage to larger geopolitical and economic concerns. While the Nationalists' China Lobby had largely faded away, a formidable array of business leaders, scholars, diplomats, and officials were determined to improve PRC-US relations by supporting the one China policy.

INDEPENDENCE ACTIVISTS IN POWER: PRAGMATISM AND COMPROMISE

Despite arrests after the Kaohsiung Incident and continued intimidation, non-Kuomintang politicians and intellectuals grew more vocal, and in 1986 formed the DPP (*Minzhu jinbudang*), the first meaningful opposition the Nationalists had faced since the retreat to Taiwan. The opposition's assertiveness coincided with the Nationalists' flexibility. Chiang Ching-kuo had recognized the need to legitimize the regime by bringing more Taiwanese into the Nationalist Party and government ranks, and by initiating steps toward political reform. Through a process known as Taiwanization, Chiang promoted native-born Nationalists, such as Lee Teng-hui (Li Denghui), to higher ranking positions.[90] With the end of martial law in

1987, wide-ranging reforms followed, including the relaxation of controls over the press, speech, assembly, and political groups.[91] In this environment, the DPP expanded its influence upward from towns, to districts, to the province, and to national-level bodies.[92]

Separatists played pivotal roles in establishing the DPP and provided some of its most adamant support. The new party, however, made independence only one of many issues in its platform, and its leadership fiercely debated how to prioritize the quest for international recognition, democratization, rule of law, economic development, environmental protection, and a host of other domestic problems. The party was divided between the Formosa faction and the New Tide faction—both of which were more firmly rooted on the island than most of the diaspora activists. The Formosa faction, which grew out of the leadership of *Meilidao* magazine, was more moderate on the independence issue, and instead focused on winning elections. More radical DPP leaders in the New Tide faction demanded a clear commitment to independence and took a less accommodating stance toward the Nationalist Party.

DPP leaders found that electoral victory, particularly in island-wide contests, often required downplaying separatism, as voters feared a military attack from the PRC would result from a declaration of independence. Although many Taiwanese were eager to vote for an alternative to the Nationalists, they rejected any action that might threaten their hard-won economic success. In particular, attracting the support of Taiwanese business leaders, many of whom wished to invest on the mainland, required that DPP leaders emphasize their ability to protect the economic growth brought by Nationalist policies rather than to risk a violent confrontation with the PRC. During the 1990s, DPP pragmatism on the independence issue appeared to grow with electoral success and the responsibility it brought, as well as a generational change to the post-*Meilidao* generation.[93] Of those arrested after 1979's Kaohsiung Incident, only Annette Lu remains powerful. Nevertheless, the DPP became the single most important forum for further dissemination of separatist ideology, particularly as it used electoral victories to shape education, language, and cultural policies on the island.

TIM leaders lobbied the DPP more vocally to back independence, and to elect their strongest supporters.[94] After Chiang Ching-kuo's death in 1988 the Taiwan branch of WUFI began to operate in public. In 1992, WUFI held its annual meeting in Taipei—the movement's center of gravity had shifted from Japan and the United States to the island itself. The transition from adamant critics in exile to participants in the political process required compromises. Simply appealing to Taiwanese solidarity against the mainlander-dominated Nationalist regime was no longer terribly successful.

WUFI, which changed its name to the Taiwan Independence Nation Building League (*Taiwan duli jian'guo lianmeng*) in 1987, expanded its agenda to include many of the issues present in the DPP platform. For example, its 1992 platform called for the expected, such as a One Taiwan and One China solution, the establishment of a Republic of Taiwan, and the promotion of a uniquely Taiwanese culture, and also advocated greater environmental protection, safeguarding the rights of aborigines, and expanded social welfare programs.[95] WUFI—the organization continued to the use the English acronym—also toned down its anti-mainlander rhetoric by accepting the idea that the definition of Taiwanese is based on choice, not race or ethnicity: "Anyone who identifies with Taiwan, loves Taiwan, and wishes to be part of Taiwan's destiny, regardless of when they immigrated or were born on Taiwan, all will be equal citizens of Taiwan after independence."[96] By the 1990s most of the TIM had abandoned the old paradigm that portrayed all mainlanders as illegitimate intruders into Taiwan's polity.

Those who had dedicated their lives to independence had to become part of the electoral process on the island. After the implementation of democratic reforms, Peng Ming-min returned to Taiwan in 1992 and ran for president under the DPP banner in 1996. Nothing better symbolized the dilemmas of the TIM than the fact that a pro-independence politician competed as the opposition party's candidate for the presidency of the Republic of China, thus legitimating the very political system Peng and others had sworn to overthrow. The DPP platform reflected the separatist agenda, promising to "Promote Taiwan culture, incorporating modern and native cultural elements" and

> Overcome diplomatic isolation, expand international activism, and elevate Taiwan's national status. Taiwan must abandon the 'one China' policy and announce to the world that Taiwan is an independent sovereign state wishing to establish normal diplomatic relations with all peace-loving countries of the world.

The platform also directly contested the unifiers' discourse on the island's history: "The current system of standardized textbooks and curriculum in elementary and junior high schools should be abolished. Political ideology and propaganda premised on a 'great China' ideology must be strictly prohibited."[97] Peng claimed that the election of 1996 offered Taiwanese an opportunity to further the struggle of the Taiwanese people, who have "withstood centuries of foreign domination, pogroms, and political terror."[98] He lost the election to Lee Teng-hui primarily because the Taiwanese remained ambivalent over their future as a nation and unsure of the ability of this ardent nationalist to lead the state.[99] Peng's defeat strengthened those in the DPP who wished to focus on domestic issues, with independence as a long-term goal.

The TIM did not and does not control the DPP; rather it appears hostage to the party for influence. Those who felt that the party lacked dedication to independence proved unable to build a viable alternative. For example, in October 1996 the Taiwan Independence Party (*Jian'guodang*) was formed by disaffected DPP members who believed their former party lacked commitment to independence and who did not like then-chairman Shih Ming-te's willingness to compromise with other parties, such as the pro-unification New Party, in order to advance the DPP agenda in the Legislative Yuan. The party, which lost many members after Chen Shui-bian won the 2000 election, was led by academics with limited experience in administration. It never seriously threatened the DPP's base of support.

Even as the TIM struggled to define its role in a newly democratized Taiwan, a Nationalist made substantive moves toward independence. Whether out of sincere belief or more cynical motives, Lee Teng-hui undermined the movement by shifting close enough to independence to draw the mainland's wrath and gain some TIM support, but not far enough to satisfy many of the most ardent activists, particularly those in exile. Lee quietly moved up the Nationalist hierarchy to become Vice-President in 1984, then President in his own right in 1988 after Chiang Ching-kuo's death. He surprised observers not only by managing to remain in office, but also by engineering the retirement of the mainland-born premier, controlling the Nationalist Party and its vast financial resources, and winning re-election in 1990 and 1996. In both rhetoric and action, Lee drifted away from the mainlander vision of the Chinese nation and Nationalist state, but usually with carefully calculated ambiguity. Although economic, social, cultural, and political contacts with the mainland expanded dramatically during his tenure, the president antagonized Beijing with statements that cast doubt on his commitment to unification.

Lee expressed his ambivalence over unification most freely to foreign journalists, thus giving ammunition to those who associated separatism with outside interference. For example, in a November 1997 interview with an American reporter, he called Taiwan a sovereign independent state (*zhuquan duli de guojia*).[100] At least one magazine in Taiwan pointed out that his views seemed more radical than Peng Ming-min's.[101] In July 1999 Lee openly repudiated the one China principle in an interview with German correspondents, stating that the cross strait relationship was state to state (*guojia yu guojia*) in nature, or "at least a special *guo yu guo* relationship."[102] Although at first glance Lee appeared to accept the Taiwanese nationalists'

vision of the island and its ties to the mainland, the President's actual statement was less clear-cut. He emphasized that because the ROC has been an
independent and sovereign state since 1912, there was no need to declare Taiwan's independence.[103] Rather than suggesting that the Taiwanese had become a nation through choice and common experience, as independence
activists often do, he described the ROC on Taiwan as a political equal to the
People's Republic based on the continuity of its government from the mainland. Thus a Taiwan-born Nationalist had effectively appropriated the independence issue.

Lee's formulation was largely adopted by Lien Chan (Lian Zhan), the
Nationalist candidate for president in 2000, and his opponent, DPP candidate Chen Shui-bian.[104] As he had done during his earlier successful
quest for the Taipei mayoralty, Chen took a relatively moderate position
on independence during the 2000 contest. He accepted the DPP platform
favoring independence and selected a staunch separatist, American educated Annette Lu, as his vice president. Chen, who won the election with
a plurality of the votes, also reassured voters that stability and prosperity
were his first priorities. His inaugural pledge of the Five No's (not to declare independence, not to change the national title, not to put state-to-
state relations in the Constitution, not to promote a referendum on independence, and not to abolish the Guidelines for National Unification
and the National Unification Council) dismayed TIM activists, but did
not satisfy Beijing. The mainland state, party, media, and academia
brought pressure upon the "leader of the Taiwan authorities" (the term
most frequently used in the PRC) to enter into talks on political reunification on Beijing's terms. The leaders of the PRC and those on Taiwan
who still support unification decried his refusal unconditionally to accept
the '92 Consensus.[105]

During the first Chen administration, WUFI focused less on demanding
an immediate declaration of independence and more upon a series of
smaller steps that would tend to make unification more difficult. In 2002
and 2003, WUFI sought to promote the Confucian concept of "rectification
of names" (zhengming) in order to substitute "Taiwan" for China as the
government's official title. It also continued long-term projects, such as advocacy of Taiwan's admittance into the United Nations as an independent
nation, and the creation of a Taiwan passport.[106] WUFI and other related
groups have urged Chen to take a hard line against the PRC and to resist
any moves toward unification.[107] Ironically, their approach to expanding
economic ties with the mainland resembles that of the "old" Nationalists,
as they are concerned that trade and investment will create a dangerous de-

pendence upon Beijing. Lobbying efforts in the United States and Japan continue, and now focus on the potential threat from the People's Republic. Through the DPP, WUFI, and FAPA, independence supporters have taken up where the old China Lobby left off—emphasizing the need for vigilance against an aggressive Beijing.

In the run-up to the 2004 presidential election Chen began to take a more assertive stance toward independence, much to the dismay of Washington and Beijing. The President's policies seemed motivated by a complex mixture of cynical political opportunism and nationalist idealism. In light of a high unemployment rate and questions over his administration's competence, he sought to sway voters by goading the mainland government into threatening the island as it had done during the 1996 election of Lee Teng-hui. Chen, facing the last four years of his long political career, may have come to believe that he must secure his place in history by pushing the island toward permanent separation from the mainland. Further, he and other DPP leaders may feel that Taiwan consciousness has spread sufficiently as to support radical changes. Chen used an appeal to the democratic process, an island-wide referendum, to promote the principle that the island's people could vote on important issues—thus opening the door to a vote on independence in the future. After a great deal of heated debate, the president was able to include a referendum with the March 2004 presidential poll. Voters were asked to decide whether to increase Taiwan's anti-missile defenses if the PRC refused to remove hundreds of short-range missiles pointed at the island, and whether to enter talks with the PRC based on an ill-defined peace and stability framework. Chen eked out a narrow victory with 50.1 percent of the vote, although the referendum failed to obtain the required support of half of the registered voters.[108]

Despite the lack of a clear mandate, Chen expressed greater determination to push ahead with measures that will sorely test Beijing's patience, including a new constitution, to be voted upon in a referendum in 2006 and to go into effect in 2008 (perhaps just before the Beijing Olympics). He claimed that this constitution would have no impact on relations with the mainland, but would focus on clarifying the duties of the president and the division of powers among branches of government.[109] PRC officials feared that the process of constitutional revision, once begun, would quickly grow to include pro-independence clauses such as changing the name of ROC to the Republic of Taiwan. To the mainland government, Chen's plans represented a clear timetable for independence. At the very least, the President is creating a framework for Taiwanese to make this choice.

CONCLUSION

Taidu supporters have endured a half century of disappointment. In 1967, *The Independent Formosa* noted that

> The time for change should come when 1) Communist China enters into the United Nations, 2) Chiang Kai-shek dies, 3) Troops on the island of Quemoy and Matsu are withdrawn, or 4) America discontinues its military aid to the Nationalist Chinese Government. The fourth point is the least likely.[110]

Separatists witnessed all but one of these events, with few immediate results. The TIM experience is that of a disorderly, faction-ridden nationalist coalition lacking international support that is nevertheless stumbling toward success today. Political change on Taiwan did not meet independence advocates' expectations, as it was marked by gradual and peaceful reform rather than sudden revolution. TIM leaders have faced a difficult transition from exiled or underground conspirators to party politicians and lobbyists. For most of the movement's history, separatists assumed that a Taiwanese nation (here meaning a community of like-minded individuals) existed and that the Taiwanese would welcome a republic. Thus, independence required the overthrow of the Nationalist state. In the wake of democratization and Taiwanization, however, TIM advocates now influence the state through the DPP, and appear to have an increasingly confident Chen Shuibian to champion their cause. Democracy has proved a double-edged sword, as elections and survey data indicate that most Taiwanese remain ambivalent about their national identity. Even if islanders believe they are part of a Taiwanese nation, this does not necessarily mean that such sentiments will override concerns over the tangible dangers of a formal declaration of independence. In this context, the movement's leaders now find themselves working through the state in order to build or strengthen a Taiwanese national consciousness. Ironically, they utilize the same institutions that they previously attacked for forcefully Sinicizing the Taiwanese.

DPP politicians largely echo the TIM when they promote the idea of an island-wide identity that combines elements of aboriginal, Chinese, Japanese, and Western culture.[111] Policies designed to create, reinforce, or protect this culture could prove key to strengthening an imagined community and thus furthering the nation-building project. History, long a key tool of nationalists, is a good example of TIM efforts in this realm. Over the last two decades, Taiwan has experienced an explosion of interest and publications about the island's recent past. The most visible manifestation of this trend was the creation of an Institute of Taiwan History Preparatory Office within the Academia Sinica, the premier research institution in the Republic of China. This and similar organizations represented the fruits of political change, and provided an opportunity to disseminate a new version of Taiwan's history. History, in turn, offered an intellectual "sanction" for expanding support of independence. Backers of independence create their own narrative to illustrate the island's differences from the mainland, and a long-term drive for separation from outside political entities, be they Chinese or Japanese. Pro-independence scholars advocate studying the island with less reference to the mainland, and certainly not as a case study for other provinces of China.[112] Curricula and textbooks increasingly follow a "Taiwan-centered" version of the island's history, rather than the Nationalists' old narrative of the island as one province of China.[113]

From the end of World War II until the 1990s, the Nationalists' educational, cultural, and propaganda organs attempted to highlight one version of the island's history, that of Taiwan province, and to convince the Taiwanese that they were Chinese and that the government in Taipei represented China. This narrative was backed up by a brutal police state and international support. Today, the TIM is working through a democratic system to forge a new version of Taiwan's history and, by extension, identity. These gradual changes may not shift islanders toward demanding formal and permanent independence from China, but more than any single policy statement, public protest, or interest group, it might serve to make unification unthinkable to a new generation of Taiwanese. Should the island's population decide to court military conflict with the mainland by declaring independence, Chen appears to be preparing the path for that final, and fateful, break.

CHAPTER FOUR

Lee Teng-hui and "Separatism"

RICHARD BUSH

CONVENTIONAL WISDOMS can sometimes be misleading. An idea is not true simply because the great majority of people accept it. A conclusion does not become established fact merely through constant repetition. Take, for example, the common view of Lee Teng-hui's approach to Taiwan's relationship with China. The conventional belief is that Lee was bent on permanently separating Taiwan from China, or, in the usual political shorthand, he promoted two Chinas or Taiwan independence. That conclusion might be true, but if it is, it is not simply because people—and particularly those in the Beijing government—say it is. Instead, we need to examine what Lee Teng-hui said and did during his tenure as Taiwan's president. The PRC government stated its position on Lee's actions and intentions most fully and categorically in its February 2000 White Paper on the Taiwan Strait issue. The document ascribed a separatist motivation to much of what Lee did, including reform of the political structure, seeking more international space, purchasing weapons from the United States, and creating a Taiwan identity. By the end of his presidency, Beijing's indictment against him was absolute: "Lee Teng-hui has become the general representative of Taiwan's separatist forces, a saboteur of the stability of the Taiwan Straits, a stumbling-block preventing the de-

---

Daphne Dong-ling Fan and Justin Wu provided valuable assistance for this essay.

velopment of relations between China and the United States, and a troublemaker for the peace and stability of the Asia-Pacific region."[1]

THE ONE COUNTRY, TWO SYSTEMS FORMULA

Lee's stated views on the issue of Taiwan and China's unification need to be examined not only for their own sake but also because the act of defining Lee became a weapon in cross-Strait political combat. Some of the combatants have a self-interested reason in asserting what Lee stood for. To misrepresent him both distorts the historical record and complicates the management of the Taiwan Strait issue. It can also be downright dangerous if Lee's alleged course is deemed to be grounds for war, as the PRC White Paper suggested.[2] The focus here will be primarily on Lee's formal public statements and secondarily on important government statements that reflect his imprint. First, however, it is necessary to lay out the PRC position to which Lee was responding: the "one country, two systems" formula for unification. That position evolved over time, eventually crystallizing into a set of proposals that persist to this day.

An early significant formulation of "one country, two systems" was delivered on September 30, 1981, by Ye Jianying, chairman of the Standing Committee of the National People's Congress. Among his "nine points," he proposed that:

- The CCP and the KMT hold talks "on a reciprocal basis" to facilitate cooperation for national reunification (note that party-to-party talks ignores the ROC government).
- The two sides conclude an agreement on cross-Strait mails, trade, air and shipping services, visits, and various kinds of exchanges.
- After unification, Taiwan could "enjoy a high degree of autonomy as a special administrative region," and "the central government" would not interfere with "local affairs on the island."
- Taiwan could retain its armed forces.
- Taiwan's current socioeconomic system would remain unchanged, as well as its way of life and economic and cultural relations with foreign countries. Property rights would not be encroached upon.
- Various Taiwan "people in authority and representative personages" could take up PRC leadership posts.
- Taiwan people who wished to settle on the mainland could do so and would not suffer discrimination.
- Taiwan industrialists and businessmen were welcome to engage in

business ventures on the Mainland, with guarantees for their legal rights, interests, and profits.[3]

Deng Xiaoping elaborated on the idea in June 1983, in a conversation with Seton Hall University professor Winston Yang. He repeated many of Ye's points but added a few more. On judicial matters, Taiwan could exercise independent jurisdiction and the right of final judgment "need not reside in Beijing." He specified that it was "party, governmental, and military systems" that the Taiwan authorities would administer. He warned that the armed forces could not be a threat to China. He specified that the Taiwan government after unification would be a local one. And finally he warned that "complete autonomy was impossible. "Complete autonomy means two Chinas, not one. Different systems may be practiced, but it must be the People's Republic of China alone that represents China internationally."[4]

Finally, the joint declaration concerning Hong Kong that Great Britain and China signed in December 1984 added specific guidelines on how a SAR would conduct economic and cultural relations with other countries and participate in international organizations and agreements. All these ties would occur under PRC aegis.

Over the past decade, there have been hints at the margin of even better treatment. But at its core, one country, two systems remains a proposal for home rule. The central government was in Beijing. It was the exclusive sovereign, representing the state known as China in the international system. Special administrative regions were subordinate units whose governments would be staffed by local inhabitants and authorized to administer local political, economic, and other affairs.[5] Internationally, SARs were free to have economic and cultural relations with other countries. Otherwise, their activities were at the discretion of the sovereign and could not undermine the sovereign's rights and prerogatives.

EARLY RESPONSES: PARTY LINE, THEN BREAKTHROUGH

China's proposals and success in bringing off the Hong Kong Joint Declaration put Taiwan on the defensive. Its initial reaction was to set such high requirements for negotiations that they would never happen. But Beijing was not displeased with Lee Teng-hui's early statements. In the first press conference that he held as president on February 22, 1988, he endorsed unification as "the goal toward which we must continue to struggle," but said that it must occur under the Three Principles of the People of Sun Yat-sen (Taipei's response to Beijing's proposals earlier in the decade). He asserted that he had a "deep concern" for the mainland and that there was no significant difference between the people on both sides of the Strait except for spoken language. The key obstacle, he asserted, was ideological. The government in Beijing held to the "Four Cardinal Principles" (the socialist road, the dictatorship of the proletariat, the leadership of the communist party, and Marxism-Leninism-Mao Zedong Thought) whereas Taipei advocated Sun Yat-sen's objective of a free and democratic China with equal distribution of wealth. One country, two systems was unacceptable because China should have only one, free and democratic system. It was also unacceptable because it "was aimed at localizing the ROC government through united front maneuvers." United-front tactics and the resort to force, which Beijing had never renounced, were forms of pressure, and pressure was not an appropriate way to bring about reunification. Lee acknowledged that Taiwan itself had work to do on democratization. Cross-Strait progress was contingent on political reform on Taiwan, because it would force the PRC to give up the four cardinal principles and contribute to positive change on the mainland.

Lee also dwelt on the effort to create an independent Taiwan, which he acknowledged might worry Beijing. He said that the independence movement was illegal, contrary to history, and lacking in support. It was "one of the greatest destabilizing factors in Taiwan today." As far as he was concerned, the Taipei government's policy was clear. "We stick to a 'one China' policy; that is, China must be reunified."[6]

In reading Lee's statements, one is struck first of all by how conventional they are. As one might expect, he reflected the standard position of the government that he had headed for little more than a month. The tone is ideological, in that the fundamental obstacle to reunification is the difference between the two systems. The stance is reactive and defensive. But the stated goal is the same as it had been for four decades: unification on our terms.[7]

On the other hand, it is striking that Lee's initial discussion covers most of the issues that would make up the Taiwan Strait issue for the duration of his presidency. Is Taipei committed to unification? (Yes.) What is the status of the Taipei government relative to the Beijing government? (Not a local government.) What is its view of one country, two systems? (Opposed.) What is its view of a Republic of Taiwan? (Opposed.) Does the difference in political system matter? (Yes, to the extent that it is a precondition for progress.) Does PRC pressure contribute to an acceptable solution? (No, to the extent that Taipei insists that Beijing renounce the use of force.) Will Taiwan permit contacts with the mainland in the absence of a political resolution? (Only cautiously.)

Over the course of the next two years, Lee elaborated on this basic position and added an element that would have profound implications for relations with Beijing. That was Taiwan's desire for an international role. In his Constitution Day speech in December 1988, he complained that Beijing was using, "any means to isolate us diplomatically and diminish our international status." He repeated that theme after a visit to Singapore in March 1989, when he was received as "President Lee of Taiwan," and cited the need to break through the framework that he said had been imposed on Taiwan in 1971, when the PRC entered the United Nations and Taiwan departed. He complained that other countries' concept of "one-China" was hurting Taiwan. This was also an early instance in which he uttered the formulation, that the ROC was "an independent sovereign state."

A gloss is required on that formulation. First of all, this was not new with Lee. Chiang Kai-shek stated it at the time the ROC left the United Nations and Chiang Ching-kuo said it in December 1978 in his formal response to the U.S. termination of diplomatic relations with Taiwan.[8] Second, I have always felt that the original Chinese formulation—*Zhonghua Minguo shi yige zhuquan duli de guojia*—conveys a somewhat different meaning from how the ROC government renders it in English. A more precise English translation would be, "The ROC is a state whose sovereignty is independent," or "whose sovereignty is independently derived." Some have suggested that the most accurate and straightforward translation would be, "The ROC is a sovereign state." And indeed, specialists on international law would argue that independence from any external authority is the essential element of sovereignty.[9] In any event, if the intent had been to have the adjective *duli* (independent) apply to "state" rather than "sovereignty," Lee would not have stated it the way he did. Note also that the subject of the sentence is "the ROC." If "Taiwan" had been the subject, the formulation would have had a more radical implication. Lee's statement as he made it was still consistent with the unification of China, but he was making an important point about the nature of the governing authorities that he called the Republic of China.

The main reason why Lee's statements in the first two years of his presidency were consistent with past ROC positions was that he was relatively weak, a Taiwanese in a leadership that was still relatively Mainlander in its membership. Also, he wanted to pursue democratization before moving to cross-Strait issues. And his reelection in March 1990 was not assured. The opposition within the KMT was such that Lin Yang-kang, a former provincial governor and premier with strong support from the business community, challenged him for the presidency. Students were demonstrating for reform. He would eventually win reelection but had to agree to General Hao Pei-tsun as premier. Once elected, however, he was free to transform the Taiwan political system and bring about an approach to mainland policy that was qualitatively more systematic than the one he had previously adopted.

Lee used his inauguration in May 1990 as the launching pad for this new approach. He asserted that Taiwan and the mainland "are indivisible parts of China," and that all Chinese were "compatriots of the same flesh and blood" who should together seek peaceful and democratic means to achieve the "common goal of national unification." Noting the prevailing trend of democratization, Lee made the following proposal to Beijing:

> If the Chinese communist authorities can recognize the overall world trend and the common hope of all Chinese, implement democracy and a free economic system; renounce the use of military force in the Taiwan Strait and do not interfere with our development of foreign relations on the basis of a one-China policy, we would be willing, on a basis of equality, to establish channels of communication, and completely open up academic, cultural, economic, trade, scientific, and technological exchange, to lay a foundation of mutual respect, peace, and prosperity. We hope then, when objective conditions are right, we will be able to discuss our national reunification, based on the common will of the Chinese people on both sides of the Taiwan Strait.

Lee thus established three steps the PRC would have to take in order to begin communications and exchanges: democratization, renunciation of force, and diplomatic restraint. He did place Taiwan's international activities within a one-China context and stipulated that contacts were to occur on an equal basis—a concept that would be made more precise as time went on. And he promised discussions on unification when conditions were right. For the first time, Taiwan offered ideas on the process by which the two sides could get to their stated common goal.[10]

The approach that Lee announced in May 1990 was formalized in the National Unification Guidelines (NUG), which were adopted by the National Unification Council in February 1991 and by the Executive Yuan in March of the same year. The Council was the top tier of a three-tier structure that Taiwan created in 1990 for cross-Strait relations. The NUC, which Lee Teng-hui chaired, was to set broad policy parameters; the Mainland Affairs Council within the Executive Yuan (cabinet) was to set policy guidelines and supervise implementation; and the semiofficial Straits Exchange Foundation (SEF) was to conduct interactions with the PRC side and solve practical problems under MAC guidance.

The guidelines stated a single goal—to establish a democratic, free, and equitably prosperous China—and established four principles:

- The mainland and Taiwan were parts of China and unification was the responsibility of all Chinese;
- Unification should be for the people's welfare and not a subject of partisan wrangling;
- Unification should promote Chinese culture, human dignity, fundamental human rights, democracy, and the rule of law; and
- Unification should ensure the rights, interests, security, and welfare of the people of the "Taiwan area" and should be achieved in gradual phases under the principles of reason, peace, parity, and reciprocity.

The NUG also replicated Lee's idea of a multistage process but changed the details. The first, short-term stage was one of exchanges and reciprocity in which the two sides, among other things, would eliminate the state of hostility, solve all disputes through peaceful means under the one-China principle, not deny the other's existence as a political entity, and respect each other in the international community. On that basis, the institutional and legal structure for cross-Strait exchanges would be established and restrictions to contacts eased. In the meantime, Taiwan would accelerate constitutional reform and promote national development, and the PRC should carry out reform, allow open expression, and implement freedom and democracy.

In describing this first stage, the NUG altered Lee's three conditions from his inaugural address. Instead of the more ideological requirement of PRC democratization, each side had to accept that the other was a political entity. The other conditions were set out in a softer way. Moreover, all were stated as parallel and reciprocal obligations (both should resolve disputes peacefully; each should promote democracy). Taipei would later note that it had specifically formulated the "political entity" concept to foster cross-Strait interaction. The term was "quite broad," the government asserted. "It can be applied to a state, a government, or a political organization." It was a type of creative ambiguity.[11] And these steps were to be taken during the course of the first phase, not prior to it.

Unlike Lee's inaugural, which contemplated only one further stage in the unification process, the NUG proposed two. In the NUG, the second phase was to be one of "mutual trust and cooperation." Official communications would begin. Direct postal, transportation, and commercial ties (the PRC's "three links") would start. Both sides would collaborate in international organizations. And high-ranking officials would undertake mutual visits. The third phase would be one of consultation and unification, which was rather like the second stage of Lee's 1990 inaugural. A consultative organization for unification would be established and, consistent with the goals of democracy, economic freedom, social justice, and even the nationalization of the armed forces, it would discuss unification and map out a constitutional system for a unified China.[12]

Lee's next major statement came on April 30, 1991, at a press conference held in the wake of the National Assembly session that made a number of amendments to the constitution and terminated the "period of national mobilization." Lee announced that pursuant to that latter action, Taiwan "will not use force to achieve national unification." In effect, Taipei's attitude toward Beijing was no longer one of hostility. From now on, he said, "we shall regard the Chinese Communists as a political entity ruling the mainland area." The CCP was no longer a "rebel regime." Lee also endorsed the work of the National Unification Council and its guidelines. But he also restated several of the harder formulations that the NUG had omitted. He warned that if Beijing did not renounce force and if it continued to isolate Taiwan internationally, "then we shall regard the Mainland as an antagonistic political entity." He repeated his view that the ROC was a sovereign country. He suggested that Taiwan independence sentiment was not "home-grown" but a reaction to the PRC's diplomatic blockade. But he also counseled patience if Beijing did not respond positively or if it stuck to one country, two systems and the four cardinal principles. Finally he described the problems with the PRC as those of a "divided nation."[13]

In short, the Taiwan government at this time had stated the clear goal of national unification. Moreover, it had laid out a process for how to get there, a roadmap that was more detailed than anything Beijing had offered. It stated as government policy what had long been a pragmatic reality, that the use of force was an unacceptable way for it to achieve its objectives. And it had refined the issues that would be the keys to progress: the legal identity of the Taiwan government, its right to participate in the international system, and PRC renunciation of the use of force.

What was the stimulus for this more forward-looking approach? One factor, no doubt, was the pressure from Taiwan businessmen who wanted to expand trade and investment on the mainland. In retrospect, it is also clear that Lee at this time did not totally control the policymaking process, and his public statements reflected to some extent the views of others in the leadership. But more important was a shift in Lee's assessment of how to sequence action on the internal and cross-Strait fronts. He came to believe that it was imperative to maintain a balance between internal politics, cross-Strait relations, and Taiwan's international role. In the early 1990s, Lee sought to secure a breakthrough in cross-Strait relations in order to facilitate constitutional reform and democratization rather than the other way around. The logic appears to be that lifting past restrictions on political expression and competition could be better justified if the sense of the threat from the mainland declined.[14]

TOWARD A TOUGHER LINE

Lee Teng-hui's position began to shift during 1993. To be sure, the key components of the approach he had tabled in 1990–1991 remained at the center of his cross-Strait policy. That is, that the PRC had to acknowledge the ROC as an equivalent political entity, accommodate Taipei's role in the international system, and renounce the use of force.[15] Yet there was also a change in emphasis, tone, and style, plus a replacement of past ambiguity with greater clarity. Several factors seemed to be at work.

Domestic politics was certainly at play. The December 1992 election for the Legislative Yuan, the first one after the retirement of the permanent members, had changed the balance of political power. The DPP won 36 percent of the vote and 50 seats out of 162, which gave it more opportunities to criticize the government. Lee's response was to co-opt the opposition's issues in order to blunt its momentum.

In particular, Lee and the government were under growing pressure to pursue a more aggressive stance on Taiwan's global status and role. General frustrations over exclusion in international organizations gave the opposition DPP a weapon with which to challenge the Kuomintang. Since 1990 DPP proposals that Taiwan try to join the United Nations had evoked a positive public response. The government in 1993 chose to co-opt the issue and began a formal U.N. campaign. (This was consistent with Lee's longstanding demand that Taiwan have an greater international role, and he was more flexible than his foreign ministry on what Taiwan should be called.) Beijing's hard-line response to Taiwan's effort to expand its international role would only harden Lee's stance toward Beijing.[16] At the same time, the DPP was raising questions about the direction of cross-Strait relations. In the spring of 1993, for example, it criticized the government for the lack of transparency surrounding the Koo-Wang talks that were to be held in Singapore at the end of April. This challenge forced the government to limit the agenda of the talks to functional and technical issues.[17]

Lee of course was fostering this pressure by continuing the process of democratization. He thought it was his responsibility to respond to the sentiment of both elites and the public. But democratization had an instrumental value as well. Lee believed increasingly that he could strengthen his leverage vis-à-vis Beijing by releasing populist forces on Taiwan.[18]

As Lee faced growing pressure from the DPP and others, he was freed from constraints from within his own party. Prior to early 1993, he could not completely dominate mainland policy. He had had to compromise with KMT heavyweights, and his statements reflected the consensus reached within the party-state. But in February 1993, Hao Pei-tsun, whom Lee had been forced to take as premier in 1990, left his position. Around the same time, there was a reshuffle of personnel in the organizations responsible for mainland policy that solidified Lee's control over this arena. A few months later, in August, conservatives within the KMT defected to found the Chinese New Party, which began to criticize Lee for insufficient commitment to the cause of unification.[19]

But Lee was not just responding to internal political pressures. There were serious substantive issues at play. He found that as Jiang Zemin assumed greater power in Beijing, Jiang and the people around him were not as flexible as he had thought. Lee had designed the shifts in Taiwan's position in 1991 and 1992, with their symbolic commitment to one China, to give Beijing some cover, in return for which he expected flexibility as well. But Jiang did not respond.

Moreover, burgeoning economic and human contacts between Taiwan and the PRC created the need for at least semiofficial contacts and understanding. That in turn required Lee and his government to offer a more precise definition of what China was, because the PRC was insisting that any agreements be predicated on the "one-China principle." Taiwan was reluctant to comply because doing so might constitute acceptance of Beijing's claim that the Taipei authorities were a local government. That most countries in the world and the United Nations regarded the PRC government as the sole, legal government of China intensified the need to clarify matters. Thus, on August 1, 1992, the National Unification Council, which Lee chaired, passed a resolution that was significant in a number of ways. First of all, it reaffirmed adherence to the one-China principle and the position that both the geographic entities of the mainland and Taiwan were parts of China. But it then clarified how the two governments defined what "one China" meant. As the resolution stated, Beijing's position was that the China was the PRC and that after reunification Taiwan would have the same, subordinate status as Hong Kong. For its part, Taipei made a three-part assertion:

- China meant the ROC, which was founded in 1912 and was by implication a successor state to the Qing dynasty.
- The ROC's sovereignty still covered all of China, but its government's "political power" (jurisdiction) covered only Taiwan, Penghu, Jinmen, and Mazu.

- China therefore was a divided country, with two political entities ruling its respective side of the Strait.

Yet when Jiang gave the political report to the Communist Party's Fourteenth Congress in October 1992, he declared that, "We resolutely oppose 'two Chinas,' 'one China, one Taiwan,' or 'one country, two governments' *in any form*. We resolutely oppose any attempts and actions designed to make Taiwan independent." This was an outright rejection of Taipei's formula of a divided country. Jiang also reiterated the call to move toward talks on "the formal end of hostilities and gradual realization of peaceful reunification." But these talks would be between the CCP and the KMT (not the PRC government and the Taiwan authorities, as in some previous offers), thus denying the status of the ROC government.[20]

The two sides chose to paper over these differences in preparation for the April 1993 meeting between Koo Chen-fu, head of Taiwan's Straits Exchange Foundation (SEF) and Wang Daohan, head of the PRC's Association for Relations Across the Taiwan Strait (ARATS). Beijing dropped its demand that the one-China principle be mentioned in the texts of the technical agreements to be signed, and there was an exchange of communications that permitted the meeting to go forward. ARATS and SEF each stated that the two sides upheld the one-China principle (which was a factual statement at the time). They disagreed on how to talk about unification (with Taiwan a bit less definite) and on whether their differences on the one-China principle were procedural or substantive (with Taiwan emphasizing the substantive). In private, Lee began to talk more skeptically about one China.[21]

Lee became increasingly annoyed that China continued to talk of Taiwan as a subordinate unit and moved to make explicit what was implicit in the NUG's references to parity and political entity. In January 1993, while endorsing the NUC's August 1, 1992 statement, he referred to the two sides as "real, equal political entities." Clarity was necessary because, as he had put it in May 1993, the proliferation of ties between the two sides of the Strait had made serious the "question of national identity." Exchanges blurred the previously clear-cut division, and, in a comment that anticipated Lee's initiative six years later, he said that "the definition of the two sides of the Taiwan Straits became a big problem." One element of that problem was "the trap of 'one country, two systems.'" He came back to this in 1994, when he charged that cross-Strait interaction was being stalled by Beijing's refusal to recognize the fact of "separate entities ruled by two different governments" and to "treat the ROC *as an equal*." In that same year, he referred to the ROC as "a nation within a divided China."[22]

PRC rejection of Lee's overtures was even more apparent in a lengthy statement on cross-Strait relations—"The Taiwan Question and the Reunification of China"—that the Taiwan Affairs and Information Offices of the PRC's State Council issued in August 1993. The statement, which Beijing likely issued in response to Taipei's new official campaign to rejoin the United Nations, reiterated many of the standard elements of the one-country, two systems formula as developed in the early 1980s concerning Taiwan's relationship to China after unification and called again for the three links. It stated that the fact of one China, of which Taiwan was a part and whose central government was in Beijing, was the premise for unification. As with Jiang's speech, this statement reiterated the idea of negotiations—now by "the two sides"—to end the state of hostility. Like Jiang, it suggested some flexibility concerning the modalities of the negotiations, but under the one-China principle. But on Taiwan's fundamental principles—equality, renunciation of force, and an international role, there was no give. Lee had hoped that his earlier concessions would win him some running room on Taiwan's international space. It was not to be.[23]

Lee voiced increasing frustrations about the PRC's diplomatic blockade. He denied that pragmatic diplomacy was designed to create "two Chinas" but believed that it positively reinforced unification and could be a bargaining chip in cross-Strait relations. And in a hint about his future direction, he said: "I'd like to visit the United States most. But not just the United States, the United Kingdom, France, Germany, or Japan would be fine, too. Given the chance, I'd hold discussions with the U.S. president, Japanese prime minister, British prime minister, or French president."[24]

PRC commentators often cite as evidence of Lee's separatist intentions an interview that Lee gave to the Japanese journalist Shiba Ryotaro in April 1994. Beijing was particularly peeved that Lee described the KMT as a foreign regime, spoke of the "sorrow of being Taiwanese," and compared himself to Moses (suggesting, they charged, that he was going to lead the Taiwan people out of China).

Although the interview reflects Lee's change in tone, it does not represent a new direction in his substantive thinking. By and large, Lee's responses were very similar to things he was saying around the same time. When he spoke of the KMT regime he did use the term "*wailai*," which can mean foreign but also outside, or external, and so does not have just a political connotation. He raised again the matter of Taiwan's distinctive identity, and did so in a way that reflected the experiences of his generation. "If I had a chance to meet Mr. Jiang Zemin, I would tell him, 'Before discussing the Taiwan policy or national unification issue, why not study what Taiwan is first?' If they still believe as before that they should rule the people on Taiwan, it will certainly result in events like the February 28 Incident." And his reference to Moses and the Exodus came right at the end, was very brief, and was linked to the February 28 Incident. Lee as Moses was leading the people of Taiwan out of a repressive past, not out of China. To cite the Shiba interview as proof of separatist intent is an over-interpretation.[25]

On the contrary, even after Lee was freed from the constraints of KMT conservatives and under greater pressure from the DPP, all of his statements can be read as an objection to the specific kind of unification that Beijing was proposing. A China in which Taiwan was a subordinate unit with little or no role in the international community was not the kind of China Lee wanted Taiwan and the ROC to be a part of. Because Jiang had ignored Taiwan's proposals and gestures, Lee saw the need to place more emphasis on the Taipei government's fundamental equivalence to Beijing, to define what Taiwan was, and to pursue a more aggressive international agenda. As he told me in July 2003, "I changed my tactics, not my principles."[26]

1995: A MISSED OPPORTUNITY?

On January 30, Jiang Zemin made his first major speech on Taiwan policy, his famous "eight points."[27] By and large, the address reiterated many of the staples of the one country, two systems approach. He opposed Taiwan's activities in "expanding its living space internationally," which, Jiang said, were designed to create two Chinas or one China and one Taiwan. He said the PRC would refuse to rule out the use of force (because Taiwan might respond by declaring independence, which would impel China to use force) He ruled out propositions like "split the country and rule under separate regimes" and "two Chinas over a certain period of time," thus rejecting Taipei's formula of a divided nation under separate rule. He urged talks to end the state of hostilities.

But Jiang's speech did contain new elements, at least concerning tone and process. He said that consultations to prepare for the hostilities talks would be on "an equal footing." He asserted that "Chinese should not fight fellow Chinese." He said "leaders of the Taiwan authorities are welcome to pay visits in appropriate capacities," and that PRC leaders were ready to accept invitations to visit Taiwan. These formulations suggested an effort to move rhetorically in Taipei's direction.

On the other hand, Jiang's proposals were all under the rubric of "the principle of one China," adherence to which was "the basis and premise for peaceful reunification." The principle would frame the agreement to end the state of hostilities and Taipei's international role, and limit Jiang's promise that "anything could be discussed." Everything hinged on the definition of that principle, which Taipei feared would negate its sovereignty. To say that Taiwan leaders would come to China "in appropriate capacities" also raised the issue of the Taipei government's status.

Lee Teng-hui responded to Jiang's "eight points" on April 8, 1995, in an address to the National Unification Council. This was probably his longest and most focused discussion to date of cross-Strait relations. But the "six points" were just a restatement of past policy. He then laid the responsibility for the slow pace of "peaceful reunification" at the door of Beijing: its failure to accept the "84-year existence of the ROC government"; its insistence on sovereignty and jurisdiction ("ruling rights") over Taiwan and the associated islands; and its blockade of Taiwan's rightful place in the international community. He called on Beijing to renounce the use of force against Taiwan. Only if Beijing could accept the reality of "the two shores of the strait being split and separately governed" could there be progress on unification and a greater consensus on the meaning of "one China."[28]

Thus each leader repackaged past positions but did not break any new ground. If Jiang Zemin had thought a different approach to tone and process might accelerate progress on cross-Strait relations, he was disappointed. Lee had two reasons to stand pat. First of all, Jiang had not shown any substantive creativity. Second, he was working hard to score an international success, a trip to the United States, in part to gain public support for his reelection campaign and, he thought, to increase his bargaining power vis-à-vis Beijing.

That visit and Lee's speech at his alma mater, Cornell University, temporarily ended China's flexibility on tone and process. Beijing excoriated Lee, charging that he was promoting Taiwan independence, and it engaged in coercive diplomacy to restrain him. If hostility were to be avoided, China said, he would have to "return to the one-China principle."

But was that trip proof positive that Lee wished to create an independent Taiwan? The PRC (and some Americans) obviously think so.[29] Lee's journey was certainly a challenge to Beijing, and it posed for China the possibility of a trend of high-level travel. Beyond that, the logic of China's allegation is not so clear. How does the mere fact of traveling to the United States and speaking about Taiwan's democratization signify a separatist intent? It may, if one defines as separatism Taiwan's efforts to gain international support for the idea that the Republic of China existed as an equal Chinese government. But again, that sort of quest is not necessarily the same as promoting Taiwan's total separation or irrevocably opposing unification. More likely, China had to oppose Lee's trip because it was contrary to Beijing's own vision of unification, in which the PRC was the exclusive sovereign and that Taiwan's international activities should be subject to its prior approval.[30]

THE MID-1990S: A ROAD BRIEFLY TAKEN

Lee's substantive approach to China took a turn with his Cornell speech and his 1996 inaugural address. He did not totally ignore discussion of the conditions under which Taipei would move forward to unification, and sometimes failed to insist that Beijing renounce force. More important, however, was Lee's greater focus on Taiwan's political significance in the modern Chinese world. In so doing, he sought to establish the moral high ground for Taiwan and reject the idea that the PRC was on the right side of history. Addressing cross-Strait relations in this way was indirect, but it was no less profound in its meaning. And it reflected a commitment to a certain kind of unification.

This of course was not the first time that Lee had sought to suggest that Taiwan might be a model for mainland modernization.[31] But he was more ambitious in his Cornell speech of June 1995, by embedding Taiwan's recent political transformation in the broader sweep of Chinese history. He said his reform efforts were grounded in "the Confucian belief that only the ruler who provides for the needs for his people is given the mandate to rule." In effect, he claimed that Taiwan represented the fulfillment of both the best of Chinese tradition and the most advanced ideas of Western civilization. In contrast, by implication, the PRC manifested the worst of both. Democratization on Taiwan, he asserted, opened up "the most free and liberal era in *Chinese* history." He expressed the hope that, just as he had undertaken his reform effort to satisfy the aspirations of the Taiwan people for an open and competitive system, PRC leaders would be similarly inspired. "Then our achievements on Taiwan can most certainly help the process of economic liberalization and the cause of democracy in mainland China."

The other significant element of Lee's Cornell address was the introduction of the concept of popular sovereignty into the discussion of Taiwan's legal status. The people of Taiwan, and they alone, had chosen all of the members of the National Assembly for the first time in the 1991 and of the Legislative Yuan in 1992. The new National Assembly had amended the constitution further so that direct election of the president would occur for the first time in 1996. Those reforms, taken together, would provide a wholly new justification for the claim that the ROC was a sovereign state. The old rationale, more consistent with traditional international law, was that the ROC was the successor to the Qing dynasty and had existed ever since

1912. Lee's new justification was that the people through elections had constituted their government, a basis for state-creation that was more in line with ideas fostered after the French Revolution. As a sovereign state and a successful democracy, Taiwan also deserved better than the international isolation that it suffered.[32]

Lee gave these ideas his fullest elaboration in his second inaugural address in May 1996.[33] He recalled that despite its excellent traditional culture, China had suffered a series of shocks and lack of confidence in its encounter with the West. In assessing the challenge of cultural reconstruction and regeneration, he expressed the hope that "the people of Taiwan will nurture a new life culture as well as a broad and long-sighted view of life. The new Chinese culture, with moorings in the immense Chinese heritage, will draw upon Western cultural essence to facilitate adapting to the new climate of the next century." Lee went so far as to draw an analogy between the seminal role that the Wei River valley (the central plains, *zhongyuan*) had played in the flowering of traditional Chinese culture and the role that Taiwan (the new central plains, *xinzhongyuan*) would play in fostering a new Chinese culture. "Uniquely situated at the confluence of mainland and maritime cultures, Taiwan has been able in recent decades to preserve traditional culture on the one hand and to come into wide contact with Western democracy and science and modern business culture on the other. Equipped with a much higher level of education and development than in other parts of China, Taiwan is set to gradually exercise its leadership role in cultural development and take upon itself the responsibility for nurturing a new Chinese culture."

This act of historical entrepreneurship is probably the most telling refutation of the idea that Lee was opposed to Taiwan's unification with China. In the early 1990s, the thrust of Lee's statements was that political unification was possible if the terms were right. Now he asserted that Taiwan represented *the best* of China in the modern world, and that China would again become a great civilization and reach "a new height of glory if it followed Taiwan's lead." But if Taiwan was the leading edge of modern Chinese civilization, how, he would ask, could a failed PRC government set itself above the ROC or set the terms on which cross-Strait reconciliation would take place, to the point of denying that the ROC government even existed? Unification should occur under Taiwan's leadership, not that of the PRC. It should occur not only on Taiwan's political terms but on its cultural terms as well. This claim, of course, was heresy to the leaders of the PRC, who sought for themselves the exclusive mantle of returning China to world prominence, their best claim to legitimacy.

Lee did some other things in his inaugural. First of all, he reaffirmed that democratization had ushered in an era of popular sovereignty. "From now on, the people as a whole, rather than any individual or any political party, will be invested with the ruling power of the nation." Popular sovereignty was "the real compliance with the will of Heaven," which meant implicitly that Taiwan was the purest manifestation of traditional Chinese culture.

Second, he reiterated a concept that had justified his promotion of a Taiwan identity. This was *gemeinschaft*, a community based on a common experience and values (*shengming gongtongti* in Chinese). He explained it this way:

> This is our common homeland, and this is the fundamental support we draw upon in our struggle for survival. Fifty years of a common destiny forged in fortune and misfortune have united us all into a closely bound and interdependent community. The first-ever popular presidential election has reconfirmed our collective consciousness that we in Taiwan have to work together as one man.

Third, he said that Taiwan would continue to promote pragmatic diplomacy because its values were the same as those of the new international order (democracy, human rights, and so on), because it needed that space, and because it deserved respect.

And finally, Lee addressed cross-Strait relations. He deplored the century-long tragedy of Chinese fighting Chinese (an allusion to Jiang Zemin's eight points), and expressed his wish for a new era in which "Chinese should help each other." Taiwan's strategy since 1990, he said, was "*expanding cross-strait relations leading to eventual national unification.*" But the Taiwan area had to be well protected and the welfare of its people safeguarded. The PRC had "refused to admit the very fact that the Republic of China does exist" and had engaged in propaganda attacks and military exercises. In one allusion among several to John F. Kennedy's inaugural, he said, "We will never negotiate under threat of attack, but we do not fear to negotiate."[34]

Lee then offered a revised formulation regarding Taiwan's position on dialogue and political reconciliation. Much of it was not new: the ROC was a sovereign state; the two sides were separate jurisdictions that were pursuing eventual unification; Beijing had to accept "facts" and act with sincerity; and an agreement to terminate the state of hostilities was a priority. But there were also new elements. First of all, Lee introduced the idea that Taiwan was already independent and so it was neither necessary nor possible for it to declare independence. He declared his willingness to make a "journey of peace" to the mainland and to meet there with PRC leaders. And he conditioned none of this on a PRC renunciation of the use of force, a pre-

condition that was present in most of his previous statements. He did stip-
ulate that renouncing force was, along with democracy, human rights, and
peace, one of the values of the new international order to which Taiwan adhered and, by implication that the PRC did not. But nowhere did he say
that China had to renounce force before progress of some sort toward reunification could occur.

Over the next three years, Lee did not repeat his ambitious claims for
Taiwan's primacy in China's historical development, although he again referred to Taiwan as a model for mainland development. His discussion of
cross-Strait relations replayed old themes, particularly the need for Beijing
to recognize the political reality of the ROC's existence and that there was,
as he put it in his July 1998 speech to the National Unification Council,
"one divided China." In the same speech he declared, "China must be reunified," but noted that that process would be a function of democratization on the mainland (which was returning as an issue). Only once—in July
1997—did he repeat a demand that Beijing renounce the use of force.[35]

SPECIAL STATE-TO-STATE RELATIONS

On July 9, 1999, Lee granted an interview to reporters from *Deutsche Velle*.
Asked his reaction to what the journalists described as Beijing's view that
Taiwan was a renegade province of China, he responded as follows:

> Historic facts are as follows: Since the PRC's establishment, the Chinese
> communists have never ruled Taiwan, Penghu, Jinmen, and Mazu,
> which have been under the jurisdiction of the Republic of China. In
> 1991, our country amended its Constitution. . . . Consequently, the state
> organs subsequently formed will only represent the Taiwan people. The
> legitimacy of the administration of state power can only be authorized
> by the Taiwan people and has absolutely nothing to do with the people
> on mainland China. Since our constitutional reform in 1991, we have
> designated cross-Strait ties as nation-to-nation (*guojia yu guojia*), or at
> least as special state-to-state ties (*teshu de guoyuguo de guanxi*), rather
> than internal ties within "one China" between a legitimate government
> and a rebellion group, or between central and local governments.[36]

A variety of reasons are offered for Lee's decision to speak out, among
them, influencing domestic politics, building his legacy, and so on. In the
summer of 2003, he told me that he had to make the statement because international lawyers had concluded that Taiwan or the ROC was not a

state.[37] The most plausible, however, is that he believed it was necessary to define precisely Taiwan's identity and that of its governing authorities in terms of international law, in order to prepare for political negotiations with Beijing. As those talks neared, a policy of ambiguity no longer served Taiwan's interests. Nor was this a new concern. As noted above, Lee was calling attention to "the question of national identity" as early as May 1993.

What is important for purposes of this discussion is how this formulation relates to previous ones. To what extent was this a new departure for Lee—as Beijing put it, "an attempt to fundamentally change the status of Taiwan as a part of China"?

Several points are worth noting. In Lee's remarks he alludes to his 1996 inaugural, in which he asserted that popular sovereignty had become a feature of the Taiwan political system ("legitimacy of the administration of state power can only be authorized by the Taiwan people").

Second, there were hints in Lee's prior statements regarding the need more precisely to define Taiwan's legal status. In July 1997, he had said that: "China is a divided nation, ruled by two *distinct* political entities. . . . Only if Taiwan has a *definite* international status can it commence talks with Beijing on an equal footing to discuss the problem of reunification." In June 1998 he had said, "Two sides should talk about international law. In doing that, we would also be talking about sovereignty."[38]

Third, it is important to note precisely what Lee was using this new formula to oppose. It was designed to challenge the ideas that Beijing's relationship to Taipei was one of "internal ties within 'one China' between a legitimate government and a rebellion group, or between central and local governments." This was consistent with Taiwan's long-standing rejection of the one-country, two-systems formula, because that formula places special administrative regions in a subordinate status.

One can therefore conclude that Lee was making explicit what had been implicit in Taipei's position for almost a decade: that the government on Taiwan possessed sovereignty just as the Beijing government did, and so was neither a renegade province nor a local government. Nothing in these statements was a rejection of the idea that Taiwan is a part of China, or that unification was no longer an objective. Lee was addressing the status of Taiwan in international law and the terms of its relationship to that China— and *Beijing's* relationship to that China. His formulation spoke to how Taiwan was a part of China, not *whether* it was. Taiwan had previously used the term "political entity" in part because it thought that ambiguity about the ROC's sovereign nature would promote cross-Strait progress. Late in the decade, however, negotiations with Beijing on political issues were looming and Lee had gotten nowhere with his requests that the PRC acknowledge that the ROC possessed sovereignty and deserved a place in the international community. In order to enter those negotiations from a strong position, clarity had to replace ambiguity.

There is an alternative interpretation: that Lee in fact was claiming something entirely new for Taiwan. It was not just that the words *guojia* and *guo* could have a range of meanings, some more provocative than others. More significant is the clear possibility that Lee and his advisers were asserting that Taiwan was, in international law terms, a state totally separate from the Chinese state. This was in contrast to the traditional view that the ROC was the sole legal government of the Chinese state, or the more recent view that the Chinese state was divided, with two sovereign governments—the ROC and PRC.

Strengthening this conclusion is the focus in Lee's statement on the point that *constitutional* changes had limited the territorial jurisdiction of the ROC government to the islands of Taiwan, Penghu, Jinmen, and Mazu. This may relate, I would venture, to the five explicit criteria for statehood as defined by the Montevideo Convention. These are: a permanent population, effective government, capacity to enter into relations with other states, independence, and a defined territory.[39] Taiwan indubitably satisfied the first four criteria, but its stance on the latter was ambiguous. It appears, therefore, that Lee's advisers sought to provide a stronger rationale for the ROC's sovereign status; that the one point at which Taiwan did not meet the criteria for statehood in international law was defined territory; and that they then went through the ROC constitution as amended to find provisions that supported the idea that the Taipei government had a well-defined territory.[40] In addition, Lee may have been meeting another implicit criterion, that the leaders of an entity assert that it is a state. His July statement thus met that requirement as well.[41]

CONCLUSION

This discussion has had a single, very simple purpose: to lay out in detail what Lee Teng-hui said about cross-Strait relations during the twelve years and four months of his presidency. Based on his many words on the subject, a couple of conclusions are apparent.

First of all, contrary to Beijing's allegations and the beliefs of some non-Chinese, he did not advocate a Taiwan nation-state that was totally divorced from an entity called China. Even when he asserted explicitly that the Republic of China was a state on a par with the PRC, he did not regard that status as inconsistent with the unification of China and the end of the state of division between the two sides of the Strait. Throughout his presidency, he focused on the terms and conditions under which unification should take place, not whether it should. Those terms got tougher or more precise as time went on, but their object was never ruled out.

To be sure, one may argue that Lee's claims for the ROC were in fact inconsistent with unification, or that they were designed to make unification impossible. That, in effect, is the approach that Beijing has taken. From its point of view, any proposal at odds with one country, two systems, and any proposal premised on sovereignty for the Taipei government, had the effect, and perhaps the motivation, of permanently separating Taiwan from China. Lee was therefore a splittist. Yet at an abstract level, such a conclusion is justified only if those who assert it first demonstrate that national unification cannot occur among sovereign entities. And clearly, there are models where it does occur. Confederation, federations, and commonwealths come to mind. Of course, designing a workable arrangement for the cross-Strait context would not be easy. But that is different from saying that Lee was *ipso facto* a separatist by adopting the substantive approach that he did.

Second, the continuity in Lee's core principles is striking. Despite some variation over time depending on circumstances, Lee placed constant emphasis on three points: within the context of a unified China, the governing authorities in Taipei possessed sovereignty and were essentially equal to the government in Beijing; Taiwan had the right to play a significant role in the international community; Beijing's growing military capabilities and its refusal to renounce their use was an obstacle to reconciliation. For all these reasons, and particularly the first two, the one country, two systems formula was unacceptable.

How these three themes were played out did change over time. Taipei's emphasis on participation in the international community increased in the mid-1990s as domestic resentment over the island's isolation grew. Lee mounted his effort to visit the United States in order to break Beijing's blockade. Beginning with his second inaugural address, he dropped the explicit demand that Beijing renounce the use of force. And Lee publicly declared his state-to-state formula after many years of speaking of two equal political entities, probably in anticipation of negotiations on political issues. Yet these were shifts of emphasis on issues that never lost their centrality. And one may argue that Lee's statements and actions on all three were a response to Beijing's inflexible stance—for example, its refusal to accommodate a role for Taiwan in the international community and to acknowledge that the Taiwan government was qualitatively different from Hong Kong and Macau.

There is some reason, discussed above, to conclude that Lee's special-state-to-state announcement was a significant shift in position. There is no question that this formulation was a new way of talking about a fundamental issue. And there is no question that Beijing chose to read the worst into this statement. I am inclined to believe that Lee was making explicit what had been implicit in his and Taipei's views on the first of its three key, constant issues—the nature of the government in Taipei.

Lee did have a more general tendency to state issues in a way that was more provocative than some of his subordinates. His public statements about the National Unification Guidelines were somewhat less conciliatory than the guidelines themselves. And Lee was not afraid to take a tough rhetorical stance. That was part of his negotiating style, a belief that soft words were not the way to blunt PRC aggressiveness. (Close analysis would probably show his feistiness was often a response to verbal challenges from Beijing.) Issues of style aside, however, Lee was right in the mainstream of Taiwan views in the 1990s on how to approach cross-Strait relations. Public opinion polls and all major political parties shared his view that the government possessed sovereignty, that the people of the island had a right to be represented in the international system, and that the PRC's growing military capabilities were an obstacle to reconciliation. Lee helped shape that opinion, of course. It was one of the political defenses that he erected during his presidency against a too-easy accommodation to Beijing and one country, two systems (democratization, restrictions on economic interactions with the Mainland, fostering a Taiwan identity, pragmatic diplomacy, and a left-center political coalition were the others). But the cautious consensus he fostered would not have been possible if such sentiments had not already existed in latent form and if Beijing had not taken steps designed to intimidate the Taiwan populace. The issue of international space he co-opted from the opposition.

Some may claim that Lee Teng-hui formulated his position in a way that made unification impossible. His approach did make one country, two systems impossible, but for reasons that most people on Taiwan would support. And his approach did get tougher as time went on. That he did so makes sense, however. In the early 1990s, the two sides agreed to set political issues aside in order to solve practical problems and build a process of interaction. By mid-decade, however, political issues were coming to the fore. Lee was getting nowhere with his appeals that Beijing acknowledge that Taipei was an equal political entity, with all that position entailed. And the PRC was blockading Taiwan's attempt to reenter the international system at every turn. By 1998, however, Taipei had decided that it was impossible to keep political issues off the agenda. Hence the need to define more precisely the legal status of the Taiwan government. And we should recall that Lee was being asked to negotiate the permanent future of 23 million people, 12 million of whom vote. He had no choice but to be careful.

Some might argue that Lee said one thing and did another, and that his statements might sound good but his actions reveal a less-than-benign intent. Recall the bill of particulars that the PRC White Paper of February 2000 presented. Lee's "measures toward actual separation" were reform of the political structure, creating a Taiwan identity, purchasing weapons from the United States, and seeking more international space. Yet most of these steps were important for their own sake, and responded to demands from within Taiwan society. The purchase of arms from the United States was a response to Beijing's own military modernization and its refusal to renounce the use of force. All were consistent with Taipei's definition of its status as a sovereign government. None constituted *prima facie* proof that Lee intended permanently to separate Taiwan from China—*unless the only formula for unification excluded those elements.* If one looks at specifics, moreover, Lee's actions—his 1995 visit to the United States, for example—do not necessarily have the meaning that Beijing and others attribute to them.

That Beijing misperceived Lee's intentions is more than a matter of historical interest. For it raises questions about the decisionmaking system that came to such an erroneous conclusion and whether that same system is likely to make other misjudgments about its adversaries. After all, the current Taiwan government has the same fundamental views on Taiwan's sovereignty, its international role, and PRC military intentions that Lee did. Similarly, Beijing took actions based on its misperceptions that increased tensions in the Taiwan Strait area and posed challenges to the United States. Future tensions—and even conflict—born of miscalculation cannot be ruled out.

There is, of course, the possibility that Beijing understood Lee perfectly well but chose to reject his proposals for reasons that had nothing to do with his substantive views. Perhaps one country, two systems was immutable because Deng Xiaoping was its author. Perhaps it feared that if it acknowledged that the Taiwan government possessed sovereignty—that sovereignty could be shared—then Hong Kong, Macau, the Dalai Lama, and even Guangdong and Shanghai might seek to take advantage of that precedent. Perhaps it feared that Lee Teng-hui's approach to the Chinese state and its constituent elements might undermine the Communist Party's legitimacy and its claim to rule as the exclusive sovereign (and perhaps labeling Lee as a separatist was a useful way to cover its tracks).

Whatever the case, there can be no fundamental solution to the Taiwan Strait issue while the sovereignty question is in dispute. In the meantime, the disagreement will impede progress on a variety of more practical issues, such as direct transportation links. To untie this knot, either Beijing will have to give up the substantive core of one country, two systems, or the leaders and people of Taiwan will have to abandon their claim that their government possesses sovereignty. Loosening the knot in order to untie it will require some understanding of why it got tied in the first place.

CHAPTER FIVE:

China-Taiwan Economic Linkage:

BETWEEN INSULATION AND SUPERCONDUCTIVITY

T. J. CHENG

CHINA AND TAIWAN are an uncommon dyad. In general, trade and investment are minimal and minimized between political rivals.[1] Yet, a dense economic nexus coexists with deeply entrenched political conflict across the Taiwan Strait. Although security relations are often strained and political détente remains elusive, cross-Strait economic interaction has been intensifying since the early 1990s. Moreover, the pattern of economic interaction in this uncommon dyad is utterly asymmetric. The weaker party (in terms of size, population, and military might), Taiwan, has become substantially more dependent on the stronger party, China, for export and investment opportunities. Furthermore, the weaker side is a democracy with active interest group and national identity politics, while the stronger side remains a Leninist regime that has proclaimed jurisdiction over, and has intimidated, Taiwan. Yet, on a per capita basis, Taiwan has sent more capital to China than has any other country.[2] All these factors raise the question of whether economic inter-

Thanks are due to Nancy Bernkopf Tucker, Deborah Brown, Robert Sutter, Alan Wachman, and the participants at a workshop conducted by the Department of State, Georgetown University and George Washington University for their comments on an earlier draft of this essay. I also gratefully acknowledge the receipt of a semester research assignment from the College of William and Mary to pursue this project.

action across the Strait would jeopardize Taiwan's security, economy, and political autonomy.

This essay examines the nature of economic linkage across the Strait and its implications for Taiwan, by looking at the question in general, and also through a case study of the semiconductor industry. Section I discusses the volume, directional flows, and composition of trade and investment as well as various policies that attempted to shape multiple dimensions of increasingly asymmetric interdependence across the Strait. Policies made in Beijing have remained steady, subtle, and effective, while policies made in Taipei have gone through major transformation, and their intended consequences have been elusive at best.

Section II explores the putative and actual impact on Taiwan of growing trade and investment in China. Asymmetric economic interdependence does not seem to give Beijing leverage to coerce Taipei, nor does it necessarily turn Taiwan businessmen (dubbed *Taishang* in the literature) into a pro-unification force. *Taishang* have tended to advocate economic policies that are more compatible with the preferences of leaders in Beijing than those of leaders in Taipei. Although economic ties with China have contributed to Taiwan's industrial upgrade, the warning signs of an industrial "hollowing-out" are looming in Taiwan.

Section III provides a case study of the semiconductor industry, the most advanced segment of the broadly defined microelectronic industry. Microelectronics has long been the mainstay of Taiwan's manufacturing sector. The recent decision by the Taiwan government conditionally to lift the ban on Taiwanese firms' production of IC (integrated circuits) in China raises the question of whether it is possible to modulate economic interaction across the Strait and preserve political "semiconductivity" or whether the ties are escalating into "superconductivity."

The final section of the essay addresses the current efforts on the part of Taiwan to upgrade and diversify its industry, in general, in order to maintain its economic resilience. Instead of discouraging businesses from going to China or directing them to Southeast Asia, the Taiwan government is helping them to continue to use Taiwan as their base to globalize their operations and production. The final section then concludes that continued globalization is the only antidote to the much feared "mainlandization" of Taiwan's economy.

This essay avoids using the term economic integration to characterize economic relations across the Strait. Economic integration is a goal-driven process that nation-states legally commit to and consciously promote. Each step in the ladder of economic integration, from a preferential trade arrangement, free trade agreement, customs union, common market, to an economic union, is based on a contractual arrangement. Cementing any such agreement between Beijing and Taipei will be a daunting task, as such agreement may be construed as a contract between two sovereign powers, or a prelude to political unification. The Beijing regime and both pro-unification and pro-independence forces in Taiwan will question the ulterior motive of any proposal for economic integration across the Strait. Proposals will abound, but the probability of any one being accepted is low.[3]

I. DEEPENING OF ECONOMIC TIES

Taiwan's trade with China began in the mid-1980s and the volume of trade has increased ever since. As table 5.1 shows, China absorbed 3.21 percent of Taiwan's total exports in 1985; the share went up to 24.68 percent in 2002, while the share of Taiwanese goods among China's imports grew from 2.34 percent to 10.92 percent during the same period. The rate of increase has been particularly noticeable since the early 1990s, a trend hardly arrested by the 1995–96 missile crisis,[4] the 1999 "two states theory" crisis,[5] China's intimidation during the March 2000 Taiwan presidential election,[6] or the SARS crisis in the spring of 2003.[7] Exports to Taiwan as a portion of China's total exports and imports from China as a portion of Taiwan's total imports have remained at low single-digit levels throughout the period. China thus is an important destination for Taiwanese goods and Taiwan is a significant source of China's imports. However, Taiwan is not a crucial export market for China, while China is not high on the list for Taiwan's outsourcing. Thus, the movement of goods is predominantly westward from Taiwan to China, resulting in a huge trade surplus in Taiwan's favor, US$23.5 billion (all future $ amounts are in US dollars) in 2002, which made up for Taiwan's overall trade deficit with its other partners of $4.45 billion, yielding Taiwan's total trade surplus of $18.05 billion.[8]

Intermediate and capital goods were main Taiwanese exports to China in the 1990s. The most important change throughout the decade was the declining share of textile goods and the drastic increase of the share for machinery and electrical goods, reaching close to half of Taiwan's total exports to China in 2001 (see table 5.2). The imports from China to Taiwan used to be agricultural goods, but beginning in the second half of the 1990s, semi- and finished labor-intensive products began to loom large, indicating that the division of labor in production was improving.

The cross-Strait trade pattern has been shaped by the pattern of direct investment. There have been three waves of Taiwanese investment in China so

TABLE 5.1 TRADE INTERDEPENDENCE ACROSS THE STRAITS

Years	Taiwan's Export to China ($Millions)	Taiwan's Import from China ($Millions)	Export to China (% of total export)	Import From China (% of total import)	Export to Taiwan (% of total export)	Import From Taiwan (% of total import)	(X+M/ Taiwan's GDP)	(X+M/ China's GDP)
			TAIWAN'S TRADE DEPENDENCE ON CHINA		CHINA'S TRADE DEPENDENCE ON TAIWAN		TRADE VOLUME AS A SHARE OF GDP	
1981	385	75	1.70	0.35	0.34	1.75	102.3	-
1982	195	84	0.88	0.44	0.38	1.01	95.1	-
1983	201	90	0.80	0.44	0.40	0.94	97.4	-
1984	426	128	1.40	0.58	0.49	1.55	100.1	-
1985	987	116	3.21	0.58	0.42	2.34	93.1	23.05
1986	811	144	2.04	0.60	0.47	1.89	94.1	-
1987	1,227	289	2.28	0.83	0.73	2.84	95.4	-
1988	2,242	479	3.70	0.96	1.01	4.06	95.5	-
1989	3,332	587	5.03	1.12	1.12	5.63	89.6	-
1990	4,395	765	6.54	1.40	1.23	8.24	88.4	29.98
1991	7,494	1,126	9.84	1.79	1.57	11.75	88.2	33.43
1992	10,548	1,119	12.95	1.55	1.32	13.09	83.4	34.24
1993	13,993	1,104	16.47	1.43	1.20	13.46	84.9	32.54
1994	16,023	1,859	17.22	2.18	1.54	13.85	84.2	43.59
1995	19,434	3,091	17.40	2.98	2.08	14.71	92.8	40.19
1996	20,727	3,060	17.87	3.02	2.03	14.93	90.1	35.55
1997	22,455	3,915	18.39	3.42	2.14	15.77	93.4	36.22
1998	19,841	4,111	17.94	3.93	2.24	14.16	60.9	34.28
1999	21,313	4,522	17.52	4.09	2.32	12.86	92.9	36.43
2000	25,010	6,223	16.86	4.44	2.50	11.11	105.1	43.91
2001	21,946	5,902	17.86	5.50	2.22	9.01	93.8	43.98
2002	32,231	8,775	24.68	7.80	2.70	10.92	97.9	-

Source: Investment Commission, Ministry of Economic Affairs, Republic of China, *Statistics on Overseas Chinese & Foreign Investment and Outward Investment*, various years.

far. The first one began in the late 1980s in the wake of Taiwan dollar appreciation and the removal of restrictions on capital outflow.[9] Taiwanese businesses were predominantly small- and medium-sized enterprises (SMEs) in labor-intensive traditional sectors, such as garments, shoe-making, and low-end consumer electronics, seeking lower labor costs to defend their export market share in the West. Initially, most *Taishang* went to Southeast Asia, but more and more found their way to China, especially after 1989, as multinational corporations (MNCs) were suspending or withdrawing their investment in China.

China patriarch Deng Xiaoping's tour to South China to outmaneuver the conservatives in Beijing and to re-ignite reform, as well as the first cross-Strait talk (the Koo-Wang meeting) of the spring of 1993, ushered in the second wave of Taiwan's investment.[10] While the rush of SMEs continued, larger and mostly public-listed companies joined the march as well. (Notice that the spike in the 1993 statistics in tables 5.3 and 5.4, below, was in part due to belated registration with the Investment Commission, Ministry of Economic Affairs, Taiwan, by those who went to China for investment surreptitiously during the previous years.) Most large firms, especially those in the petrochemical industry, went to China in order to supply intermediate goods to SMEs in proximity and to look for cheap and accessible land for expansion. As in the first wave of "China fever," the push factor was in play as well. As the environmental movement and middle-class demand for quality of life gained momentum, most counties and townships in Taiwan were simply hostile to big and potentially polluting investment items.[11]

Other big firms, especially those in the food processing industry, began to penetrate China's market. Some big firms also eyed infrastructure projects. In bidding for membership in the General Agreement on Tariffs and Trade (GATT) and, since 1994, the World Trade Organization (WTO), China sometimes unilaterally reduced tariff rates, but its market remained quite closed to foreign firms. Taiwanese firms in upstream and midstream production had to go behind China's tariff wall to supply the export-oriented, downstream Taiwan concerns that had already migrated to China. China's domestic market was not necessarily wide open to *Taishang*. In the petrochemical industry, state regulated prices and other non-tariff barriers were protecting PRC state enterprises.[12] But *Taishang* were pre-positioning themselves in a market that was expected to expand and liberalize.

Firms in the information technology sector spearheaded the big third wave of investment beginning in the late 1990s. As early as 1995–96, firms manufacturing computers and peripherals already had begun to venture into the Guangzhou area. But the exodus from Taiwan has been most noticeable since 1998, and this time around mostly to the Shanghai area. Some

TABLE 5.2 MAJOR EXPORT COMMODITIES FROM TAIWAN TO MAINLAND CHINA VIA HONG KONG

	2000 / JAN.–JULY		1999			1998		
Rank	HS Code	Share(%)	HS Code	Share(%)	Rank	Rank	HS Code	Share(%)
1	847330	8.14	847330	7.58	1	1	847330	5.51
2	854213	4.71	854213	2.79	3	-	-	-
3	390330	3.47	390330	3.07	2	5	390330	2.4
4	854230	2.87	854230	1.94	8	-	-	-
5	540742	2.41	540742	2.58	5	3	540742	3.12
6	590310	2.36	590310	2.74	4	2	590310	3.19
7	850490	2.05	850490	1.9	9	10	850490	1.87
8	540752	1.88	540752	2.07	7	9	540752	1.92
9	600293	1.64	600293	2.09	6	4	600293	2.73
10	392042	1.56	392042	1.89	10	6	392042	2.21
11	854219	1.54	-	-	-	-	-	-
12	900691	1.41	900691	1.06	18	-	-	-
13	852990	1.39	852990	1.35	13	-	-	-
14	390319	1.34	390319	1.24	16	17	390319	1.14
15	410422	1.22	410422	1.25	15	12	410422	1.48
16	600243	1.15	600243	1.26	14	13	600243	1.37
17	590320	1.07	590320	1.11	17	16	590320	1.16
			854040	1.67	11	7	550320	1.98
			721934	1.58	12	8	540233	1.94
						11	540243	1.86
						14	854040	1.25
						15	721934	1.24

Note:
1. Only items with at least 1% of total exports are listed above.
2. HS codes are described as follows:

   HS 847330: Automatic data processing machines and units thereof; magnetic or optical readers or scanners
   HS 854213: Metal oxide semiconductors (MOS technology)
   HS 854230: Other monolithic integrated circuits
   HS 850490: Static converters & parts
   HS 854219: Circuits obtained by a combination of bipolar and MOS technologies (BIMOS technology)
   HS 852990: TV & parts

Source: www.mac.gov.tw, *Cross-Strait Economic Statistics Monthly*, various years

TABLE 5.3 TAIWAN'S OUTBOUND INVESTMENT BY DESTINATION
(% SHARE OF THE TOTAL)

	CHINA	HK	SINGAPORE	ASEAN4	BRITISH TERRITORIES (INCL BRIT VIRGIN IS.)
1989	n.a.	n.a.	n.a.	n.a.	n.a.
1990	n.a.	n.a.	n.a.	n.a.	n.a.
1991	9.5	10.9	0.7	37.7	14.6
1992	21.8	4.8	0.8	24.7	21.1
1993	65.6	3.4	1.4	4.3	4.0
1994	37.3	4.9	3.9	7.3	22.1
1995	44.6	4.1	1.3	7.6	15.1
1996	36.2	1.8	4.9	9.5	23.8
1997	60.0	2.0	3.2	4.5	14.5
1998	38.2	1.3	3.0	3.9	34.5
1999	27.7	2.2	7.2	3.6	30.1
2000	33.9	0.6	2.9	1.5	29.3
subtotal					
1991–1997	47.8	3.6	2.6	9.4	14.9
subtotal					
1998-2000	33.6	1.2	4.0	2.8	31.1
Total					
1991–2000	41.7	2.6	3.2	6.6	21.8

Source: Investment Commission, Ministry of Economic Affairs ROC, *Statistics on Overseas Chinese & Foreign Investment and Outward Investment*, December 2000.

firms went to China to tap the domestic market, but most firms migrated for lower labor costs, as Western firms began to request their Taiwanese sub-contractors to use China's production costs as the base to quote prices.[13] Land and labor costs in China are substantially lower than those in Taiwan. Moreover, these firms have not encountered difficulties in receiving payments for their export-oriented goods, a problem that has been endemic to foreign firms that sell their goods in China's domestic market. Since 2000, companies in the semiconductor industry—chip making, designing, testing, and packaging—have also been poised to invest in China, a story we shall return to in Section III. Meanwhile, cement, real estate, banking, and other local market-oriented industries are either queuing up for entry to China (banking and real estate) or stepping up their investment in China (cement and other sectors).

TABLE 5.4 TAIWAN'S OUTBOUND INVESTMENT TO CHINA—BY INDUSTRIES

Unit: million; %

Year / Industry	2002 Value	2002 %	2001 Value	2001 %	2000 Value	2000 %	1999 Value	1999 %	1998 Value	1998 %	1997 Value	1997 %	1996 Value	1996 %	1995 Value	1995 %	Accumulation of 1991-1994 Value	%
Electronic and Electric Appliances	2618.7	39.0	1254.8	45.1	1464.8	56	537.8	42.9	759.0	37	875.0	20	276.9	23	214.8	20	668.2	15
Chemicals	474.4	7.1	163.8	5.9	110.78	4.2	143.0	11.4	146.8	7	231.2	5	98.8	8	94.6	9	294.7	7
Plastic Products	398.8	5.9	156.1	5.6	184.78	7.1	99.1	7.9	64.2	3	349.1	8	63.6	5	62.7	6	512.5	11
Machinery Equipment & Precision Instruments	665.8	9.9	242.3	8.7	145.2	5.6	59.3	4.7	74.6	4	247.3	6	39.9	3	29.5	3	355.4	8
Food and Beverage Processing	152.9	2.3	58.4	2.1	43.253	1.7	58.3	4.7	70.0	3	330.1	8	121.7	10	117.4	11	534.7	12
Basic Metals & Metal Products	631.5	9.4	193.8	7.0	183.85	7.1	104.5	8.3	126.8	6	396.0	9	128.1	10	116.8	11	364.2	8
Textile	127.5	1.9	22.5	0.8	39.588	1.5	34.3	2.7	129.5	6	208.5	5	96.9	8	60.9	6	265.8	6
Others*	1653.5	24.6	692.4	24.9	434.91	17	216.7	17.3	663.7	34	1,697.10	39	403.3	33	396.0	34	1,556.20	33
Total	6723.1	100.0	2784.1	100.0	2607.1	100	1,252.8	100.0	2,034.6	100	4,334.3	100	1,229.2	100	1,092.7	100	4,551.70	100

Sources: Investment Commission, MOEA, ROC.

Note: * including: non-metallic minerals; transport equipment; machinery equipment and others.

**The surging amount of 1997–98 are partly because of the extension of deadline for approval by Taiwan government. Lagged statistics are combined with the original data here.

It is unknown exactly how much of Taiwan's direct investment (versus portfolio investment) is lodged in China, for many Taiwanese firms routed through many other locales to reach China, hence they are not registered or are wrongly classified in Taiwan's statistics. The number and amount of Taiwan's investment cases are certainly better reflected in China's statistics, but they are not fully captured there either. As of the second half of 2002, the official figure for Taiwan's cumulative direct investment (actual, not approved, investment) in China was $25.2 billion (and 26,497 cases) according to Taiwan's Ministry of Economic Affairs statistics, and $33.2 billion according to China's statistics. A more realistic figure was $66.8 billion, according to Taiwan's Central Bank, which includes in its estimates Taiwan's investment in China via tax havens. Some private sector estimates based on insiders' money transfer experiences were as high as $100 billion, which was not entirely incredible. If we assume that Taiwan's investment in British territories (the Virgin and Cayman islands) eventually found its way to China, then China absorbed 63.5 percent of Taiwan's total outward direct investment between 1991 and 2000 (see table 5.3).

Table 5.4 shows the changing composition of Taiwan's investment in China during the 1990s. The shares of plastic products, food processing, and textiles shrank drastically, while chemicals, machinery and basic metals fluctuated to different degrees. The shares of electronics and electric appliances grew steadily and expanded most drastically after 1998, indicating that the information technology sector has indeed been the mainstay of Taiwan's investment in China since 1998. This compositional change of investment also resulted in Taiwan's growing exports of machinery and electrical products to China, as mentioned above, and as table

TABLE 5.5 OVERSEAS PRODUCTION OF TAIWAN'S ELECTRONICS, ELECTRICAL, AND INFORMATION SECTORS

YEAR	OVERSEAS OUTPUT AS A SHARE OF TOTAL OUTPUT	OUTPUT FROM MAINLAND AS A SHARE OF OVERSEAS OUTPUT	OUTPUT FROM MALAYSIA & THAILAND AS A SHARE OF OVERSEAS OUTPUT
1995	28	50	44
1996	32	53	40
1997	37	62	31
1998	43	67	23
1999	46	72	20
2000		73	

Source: www.mem.com.tw, *Micro-Electronics*, 2000.

5.5 shows, a higher ratio of mainland output in total overseas output (which by itself was already increasing) of Taiwan's electronic, electrical, and information sectors.

Market conditions called for *Taishang* to trade with and invest in China. But policies of various sorts did intervene; obviously Chinese governments at all levels induced Taiwanese investment, while the Taiwan Government restrained it. Taken as a whole, *Taishang* responded more to market conditions than the policies, and more to China's than Taiwan's policies.

China's overall policy has two sides: one pertains to the protection of Taiwan investment, the other is related to incentives. Protection of Taiwan's investment was first pronounced in Marshall Ye Jianying's Nine Points in 1981, then in the State Council's 22 Articles in 1988. It was incorporated in the Investment Protection Law enacted by the National People's Congress in 1994, and the Implementation Regulations for this law promulgated by the State Council in 1999. The promise to protect *Taishang* investment is obviously based on the China central government's unilateral commitments (rather than on a bilateral agreement). When it comes to incentives, tax concessions (two years of corporate tax exemption plus three years of 50 percent reduction) and land provision (via construction of industrial estates) are two main components. These incentive packages are sector-specific, even firm-specific, and vary from locality to locality, but general trends are discernible. In the early 1990s, foreign direct investment (FDI) versus foreign borrowing became the main mode of capital inflow for China, and the intent was to use FDI (including *Taishang* investment) to create jobs and promote exports.[14] Labor-intensive, export-oriented SMEs fit the policy need, and their investment in various forms (joint ventures, wholly owned subsidiaries, or simply subcontracting, cooperative production arrangements) was welcome. In the mid-1990s, the government went after the capital-intensive and land-using sector as well, a new drive in tandem with the establishment of industrial estates. Indeed, big Taiwanese firms had even been invited to participate in infrastructure projects.[15] Then in the post-1997 era, the development of high technology sectors became a leadership project for newly appointed premier Zhu Rongji, and Taiwanese firms in the information technology sector have been on the priority list for invitation.[16] In her pathbreaking visit to Taiwan's Hsinchu Science and Industrial Park in 1998, Zhu Lilan, China's Minister of Science and Technology, called for the synergy of system engineers and computer scientists across the Strait.[17] In general, China's policies to attract Taiwan's investment in the early and late 1990s were more successful than in the mid-1990s.

Taiwan's policy was initially reactive, but quickly became restrictive. Typically, its private sector took the lead, bypassing existing policies, and then policy measures followed. The post-facto regulations allowed indirect trade and investment under a tripartite scheme: permissive, prohibitive, and special case, and required a permit for each transaction, which was subject to review regarding national security and the impact on the domestic economy. The overall thrust of the policy was to regulate economic flow in such a way as to support political initiatives. Initially, the Taiwan government hoped to leverage Taiwan's trade and investment in China for political concessions (that China should renounce the use of force toward Taiwan, treat the Taipei regime as an equal to the Beijing regime, and not interfere with the development of Taiwan's diplomatic relations).[18] With or without official permission, *Taishang*, primarily of small- and medium-size enterprises, traded with the mainland, mostly via Hong Kong, and poured investment into coastal China, hoping to maintain their market share in American and European markets, leading the government to pursue a "Go South" policy in 1994.

The "Go South" policy was meant to direct Taiwan's outward investment away from China and toward Southeast Asia. The Ministry of Economic Affairs "adopted" the Subic Bay industrial estate project in the Philippines and "persuaded" the KMT's Central Investment Company to finance the development of an industrial zone in Vietnam's Ho Chi Minh City. The government also assiduously promoted investment in Malaysia and Thailand. The "Go South" policy failed to stem the tide, however. Although Taiwanese investment in China and Southeast Asia was roughly equal at the end of the 1980s, the former dwarfed the latter by four to one in the mid-1990s. Taiwan's exports to China also swelled, as Taiwanese firms shipped more machinery and intermediate goods to China to support their new ventures.

The 1995–96 missile tests temporarily slowed down *Taishang* investment in China, but not cross-Strait trade. As soon as President Lee Teng-hui sent out an olive branch in his inauguration speech in May 1996 by proposing to make a peace journey to China, Taiwan's direct investment in China rebounded strongly, leading the government to issue a policy of "go slow, be patient" (*jie-ji yung-ren*) in late August 1996. This "Go Slow" policy forbade the *Taishang*'s participation in any infrastructure project on the mainland, restricted investment in the high-tech sector there, and subjected mainland-bound projects of any type exceeding US $50 million to approval on a case-by-case basis.[19]

The "Go Slow" policy constrained Taiwan's investment on the mainland. Some firms abided by it, many bypassed it via a third place, which explained the sudden rise of Taiwan's investment in British territories in the Caribbean region. To those firms not making investments in China, the policy was unfair; for those surreptitiously investing in China, it was ineffective; and to both groups, it was an unnecessarily self-limiting policy.

Toward the end of the decade, the "Go Slow" policy drew criticism from most business sectors, in particular from the high-tech sector, forcing the government to switch to the current policy of "active opening, effective management" (*ji-ji kai-fang, you-xiao guan-li*) to manage economic ties with China, an issue that Section III will address.

II. IMPACT: PUTATIVE, REAL, AND POTENTIAL

The deepening economic ties with China are so lopsided that three concerns have often been raised regarding their negative impact on Taiwan. First, China seemingly is in a position to use Taiwan's economic dependence as leverage to coerce Taiwan politically and militarily. It is feared that, *Taishang*, so glued to the Chinese economy, could unintentionally become a liability for Taiwan's security and autonomy, creating a "hostage effect," a term used in Taiwan's public discourse. This essay submits that the probability for China to impose economic sanctions on Taiwan remains low in the foreseeable future, because of the high costs of replacing Taiwan's investment and suspending trade with Taiwan. A second concern is that the *Taishang* could unwittingly become a political force championing the cause on behalf of, if not at the behest of, Taiwan's political adversary. In public policy discourse, this is often described as the "Fifth Column" effect, a condition under which *Taishang* could inadvertently become political agents for the other party. This worry is probably unwarranted, as *Taishang* are not necessarily for unification. Although their interests have led them to lobby the Taiwan government for policy change, their behavior is akin to what other foreign enterprises (including those in the United States) do to their home governments. The third concern has to do with the harm that economic linkage might cause to Taiwan's economy, called the industrial "hollowing out" effect in public discourse. In fact, the exodus of *Taishang* to China (and to Southeast Asia earlier) has entailed beneficial industrial effects in Taiwan. However, the *Taishang*'s rush to China may now threaten to "hollow out" Taiwan's industry.

Are *Taishang* giving China leverage over Taiwan? Chinese leadership has publicly stated its intention to use economic linkage across the Strait for political purposes (*yi-jingji-cu-zhengzhi*), and to use the private sector to "compel" the Taiwan government to yield to the Beijing regime's plan for unification (*yi-min-bi-guan*).[20] Citing a People's Liberation Army internal document, Taiwan's Vice President Annette Lu has warned that China is deepening Taiwan's dependence on the Chinese economy, while preparing for a military showdown in 2010, by which time the resistance to unification is expected to be further enhanced.[21]

The worry about China's likely economic coercion of Taiwan for political subjugation is based on the two following considerations. First, in general, export dependency creates more vulnerability than import dependency, as alternative export markets are more difficult to find than alternative import sources, oil being a notable exception. Export markets need to be nurtured and earned, while substitute imports can be easily secured if one is willing to pay a higher premium. In 2002, Taiwan depended on China to absorb 25 percent of its exports, while China relied on Taiwan for only 11 percent of its total imports. Indeed, beginning in 2002, China supplanted the United States to become the number one export market for Taiwan. Second, FDI in one's political adversary is even riskier than trade dependency. In trade, two sides swap goods, but in FDI, firms are stuck in a host country. In general, foreign firms have bargaining power before making the location choice for their direct investment, but once the choice is made, the power shifts to the host government, as relocation is often costly and foreign firms' operations hinge on logistical support from the host country.[22] Recall that Taiwan has invested more than any other country in China on a per capita basis, and that China has assiduously disputed Taiwan's sovereignty.

However, the probability of imposing sanctions on Taiwan might be low given that the cost of doing so would be very high for China. First, Taiwan's export dependence on China needs to be understood in a broader context. Although *Taishang* ship many Taiwanese goods to China, they also sell many Chinese goods abroad. It is estimated that *Taishang* exported 85 percent of what they produced in China in 1992, 70 percent in 1996, and 45 to 50 percent in 1998, and their exports accounted for 14.4 percent of China's total exports in 1994 and 14 to 22 percent in 1996.[23] Moreover, the United States—the security guarantor for Taiwan—is China's most significant export market and the principal source of China's earnings. As Nicholas Lardy of the Institute of International Economics points out, the sharp drop of Taiwan's export market share in labor intensive sectors in the United States and Japan coincided nicely with the sudden rise of China's exports in these sectors and markets, as well as with the influx of Taiwan's investment in China in these sectors.[24] In a sense, the United States continues to be Taiwan's largest trade partner, as it used to be, only now Taiwan's exports are routed through the assembly lines in China.[25] Breaking the trade and investment ties across the Strait would mean an instant reduction of more than 14 percent of China exports and a major disruption of Sino-American trade ties.

In addition, many of China's imports from Taiwan are capital and inter-mediate goods, crucial to China's production (versus consumption, as in the case of the import of final consumer goods). Moreover, as Taiwan's invest-ment in China continues to pile up and the division of labor across the Strait escalates, more and more trade is conducted within versus across industrial sectors, as seen from the increasing ratio of intra-industry trade or IIT.[26] One study shows that, for the manufacturing sector as a whole, the IIT in-dex grew from 0.8 in 1980 to 28.8 in 1991. Another study shows that the IIT for the manufacturing sector grew from 16 to 30.4 between 1992 and 1998, most significantly in the following sectors: electrical and electronics, trans-portation equipment, and optical equipment.[27] The higher the IIT ratio is, the more interlocking the production of the two trading partners is. A low IIT ratio means that the two trade partners are just swapping broad cate-gories of finished goods. A high IIT ratio means that parts, components, in-termediate goods, and specialized finished goods are crossing borders. Oth-er things being equal, it is more costly to break economic ties if the IIT ratio is high, for it means not only that consumption is disrupted (and substitute markets and supplies must be found), but also that production might be halted as well, affecting a nation's output and employment.

Next, while in an extractive industry, FDI, once made, tends to be at the mercy of the host government; in the manufacturing sector, this is not nec-essarily the case.[28] Firms in labor-intensive sectors, especially those with market share abroad, can be relocated to other lower wage countries. The balance of power does not necessarily shift from foreign firms to host gov-ernments once the investment is sunk, if these firms are highly engaged in R&D, carry reputed brand names and other specific assets, and command their own globally diversified production chains and/or marketing chan-nels.[29] These firms are not easily held hostage, as they can either vote with their feet (the case of most SMEs) or retain bargaining power vis-à-vis host governments (the case of many high-tech firms). Many *Taishang* are hostage-resistant. Moreover, once *Taishang* are harassed, other country's investors in China may be alarmed and FDI disrupted as well.

Finally, irrespective of whether they have mobility and asset specificity, *Taishang* are major employers and contributors to government revenue. As table 5.6 shows, *Taishang* absorbed 2 percent of urban employment in 1995, 3.9 percent in 1999, a very significant figure considering that urban unem-ployment was 4.3 percent in 1995, and 6.2 percent in 1998. *Taishang* are not essential to China's gross capital formation, but their tax revenue is enough to offset 5 percent of the central government's budget deficit. This revenue-generating function is important to the government in Beijing, considering that China's many indebted state-owned enterprises have been threatening

TABLE 5.6 TAISHANG'S CONTRIBUTION TO CHINA'S ECONOMY
(UNIT: % UNLESS OTHERWISE INDICATED)

	1995	1999
Gross capital formation	1.1	0.7
Employment	3.9 million	8.2 million
Urban labor	2.0	3.9
Industrial output	3.1	4.6
Export	14.4	22.9
Revenue of Central Gov't	1.0 (3.4 bn RMB)	1.7 (9.8 bn RMB)

Sources: The 1995 figures are Kao Chan's estimates; the 1999 figures are Tung's (see Tung 2003: pp. 59–60).

Note: budget deficits for 1995 and 1999 were 65 bn RMB and 179 bn RMB respectively. Losing revenue collected from Taishang would increase deficit by more than 5%.

to break the back of state-owned banks. Without government budgetary support, China's banking sector might go bankrupt, which would hurt the public which traditionally puts its savings in banks rather than in equity.[30] It is not too far-fetched to contend that *Taishang* are a factor crucial to social and political stability in China.

Given the above cost-benefit analysis, it came as no surprise that China's leadership in Beijing had promptly assured the safety of *Taishang* investment and China's need of them during each one of the three recent cross-Strait crises. When a few *Taishang* publicly supported the Democratic Progressive Party candidate in the March 2000 Taiwan presidential election, the Beijing regime carefully crafted its warning message, segregating the exceptional few from the rest. Interestingly, these few individuals on the presumed blacklist were not penalized and, since then, actually have invested more on the mainland.[31] This episode suggests that China probably cannot afford to lose *Taishang* as a collectivity, and was hesitant to lose even those individual *Taishang* not to the liking of leaders in Beijing.

The above cost-benefit analysis also suggests that at some high level of economic interaction, both sides have enough stake in the linkage so that it is irrelevant whether Taiwan needs China more or vice versa.[32] To use a high-rise analogy, it does not matter from which floor, the fifteenth or the twentieth, one attempts to escape a towering inferno, the same result can be anticipated. However, it is important to note that cross-Strait economic links are not static. There is no guarantee that China's stake in the linkage can become only higher, never lower. Consider this: China's state sector reform succeeds, its unemployment problem eases, its central government's budget deficit shrinks, its township and village enterprises are transformed into export-oriented SMEs, and the new entrepreneurs in Shanghai and Beijing replace Taiwanese high-tech firms as the second fiddle to Western high-tech giants. If all these were to happen, then *Taishang* on the mainland would be replaced or become "disposable." The asymmetric economic interdependence across the Strait as we understand it now will then be more likely to be leverage for political blackmail and coercion. To use the high-rise analogy again, China would then be located on the second floor, certainly with a better chance to be rescued, than a Taiwan trapped on the fifteenth floor of a towering inferno.

If *Taishang* are not hostages at least in the foreseeable future, are they agents, if only by default, promoting the cause of unification, and advocating pro-unification policies? As of today, there are about 50,000 (26,000 according to Taiwan's official statistics) Taiwanese enterprises and half a million Taiwan businessmen, including owners, their managers, and service providers, on the mainland, a sizeable ersatz social force to Taiwan.[33] Despite many telephone-based, time-series surveys on Taiwan residents' views on national identity and their stands on the future relationship between China and Taiwan, it is impossible to discern the attitudes of *Taishang* toward these issues. However, there is no reason to assume that having business interests in China *ipso facto* makes *Taishang* an active pro-unification force. Many *Taishang* were sympathetic to the Democratic Progressive Party, a party that once endorsed the idea of creating a Republic of Taiwan, during the process of democratic change. Moreover, even those *Taishang* who feel particularly at home in China realize that they can gain most when the governments across the Strait are divided and in competition for their loyalty. The maintenance of the status quo (not unification) ensures the continuation of the bidding war between Beijing and Taipei for the *Taishang*'s loyalty, a logic that is comparable to a menage à trois affair.[34] Furthermore, interviews conducted in Hsinchu and Shanghai reveal that *Taishang*, especially those in the high-tech sector, are essentially cosmopolitan, comfortable working in China, Southeast Asia, the United States, or Taiwan.[35] Some preliminary sociological studies reveal that *Taishang* are increasingly becoming modern nomads, migrating to where business opportunities abound, and dispersing their family members across many continents; and citizenship may well be a convenience.[36] Given the choice between Beijing and Taipei, though, *Taishang* probably are more inclined to give their loyalty to the latter.[37]

First, during the three periods of tension (China's missile tests and war games in the Strait in 1995–96, the proclamation of the "two states theory" in the summer of 1999, and Taiwan's second presidential election in 2000), *Taishang* opposed China's intimidation and war games. *Taishang* reacted very strongly and registered their complaints with the Beijing government during the 1995–96 missile crisis. And very few, if any, *Taishang* blamed the Taiwan government for the following two crises. Indeed, quite a few *Taishang* pointed out to Chinese leaders that the existence of the Republic of China on Taiwan was a reality that no one could deny.[38]

Second, the *Taishang*'s affinity with Taiwan's political authority is much stronger than that with China's. *Taishang* have unsurpassed political influence and connection in Taiwan; many have been appointed to the policy advisory group of the president, the board of the Straits Exchange Foundation, and to the deliberation councils of the economic bureaucracy. Political patrons seek the support of *Taishang*. In contrast, *Taishang* play third fiddle at best, and never are on an equal footing with leading the heads of MNCs from other countries, not to mention, with the members of the Chinese Princeling Party (offspring of Chinese political elite who are now active in business and financial circles). While in Taiwan, political patrons come to *Taishang*, in China, *Taishang* seek political patrons. Of half a million *Taishang* and their retainers, only one has been elected to a local-level people's congress: Tsang Yu-shou in Ningbo.[39]

Third, *Taishang* retain Taiwan's citizenship, declare income tax in Taiwan, and, in the case of male *Taishang*, render their compulsory military service. Some may have Western passports as well, but probably not China's passport, which requires one to renounce other citizenship. Although lacking a tax agreement, the Taiwan government follows the principle of no double taxation, crediting *Taishang* what they have paid to the Chinese government if their salary is dispersed from their enterprises incorporated on the mainland. All this means that *Taishang* have invested heavily in Taiwan citizenship.

Fourth, the *Taishang* mainland experience is not always a happy one. Collectively, *Taishang* carry weight in the calculations of Chinese leaders concerning cross-Strait relations, but as individuals, they can be unfairly treated at local levels. A significant number of mistreated *Taishang* have established an Association of Victimized *Taishang* to underscore a fundamental reality that protection of *Taishang*'s lives and property is weak, given the absence of an investment protection agreement between China and Taiwan.[40] Sixteen cases of personal property loss have exceeded $12 million each, and none of them has been redressed legally, even though the Chinese Communist Party issued a red-lettered decree for proper settlement. Indeed, a lawyer who had represented hundreds of cases was denied reentry to China after he made the issue public.[41] The legitimate and all too common practice of pursuing vertical integration and creating a group of affiliated companies may be viewed with suspicion and trigger tax and tariff auditing for possible interlocking trade.[42] In addition, the Chinese Communist Party has begun to implant its cells in *Taishang* enterprises.

In due course, however, some *Taishang* may decide to settle down in China and even retire there (around 6,000 Taiwan veterans have done so).[43] Costs of living, land prices, and income taxes are low while stock market and business opportunities are tempting in China. Offspring education and medical care are probably two determining factors for the *Taishang*'s choice of permanent residency. Beginning in the late 1990s, the Beijing regime has been accommodating the request for the establishment of *Taishang* grade schools, using Taiwan teachers and textbooks. So far, Donguan in Guangzhou and Kunshan in Shanghai have *Taishang* schools. The Malaysian Chinese solution (educating youngsters in "ethnic" grade schools or international schools in China and subsequently sending them to either Taiwan or abroad for higher education) has become a viable option. Medical care is more a concern, especially after the 2003 SARS epidemic. Taiwanese enterprises have entered contracts with a few designated hospitals for employees' medical care, but the service is said to be too expensive and the quality questionable.[44] No Taiwanese hospital yet has been permitted to establish facilities on the mainland, but the Beijing government has already promised to extend its socialist system of medical care without price discrimination ("national" treatment) to *Taishang*. *Taishang* have begun to fly in Taiwanese doctors and use an out of the area clause to make claims for Taiwan's national health coverage. A pattern akin to the Caribbean-Miami solution seems to be emerging: exercise self-care for small illness, return to Taiwan for major care, exploit the visiting home doctors, and use local facilities only for most urgent care.[45] Thus, if medical care and the education of offspring are no longer intractable problems for those *Taishang* thinking of settling down in China, then what Taiwan can offer to lure them back to reside in Taiwan are emotional attachment and perhaps piece of mind in a rule of law environment. But even if *Taishang* eventually choose to settle down in China, they probably will continue to stay in their enclave communities, and maintain their presumed preference for peace and prosperity under the status quo. Their opposition to forced unification or risky independence probably will not change.

Although *Taishang* are not stooges of the Chinese government, they have been pushing for policies in the direction that the Chinese government hopes to go, sometimes to the dismay of the Taiwan government. Effective policy advocacy necessitates collective action, which in turn requires the formation of business associations. *Taishang* are territorially organized into seventy associations, mostly in coastal China, but they are also active in Taiwan's industrial associations. Autonomous and self-governing, *Tai-*

shang associations work closely with the offices of Taiwan affairs at different levels of the Chinese government. Back in Taiwan, *Taishang* periodically meet with officials of the Mainland Affairs Council, and the President of Taiwan typically gives a speech at their annual meeting. *Taishang* have voiced their views on at least three policy issues: China's most favored nation (later re-designated as permanent normal trade relation) status in the United States; the Taiwan government's "Go Slow" policy; and the three direct links across the Taiwan Strait. Throughout the 1990s, *Taishang* (and American MNCs with business interests in China) had supported the granting of China's normal trade status, long before the Taiwan government went public in 2000 to "endorse" China's trade status in the United States. Since, at the time, members of the U.S. Congress linked China's human rights record and China's trade status, the *Taishang*'s stand put the Taiwan government in an awkward position. But it was over the "Go Slow" policy and the issue of the three direct links that *Taishang* were at true loggerheads with the Taiwan government.

The "Go Slow" policy started in September 1996. China defied it and the *Taishang* lamented it. At the end of the 1990s, two prominent businessmen, Wang Yung-ching and Chang Jong-fa, joined the chorus of criticism. As the head of Formosa Plastics, the largest petrochemical firm in Taiwan, Wang was the captain of traditional industry. Chang—head of the Evergreen Corporation, the world largest container shipping company—was the voice of the service sector. The fate of this policy was almost sealed when Morris Chang—the chairman of Taiwan Semiconductor Manufacturing Corporation (the world's largest IC foundry) and spokesman for the high-tech sector—also registered his disapproval in 2000. Within a year, the Democratic Progressive Party (DPP) government promised to replace the "Go Slow" policy with a managed liberalization policy in a blue-ribbon national economic conference in 2001, and subsequently expanded the scope of permitted investment in China. Business continued to push for lifting the ban on investment in the high-tech sector, a case to which we shall return.

The most protracted policy conflict between *Taishang* and the Taiwan government revolves around the issue of three direct links across the Strait. In its initial formulation, the three direct links—proposed by China in the early 1980s—were for direct mail exchange, telephone contact, and transportation. In due course, the trio was re-constituted, now referring to direct communication, trade, and transportation. Liberalization in telecommunications solved the problem of the first direct link. For the other two links, the Taiwan government established an overseas transshipment center in Kaohsiung and made special arrangements with seaports of neighboring countries (for a technical detour of ocean shipping to obtain documents without actually unloading and reloading cargo) in the second half of the 1990s. Direct air links remain an intractable problem, as they are politically and militarily sensitive, involving the issue of immigration and the use of airspace. The SARS epidemic dampened the *Taishang*'s zeal for direct air links and revealed the virtue of keeping a *cordon sanitaire* across the Strait. However, as the epidemic subsided, the request for this link resumed. To be fair to *Taishang*, it is important to note that they never advocated direct air links on China's terms, which until recently, required Taiwan to accept Beijing's One China Principle, and by logical extension, to define cross-Strait aviation as a special domestic flight. *Taishang* also have been submitting various plans that would not compromise national security, such as permitting airfreight and day flights only, at first. In this light, *Taishang* have not been doing China's bidding, but only promoting their business interests, as any business group would do. In fact, the American Chamber of Commerce in Taiwan has long been advocating the free flow of goods, services, and personnel across the Strait, and the head of the American Institute in Taiwan has also urged the Taiwan government to let cross-Strait economic interaction unfold in "natural progression."[46]

Taishang have not been able to persuade the DPP government to establish direct links although some compromises have been tried. Taipei implemented the mini-links via two outer islands, Jinmen and Mazu, limiting them to those who hold special permits. At the Chinese end, only Fuzhou and Xiamen permitted entry. Charter flights were introduced, but for inbound travel only. The highly competitive presidential election in March 2004 created a rare window of opportunity for *Taishang* to push for direct links and other cross-Strait issues. Both the DPP and opposition parties bid against each other for the loyalty of *Taishang*, who accounted for 3 percent of eligible voters in Taiwan (the margin of victory turned out to be only 0.2 per cent). However, locked in a dead-even electoral campaign, President Chen only promised to expand the scope of mini-links, permit two-way charter flights, and expand *Taishang*'s health care- and education-related welfare coverage. There appear to be clear constraints on the degree to which *Taishang* can persuade the DPP government to alter its cross-Strait policy.

The concern about the economic impact of Taiwan's investment abroad, especially in China, is reflected in the debate on the "hollowing out" of Taiwan's industry. The departure of Taiwan's SMEs since the late 1980s led to a fear that jobs would be lost, domestic investment would decline, and the manufacturing sector would shrink. Factory closure dominated the news at the turn of the 1990s. The negative net FDI (outflow exceeds inflow) in the manufacturing sector first appeared in 1987, was significant in 1989, and has remained so ever since 1993 (with the exception of 1995). And the share of the manufacturing sector in GDP dropped steadily from 39.4 percent in 1986 (the peak year of the postwar era) to 25.3 percent in 2001.

The "hollowing out" warning proved to be a false alarm; indeed, at least until the late 1990s, outward FDI has contributed to industrial upgrading rather than to an industrial decline in Taiwan. Evidence abounds. First, as economist Tung Chen-yuan has carefully demonstrated, outward FDI to China brought Taiwan a significant, high level of foreign exchange earnings between 1989 and 1997.[47] Second, most medium and large firms active in outward direct investment have continued to invest and expand their production in Taiwan, according to Ministry of Economic Affairs' surveys of Taiwan enterprises in 1996 and 1998. Third, while most emigrated SMEs had either reduced or terminated their production in Taiwan,[48] their overseas operation did lead them to procure intermediate and capital goods from big firms in Taiwan. Their acquisition was reflected in the changing trade pattern between the two sides of the Strait. Fourth, the technology intensity of Taiwan's overall exports continued to grow (see table 5.7). Finally, as shown in table 5.8, the unemployment rate actually declined after 1986 and remained extremely low through the mid-1990s, while labor productivity for the same period increased drastically in comparison with the preceding ten years.[49] Although the share of the manufacturing sector in Taiwan's GDP decreased and the share of the service sector increased, these developments were entirely expected. All matured economies in the West have gone through such structural changes.

TABLE 5.7 EXPORT COMMODITIES BY INTENSITY OF INPUT FACTOR FOR TAIWAN, 1982–2001

	DEGREE OF LABOR INTENSITY			DEGREE OF CAPITAL INTENSITY			DEGREE OF TECH INTENSITY		
	high	mid	low	high	mid	low	high	mid	low
1982	47.2	30.8	21.9	26.9	45.4	27.6	18.3	32.6	49.1
1985	45.9	35.6	18.5	24.5	48.7	26.8	18.8	33.6	47.6
1990	41.0	38.3	20.7	28.9	50.5	20.5	26.7	38.6	34.7
1995	36.4	40.6	23.0	31.9	56.5	11.6	36.5	41.4	22.0
1997	34.9	43.1	22.1	30.3	60.6	9.1	39.7	41.1	19.2
2000	37.6	41.2	21.2	28.1	64.4	7.5	42.5	43.2	14.3
2001	34.4	42.8	22.8	29.6	62.6	7.9	45.5	40.7	13.8

Source: Council on Economic Planning and Development, *Taiwan Statistical Data Book*, 2002.

TABLE 5.8 UNEMPLOYMENT RATE IN TAIWAN

YEAR	AVERAGE RATE
1986	2.66
1987	1.97
1988	1.69
1989	1.57
1990	1.67
1991	1.51
1992	1.51
1993	1.45
1994	1.56
1995	1.79
1996	2.60
1997	2.72
1998	2.69
1999	2.92
2000	2.99
2001	4.57
2002	5.02

Source: Department of Statistics, Ministry of Economic Affairs, *Domestic and Foreign Express Report of Economic Statistics Indicators*, March 2003.

Industrial upgrading is often an outcome of "defensive" FDI, where high labor costs, a worsening investment environment, and currency appreciation force SMEs in traditional sectors to escape abroad in order to safeguard their business stake, thereby indirectly benefiting the home economy. FDI in Southeast Asia by Japanese SMEs in the 1960s and 1970s belonged to this genre. It promoted Japanese economic expansion abroad and industrial upgrading at home. Taiwan was clearly replicating this experience.

Since the second half of the 1990s, however, Taiwan's FDI has been more of an "expansive type," threatening to create an industrial "hollowing out" effect. The expansive type of FDI is one where oligopolistic competition leads major firms in capital-intensive and high-tech sectors to move abroad to exploit their technological edge when a product is maturing and the patent is ending.[50] In doing so, these leading firms are likely to bring with them all other supporting or affiliated firms in the long industrial chain, featuring a procession of what one may call "the moving pack." If major "industrial clusters" are all drained, and if the home economy is left without a new growth sector, such kinds of FDI may lead to significant investment and employment losses in the home economy. As economists Keith Cowling and Philip Tomlinson point out, Japan has been overzealously engaged in FDI in the wake of large-scale currency realignment under the 1985 Plaza Accord, helping to send the Japanese economy into a decade-long recession, and to perpetuate the problem of structural unemployment.[51] A recent study of the Taiwanese economy identifies some early signs of industrial "hollowing out" beginning in the late 1990s, when Taiwan's restive information technology sector started advancing to China.[52]

As revealed in table 5.8, unemployment rates in Taiwan have been creeping up since the mid-1990s. The high-tech sector by itself is not particularly job-creating, but it has tremendous purchasing power, essential to the expansion of the service sector. Once a high-value added manufacturing sector is gone, soon so will be high value-added service sectors.[53] Gross fixed capital formation as a share of Taiwan's GNP remained steady in the second half of the 1990s, but its overall labor productivity has grown at a slower pace (see table 5.9). Moreover, in 2001, Taiwan's unemployment rate for the first time in more than three decades jumped to 4.96 percent, its gross fixed capital formation dropped below 20 percent, and its GDP grew negative 2.2 percent, all record-breaking figures. Economic downturn continued in 2002, with an even higher unemployment ratio, 5.2 percent. Ob-

TABLE 5.9 CAPITAL FORMATION, THE MANUFACTURING SECTOR, AND LABOR PRODUCTIVITY

YEAR	GROSS FIXED CAPITAL FORMATION	MANUFACTURING SECTOR	LABOR PRODUCTIVITY	LABOR PRODUCTIVITY
	(% of GNP)	(% of GDP)	(NT$ 1,000)	1996 = 100
1976–80	27.6	35.1	328	40
1981–85	23.2	36.4	410	49
1986–90	20.1	36.7	552	63
1991–95	23.7	30.5	726	86
1996–01	22.0	26.9	938	116
1996	22.2	27.9	847	100
1997	22.5	27.8	893	107
1998	23.4	27.4	922	112
1999	22.7	26.6	962	120
2000	23.1	26.4	1007	127
2001	18.4	25.6	996	132

Sources: For labor productivity, see Lin Wu-lang, 1997, p.32; for gross fixed capital formation and manufacturing, see *Taiwan Statistical Data Book*, 2002, pp.54, 57.

viously the global recession (caused by the burst of the Dotcom bubble and then the 9/11 terrorist attacks) and policy uncertainty (caused by the first transfer of power between political parties in Taiwan's history) have contributed to Taiwan's economic contraction. But the massive exit of Taiwan's electronics industry to China that began in 1998 made the specter of industrial hollowing out in Taiwan even more imminent and threatening. Although Taiwan's electronics firms continue to perform well in world markets (leading firms even have gained market share),[54] their operation and production facilities are increasingly relocated abroad. It was against this macro-setting that leading semi-conductor firms pronounced their intention to set foot in China, sending a shock wave through the core of Taiwan's economy and polity, and leading to a grand policy debate, an episode to which we now turn.

III. THE CASE OF THE SEMICONDUCTOR SECTOR

During the second half of the 1970s, Taiwan avoided a Korean-style big push strategy for massive expansion of capital-intensive, heavy, and petrochemical sectors. Instead, Taiwan steadily nurtured the information technology industry, primarily via its newly established Industrial Technology Research Institute.[55] Thanks to this institute's manpower training, its introduction of Western knowhow, its sponsorship of research and development consortia, and the return of previously U.S.-based Chinese researchers, Taiwan quickly made inroads into the computer industry (and its peripherals) and the semiconductor industry.[56] By the early 1990s, Taiwan had emerged as the third largest computer hardware-producing country, next to the United States and Japan, and the largest foundry (i.e., chip-maker) in the world.[57] The semiconductor sector—the core of the broadly defined information technology sector—used to be dominated by integrated device manufacturers, such as Intel and Samsung (a rather distant second), which not only design and develop chips but also manufacture them in their own facilities. Taiwan Semiconductor Manufacturing Corporation (TSMC) and United Microelectronics Corp (UMC) pioneered the foundry model. A foundry maintains expensive manufacturing facilities (or fab) and produces on order from chip-designing and developing "fabless companies," such as Qualcomm and Nvidia.[58] TSMC and UMC changed the structure of the world's semiconductor industry, captured around 70 percent of the foundry market, and spawned a significant number of Taiwanese chip designers and developers (including the fifth and sixth largest firms in the world) as well as IC testing and packaging

companies. Most semiconductor firms in Taiwan were founded by re-
turnees from U.S. high-tech firms, and clustered in Hsinchu Science Industrial Park, not far from two premier research universities, weaving a
dense social and production network in the Hsinchu-San Jose community.[59] As of 2000, TSMC and UMC made mainly 8 inch wafers, using 0.13
micron circuits, but they were capable of making 12 inch wafers, and were
developing a 0.1 to 0.09 micron technique.[60]

For Taiwan, wafer fabrication symbolizes national pride, epitomizing
the success of its information technology industry. Crowned by the two
leading foundries, TSMC and UMC, this industry accounts for one-third
of total manufacturing outputs, and 50 percent of exports (and exports
are 30 percent of GDP). Taiwan leads the world in the production of
many products (see table 5.10) and leads East Asia in entrepreneurship in
the information technology sector. Long before the DPP government
took power from the KMT in May 2000, low-end and labor-intensive
manufacturers had found their way to the mainland, including firms producing the PC 486 model, motherboards, monitors, and PC peripherals.
The government was also on the verge of approving the plans by major
notebook computer makers to invest in China.[61] However, the government had been wary of the direct investment by Taiwanese firms in any
kind of wafer fabrication in China, allowing only the 0.25 micro technique to be sold to China. In line with the "Go Slow" policy, the govern-

TABLE 5.10 TAIWAN'S PROMINENT PRESENCE IN THE PRODUCTION OF
PC AND PERIPHERALS (1999)

	ITS WORLD MARKET SHARE (%)	SHARE OF ITS OVERSEAS POWERHOUSE OVER WHOLE PRODUCTION (%)	UNIT PRICE (USD)
Notebook	49	3.3	10,901
Monitor	58	73.3	1,589
Desktop PC	19	86.0	369.4
Masterboard	64	40.5	75.4
Switches	70	94.0	21.7
PC Case	75	78.0	18.8
CD/DVD Drive	34	80.5	357
Scanner	91	58.0	422
Graphic Card	31	63.0	45.6
Keyboard	68	57.0	64

Source: www.mic.iii.org.tw

ment's position was clear: selling medium-level technology to China was fine, direct investment in China's chip-making was not. Yet, world market conditions and China's industrial policy quickly led the semiconductor makers, especially TSMC, to challenge the Taiwan government's "Go Slow" policy.

A new reality in the world semiconductor markets set in right after the turn of the new century. The burst of the IT bubble exposed the problem of overcapacity in global IT production that the exuberant Internet revolution and the Y2K boom helped to create. In 2001–2002, leading foundries had only a 70 percent utilization rate. The only market that was not contracting was China, where the demand for IC was expected to grow from $25 billion in 2002 to $41 billion in 2005. A policy shift, however, had long preceded the market signal. Beginning in 1997, China, under the first post-Deng leadership, had been assiduously pursuing WTO membership, which required an accelerated reform of the state sector. Around 27 million state sector employees were supposed to be laid off between 1998 and 2002; attracting FDI to help to expand the economy and alleviate the unemployment problem became a top priority. But the new leadership (both Jiang Zemin and Zhu Rongji were scientists and engineers by training) also called for FDI in the high-tech sector, which, although not as prone to creating jobs as traditional industries, contributed to upgrading traditional sectors and absorbing skilled labor. The Asian financial crisis slowed state sector reform, but, as alluded to above, it led the leadership to believe that the high-tech sector helped an economy (viz. Taiwan) to stave off major financial crises. Having successfully induced Taiwanese firms in the computer industry and its peripherals to migrate to China, Chinese officials turned explicitly to semiconductor firms. On June 27, 2000, in a meeting with a delegation from Taiwan's Chinese National Federation of Industries, Minister of Science and Technology Zhu sent the following signals to Taiwan's semiconductor industry: tax incentives were under consideration; visits by TSMC and UMC heads were welcome; FDI was likely to receive national treatment upon China's WTO entry.[62] Meanwhile, Western and Japanese MNCs were eyeing China 's semiconductor market. In July 2000, Motorola (the second largest mobile phone maker in the world) discussed with China the construction of a chip plant; NEC also looked to build one in China. It was under these new market conditions and China's new policy initiative that TSMC urged the Taiwanese government to overhaul its policy on investment by the *Taishang* in China's semiconductor sector.

It took Taiwan two years to change the policy, and an additional year to make specific decisions on TSMC's application to build a foundry in China. The arduous process of policy change was a function of interplay among business pressures, government responses, and public concerns and involvement. This protracted process vividly shows Taiwan's dilemma regarding the management of its economic ties with China. The following is a summary of the interaction among the parties concerned throughout the four phases.

The first encounter between the industry and the government was a brief one. In spring 2000, Morris Chang stated that TSMC must have production facilities (presumably 8-inch wafer foundries) in China to meet the growing IC market demand there, and that in ten years, her market would overtake Japan's to become the second largest in the world. In the early summer, Advanced Semiconductor Engineering Inc, the world's number two packaging and number one testing company, also called for a new policy. In response, the government "relaxed" the regulations by permitting Taiwanese firms to build 6-inch wafer fabs and post-production testing and packaging facilities in China, and, furthermore, promised to review the regulations. TSMC and other leading firms did not bypass regulations to venture into China, unlike firms in many other industries during the 1990s. In fact, TSMC accelerated the construction of its Fab Six (including its last new 8-inch site and its first 12-inch facilities in Taiwan), which was completed and put into operation ahead of schedule in the spring of 2000. Furthermore, Morris Chang even announced that new investments would be mainly based in Taiwan for the next 5 to 10 years and that TSMC would not invest in China for at least four years.[63] Essentially both sides settled for a moratorium. Meanwhile, the government was being overwhelmed by the partisan conflict over the construction of the fourth nuclear power plant.

The advent of a few wafer-producing corporations in China, the anticipated entry of China into the WTO, the burst of the Dotcom bubble, and the onset of economic recession rekindled the issue in the second half of 2001. In early summer, Morris Chang made a trip to China for a preliminary study of TSMC's investment there. In late summer, the government convened an Economic Development Advisory Conference to build a consensus on the strategy for economic revival. This conference provided a forum for business collectively to air its grievances regarding the investment environment in Taiwan, to condemn the "Go Slow" policy, and to demand the establishment of direct links across the Strait. The government promised to replace this policy with a managed liberalization policy. In implementing this new policy, the government drastically increased the scope of permissive imports from China from 2,000 items to nearly 5,000 items. Direct remittance across the Straits also became possible, making it unnecessary for an investor to work through a third place. Furthermore, the scope of permissive investment was greatly expanded, now including 122 high-

tech items, such as notebook computers, mobile phones, and DVD players. Finally, the government raised the ceiling of the investment amount
from $50 million to $80 million per project that would be subject to the
special review process. However, the government remained hesitant in
lifting the ban on the construction of 8-inch wafer foundries in China,
drawing sharp criticisms from the semiconductor industry. When the new
cabinet (formed after the December 2001 legislative election) appeared to
be caving in to business pressure in late January 2002, the opponents of the
industry were galvanized. President Chen Shui-bian intervened to prevent
any policy decision and suggested a "rational debate."[64]

The grand debate in March 2002—the third phase of the saga—saw a
full mobilization of both camps, and close scrutiny of each argument. Tables 5.11 and 5.12 list the supporters and opponents of the issues and the
main points that were advanced. Key advocates came from the high-tech
sector, two unification-leaning political parties, the KMT and the People's

TABLE 5.11 THE LINEUP OF SUPPORTERS AND OPPONENTS OF
TAIWAN SEMICONDUCTOR FIRMS' INVESTMENT IN CHINA

	SUPPORTERS	OPPONENTS

Associations	Taiwan Semiconductor Assn.
	Taipei Computer Mfg Assn.
	National Assn. of Industry
	  & Commerce
	Chip designers already
	  positioned in China
		Taiwan assn. of teachers
		Taiwan engineers assn.
		North American Assn. of
		  Taiwanese Prof

Political parties	Kuomintang & People's First Party	Taiwan Solidarity Union
Opinion leaders	Lee Yuan-tse (Academic Sinica)	Lee Teng-hui (former president)

Think tanks	Chung-hua Institute of Econ
	  Research (researchers)
		Taiwan Institute of Economic
		  Research
		Taiwan Thinktank
		Chung-hua Institute of Econ Research
		  (leadership)

Government	Vice-premier (head of Council
	  on Economic Planning and
	  Development)
	Ministry of Economic Affairs
		Mainland Affairs Council
		National Security Council

Source and notes: compiled by author; President Chen was non-committal while Vice-President Lu
initially opposed, but later on, gave conditional endorsement.

First Party (which both gave their blessings, but avoided joining the battle), the president of Academic Sinica, and some researchers in an economic affairs think tank.[65] Among the most ardent critics were those university professors and researchers in favor of separating Taiwan from China politically, the Taiwan Solidarity Union (TSU), former president Lee Teng-hui, and a coterie of researchers housed in various think tanks.[66] The DPP as a party deferred to the DPP government, which showed conflicting tendencies. The vice-premier (concurrently the head of Council of Economic Planning and Development) and the Ministry of Economic Affairs were more inclined to support the industry, while the Mainland Affairs Council and the National Security Council were not enthusiastic. The president was noncommittal, while Vice President Lu initially staunchly opposed lifting the ban but subsequently gave her conditional approval.

Essentially, the industry advanced three major arguments and one minor one.[67] First, if Taiwanese firms were not permitted to go to China, firms from other countries would not hesitate to fill the void and cheerfully exploit China's expanding domestic market. Taiwanese firms had no monopoly in technology; indeed, any firm's technological edge was temporary. Second, the fabs had to be close to customers if they were to survive.

TABLE 5.12 SEMICONDUCTOR FIRMS' INVESTMENT IN CHINA: PROS AND CONS

PROS	CONS
Three core arguments	Three core arguments
1. Taiwan has no monopoly of technology; it gives up China market, others would grab it.	1. Taiwan's market share hinges on innovative production, not monopoly of technology; others can produce, but not displace with Taiwan's foundries
2. Proximity to customers is crucial.	2. Key is market access, not proximity; China cannot keep market closed under the WTO rules
3. The industry has high depreciation cost; Taiwan's surplus capacity be used in China.	3. Once a foundry migrates, other supporting firms will follow, given the clustering nature of the industry.
One supplementary argument	One supplementary argument
4. Unparalleled investment environment in China	4. FDI in China amounts to feeding the tiger.

Source: Compiled by author.

Third, many facilities for 8-inch wafer fabrication were idle in Taiwan, equipment was costly, and failing to move to China would hurt the chance to develop and expand 12-inch wafer fabs in Taiwan. The final argument pertained to the asymmetric investment environment across the Strait. China was offering tax incentives and abundant high-tech manpower to Taiwanese firms, which were suffering from water and power shortage in the Hsinchu Industrial Park. This argument, however, was quickly dropped since for years Taiwanese firms had been the main beneficiaries of tax incentives in Taiwan and experienced Taiwanese workers could be expected to have higher productivity. Furthermore, the Taiwan government rapidly addressed logistic problems. As to its policy recommendation, the industry urged that the government lift the ban without any delay, for a delay of two years would mean the loss of the China market forever.

The opponents refuted or qualified the three core arguments the advocates presented.[68] First, the industry underestimated its own competitiveness by assuming that other makers would grab the China market if TSMC and UMC were not permitted to go to China. Yet, Dutch, Japanese, and Canadian investment had not been very successful in China. The impressive market share of Taiwan's foundries (77 percent of world production value, far ahead of Singapore) was not derived from better equipment, lower costs of skilled labor, or a monopoly on technology, but rather from their innovative techniques and management, as well as from the "clustering effects" in Hsinchu Science Park. Second, proximity to market was not a necessity for the foundries to prosper, otherwise TSMC and UMC should have been established in the United States and major markets rather than in Taiwan. Access to the China market was a legitimate concern, as an increasing domestic market could tempt Chinese (or any) government to erect tariff or non-tariff barriers in order to induce MNCs to provide direct investment, thereby facilitating technology transfer. On the other hand, WTO rules should enable Taiwanese firms to remove barriers to market entry. Third, although surplus facilities for 8-inch wafer fabrication could not sit idle, their relocation to China would run the risk of "hollowing out" Hsinchu Industrial Park, as all supporting industries would migrate as well, turning the Hsinchu region into a Jurassic park. The 8-inch wafer fabs should not leave for China before the 12-inch wafer fabs reached a phase of mass production in Taiwan. The fourth assertion was a national security argument: selling old equipment to China, not to mention bringing in capital and relatively advanced technology, could "feed the tiger." Indeed, permitting high-tech personnel to work in China was tantamount to assisting the enemy. Most opponents ignored this or downplayed it. The opponents prescribed an embargo as the best option for Taiwan, but warned that condoning the perpetrators (those who defected from Taiwan to establish foundries in China) while restricting law-abiding TSMC and UMC from going to China, was the worst option.

The fourth and current phase began in April 2002, when the government decided to lift the ban on investment in China, but promised to modulate the pace and the terms of investment on 8-inch wafer production there. In conjunction with this decision, the government spurned the proposal to restrict the free flow of high-tech personnel across the Strait, but committed to drafting the National Technology Protection Law, a law akin to a technology export control regime that many Western nations have. A victory for the semiconductor industry, the current policy measure does not give the industry carte blanche. TSMC and UMC must apply for approval in two phases. The first phase is for the approval of financing arrangements for initial investment; the second is for the approval of relocating the equipment. It is understood that the bulk of capital for 8-inch wafer production will be raised in China and that the approval for the second stage application hinges on the performance of each company's 12-inch fabs in Taiwan. Disappointed with the policy shift, the opponents swore to oversee the approval process.

TSMC submitted a Phase-I application in September 2002, which took the Investment Commission of the Ministry of Economic Affairs six months to review. TSMC planned to transfer $371 million from its headquarters and raise $418 million from Chinese banks, and expected to draw $109 million from the revenue of the proposed plant to finance its $898 million factory.[69] The TSU—which remains an ardent critic of the new policy—demanded, among other things, that a technology protection law be enacted, and that TSMC's construction of 8-inch wafer fabs in China could begin only after its 12-inch fabs in Taiwan had reached the "economy of scale in production." Given that the Legislative Yuan was close to summer recess, it was impossible to resume debate, let alone pass, the technology protection law.

The premier eventually was able to neutralize the opposition by promising to punish the perpetrators (former TSMC employees who betrayed the company and struck a deal with the PRC to build two 8-inch fabs in Shanghai, see below), and to enhance anti-dumping measures to prevent cutthroat competition from China's fabs. TSU defined "economy of scale in production" as 20,000 wafers per month, with a 70 percent yield rate. But TSMC opposed having a strict definition. The premier promised to consult with experts regarding the yield rate, output value, and market condition when reviewing the Phase II application.[70] In late February 2003, the Phase-I application was approved.

Thus, it took two years for the government to decide to lift the ban on the semiconductor industry's investment in China and another six months tentatively to approve the Phase-I application. The industry welcomed policy change, but lamented the high opportunity cost of protracted and belated policymaking. In Morris Chang's own words, "Had we been allowed to go in the year 2000, the new players in Shanghai would not have been so cocky." However, the opponents warned of the risk of opening a floodgate that would accelerate the process of hollowing out. Did the policy change do more harm than good to Taiwan's semiconductor industry? Did Taiwan lose or is it losing the industry as a consequence of this most dramatic, emotionally charged, and, to many, unduly delayed policy shift? Answering these questions requires a close examination of "the rise of China" in this sector, when Taiwan was internally consumed in a protracted policy battle.

During the 2000–2003 period, many firms came into being in China to the dismay of TSMC. Local governments in Shanghai, Beijing, Shenzhen, Xian, and Chengdu dived into wafer production, while Shenyang and Harbin also tried to join the fray. Some $8.5 billion were invested. In Shanghai alone, eleven firms were formed. Of all the new players, only two may be able to reap profit in the very near future, namely Zhongxin (Semiconductor International Corporation) and Hungli (Grace Semiconductor Corporation), both located in Shanghai, and established (in the case of the former) or assisted (in the case of the latter) by former cadres of TSMC and with PRC's capital input.[71] According to the estimates by these two firms, their and other local production can only meet 30 percent of domestic demand in 2005.[72] It would appear that the China market has room for all latecomers.

Two new developments surprised TSMC. The first blow is that Zhongxin is closing the technology gap. When Zhongxin and Hungli began to invest, they expected to use 0.25 micron for medium- and low-price end products. And yet, due to the 2001 recession, western integrated device manufacturers slowed construction of their own fabs and transferred know-

TABLE 5.13 WELDING TECHNOLOGY LICENSED TO SMIC IN 2002–2003

TECHNOLOGY	PRODUCTS	LICENSORS	REMARKS
0.13 micron	DRAM (stacked)	Elpida (US)	
0.13 micron	DRAM (unspecified)	Texas Instrument	with fab order
0.14 micron	DRAM (trench)	Infeneon (Germany)	products be sold back
0.15 micron	SRAM	Toshiba (Japan)	with fab order
0.18 micron	Logic	Chartered (Singapore)	

Source: Compiled by author.

TABLE 5.14 MAJOR TYPES OF CHIP PRODUCTION AND THEIR
MARKET SHARES IN 2002

PROPORTION OF MARKET SHARE	TYPES OF CHIPS
34%	Logic, a kind of programmed chip for input/output operation; used in remote control device, cell phones, voice distinction machine and so on.
27%	Analog, used in microphones, speakers, displays, wireless device.
26%	MPU or micro-processing unit
17%	DRAM or dynamic random access memory; used in PC; DVD players, high definition TV, 3G handsets
10%	MCU or micro-controlling unit
9%	Flash, a memory chip used in portable device
6%	DSP or digital-signal processors, used in cell phones, DVD players, digital TV
24%	Other (including SRAM or static random access memory)

Source: IDC; the 2002 percentiles were reported in *Topics*, April 2003, p.54.

Notes: Flash memory chips are able to store information when power is turned off; DRAM needs constant charge; hence Flash and DRAM are complementary.

how to the two firms.[73] Zhongxin, in particular, was able to sign many technology licensing agreements with major foreign IC manufacturers (see table 5.13).[74] In May 2003, MoSys certified its 1T-SRAM (static random access memory) using the 0.18 micron technique. Currently building its first 12-inch fab in Beijing, Zhongxin vows to use 0.13 micron technology soon. Notice that the plant in which TSMC is going to invest will use 0.25 and 0.35 micron technology to produce 8-inch wafers for the China market.[75] The second surprise is that SMIC is not just catering to China's market, as previously announced and widely predicted, but producing for foreign markets as well, albeit on a very small scale. SMIC used a low-price lure to receive a DRAM (dynamic random access memory) order from IC manufacturers. The two new Chinese firms may be chipping away TSMC's and UMC's international market share.

The challenge that the IC foundries in China pose to Taiwan's semiconductor industry is real, but not yet as serious as the policy critics have predicted. China's two leading firms remain primarily foundries for one type of chips, DRAM. As table 5.14 shows, the DRAM market was less than a quarter of the IC product in 2002. Low profit margins for DRAM have long reduced TSMC and UMC's appetite for orders for this kind of memory chip. China's semiconductor firms certainly will do their utmost to break into more lucrative IC markets (such as those for Logic or DSP, digital-signal processor chips, which are harder to make).[76] Western firms may be willing to transfer technology, for example, in Logic IC in exchange for lower priced wafers. But due to the long duration of certification, and the wide gap between two leading firms and the rest, integrated device manufacturers and fabless IC designers are unlikely to give high-end orders to China's fabs. Moreover, given that Taiwanese firms currently have higher yield rates and better service, Chinese firms will not win over international orders unless they reduce their prices by more than 30–50 percent.[77]

Furthermore, by the end of 2004, the two leading Chinese firms will be producing up to 25 percent of Taiwan's 8-inch wafer outputs. The bulk of the Chinese foundries' output still uses the 0.25 micron technique, and China's domestic market is huge enough to absorb TSMC's foundries, even if they are yet to be constructed in China.[78] More importantly, although the growth rate of China's semiconductor market is impressive, the total amount of its market demand will still be barely over the single-digit level. If there was any consensus in the grand policy debate in March 2002 on the future of Taiwan's semiconductor sector, it was that all parties agreed that China's market should be only a component of Taiwan's strategy to thrive in the global market.

IV. MANAGING ECONOMIC TIES WITH CHINA

Approving TSMC's investment in China denotes the shift away from the "Go Slow" policy, which sought to contain, restrict, and discourage the *Taishang*'s rush to China. In its place is a guided liberalization policy that aims to lift control on, but monitor and manage the outflow of investment. Operationally, the current policy has four objectives. First, the government wants to make the *Taishang*'s investment in China transparent, so as correctly to track the flow and stock of Taiwanese capital bound for China. Second, the government wants to minimize the *Taishang*'s use of Taiwan capital for their China operations, in order to diversify their capital base and to keep them from draining Taiwan's capital. Third, the government wants to see the *Taishang*'s profits earned in China at least partially repatriated to Taiwan in the form of dividends to domestic shareholders. Finally, the government wants the *Taishang* to use Taiwan as a research, development and management center for their overseas operations, and to use Taiwanese banks' overseas banking units as a mechanism for their overseas financial management.[79]

The liberal nature of the new policy did lead *Taishang* to either timely or belated registration of their investment with the Taiwan government (which explains the spike of 2002 in table 5.4, above). However, a good number of the *Taishang* remain *incognito*, and there have been many illicit investments, using overseas sister companies to bypass the new regulations in sensitive sectors, such as semiconductors. The government did impose fines on three cases of unauthorized Taiwanese investment in China, the first punitive action ever taken against *Taishang* in democratic Taiwan. But the legal ground to compel their divestment was not particularly strong, while the fines were too small to deter any future offenders.[80] Indeed, that TSMC and UMC have been law-abiding firms might have been partly due to the government's shareholding as well as their age-old, intimate ties with the government's research arm, the Industrial Technology Research Institute.[81] Many firms have not received government capital injection, and some firms are either uninterested in the Institute's technology or ungrateful concerning its previous support. These firms will not hesitate to extend their operations to China without reporting to the government, or even leave Taiwan altogether for China, as in the case of the CEO of Zhongxin. Recall that the restriction of capital outflow was removed in the late 1980s, and that the practice of transfer pricing across national borders is prevalent among sister companies.

That the perpetrators in the crucial semiconductor sector have not been actively prosecuted suggests that the government realizes the limited utility, if not complete futility, of using injunctions or punishment to "manage" the *Taishang*. Ever since the adoption of the managed liberalization policy toward Taiwan's investment in China, the government under the DPP—a party that used to side with labor and environmentalists vis-à-vis business—has been seeking alliances with leading firms in the high-tech sector.[82] Taiwanese firms are not a "technonational" type, unlike Korean firms, which are huge, ambitious, and obsessed with their own brand names and in-house technology, but in nearly complete collaboration with the government. But Taiwanese firms are not of a "technoglobal" type, either, unlike Western MNCs, which are resourceful, globally established, and completely dependent on their own labs rather than on government-funded research for technology. Taiwanese firms, in political scientists William Keller and Louis Pauly's apt characterization, are "technohybrid," located in the middle of the technonational-technoglobal continuum. Taiwanese firms are more likely to thrive with their government's promotion of their joint ventures with Western and Japanese firms, as well with its "logistic" support, such as the provision of industrial estates, manpower training, and R&D consortium arrangements.[83]

To keep the *Taishang* rooted in Taiwan, the government has launched a series of programs to improve the investment environment (such as easing the acquisition of industrial land and accelerating the inflow of talent) and to weave dense, interlocking industrial clusters, thereby raising the opportunity cost of leaving Taiwan. These programs are subsumed under the "Challenge 2008 National Development Plan," adopted in early 2002. The plan attempts to move Taiwan's economic structure from one that is based on manufacturing to one that will be based on innovation (or R&D) and will be more diversified. The central piece is the "two trillion and twin-star project." Through this project, the government hopes to raise the output value of the semiconductor and image display industries to $28.5 billion each, and to nurture the digital content (DVD, data-processing and transfer, software) and biotechnology sectors into star industries, all by 2006.

The "two trillion and twin-star" project is a strategic response to China's pursuit of Taiwan's semiconductor industry. Essentially, the project is an attempt to enhance the technological level and capacity of this sector on the one hand, and use it to foster other industrial sectors on the other. The leading fifteen firms in Taiwan's semiconductor industry had a combined revenue of $ 14 billion in 2002. If their revenue grows by 20 percent a year, the "one trillion" goal will be easily within reach in 2006. Undoubtedly, part of the growth will come from the China market, thereby paradoxically inducing the leading firms to begin or expand operations in China. But the recovered world market and expanded domestic market should help to keep the bulk of semiconductor production in Taiwan. Expanded domestic demand for semiconductors may come from the image display sector, one that is already quite sizeable in Taiwan, and two new sectors to be fostered, digital content and biotechnology.

The image display sector is probably the most promising new sector for Taiwanese industry. The output value for TFT-LCD (thin-film-transistor, liquid crystal display)—the flagship product of the sector—was $6.9 billion in 2002, double that of 2001.[84] If this industry is able to grow by 42 percent a year, it should be able to reach the goal of $28 billion as well in 2006. The most formidable competition is from Korea, not China.[85] As in the semiconductor industry (where Korea opted for integrated device manufacturing and national brand, Taiwan for foundry and for alliance with Western firms, initially), Taiwan began with manufacturing on foreign firms' design, quickly moved to designing, and has begun to attract leading foreign upstream manufacturers to Taiwan. To be in close proximity with its major customers, AU, Quanta, and Chi-Mei, Asahi has decided to invest $0.1 billion in Taiwan to produce ultra large glass substrates, the first of its ventures outside Japan. With this factory, Taiwan will surpass Korea to become the leading supplier and users of TFT-LCD.[86] Meanwhile, the significant expansion of TFT-LCD production has led to rapid growth and upgrading of supporting and downstream industries, such as notebook and desktop PCs.[87] Equally significant is that the TFT-LCD and semiconductor sectors are jointly spawning new industrial clusters. In fact, the digital television manufacturing cluster has taken shape in Taiwan, as makers of all major systems are all present, and the supplies of materials, chip-design and chip-making techniques, and flat panel production are all within reach.[88]

Digital content and biotechnology are the other two sectors earmarked for promotion. Taiwan probably has more advantages than China in the digital content sector, where traditional content (media, entertainment, publication, and software) and digitalized communication converge. China may have a larger supply of personnel, but its e-generation is yet to come of age, and its lack of political and civic liberties may constrain the creation, development, and distribution of digital products and service. The design and production of high-end IC also can help Taiwan to jump start the digital content sector. For the biotech sector, however, China is probably better endowed than Taiwan. China has yet to establish venture capital companies—essential to capital-intensive biotechnological research—and enhance its intellectual property rights regime, but it has more researchers and a much larger and more stratified sample pool of research materials, such as DNA from a variety of climate zones.[89] The government in China is also more inclined to support the biotechnology sector than the digital content sector, as the development of the former is less politically subversive than that of latter. Taiwan's only comparative advantage in the biotechnology sector probably lies in processing and transmitting biotechnology related data. It is thus natural for the newly created Nankang software industrial park to house three types of Taiwanese and foreign firms, software and other digital content firms, IC design, and biotech firms.[90]

However diversified Taiwan's industry may become, it will be difficult, if not impossible, to dilute economic ties across the Strait. Dense economic ties with China will remain an inescapable reality to Taiwan. Given the adversarial relationship across the Strait, political, security, and other noneconomic risks that the dense economic linkage with China may entail should not be overlooked, however remote they appear to be. Incorporating China's operations into Taiwanese firms' global strategy and keeping the *Taishang* anchored in Taiwan's economy may not minimize noneconomic risks. But at least such strategies will sustain Taiwan's economic gains in China and help to deal with the emerging problem of Taiwan's "industrial hollowing out."

Paradoxically, while the DPP Government's capacity to manage Taiwanese capital flow to and trade with China remains limited, the *Taishang's* ability to sway the government's policy toward China is also highly circum-

scribed. As shown in Section I, *Taishang* ventures in China have been crucial to Taiwan's export expansion and foreign exchange earnings. Elected to
office with only 39 percent of votes cast, President Chen did make an effort
to accommodate the request from the business community (especially the
high-tech sector) to phase out the unpopular "Go Slow" policy. But the
government pursued its new policy of managed liberalization with great
caution, often to the dismay of the *Taishang*. Moreover, when Taiwan's status is at stake, business requests are taken note of but not granted, the three
links issue being the prime example. As analyzed in Section II, *Taishang*
ventures in China might also create problems for Taiwan's security, politics,
and economy—a concern that serves to discount *Taishang* political influence. The *Taishang* are also essential to China's economy, indicating that
Beijing cannot always use them as a political instrument to coerce Taiwan.
Hence, *Taishang* may not constitute an effective constraint on President
Chen's policy agenda now that, in the wake of the March 2004 presidential
contest, his support base has expanded to half of the voters and there is no
reelection battle for him to fight.

CHAPTER SIX

Taiwan's Defense Reforms and Military Modernization Program:

OBJECTIVES, ACHIEVEMENTS, AND OBSTACLES

MICHAEL D. SWAINE

MAINTAINING PEACE and stability across the Taiwan Strait is absolutely vital to the continued prosperity and security of the Asian region, as well as to stable relations between the People's Republic of China and the United States. Unfortunately, it is becoming increasingly difficult to achieve this objective, given the instabilities resulting from Beijing's steadfast opposition to the apparently relentless efforts of the Republic of China (hereafter referred to as the ROC or Taiwan) to achieve permanent separation from the mainland. The resulting political tensions have led to a complete collapse of the past common understanding between the two sides regarding the present and future status of Taiwan. In the absence of a resumption of a cross-Strait understanding through dialogue, stability for each side is increasingly (though not solely[1]) dependent on military deterrence. For China, such deterrence is directed at preventing any final consolidation of Taiwan's separate status; for Taiwan, it is directed at preventing China—with the assistance of the United States—from attempting to use force to compel reunification on Beijing's terms.

Yet Taipei's ability to deter the mainland is an issue of growing concern for many observers, given both Taiwan's anemic economic performance and low level of defense spending, and China's increasing military prowess and apparent emphasis on acquiring the capability to strike Taiwan quickly before Washington can react. Many questions remain unanswered regarding, for example, Taiwan's ability and / or willingness to develop a more realistic and coherent military strategy, to more accurately evaluate, acquire and deploy a range of sophisticated weapons and support systems, to create a more integrated overall force structure, and to increase popular support for the armed forces by ensuring civilian controls and more transparent internal military processes. In order to resolve these and other questions, many observers believe that Taipei must follow through on a comprehensive and in-depth program of defense reform and modernization that has been underway for several years.

This article examines that program in considerable detail. The first section looks at the basic objectives and challenges confronting Taiwan's defense reform and modernization efforts. The second section provides an overview of the accomplishments to date and the remaining obstacles confronting the achievement of those objectives. The third section assesses the underlying reasons for the failures and successes experienced by the defense reform and modernization program thus far. A final section comments on the prospects for the future and the implications of the preceding analysis for United States policy and U.S.-ROC relations.[2]

I. OBJECTIVES

Taiwan's defense reform and modernization efforts are focused primarily on four key issue areas: 1) civil-military relations; 2) military streamlining and restructuring; 3) national security and military strategy; and 4) weapons and technology procurement. The ROC government is attempting, with assistance from the United States, to correct significant deficiencies in each of these areas, in order to develop a more professional, capable, and transparent military that is more responsive to Taiwan's democratic leadership and norms and more capable of meeting the growing challenge posed by the Chinese military. The major reform or modernization objectives in each of these four areas and the intended means of attaining them will be examined in order.

TO ESTABLISH DEMOCRATIC, NONPARTISAN, CIVILIAN CONTROL OVER THE MILITARY

One of the most important objectives of defense reform is the effort to depoliticize the ROC military and to place it entirely under an institutionalized, open, and reasonably transparent system of popularly elected, civilian governmental control responsive to the public. These goals gradually emerged as a consequence of the democratization of Taiwan's political system and in reaction to the historical legacy of the ROC military as a highly insulated and secretive institution, under the direct and virtually exclusive control of the president and his immediate subordinates. Prior to democratization, all significant military-related decisions were made by a very small number of professional military officers or former senior officers in very high political posts. The ROC president completely dominated basic decisions regarding Taiwan's national security and defense strategies, force structure, and even operational doctrine, while the General Staff Headquarters (GSH) was in control of narrower policy-related issues, and the armed services controlled various war fighting issues separately.

Even more important, under Chiang Kai-shek and Chiang Ching-kuo, the ROC military had functioned as a party-controlled army in service to the Chinese Nationalist Party or Kuomintang (KMT). Specifically, during that period (from the 1950s to the 1980s), the military primarily served the KMT's objectives of: a) remaining in power on Taiwan as the dominant representative of mainland Chinese interests and prerogatives; and b) challenging and eventually overcoming Chinese communist control over the mainland. These objectives became increasingly problematic as Taiwan democratized during the nineties—leading to the rise in political power on the island of the native Taiwanese population—and as the communists consolidated control on the mainland and the PRC's military power and political-economic influence within the international community increased. In addition, the resulting nativist opposition political movement led by the Democratic Progressive Party (DPP) wanted to ensure that the military would obey any non-KMT-led government that might win election in the future.[3]

In very recent years, the impetus for greater openness and democratic control over the ROC military gained even more momentum as a result of several major corruption cases involving illicit payments between foreign and domestic defense industry contractors, officials, and senior ROC military officers on the one hand, and government bureaucrats on the other hand, over the procurement of major weapons systems from abroad. These widely publicized cases heightened public awareness of the need for significant structural and procedural reforms of the military designed to open it up to civilian scrutiny and subject it to clear, enforceable legal strictures.

Efforts by Taiwan's democratic political leadership to exercise greater control over the military have been obstructed by both specific organizational features of the civil-military command system and the near-total absence in Taiwanese society of civilian expertise regarding military matters. The former obstacle centered on the persistence of a dual authority structure over the armed forces: a parliamentary line of authority between the premier, the minister of defense, and the chief of the general staff (CGS) for ordinary administrative matters and a second direct line of command authority between the president and the CGS for operational matters.[4] This structure complicated lines of command and control between the government (i.e., the president and the premier) and the armed forces and made it virtually impossible for the Legislative Yuan (LY) directly to examine and question the policies and actions of the professional military, in the person of the CGS. The CGS could claim that his direct link to the president placed him (and the uniformed military) outside the premier-led parliamentary system and hence exempted him from LY questioning regarding operational matters.[5]

The latter obstacle is much more deeply rooted and hence difficult to change. The lack of civilian expertise on military issues derives from the secretive and exclusionary nature of Taiwan's military system in the past, the overall low emphasis placed on military affairs and the pursuit of a military career among most ROC civilians, and the simple fact that the teaching of military-related matters was carried out exclusively within the professional military education system. The resulting near-monopoly of military expertise by the armed forces tended to reinforce the prerogatives exercised by the professional military and increased resistance to establishing effective civilian oversight. In this system, the formal position of the minister of defense was not very significant. The influence of any individual minister was largely based on his prestige, which often derived from the fact that he had previously served as CGS. Although the minister of defense was routinely subjected to LY interpolation, he had no power over military matters.[6]

In response to the above problems, the LY ratified two major defense reform laws in January 2000: the National Defense Law (NDL) and the Ministry of National Defense Organization Law. These laws focused the reforms on three major areas: 1) the depoliticization of the military; 2) the creation of a single civilian chain-of-command under the president, the premier and minister of defense along with the strengthening of the overall authority of the Ministry of National Defense (MND); and 3) the development of extensive levels of civilian expertise within the MND.[7] The elimination of the dual chain-of-command in favor of a single line of authority from the CGS-led professional military to the minister of defense, the premier, and ultimately the president as commander-in-chief would clarify the system of command and control and expose the CGS and other senior military officers to direct oversight and examination by the LY, especially over planning, budget, and procurement issues.[8] Other closely related changes would reportedly strengthen the joint operational authority of the GSH over the individual services by transferring many of the current responsibilities and powers of the service headquarters to the GSH. The CGS would directly command several unified or joint warfare centers, including four military theaters on Taiwan, one each on Penghu and the offshore islands, and the two naval fleets. The three service headquarters would in turn be downgraded to the level of individual subordinate commands and focus primarily on operational training and doctrinal development.[9]

In order to strengthen the capabilities of the MND, the defense laws also aimed at increasing the specialization of units within the ministry. The MND would be divided into three major divisions: policy, armaments, and military operations. The first two divisions would be directed by two vice ministers, and the third division would be under the CGS. Within these three divisions, some offices would be transferred from the GSH and some would be formed from old units.[10] In addition, the transfer of many roles and functions from military staff offices to new civilian-led MND offices will assist in the effort to strengthen the training of civilians in defense matters. Related to this issue is the desire over the long term to introduce civilian management techniques and systems into the military and generally to increase the number and capabilities of civilian appointees within the military establishment. The national defense law requires one-third of MND officials to become civilians, ostensibly by the end of 2003. U.S. assistance and advice in the effort to increase civilian control over the military is critical.[11]

Taken as a whole, these changes, could significantly shift control over basic military decisions (including warfighting operations) from the individual services to the GSH and—most importantly—to the minister of national defense and his senior subordinates. Under this new structure, and with the strengthening of the MND as an institution, the Minister of Defense and his many civilian subordinates would become key players in the operational chain of command. Perhaps even more important, the MND itself—and not the professional military—would become the center of gravity on critical decisions in such areas as strategic planning, acquisition, and budgeting.[12]

TO RESTRUCTURE, STREAMLINE, AND MODERNIZE THE ARMED FORCES

Most of Taiwan's political and military leaders recognize the need to carry out a basic restructuring and modernization of the armed forces, primarily in response to the changes that have taken place in the mission objectives and threat perceptions of the Taiwan military during the past decade. Today, Taiwan faces a growing, more complex threat from China in the form of a modernizing, multidimensional People's Liberation Army (PLA) possessing a growing number of short-range ballistic missiles, advanced strike aircraft, improved diesel submarines and surface ships, a possible amphibious attack capability, information warfare and psych-ops units, and likely fifth column elements.[13]

For the proponents of reform and modernization, Taiwan's changing threat environment requires a fundamental restructuring and streamlining of the armed forces and the acquisition of a vast range of new capabilities and operational procedures to deter and, if necessary, to repel a PRC attack. Specifically, the longstanding historical emphasis placed on Taiwan's ground forces in determining the overall size, disposition, and internal pattern of decisionmaking authority within the armed forces, along with the overall "stove-piped" nature of the ROC military structure as a whole (in which the separate armed services operate largely independently of one another—discussed below), should be fundamentally revised, if not eliminated altogether. These features should be replaced by a smaller, more integrated, joint, and balanced force, possessing lighter, more mobile ground units, greatly improved naval and air capabilities, better surveillance and battle management systems, quicker response times, increased survivability (including both passive and active forms of defense against missile and air attack), and enhanced deterrence capabilities.[14]

Thus, the first priority in structural reform is to reduce further the overall size of Taiwan's military, from an existing level of approximately 370,000 personnel to approximately 325,000, as envisioned by the so-called *Jing Jin* force consolidation program. This is supposedly to be accomplished over a three year period, by eliminating 15,000 positions per year between 2004 and 2006.[15] However, for some reform advocates, the ultimate goal of the force reduction effort is to reach a level of approximately 275,000 personnel, although no time period has yet been specified for this reduction.[16] Beyond personnel reductions, other elements of the program include reducing the number of levels in the chain of command, merging or consolidating military educational institutions, streamlining high-level staff units, and reducing the number of general officers, especially in the ground forces. There has also been some discussion—most recently by President Chen Shui-bian[17]—of moving away from a conscription force toward a partial or an all-volunteer military, in order to strengthen discipline and morale and to facilitate longer terms of service. The latter is viewed as necessary for the enhanced training levels required to attain the more sophisticated capabilities of the future Taiwan military.[18] There is also discussion of establishing a more professional noncommissioned officer (NCO) corps, to improve training and to give more responsibility and opportunity to junior officers, in response to the perceived need for more initiative at local levels.[19] Reportedly, some have also voiced a desire to include more women in the military, especially if a volunteer force emerges.[20]

Taiwan's force structure improvements require the acquisition of more powerful and mobile ground, air, and naval combat platforms, as well as improved anti-submarine warfare (ASW) and air and missile defense capabilities, and more potent joint warfare, early warning (EW), reconnaissance, surveillance and battle management systems. These ostensibly include submarines, P-3C ASW aircraft, Kidd-class and possibly AEGIS-equipped frigates and destroyers, more capable air-to-air, air-to-surface, and surface-to-surface missiles, more advanced attack helicopters, improved Patriot ballistic missile defense systems, and long-range EW radars, including tactical radar upgrades, and improvements in command and control, communication, computers, intelligence, surveillance, and reconnaissance (C4ISR) capabilities.[21] Strengthening jointness and rapid reaction capabilities, especially between the ROC Air Force and the ROC Navy, is also a key modernization objective. In addition, the development of a more survivable force requires a variety of passive defense measures, including the hardening of air bases, command, control, and communication facilities, and other vital military and political locations, generally using steel-reinforced concrete. U.S. assistance in virtually all of these areas is critical, as discussed below. Finally, some observers argue that the Taiwan military must also establish a more credible deterrent by acquiring limited but potent offensive strike capabilities to attack targets on the Chinese mainland. This highly controversial argument is examined below.

TO STRENGTHEN OVERALL NATIONAL SECURITY AND STRATEGIC PLANNING

For some observers, it is more important for Taiwan to strengthen its strategic planning process than simply to acquire various new weapons and weapons systems, streamline the military structure, or more effectively coordinate military operations within and among the services. Without a comprehensive, integrated national security and strategic planning system, it becomes extremely difficult to link threat perceptions to strategic priorities, military doctrine, operational doctrine, and force structure requirements in a way that maximizes the ability of Taiwan's scarce military assets to protect vital national interests. And in the absence of such organic links, it in turn becomes extremely difficult to assess such vital questions as: what types of weapons systems are absolutely essential for Taiwan's defense? How are they to be used most effectively? What level and type of jointness and operational training are required among the services, and to what end? How should Taiwan's most critical military assets be deployed to maximize their deterrence and warfighting capabilities in a crisis or conflict? How should such deployments relate to possible American force deployments during a crisis or conflict? And to what extent are offensive weapons and operational doctrines required for Taiwan's defense?

Historically, the ROC government has lacked the tradition, experience, and incentives to establish an integrated and systematic national security and strategic planning process. For decades, Taiwan's national security approach and military strategy were largely determined by the legacy of the KMT's experience on the mainland, the army's dominance over the ROC military, the personal views of President Chiang Kai-shek and the CGS-dominated military system, and—before America's de-recognition of the ROC government and resulting abrogation of the U.S.-Taiwan security treaty in 1979—the priorities of the overall U.S. security strategy in the Western Pacific. Taiwan's overall national security and foreign policy objectives were largely dictated by the KMT's rivalry with the Chinese Communist Party and its claim of authority over the mainland.[22]

In recent years, the shift from the ground force-centered, offensive mission of retaking the mainland to the essentially defensive mission of protecting Taiwan from a multipronged PLA attack have raised the importance of both air and naval forces to Taiwan's defense. And yet the resulting overall strategy of "effective deterrence" (*youxiao hezu*) and "resolute defense" (*fangwei gushou*) has been translated into a relatively simple doctrine of air-to-air, naval-to-naval, and ground-to-ground force interdiction marked by almost no operational interactions between the services, weak levels of both intra- and inter-service command, control, and communication, the maintenance of very sizeable ground forces, and an orientation toward retaining significant forces in reserve in order to "hold on" until U.S. assistance arrives.[23] Overall, according to knowledgeable observers, no true J-5 planning and command structure and process existed and significant perceptual and procedural gaps emerged between the GSH and the individual service commands.[24] Moreover, since 1979, Taiwan's specific force structure—and hence the effectiveness of its defense strategy—became highly dependent upon arms sales decisions made in Washington.

In the absence of a more sophisticated, comprehensive and integrated defense strategy, decisions regarding weapons acquisitions, operational doctrine, deployments, and changes in force structure became highly subject to the political and personal motivations and views of senior ROC political leaders (and in particular the president), the vagaries of inter-service rivalries (in which the ground forces have long held a privileged position), and the opportunities and pressures presented by the United States, as Taiwan's sole security partner and source of its major military weapons systems. A more transparent, systematic, pragmatic, and institutionalized national security and military strategic planning process would provide a much more credible and convincing set of standards for determining the critical elements of Taiwan's overall military modernization and reform effort. Such an accomplishment would in turn permit Taiwan to deliver more convincing arguments to the United States, the LY, and other interested and influential players regarding its weapons requirements (or non-requirements[25]), to adjudicate disputes among the armed services more effectively, and in general to reduce the level of arbitrary or personal influence exerted on the entire process.

The above deficiencies clearly suggest the need for Taiwan's civil-military defense establishment to develop a broad range of conceptual approaches and models, procedures, processes, and institutional structures for conducting strategic assessment, planning, and implementation. This task is, of course, not nearly as complicated as in the case of a large state with a wide array of security concerns and threats, such as the United States. Taiwan obviously faces a very clear security challenge from a single source. Nonetheless, the development and implementation of the most effective military strategy for meeting that threat presents significant challenges.

First, China is a very large potential adversary possessing significant resources and growing military capabilities, especially in the areas of air, missile, and submarine attack. Second, the main island of Taiwan is located less than 100 nautical miles from China and can be reached quite rapidly from the mainland by air; at the same time, the Taiwan Strait acts as a defensive barrier against ground assault. Third, the island itself is relatively narrow with many mountainous areas along the east coast, offering little opportunity for maneuver and defense-in-depth.[26] Fourth, Taiwan itself has relatively limited resources and is highly dependent upon a single foreign source for much of its military hardware and systems. It is also reliant to a significant degree upon that same source for military assistance in the event of a serious military threat from China. Fifth, Taiwan's national identity and foreign policy are to a great extent in significant flux as a result of democratization and the resulting Taiwanization and de-Sinification of the society and polity.

These factors suggest that the Taiwan military must develop a military strategy that: 1) is highly efficient in the use of limited resources; 2) effectively integrates early warning and rapid response capabilities; 3) maximizes the application of military counter-measures (especially significant offshore operations) against the most likely and most potent threats from the PLA; 4) at the same time, does not inadvertently provoke a PLA attack during a crisis or unnecessarily escalate an existing conflict; and 5) reinforces to the maximum extent possible whatever assistance is provided by the United States in a crisis or conflict. In addition, whatever military strategy Taiwan develops must be consistent with its changing national security and foreign policy objectives. This is a tall order.

Taiwan has turned to Washington for critical advice and assistance to develop its national security and military strategy and strategic planning process. It is seeking to study and to some extent to emulate the methodologies and structures basic to the integrated and robust national security and military strategic planning system employed by the U.S. executive branch and the Department of Defense. In the former area, Taipei seeks to strengthen national security planning and to improve interagency coordination among all agencies with relevance to foreign affairs and defense by, first, enhancing the strategic planning capability of the existing National Security Council, and, second, strengthening the NSC's contacts with the Taiwan military and its overall coordination role in civilian and military areas. In the area of military strategy, Taiwan's Ministry of Defense is working to acquire in-house capabilities to develop military strategic plans that more effectively link threats with doctrine, force structure, procurement, training, and military purchases, to conduct war gaming and short, medium, and long-term assessments of the changing PRC threat, to foster greater jointness among Taiwan's armed services, and to integrate the relevant activities of subordinate organs within the MND and the armed forces.

TO IMPROVE THE EFFICIENCY AND INTEGRITY OF THE PROCUREMENT PROCESS AND TO DIVERSIFY THE SOURCES OF PROCUREMENT AND INCREASE THE INDIGENOUS PRODUCTION OF WEAPONS SYSTEMS

For many years, public confidence in Taiwan's military has been undermined by repeated corruption scandals involving the procurement of extremely expensive weapons systems from the United States and other foreign suppliers. These scandals have usually witnessed the payment of various types of bribes or kickbacks by defense contractors or their agents to Taiwan military officers within procurement offices.[27] Moreover, members of the LY and segments of the public have been unsupportive of significant defense outlays because of a strong suspicion that U.S. business circles (perhaps with collusion from the Taiwan military) drive U.S. policy regarding weapons sales, resulting in inflated prices or efforts to dump obsolete weapons on Taiwan.[28]

These concerns have resulted in support for efforts to create a more transparent, objectively based, and institutionalized weapons procurement process, to diversify the sources of weaponry, and to develop a stronger indigenous production base for many weapons systems. The above-outlined effort to restructure and strengthen the MND includes the establishment of a more professional, single-decision-point MND Armaments Bureau led by a vice minister of armament. This office develops strategies for procurement of weapons and equipment, plans for the development and indigenous production of defense related technologies, and would in general provide extensive support for weapons acquisition by the armed services. It oversees and enforces the implementation of the entire procurement process on the basis of an extensive body of rules and regulations that have been established in recent years. The effort to establish clearer standards and criteria for assessing Taiwan's defense needs (involving a better mutual understanding between Taiwan and the United States of what constitutes a "significant upgrade" of specific weapons systems or capabilities) is also seen as essential to this process.[29]

II. ACCOMPLISHMENTS AND SHORTCOMINGS

Taiwan's defense reforms and modernization program have thus far produced some notable advances. However, many key areas continue to exhibit little real progress, or are advancing at an excessively slow rate. And some areas deemed successful at present are apparently succeeding primarily because of external pressure by the United States, and not as a result of genuine internal reform and change.

In the realm of civil-military relations, the effort to depoliticize the military and to expose it to public scrutiny has achieved perhaps the most obvious successes. First and foremost, the dual-track authority structure between the senior ranks of the uniformed military and the civilian leadership has been abolished, in favor of a single chain-of-command within the premier-ministry structure. Although the president retains supreme power over the military as commander-in-chief, the CGS is now unambiguously subordinate to the MND and thus subject to LY oversight and interrogation. In fact, the LY and the media now have access to a wide variety of military and civilian officers and officials within the MND and the military chain-of-command. This has opened the entire military to the sometimes glaring eye of public scrutiny and the oft-times ill-informed criticisms of various politicians. Second, the formal influence of the KMT over the military has been abolished. No longer a party-army dedicated to advancing the goals of a single political entity, the Taiwan military is now more genuinely associated with the government and the national constitution, regardless of which party rules.[30]

In contrast, the far more challenging effort to establish genuine civilian control over the military has thus far exhibited only limited success.[31] On the surface, the civilianization of the MND is proceeding according to plan. One-third of approximately 600 key positions within the ministry were filled by civilians by the end of 2003, as required by law.[32] However, knowledgeable insiders strongly suggest that this formal change will not translate into a genuine increase in civilian authority within the MND, or, more broadly, into an increase in civilian control over the military over at least the short to medium term. This is because many of the civilians staffing the MND are actually retired military officers. Moreover, the government has yet to develop an accepted, regular process for recruiting both government and nongovernment personnel into the MND, and it has not yet devised an examination for prospective MND staffers.[33] It also lacks a regularized process for the granting of security clearances to civilian government officials whose positions require access to classified information. A recently proposed personnel security plan has generated strong opposition from KMT legislators and others who argue that it could be used as a tool of political persecution.[34]

The effort to restructure, streamline and modernize the Taiwan military has also experienced mixed results thus far. Taiwan is moving ahead with its plans to reduce the size of the armed forces and to examine alternatives to conscription. The *Jing Shi* streamlining and consolidation program, put into effect in July 1997, decreased the number of military personnel to less than 375,000. As indicated above, the military is to be reduced by a further 45,000 personnel within three years under a follow-on consolidation plan. Moreover, the MND has reportedly formed a special task force to embark on research into an alternative recruiting system for military service instead of the present two-year compulsory service system. It recently unveiled measures to introduce limited voluntary military service on a trial basis, apparently as part of an effort to move to a partial volunteer military in each service as an experiment. Finally, the MND might also seek to streamline by cutting back on the political warfare apparatus of the Taiwan military. This apparatus is a holdover from the KMT party-army era, when the apparatus served largely to propagandize the idea of reunification and strongly opposed the pro-independence stance of the DPP.[35]

However, on the negative side, little agreement exists over the specific contents of Taiwan's future force reductions, e.g., which services and which units are to be cut. And debate continues over the ultimate size and structure of any reductions beyond the initial 45,000 personnel, despite the ultimate objective of 275,000 cited above. A DPP study made public in late March 2003 stated that the size of the military should be reduced far below current planned levels, to approximately 256,000 (largely by trimming more personnel from the ground forces), and that spending on personnel should be cut to 40 percent of the total defense outlay, down from the present 56 percent, in order to free NT$36 billion each year for weapons procurement.[36] Yet the ROC Army continues to resist mightily any major reduction in ground forces (as discussed in greater detail below), as well as other aspects of the military streamlining effort. Ground forces still constitute more than half of Taiwan's armed forces. And enormous resistance remains to anything beyond the above-mentioned highly limited experiments with volunteerism, despite Chen Shui-bian's verbal support for this objective.[37] For many knowledgeable observers, the shift to a volunteer force would be very costly, and many fear it could reduce the size of the military below necessary levels. Finally, debate remains unresolved over what to do with the military's political warfare system. It has reportedly stopped espousing the reunification ideals of the KMT, yet still employs thousands of personnel. Although the MND and CGS will probably retain the system, they would likely focus it largely on welfare and morale, reduce its funding, and downgrade the head of this system to a lieutenant general.[38]

The restructuring and modernization of Taiwan's armed forces are also showing signs of progress, in most cases with U.S. assistance. And yet much remains to be done. The United States has enormously expanded the pace and scope of its weapons sales, advice, and direct assistance to Taiwan in many areas. In April 2001, Washington agreed to sell Taiwan (or to assist Taiwan in obtaining) an unprecedented level of advanced early warning and reconnaissance aircraft, surface naval combatants, submarines, and various types of technical assistance and support. After lengthy discussions, Washington and Taipei apparently reached agreement on the acquisition of virtually every major item approved at that time.[39] Among these military systems, long-range, early warning radars, missile defense, ASW platforms, and improvements in C4ISR for Taiwan's air, sea, land, and joint defense platforms as well as command and operation centers reportedly enjoy the highest priority. (These weapons and support systems will be discussed in greater detail below.)

In addition to providing major weapons and support systems, the U.S. Defense Department has conducted over a dozen assessments and studies of Taiwanese military capabilities during the past three years, including in-depth examinations of Taiwan's ability to defend itself against air attacks, naval blockades, and military landings.[40] It has also undertaken a study of Taiwan's C4ISR systems and is providing mobile training teams and other assistance packages in such specific areas as battle management/C4ISR-joint operations and joint air defense doctrine,[41] missile defense, logistics, information warfare, defense-related modeling and simulation, and defense counter-air operations. Washington is also providing Taiwan with access to U.S. national military assets, such as early warning sensors, and has carried out a strategic survey of vulnerabilities in the island's military and civilian infrastructure. Moreover, since 2001, the U.S. military has sent representatives to Taiwan's annual military exercises, as part of expanding efforts not only to provide advice on warfighting issues, but also to coordinate with the Taiwan military in order to reduced the likelihood of friendly fire incidents in a conflict with the Mainland, and to improve coordination of noncombatant evacuation operations of U.S. personnel during a military crisis.

In all, there are reportedly now more ongoing U.S. military programs with Taiwan than with any major U.S. ally. In order more effectively to supervise and coordinate Taiwan's rapidly expanding defense cooperation with Washington, the MND formed a unified window or coordination unit—the U.S.-Taiwan Military Cooperation Group (UTMCG)—on May 1, 2002, under the auspices of Vice Admiral Lee Hai-tung. This unit is responsible for channeling all defense cooperation programs with the United States, even though many programs are actually being coordinated through the MND's Strategic Planning Department, discussed below.[42]

Finally, Taiwan continues to move forward with efforts to attain both offensive and defensive capabilities against PLA naval, air, and missile attacks. The ROC military has apparently decided—despite considerable hesitation and under significant U.S. pressure—that it must acquire several batteries of PAC-3 Patriot ballistic missile defense systems. It is also reportedly contemplating the acquisition of more advanced, so-called "upper-tier" missile defense systems—such as AEGIS-equipped destroyers with the advanced anti-missile Standard-Missile-Three (SM-3) and the ground-based Theater High-Altitude Air Defense System (THAADS)—assuming these systems come on line over the next few years.[43] In addition, a long-standing short-range ballistic missile program reportedly remains active, as well as a more recent attempt to develop land-attack cruise missiles. Both undertakings are part of a larger effort to acquire a limited offensive strike capability against the mainland, discussed below.[44] At the same time, passive defense capabilities have been strengthened at some key military sites. For example, a program to harden air bases and critical communication centers is underway, along with the rapid runway repairs program. In the latter case, equipment has been procured and a viable training program has been implemented.[45]

As a result of both U.S. assistance and Taiwan's own efforts, the quality of the ROC armed forces has without doubt increased in recent years. In the view of knowledgeable observers within the U.S. government, individual ROC front-line military units are generally well-respected, their operators reasonably well-trained and in some notable cases (e.g., air force units) functioning at a higher level of readiness, and the equipment on major weapons platforms such as surface ships is well-maintained. Moreover, specific combat units have reportedly improved their ability to fight at night and some progress has been attained in eventually creating joint warfighting capabilities among the services.[46]

On the negative side, serious problems remain in coordination, communication, integration, and planning among Taiwan's fighting units—all absolutely critical areas for creating the kind of force that can more effectively deal with the growing Chinese threat. Although concerted efforts are being undertaken by Taiwan with U.S. assistance to improve performance in each realm, progress remains relatively slow and internal debates in Taiwan (as well as differences with Washington) continue over the proper concept and configuration that should guide each area of modernization. Equally important, most approved weapons systems have yet to be acquired, much less made operational, and the pace of acquisition remains slow. Most notably, the purchase date for several weapons (e.g., most systems approved in April 2001), the specific amount of money required for the acquisition or development of individual systems (e.g., of advanced ASW aircraft), and the production location of some major weapons (e.g., modern diesel submarines), remain largely undetermined.[47] And in some instances, differences remain between Washington and Taipei over the priority to be accorded some weapons, such as Paladin self-propelled howitzers (strongly desired by the ROC army) and the above-mentioned attack helicopters.[48] In addition, some important elements of the modernization effort—such as the C4ISR system—are allegedly being constructed on the basis of an inadequate understanding of their true potential. Specifically, the objectives of increasing overall battlefield awareness and local unit initiative are reportedly not sufficiently emphasized.[49]

Although the Chen Shui-bian government decided in the autumn of 2003 to establish a special budget of over $15 billion to purchase several of the major weapons approved in April 2001, and even though the Ministry of Defense has more recently submitted a draft budget in support of this decision, it is by no means certain that the LY will approve the required funds.[50] Moreover, although some knowledgeable observers believe that the Taiwan military can develop the skills to operate the kinds of sophisticated weapons systems supplied by the United States, this will require major changes in training and require a considerable amount of time. In addition, the above-mentioned civilian and military infrastructure vulnerability study is still pending, and some observers fear that the hardening and the runway repair efforts are not being fully implemented. In the former area, progress is reportedly hampered by the Taiwan military's insistence that it can only study and protect military—not civilian—facilities. In the latter area, lack of sufficient progress is apparently due to inadequate personnel and unenergetic leadership. Finally, efforts to develop indigenous capabilities (e.g., Taiwan's ballistic missile and anti-ballistic missile programs) are reportedly experiencing technical problems, especially regarding guidance systems.[51]

Perhaps most troubling is the fact that much of the momentum behind Taiwan's effort to carry out improvements in both hardware capabilities and supporting "software" infrastructure and C4ISR systems is still largely provided by the U.S. government, for reasons discussed below. One notable exception is in the area of offensive weaponry such as ballistic missiles, also discussed below. U.S. officials told Taiwan officials at the second U.S.-Taiwan defense conference in February 2003 that Taiwan should spend more on its own defense and move more quickly to acquire specific systems such as the PAC-3 missile defense system.[52] This message was reiterated by a U.S. delegation—led by Mary Tighe, the Principal Director for Asian and Pacific Affairs in the Office of the Secretary of Defense (OSD)—that visited Taiwan in March 2003, and by messages delivered to the Speaker of the LY, Wang Jin-pyng, when he visited Washington in summer 2003.[53]

The effort to establish an integrated, comprehensive strategic planning process exhibits major shortcomings. To be sure, organizational changes have been undertaken in some areas. For example, a Strategic Planning Department (SPD) and an Integrated Assessment Office (IAO) were established within the MND in 2000, both modeled after similar offices within the Department of Defense.[54] The SPD (directed by a navy vice admiral) is charged with overseeing the implementation of the entire defense reform process, in support of the minister of defense, as well as with developing a comprehensive strategic planning process, analyzing Taiwan's strategic environment (especially over the near term, i.e., 1–5 years), and promoting security cooperation and exchanges with foreign militaries. The IAO (directed by an Air Force lieutenant general) is responsible for analyzing the specific nature of the threat to Taiwan in both the medium and long term (10–20 years), and for developing and analyzing various types of military scenarios or contingencies that might emerge (using, among other means, defense modeling and simulation techniques developed at the U.S. Pacific Command), in order to assess Taiwan's military strategy, plans, force structure, military capabilities, and resource allocation.[55] However, the SPD and IAO are both understaffed and lack a sufficient number of skilled personnel to perform these duties. Moreover, some uncertainty remains as to the specific division of labor between the two organizations, thus producing some rivalry. The MND is currently in the process of reassessing its initial institutional arrangements under the reforms, and is scheduled to finalize those arrangements in 2004.[56] As a result of this ongoing process, the specific missions of and authority relationships between the SPD and IAO, and the respective relationship between these organizations and the MND, have yet to be determined.[57]

On the conceptual level, efforts to develop a comprehensive and integrated national security strategy and to improve interagency coordination in the national security and defense arenas have enjoyed notable but still very limited success to date, according to knowledgeable observers. Regarding the former effort, Taiwan has received increasing amounts of input from the United States in recent years. Several forums for security dialogue between Washington and Taipei now exist, including the annual U.S.-ROC Monterey Talks held in Monterey California, and the U.S.-Taiwan Defense Review Talks, which include officials from the Office of the Secretary of Defense (OSD) and their policymaking counterparts from the Taiwan MND. The former focuses largely on national security and military strategy-related issues while the latter focuses largely on defense policy issues, as well as weapons acquisitions.[58]

As these interactions proceeded, Taiwan's NSC initiated the development of a comprehensive national security strategy. The intent of this effort is to create a strategy that can be supported by all segments of the political leadership in Taiwan and the public at large, as well as the U.S. government. However, this effort has been hampered by Taiwan's intensifying national identity crisis, which pits advocates of an entirely separate Taiwanese sense of nationhood against advocates of some form of future social and political association with mainland China. This crisis prevents any agreement on issues relating to the scope and tenor of Taiwan's national security interests beyond protection of the home islands and the advancement of Taiwan's diplomatic stature.[59]

More concretely, as indicated above, in the strategic planning process, a greater emphasis has been placed on the notion of "jointness" among the armed service. However, an overall military strategy of deterrence and defense that integrates the separate missions of the individual services into a coherent whole has yet to appear.[60] In the absence of such a strategy, it is difficult to determine what level and type of jointness might be best for Taiwan. In the view of some observers, the interests and concerns of Taiwan's ground forces continue to dominate efforts to develop military strategy and doctrine. This point is discussed in greater detail in the next section.

Concerning the effort to improve interagency coordination, there is evidence of greater involvement and coordination among relevant agencies in interactions with the U.S. government, e.g., at the above-mentioned Monterey Talks.[61] However, a systematic, institutionalized internal interagency process has yet to emerge within the ROC government. The National Security Council does not play a strong coordinating role among national security and defense-related agencies, and no equivalent exists to the so-called Principals Group of the U.S. government, consisting of the heads of all major national security-related agencies.[62]

Finally, attempts to improve the procurement process and the level of indigenous weapons production have exhibited the least amount of substantive progress to date. Some advances have occurred in combating corruption and in raising the level of transparency in the procurement process. The MND has established the above-mentioned Armaments Bureau under a vice minister, and policies, strategies, and plans regarding the weapons procurement process have reportedly witnessed some improvements as a result. However, the growing statutory involvement of the LY in the evaluation and approval of major weapons systems has opened the procurement process up to enormous amounts of political manipulation and slowed the effort to move forward with acquisitions agreed upon by the Taiwan military and the executive branch.[63] Moreover, according to insiders, Taiwan has yet to adjust fully to the end of the annual foreign military sales (FMS) process with the United States. Sales can now theoretically be made at any time there is a perceived need for a significant increase in Taiwan's self-defense capabilities. However, Taiwan's defense planning process is not yet sufficiently developed to provide clear guidance on acquisition decisions, including a mutually agreed upon definition of what constitutes a "significant upgrade" of weapons systems, as mentioned above.[64]

III. UNDERLYING FACTORS

On the basis of the foregoing analysis, and the views of knowledgeable observers, it seems that much of the progress witnessed thus far in the reform effort can be attributed to four sets of factors: First, the existence of strong political support from above and general agreement in society regarding some very specific changes, such as the depoliticization of the military and the strengthening of civilian access and control. Second, the existence of clear economic pressure in support of cost reductions, e.g., regarding the effort to decrease the overall size of the military. Third, the relative ease of applying certain technical or training "fixes" to specific military units, e.g., regarding advances in readiness and night fighting capabilities among individual services. Fourth, the continuous, growing external pressure for reform exerted by the United States, e.g., regarding many arms acquisitions, improvements in military support systems, and organizational restructuring. However, with the possible exception of U.S. pressure, these motivating factors cannot ensure the success of those reforms that require deeper conceptual, attitudinal, and structural changes in the system.

Many underlying obstacles still exist to the implementation of such reforms. First, as suggested above, successful reform requires a sea-change in the way Taiwan's civil-military leadership makes decisions. Taiwan's new democracy and the accompanying need for deeper and broader levels of civilian involvement and control in the decisionmaking process, as well as the increasing size and complexity of the threat posed by China, together demand the greater institutionalization of the decisionmaking process, the expansion of military expertise into civilian areas, the creation of a GSH with genuine joint warfighting functions, and the overall dispersal of authority across both civilian and military agencies.

Strong and energetic political and military support from the very top of the leadership structure is necessary to overcome the deeply rooted interests that resist such changes. And yet such support is arguably absent or at least insufficient at present. Some observers argue that the impetus behind defense reform dropped significantly when former ROC Air Force chief, Chief-of-the-General-Staff, Minister of Defense, and Premier General Tang Fei retired within one year after the advent of the Chen government in March 2000. Tang was a major force behind the reform effort. Beginning in the mid-1990s, he was the leading figure among a strong group of reformers within the Taiwan military that included many air force and navy officers and even a few army officers. These individuals accepted the direction that democracy was taking in Taiwan and understood the need for true reform in the military. However, most of the more vocal of these officers were eventually driven into retirement or marginalized, except for a very few individuals such as Tang Fei. After Tang's departure from the government, support for reform within the military largely fell to individuals such as his successor and former Chief-of-the-General-Staff and ROC army chief Tang Yiau-ming. Although Tang Yiau-ming, a native Taiwanese, is reportedly supportive of many aspects of reform, his army background, previous strong rivalry with Tang Fei (in which he reportedly tended to oppose whatever Tang Fei supported) and allegedly limited strategic vision led many individuals to conclude that military (and in particular army) resistance to many reforms remained steadfast. Tang Yiauming, in turn, took the occasion of the presidential election in March 2004 to announce his intention to retire from the post of minister of defense. His replacement, Admiral Lee Jye, the incumbent CGS, is relatively unknown to Americans, but, according to one knowledgeable observer, he is viewed as more reform-minded by Taiwan's political leadership (along with being a strong advocate of submarines).[65]

Of equal importance, the extent of high-level civilian political support for defense reform has lagged significantly during the past two years. After taking office in 2000, Chen Shui-bian attempted to court the military and champion the cause of military reform by visiting military sites and making supportive speeches. However, he has pulled back from this effort in recent years. According to many observers, Chen Shui-bian became less able and willing to press forward with defense reform because of growing domestic problems, including his unending struggle with the political opposition, the resulting policy deadlock within the ROC government, the sagging Taiwan economy, and increased pressure from Beijing. Moreover, from mid-2003 to March 2004, his energies were clearly focused on getting reelected and he reportedly did not want to expend significant amounts of political capital pressing hard for controversial and strongly resisted changes in the military. Some of Chen's supporters also wondered why the government should spend billions of dollars on modernizing the military when such outlays will probably produce little if any political support. Many such individuals reportedly feel that money spent on the military will only be taken away from other uses of far greater benefit to the public. They argue that most ordinary soldiers are conscripts with little interest in improving the armed forces, and most senior officers are mainlanders who evince little sympathy for the Chen Shui-bian government. In fact, many senior officers reportedly remain strongly supportive of the "one China" concept and are intensely bitter toward what they see as Chen Shui-bian's efforts to create a new Taiwan identity that rejects any future political association with mainland China, of whatever form.[66]

Finally, on some very specific defense modernization issues, concerted action is complicated by basic political considerations. For example, many observers believe that any effective effort to harden soft targets such as civilian and military leadership compounds, power grids, energy generation sites, fuel storage facilities and other vital infrastructure would require a prior level of public concern over the very real possibility of a Chinese attack and a concerted level of support for civil defense that no Taiwan politi-

cian is willing to generate or uphold.[67] And yet, despite all these considerations, some observers believe that Chen might move with greater determination to implement defense reform now that he has been reelected (and
thus no longer needs to run for office), and especially if he obtains a workable majority in the LY in December 2004.

At lower levels of the political-military system, deeply rooted resistance
remains to many fundamental reforms. For example, service rivalries continue to obstruct many initiatives. The Taiwan army—still a dominant influence within the armed forces—generally exhibits strong and effective
resistance to reducing the physical size and strategic importance of the
army, for reasons discussed in greater detail below.[68] Moreover, some important institutional restructuring requires overcoming resistance within
the military leadership—and especially army leaders—to the elimination
of certain high-level billets. As previously mentioned , the effort to create
a more representative GSH less dominated by the views of the CGS and
possessing greater authority over operational matters requires moving
both policy-related and operational command functions from the individual service headquarters to the GSH. The latter move would involve the
transfer of the existing commanders-in-chief of the individual service
headquarters to the GSH, replacing the current deputy chiefs-of-staff.
However, the elimination of these very senior GSH positions would require the removal of several general-rank billets, and is thus strongly resisted by elements within the military.[69]

In addition, many military officers continue to resist any required time
line or quotas for placing civilians within the MND. They fear a loss of defense capability by placing authority in the hands of inexperienced civilians.
Also, there is little incentive or means to develop defense expertise among
civilians at present. Military and defense education are dominated by the
professional military, and many structural and procedural impediments
exist to developing greater civilian expertise. One major systemic obstacle
derives from the limited number of political appointees in government organizations. For example, within every ministry, only the minister and vice
minister(s) are political appointees, while all other posts are filled from the
civil service system. As a consequence, trusted civilian supporters of the political leadership cannot develop critical defense experience by working
their way up the hierarchical ladder within the MND. There is also a lack of
adequate positions for civilians to work as regular MND staff. In the past,
all such staffers have been graduates of military academies, while civilians
mostly dealt with secretarial matters and could be employed only on a contractual basis They were not listed as regular staff.[70] Also, as indicated
above, the Executive Yuan has yet to devise a certification examination for

prospective MND staffers. It will take a considerable amount of time to alter this system and develop the necessary military expertise among civilians. And this effort is further complicated by the fact that a significant cultural stigma continues to attach to serving in military related positions.

Another systemic challenge to defense reform resides with the Legislative Yuan. Several factors serve to undermine the LY's effort to improve the transparency, responsiveness, and efficiency of the military by overseeing and approving critical aspects of defense reform and modernization, such as the defense budget and the procurement process. First, the sharply divisive, zero-sum nature of Taiwan politics has produced exceedingly high levels of political manipulation and policy deadlock within the LY and in relations between the LY and the Executive Branch. Many Pan-Green members of the LY remain highly suspicious of large segments of the officer corps—and in particular the army—which they still regard as a bastion of pro-mainlander influence. Moreover, LY members from virtually all political parties still view the military leadership as excessively secretive and prone to corrupt or insider dealings with foreign and domestic defense corporations. These suspicions contribute to efforts by many LY members to reduce defense outlays in general and the size of the army in particular.[71] Most recently, some LY members also reportedly resist large increases in defense spending because: a) they do not see the need for such outlays, given the virtual security guarantee provided to Taiwan by the U.S.; and b) they believe the dismal state of Taiwan's economy prevents such outlays. Moreover, as suggested above, the public as a whole continues to evince little support for any significant increase in defense spending.[72] As a result of such factors, Washington is concerned that all future major procurement programs will face protracted debates and politically driven opposition, as occurred with the recent controversial decision to acquire Kidd-class destroyers.[73]

Second, the level of defense expertise among LY members remains extremely low, largely as a result of: a) the general lack of such expertise within civilian society as a whole; b) the small size of the professional staffs that provide expertise for LY members on a variety of relevant subjects; and c) the absence of incentives within the LY to acquire such expertise. Few benefits accrue to LY members as a result of service on the LY National Defense Committee, given both the public's lack of interest in defense matters and the fact that the committee does not wield much power or influence within the overall LY committee system. In the absence of real knowledge on defense matters, many LY members rely on rumors, often inaccurate press reporting, or their own political biases to formulate their views.[74] Hence, LY consideration of budget, procurement, and other defense issues is often ill-informed or, worse yet, deliberately obstructionist, thus contributing to a sense of resentment and suspicion within the professional military.[75] In addition, the above features of the LY contribute to the increasingly lengthy process involved in obtaining LY approvals, now extending to almost three years.[76] In short, on balance, the LY serves more as an obstacle than a facilitator of defense reform and modernization. And yet its role is increasingly critical to the ultimate success of those efforts.[77]

As indicated above, Taiwan's current economic weakness also plays a role in obstructing the modernization effort, by reducing capabilities and incentives to undertake potentially costly downsizing, streamlining, and weapons / software / C4ISR improvements. In 2001, Taiwan's GDP dropped to negative 2.18 percent and the unemployment rate reached a record high of 4.57 percent. The Directorate General of Budget Accounting and Statistics estimated that the SARS outbreak would cut GDP growth in 2003 to less than 3 percent, although it ultimately reached 3.24 percent.[78] Largely as a result of such declines, Taiwan's defense spending has not increased in real terms over the past several years. The proposed FY03 defense budget of US$7.69 billion (NT$261.5 billion) was up only very slightly, i.e., about the same as the projected rise in inflation. Moreover, defense spending has declined steadily as a percentage of Taiwan's GDP over the past several years. It accounts for just 14.7 percent of the projected total government budget for FY03, and only about 2.8 percent of GDP, which is less than other countries facing major military threats, such as South Korea and Israel. And personnel expenses continue to occupy over 55 percent of total defense outlays (far exceeding both operational costs and military purchases), while investment in training lags. In recent years, the share of the defense budget allocated to purchasing new weapons and equipment has declined as the proportion of defense expenditure allocated to personnel expenses has increased.[79]

ROC officials have recently indicated that defense spending will increase by 4 percent and acquisitions increase by 30 percent in FY04. However, such increases are viewed in the United States as minimal. Moreover, as indicated above, it remains problematic whether Taiwan will allocate the funds necessary to purchase a total of approximately $30 billion in approved US weapons sales.[80] Taiwan's total annual acquisition budget is usually approximately $400–500 million, thus requiring either special appropriations for virtually every significant purchase or a significant increase in the annual budget.[81] In all, economic pressures exacerbate the existing tendency to view the price of U.S. weapons sold to Taiwan as excessively expensive.

In addition to the above largely systemic factors, defense reform and modernization are also hampered by Taiwan's continued failure to develop a more sophisticated set of agreed-upon national security and defense strategies. Debates over such strategies continue, reflecting the influence of a myriad of factors, including vested service interests, political and financial considerations, and differing views over the urgency of the Chinese military threat posed to Taiwan and the likely type of military assault the PLA might launch against the island. Ultimately, however, the persistence of such debates is a clear confirmation of the inability of Taiwan's political process to produce an individual or group with the power, ability, and determination to overcome such divisive forces.

The most significant strategic debates are over issues such as the relative size and importance of air, naval, and ground forces and the utility of developing an offensive strike capability against China. In the former debate, the dominant school of thought believes that Taiwan must develop a military strategy centered on the development of truly potent air and naval forces. Without such capabilities, it is argued, Taiwan would be unable to deter or defeat the most likely type of PLA attacks, such as an air and missile barrage, a naval blockade, or an amphibious assault (which requires air and naval superiority for success). Moreover, air and naval forces would be especially important in deflecting a rapid, intense PLA strike against military, communication, infrastructure, and political centers, according to proponents. Such a decapitation-centered "fait accompli" strategy is viewed as particularly likely by some analysts, and might occur before United States forces could appear on the scene. Proponents thus argue that the continued maintenance of huge, costly ground forces simply diverts scarce resources and energies away from the development of far more important air and naval capabilities. To support such capabilities, Taiwan should develop small, light, and highly mobile ground forces able to respond quickly to limited PLA ground assaults.[82] Proponents of this view unsurprisingly include senior naval and air force officers, as well as many U.S. military advisers and experts. In addition, some members of the Pan-Green alliance reportedly support such a strategy as a means of reducing the influence of the army.

The opposing minority viewpoint believes that Taiwan must retain sizeable ground forces, for both military and political reasons. Militarily, such forces are absolutely vital, it is argued, in preventing the PLA from achieving any *final* victory by seizing the island of Taiwan; without such a seizure, whatever military strategy the PLA might adopt would fall short of success. Moreover, proponents of this view argue that Taiwan's air and naval forces will never be able to attain the size and capabilities necessary to defeat a massive PLA air and naval attack. They believe the PLA would be quite willing to sacrifice large numbers of inferior aircraft and ships to deplete

Taiwan's capabilities, thus leaving the island defenseless, especially if the army has been heavily reduced in size. Thus, for these advocates, from whatever military vantage point one examines the problem, the only sure guarantor of Taiwan's survival (presumably until U.S. forces arrive on the scene) are sizeable ground forces. Politically, a sizeable ground force presence can also serve as a vital source of leverage for Taipei in any negotiations that might ensue during or after a conflict with China. Some observers are concerned that Beijing and Washington (or Washington alone) might attempt to compel Taipei to accept terms for resolving a conflict that do not serve Taiwan's interests. Without substantial ground forces, they argue, Taiwan will have little ability to resist such pressure. This minority argument in favor of ground forces persists within the strategic debate— and thus reinforces efforts to resist major reductions in the size of the ground forces—because it is supported by significant numbers of senior army officers, as well as some Taiwan strategists and scholars.[83]

The debate over the utility of offensive weapons has become sharper in recent years. Two basic schools of thought exist among proponents. One group argues that the acquisition of an offensive conventional counterforce capability is necessary to deter China from launching a conventional attack against Taiwan, and if deterrence fails, to degrade significantly China's ability to sustain such an attack against Taiwan. These forces would consist essentially of several hundred short-range ballistic missiles (SRBMs), land-attack cruise missiles (LACMs), and air assets armed with standoff attack weapons capable of striking China's ports, theater command, control, and communication nodes, and missile launch sites, as well as enhanced offensive information warfare capabilities.[84] Some advocates even argue that such capabilities might be used preemptively, to derail a PLA strike before it is launched.[85] The second group argues that Taiwan must focus on acquiring offensive strategic countervalue capabilities to threaten major Chinese cities in Central and Southern China, such as Shanghai, Nanjing, Guangzhou, and even Hong Kong. These would consist essentially of a relatively small number of intermediate-range ballistic missiles (IRBMs) or medium-range ballistic missiles (MRBMs) with large conventional or perhaps even nuclear or biological warheads, intended purely as a deterrent against an all-out Chinese assault on Taiwan.[86]

Political leaders of both the Pan-Blue and the Pan-Green coalitions have at times seemed to support, or at the very least express sympathy for, one or both of these arguments. When he was running for president in 1999–2000, Chen Shui-bian advocated what many observers regard as an offensive-oriented policy, explicitly calling for a change in Taiwan's defense strategy from "pure defense" to "offensive defense" (gongshi fangyu). This formulation abandoned the "old concept of attrition warfare" in favor of an emphasis on "paralyzing the enemy's warfighting capability" and "keeping the war away from Taiwan as far as possible."[87] A key principle of Chen's platform was the "decisive offshore campaign" or "decision campaign beyond boundaries" (*jingwai juezhan*), calling for Taiwan's military to "actively build up capability that can strike against the source of the threat" using enhanced naval and air forces as well as joint operations and information warfare.[88] Not to be outdone, during the 1999 presidential election campaign, KMT candidate Lien Chan explicitly stressed the importance of long-range offensive missiles as the pillar of a second strike capability for Taiwan.[89] Advocates of an offensive strike capability also include individuals who are concerned with the high cost of acquiring more sophisticated defensive weaponry from the United States during hard economic times. They view offensive weapons such as ballistic missiles as a less expensive, more cost effective means of deterring China. This group also includes some army officers, who view the deployment of such weapons as a means of avoiding the acquisition of more sophisticated and costly air and naval forces, and thus as a means of maintaining large ground forces.[90]

There are many opponents to the acquisition of either type of offensive capability, however. These individuals point out that Taiwan could not develop a large enough offensive counterforce capability credibly to threaten the extensive number of potential military targets existing on the Mainland. Moreover, it would likely prove extremely difficult to locate and destroy China's large number of mobile SRBMs, while Taiwan's relatively small missile force and infrastructure would be a top priority target for Chinese missile, air, and special forces attacks. In addition, an offensive countervalue capability designed to threaten Chinese cities would be of very limited value, opponents argue, because: a) the Chinese would likely be undeterred if Taiwan were only able to threaten Central and Southern cities and not Beijing; and b) any type of credible countervalue capability would almost certainly require WMD warheads, which the United States would oppose. An offensive countervalue capability would thus likely prove to be inadequate and could greatly exacerbate U.S.-Taiwan relations. It might also provoke a massive preemptive Chinese strike, or at the very least a massive Chinese counterstrike that would almost certainly devastate Taiwan.[91]

Opponents of an offensive deterrent include significant numbers of scholars and military strategists, as well as many individuals within the United States government. Many knowledgeable American observers think that Taiwan is largely wasting its time, effort, and resources on acquiring genuine counter-force offensive capabilities.[92] Also, from the U.S. perspective, the possession of significant offensive weapons by Taiwan injects a potential element of unwanted instability into the equation. In a political-military crisis, Taiwan might use such weapons to retaliate against the mainland without the consent of the United States. China might mistake such an attack as coming from the United States, thus inviting retaliation against the U.S. mainland. To many U.S. observers, Taiwan seems to be developing some offensive systems without a clear sense of how they will be used.

Efforts to strengthen indigenous weapons production arguably confront a wide array of deeply rooted barriers. Any effort to indigenize Taiwan's arms production confronts significant economic costs and a steep technology curve. Taiwan does not have the industrial base or funding required to serve as a prime defense contractor on a major new weapons system, in the opinion of some knowledgeable observers. Hence, this is viewed by many as a very long term objective, and probably one that will never reach the desired level. Moreover, although Taiwan would certainly like to diversify its weapons procurement sources, this goal remains virtually impossible to achieve over at least the medium term, given Taiwan's relative diplomatic isolation and China's willingness to level political and economic costs against any country that is willing to supply Taiwan with weapons.

Finally, and by no means least important, many of these problems are exacerbated by the existence of a type of "military culture" within the ROC armed forces that is highly cautious, conservative, and risk averse. In this culture, subordinate officers and soldiers hesitate to make even minor decisions without the approval of higher ups. Innovation and initiative are not highly prized at any level of the system, and the existing NCO corps is not given the responsibility and authority appropriate to their position as critical intermediaries between the senior officer corps and ordinary soldiers. As a result, many structural and procedural reforms, as well as acquired military systems, do not realize their intended potential.[93]

IV. PROSPECTS FOR THE FUTURE AND IMPLICATIONS

The above analysis indicates that Taiwan's defense reform and modernization process remains beset with multiple problems and obstacles. Nonetheless, if Washington continues to press hard for change and the ROC government continues to recognize the value of responding positively, albeit incompletely, to such pressure, there is little doubt that advances will continue. Specifically, it is likely that Taiwan will acquire several additional key weapons and support systems approved by the United States. In particular, improvements in C4ISR, jointness, and training, and the acquisition of new destroyers, PAC-3 ballistic missile defense batteries, long-range, early warning radars and associated equipment, and more so-phisticated ASW systems will almost certainly occur over the medium term, i.e., within the next five to seven years.

Second, the effort to strengthen, streamline and civilianize the administrative hierarchy in charge of military affairs will doubtless continue. The MND will acquire more expertise and direct line control over key military planning and operational control decisions, absorbing many of the past functions of the professional military command structure. Moreover, lines of authority and internal decision making processes and outcomes will no doubt become more transparent to the public and the LY.

Third, the size, configuration, and orientation of the armed forces will continue to adjust to the demands of creating a more credible set of deterrence and defense capabilities. In particular, the army will become smaller, the air force and navy will receive greater attention and exert greater influence over defense restructuring and streamlining, and all military services will carry out limited experiments in volunteerism.

Fourth, the MND will produce a seemingly more integrated and coordinated strategic planning process, centered in the Strategic Planning Department and the Integrated Assessment Office, with input from both the civilian national security leadership above and the uniformed services below.

Finally, the arms procurement process will likely become less corrupt, more efficient, and slightly less dependent on a single source of foreign military hardware.

Such likely advances will almost certainly enhance the overall capability of Taiwan's armed forces. Yet it remains far from certain that they will together produce improvements in Taiwan's deterrent and warfighting capabilities sufficient to influence greatly both Beijing's overall political, diplomatic, and military strategy toward Taiwan and any specific decision to apply coercive measures or outright force in a crisis or military conflict. Thus far, there has been little evidence of enormous PLA concern over the advances taking place in ROC military capabilities per se. China's greater concern seems to remain focused, as in the past, on the deepening U.S.-ROC military-political relationship. In addition, it is uncertain whether the above likely advances will produce levels of efficiency, transparency, and accountability in the defense sector sufficient to generate significant levels of public trust and support, at least over the short to medium term. As indicated above, the Taiwan public's distrust of the military and its general disinterest in greatly increasing the military's capabilities are deeply rooted.

Overall, the above improvements in reform and modernization could amount to only marginal overall advances, based on the objective of achieving a lowest common denominator set of changes designed to placate the most significant U.S. concerns, ensure the quiescence of key institutional participants such as the ROC army, and avoid alarming the public and key social interest groups in Taiwan. In other words, the more difficult political, bureaucratic, financial, and conceptual decisions required to achieve the stated objectives of the defense reform and modernization process could very likely be postponed or avoided altogether for many years.

To achieve such ambitious objectives will require:

- A more capable, united ROC political leadership at the top that is willing to take on the many challenges confronting the reform and modernization process in a more determined manner.
- A clearer recognition within both the elite and among critical segments of society of the urgency of the threat posed by an increasingly capable PLA, and of the urgent need for Taiwan to deal with that threat in a more capable manner.
- A deeper level of agreement among political elites and the armed services regarding the most optimal defense strategy and related force structure needed to meet that threat.
- A clearer understanding between the United States and Taiwan of the relationship between their respective core strategic and operational objectives in deterrence and defense.

It is probably impossible to meet such requirements over the short to medium term, given the depth and complexity of the obstacles and concerns involved, and the sensitivity of many issues, especially concerning U.S.-Taiwan relations.[94] As suggested above, persistent differences remain between Washington and Taipei regarding: military investments and weapons production priorities, the level and type of technology transfer to Taiwan, and the respective roles and missions to be performed by the U.S. and ROC militaries in the event of a crisis.[95] Adding to these difficulties, in recent months, U.S. officials have expressed intense displeasure over leaks from Taiwan sources of various types of defense cooperation programs with the island, including classified information. Some U.S. observers reportedly suspect that such leaks might be politically motivated, to demonstrate U.S. support of Taiwan through disclosure of classified agreements.[96]

Beyond these difficulties, perhaps the most fundamental underlying obstacle to a deepening of the reform and modernization effort is the ongoing zero-sum nature of political competition in Taiwan, combined with the intensely cynical, opportunistic, and sometimes corrupt attitudes so evident among politicians. As long as the opposing Pan-Green and Pan-Blue political coalitions continue to refuse to cooperate with one another in many critical policy arenas such as economics, cross-Strait relations, and defense, any ROC government will find it extremely difficult to develop and sustain costly, unpopular, and potentially divisive defense reform and modernization efforts. In all, it will remain very difficult to push forward with defense reform under conditions in which the president, much of the military, and the Legislative Yuan regard one another with intense suspicion, when force modernization remains highly dependent on the vagaries of U.S. support and assistance,[97] and when the public is left largely uninformed about the potentially lethal nature of the threat posed by the Chinese military. And of course it is by no means certain that the highly risk averse military culture of the ROC armed forces will be rectified any time soon.

However, even if a sufficient level of unity, agreement, and determination are attained over the near term, many observers argue that Taiwan is already too far behind in the reform effort to improve its military capabilities appreciably before any crisis might emerge across the Taiwan Strait. Specifically, the U.S. government worries that Taiwan's defense reforms and modernization will not take effect early enough to deal with the possible emergence of several major PRC military capabilities by 2007–2010 or even earlier.[98] Few of the pending weapons acquisitions or institutional and procedural changes of the reform effort will take full effect before that time period. Moreover, these concerns are intensified by a growing suspicion within the Defense Department that Beijing is now placing a top priority on acquiring the capability to launch a rapid, "fait accompli" decapitation strike against Taiwan's political and military centers before the United States can respond. Countering such a contingency requires the acquisition by Taiwan of genuinely potent military capabilities over a relatively short period of time. Thus, there is increasing movement by the U.S. to implement as soon as possible several "quick-fix measures" aimed at greatly enhancing Taiwan's joint operational capabilities and improving response and readiness over the near term. These center on efforts to achieve greater force integration and coordination using new C4ISR systems, to improve overall defense and operational planning, and to strengthen passive defense capabilities, especially at critical military and political sites.[99]

Yet even the attainment of these *relatively* modest short-term objectives faces significant obstacles. Despite the surface appearance of unity and enthusiasm for such changes expressed by the ROC government and military, considerable debate, and even some resistance, remains concerning many of these undertakings. For example, as Michael Chase discusses in his chapter in this volume, a persistent and possibly widening difference remains between senior leaders in Washington and Taipei regarding the true urgency of the military threat posed by the PLA.[100] Moreover, well-informed observers insist that some essential defense efforts (e.g., the hardening and guarding of key leadership locations, command and control centers, and energy and supply networks) are simply not being done, while the kind of near-term improvements envisioned in some critical areas (e.g., C4ISR and long-range early warning radars) will fall short of desired expectations, due largely to financial constraints or technology problems.[101]

Most if not all of these difficulties must be overcome or at least greatly reduced in the near term if Taiwan is genuinely to enhance its combat sustainability and thereby either credibly deter the PLA or lengthen the time the United States has to respond to a conflict in the Taiwan Strait. To facilitate this undertaking, Washington should make more concerted efforts to communicate a clear and consistent message to Taiwan's political and military leadership regarding its views and preferences in all areas of defense reform and modernization, while supporting Taipei's efforts to resolve its own internal differences and to clarify its strategic objectives.[102] In addition, the United States should make greater efforts to aid Taiwan in the development of civilian military expertise and to provide assessments of military areas that more accurately reflect the specific characteristics of Taiwan's political, military, and social situation. But ultimately, it will be up to Taiwan's leaders to overcome the many internal challenges remaining to their defense reform and modernization efforts.

Finally, the U.S. government must also make much greater efforts to coordinate the Pentagon's increasingly robust attempt to strengthen Taiwan's defense capabilities with the larger political and diplomatic objectives of the U.S.-China relationship. Although there is little doubt that the ROC military must be strengthened significantly to deal with an arguably more ominous PLA threat, Taipei's (and Washington's) resulting increase in deterrent and warfighting capabilities must be balanced by an equally effective effort to reassure Beijing that such capabilities will not be used to shield Taiwan from attack during a move toward permanent and full independence. In other words, increased military capabilities alone will not maintain stability across the Taiwan Strait, and could even precipitate a conflict if mishandled. This balancing act will require a much clearer understanding by Washington and Taipei of both the requirements and the limitations of their mutual effort to carry out defense reform and modernization in Taiwan.

CHAPTER SEVEN

U.S.–Taiwan Security Cooperation:

ENHANCING AN UNOFFICIAL RELATIONSHIP

MICHAEL S. CHASE

TODAY, TAIWAN is one of the most dangerous flashpoints in the Asia-Pacific and the issue most likely to lead to conflict between the United States and China. In fact, for nearly five decades, Taiwan has been one of the central dilemmas in U.S.-China relations. Even during the 1970s and 1980s, when the United States and China cooperated to balance the threat posed by the Soviet Union, differences over Taiwan were among the most intractable problems in the relationship between Washington and Beijing.[1]

America's unofficial relationship with the island, especially U.S.-Taiwan security cooperation, is peculiarly controversial and divisive for Washington and Beijing. As a condition of normalization of its relationship with China in 1979, the United States abrogated the 1954 U.S.-ROC Mutual Defense Treaty, but Washington has maintained a strong, if somewhat ambiguous commitment to the island's defense as part of its unofficial relationship with Taiwan, in accordance with the 1979 Taiwan Relations Act (TRA). In the words of two former Pentagon Asia specialists, "Washington's official relationship with Beijing on the one hand and its unofficial re-

The author would like to thank Michael Lostumbo, James Mulvenon, Nancy Bernkopf Tucker and several other reviewers for their comments on draft versions of this chapter.

lationship with Taipei on the other represent perhaps the most complex foreign policy balancing act in the world today."[2] Stability in the triangular relationship between Washington, Beijing, and Taipei has been preserved since 1979 by "a complex and arguably somewhat contradictory set of official agreements and unofficial understandings," including the 1972, 1979, and 1982 U.S.-China joint communiqués.[3] This set of agreements and understandings in turn was supported by a consensus among all three parties that Taiwan was part of "one China," as reflected in the 1972 Shanghai Communiqué, in which Washington stated, "The United States acknowledges that all Chinese on either side of the Taiwan Strait maintain there is but one China and that Taiwan is a part of China."

As a result of the political changes that unfolded in Taiwan in the 1980s and 1990s, however, the consensus underlying those agreements and understandings has begun to unravel. At the same time, Beijing's cross-Strait policy has done little to accommodate Taiwan's political transformation, and the heavy-handed implementation of "one country, two systems" in Hong Kong has made the PRC's preferred approach to unification even less attractive to the people of Taiwan. These trends further complicate an already extremely difficult balancing act for U.S. policymakers, as reflected by President Chen Shui-bian's insistence on holding a referendum to coincide with the March 2004 presidential election, despite President Bush's public admonishment in December 2003 that Washington viewed the initiative as a potentially provocative attempt to change the status quo.[4]

Notwithstanding the friction this episode produced, the view of observers in Washington, Taipei, and Beijing is that the U.S.-Taiwan security relationship is closer today than it has been at any time since 1979.[5] Taiwan's status as the largest recipient of U.S. foreign military sales and training in the Pacific Command's area of responsibility underscores this point. Security cooperation between the United States and Taiwan, however, is not limited to arms sales. On the contrary, as the U.S.-Taiwan security relationship has evolved over the past five years, the focus of cooperation has shifted increasingly to "software" issues, such as training and education, defense policy dialogue, the reform of Taiwan's defense bureaucracy, and assessments that are designed to help the island enhance the capabilities of its military, improve its procurement procedures, and better integrate the weapons it purchases from the United States. At the same time, however, emerging differences between Washington and Taipei over weapons procurement and threat perceptions may complicate efforts further to enhance U.S.-Taiwan security cooperation. Taiwan's perception that China is unlikely to use force, coupled with its apparent assumption that the United States would back it in any conceivable conflict scenario,

complicates Washington's efforts to encourage Taipei to commit the resources that are required to improve its own defense capabilities. Both
sides must take steps to address these emerging problems.

Perhaps an even larger challenge for the United States is helping Taiwan
improve its defense capabilities without undermining U.S.-China relations
and cross-Strait ties. The overriding policy objective for the United States
is preventing conflict in the Taiwan Strait. Accordingly, Washington must
continue a longstanding balancing act, finding a policy equilibrium that
will allow it to deter Beijing from resorting to force while at the same time
discouraging Taipei from undertaking unduly provocative actions. Washington must strengthen deterrence by helping to improve Taiwan's defense
capabilities and furthering the island's defense reforms, but it must also
reassure Beijing that it does not support independence for Taiwan. This is
becoming an increasingly precarious tightrope act for the United States,
especially given the possibility, following his controversial victory in the
March 2004 presidential election, that President Chen may press forward
with plans to hold an island-wide referendum on a new constitution, a step
that could trigger a cross-Strait conflict if Beijing regards it as equivalent to
a formal declaration of independence.

U.S.-TAIWAN MILITARY-TO-MILITARY RELATIONS SINCE 1979

SECURITY COOPERATION CENTERED ON ARMS SALES, 1979–1997

The breaking of formal diplomatic relations with the ROC and termination
of the 1954 US-ROC Mutual Defense Treaty were part of the process of the
normalization of relations between the United States and China that cul-
minated in 1979 with the establishment of official diplomatic relations between Washington and Beijing.[6] This led to charges, reiterated to this day
by many Taiwan officials and analysts, that the U.S. had "abandoned" and
"betrayed" its erstwhile ally.[7] Nevertheless, Washington maintained a
strong interest in Taiwan's defense, as embodied in the 1979 TRA, and continued to sell arms to the island even after signing the August 17, 1982 U.S.-
China Communiqué.[8]

During this period, security cooperation was centered primarily on
arms sales. For Taipei, the point of many of the arms purchases was to
demonstrate the strength of Taiwan's relationship with the United States
and to symbolize the extent of U.S. support for Taiwan. Domestic political considerations and rivalries between the branches of the Taiwan
armed services were also important drivers of the arms procurement

process. For Taiwan, the deterrent effect was the primary reason for most arms purchases.[9]

Throughout the 1980s, and the first half of the 1990s, not only was the U.S.-Taiwan defense relationship focused largely on arms sales, it was also "highly ritualized," according to U.S. officials. Visits to Taiwan by U.S. military personnel were restricted to the O-6 level (a captain in the U.S. Navy; a colonel in the Army, Air Force, and Marine Corps) and below, and only visits that were related to the arms sales process were permitted. Department of Defense civilian personnel above the rank of GS-15 were not allowed to visit Taiwan and U.S.-Taiwan exchanges focusing on operational matters were strictly limited.

Broader problems in the U.S.-Taiwan relationship hampered the development of deeper security cooperation throughout the 1980s. In the late 1980s, Taipei reportedly demonstrated renewed interest in a clandestine nuclear weapons program, which the United States once again forced it to abandon.[10] Perhaps more importantly, Taiwan was not yet a democracy, and there was still strong criticism of human rights abuses in Taiwan from members of the U.S. Congress.[11] In the early-to-mid 1980s, human rights violations and the suppression of the opposition movement in Taiwan were points of tension in U.S.-Taiwan relations.[12] In the 1990s, however, Taiwan's remarkable political transition provided a new rationale for U.S. assistance to and interaction with the island's military. According to scholars and former U.S. officials, it was Taiwan's continued economic development and especially political change that helped to increase U.S. support for the island. In the words of Chas W. Freeman, Jr., former assistant secretary of defense for international security affairs:

> As Taiwan's economic prosperity has advanced and its democratization has proceeded, it has had an easier and easier task of selling itself in the United States, since it has, in fact, become increasingly admirable as a society, and its natural affinities with Americans have grown, rather than diminished.[13]

Against this background of change in Taiwan, the Clinton administration in 1993–94 undertook a review of Taiwan policy. The review approved several modifications of U.S. policy toward Taiwan, including protocol changes for some meetings in Washington and occasional visits to Taiwan by cabinet-level economic officials.

Nevertheless, limits on U.S.-Taiwan security cooperation remained in place. In the years between the normalization of U.S.-PRC relations in 1979 and the 1995–96 crisis in the Taiwan Strait, U.S. military and civilian defense officials had relatively little contact with their Taiwan counter-parts. There were no strategic discussions, only the annual U.S.-Taiwan arms sales talks.

Throughout much of the 1990s, U.S. thinking about a potential Taiwan Strait conflict continued to be "based on little knowledge of Taiwan de-fense planning and no significant pre-crisis interaction between the two militaries."[14] Most U.S. policymakers and observers agree that the 1995–96 Taiwan Strait crisis was a critical turning point in the long and tortuous history of U.S.-Taiwan security cooperation.[15] According to two astute ob-servers, "The events of 1995–96 caused some in the Pentagon to rethink the relationship."[16] The crisis surrounding the PRC military exercises and mis-sile tests that followed the visit of then-president of the ROC Lee Teng-hui to Cornell University in 1995 gave rise to two primary sources of motiva-tion for increased interaction and diversification of the U.S.-Taiwan secu-rity relationship. First, the crisis revealed that the United States knew very little about the Taiwan armed forces. In the words of one U.S. official, in 1995–96, the U.S. and Taiwan found themselves "standing shoulder to shoulder, almost, but we realized we didn't even know each other."[17] The crisis made clear that for Taiwan and the U.S. "poor channels of commu-nication and a high degree of unfamiliarity would pose serious problems if fighting were to break out."[18] Communications were so inadequate that U.S. officials felt they knew more about the PRC than about Taiwan. The relative lack of interaction between the U.S. and Taiwan militaries had left the United States with a limited understanding of the problems faced by Taiwan's armed forces. At the same time, it was becoming increasingly clear that the rising generation of Taiwan military officers had little expo-sure to the United States. The isolation of the Taiwan military was so se-vere, it was as if the Taiwan military "was stuck in a time warp," according to a former U.S. government official. Moreover, growing worries about PRC military modernization contributed to the intensification of concerns in Washington about the lack of coordination between the U.S. and Tai-wan militaries.[19]

ENHANCING AND DIVERSIFYING U.S.-TAIWAN SECURITY COOPERATION, 1997–PRESENT

The conventional wisdom holds that the second Bush administration is largely responsible for strengthening U.S.-Taiwan security cooperation. To be sure, U.S.-Taiwan security cooperation has been enhanced under George W. Bush's administration. It is important to note, however, that present trends in U.S.-Taiwan defense relations began to take shape during the latter years of Clinton's presidency.[20] Since the 1995–96 crisis in the Taiwan Strait, the security cooperation relationship has been marked by continuity more than discontinuity. "What we're seeing now is an augmentation of what Campbell started," one U.S. official said, referring to the "software" initiatives Kurt Campbell undertook during his tenure as deputy assistant secretary of defense for Asian and Pacific affairs in the Clinton administration.

The series of "software" initiatives stemmed from the realization during the 1995–96 Taiwan Strait crisis that selling hardware to Taiwan was not enough, particularly if Taiwan was unable effectively to integrate and employ the arms it purchased from the United States. Moreover, the difficulties the United States encountered in fighting alongside even its closest allies during the Gulf War suggested that working with Taiwan in a conflict would be impossible unless the United States undertook efforts to improve Taiwan's defense capabilities. According to a 2000 DOD report to Congress:

> These non-hardware programs serve multiple purposes. Functional non-hardware initiatives address many of the shortcomings in Taiwan's military readiness that were identified in the February 1999 *DOD Report to Congress on the Security Situation in the Taiwan Strait*. They allow Taiwan to better integrate newly acquired systems into its inventory and ensure that the equipment Taiwan has can be used to full effectiveness. These initiatives provide an avenue to exchange views on Taiwan's requirements for defense modernization, to include professionalization and organizational issues, and training. Exchanges and discussions enhance our ability to assess Taiwan's longer-term defense needs and develop well-founded security assistance policies. Such programs also enhance Taiwan's capacity for making operationally sound and cost effective acquisition decisions, and more importantly, to use its equipment more effectively for self-defense.[21]

Some of the initiatives designed to address these problems were focused on training, logistics, "jointness," and C4ISR issues. The United States has sent a series of assessment teams to Taiwan to gather data and identify problems that the U.S. might help Taiwan to address (these initiatives are described in detail below). At the same time, however, this effort was constrained. The challenge for the United States was helping Taiwan to improve its capabilities without exceeding the boundaries of its understandings with Beijing in a way that could spark the very crisis it was trying to prevent.

The difficulty of striking this balance was evident in the effort to engage Taiwan in discussions of national security and defense policy issues. It was believed that it would not be possible for the United States and Taiwan to hold talks on strategy in Washington, so it was decided that the talks would be held in Monterey, California (strategic defense dialogues are discussed in greater detail below). The first of these sessions was held in December 1997. In addition to the so-called "Monterey Talks," the U.S. deputy national security adviser reportedly held several meetings with his Taiwan counterpart in New York City.[22] According to U.S. observers, in the late 1990s private meetings took place among representatives from the United States, Taiwan, and Japan in which delicate messages were communicated to Taiwan.[23]

In the first 18 months of the Bush administration, U.S.-Taiwan defense relations became even closer, both symbolically and substantively. In April 2001, President Bush said on the ABC News program *Good Morning, America* that the United States would "do whatever it takes to help Taiwan defend itself." In March 2002, Deputy Secretary of Defense Paul Wolfowitz reiterated the President's statement at the U.S.-Taiwan Business Council's defense industry conference in Florida.[24] These statements, as well as the increasing scope and tempo of security cooperation between the United States and Taiwan, as reflected by Taiwan Defense Minister Tang Yiauming's meetings with Deputy Secretary Wolfowitz and other U.S. officials at the abovementioned Florida defense industry conference and the observation of Taiwan's military exercises by U.S. military personnel, have led some observers to argue that the Bush administration has altered U.S. policy. Some have even proclaimed the death of the longstanding U.S. policy of "strategic ambiguity," which was designed simultaneously to deter Beijing from using force to resolve the Taiwan issue and discourage potentially provocative actions on the part of Taipei by remaining vague about the conditions under which Washington would intervene in a crisis.[25]

Although the Bush administration has gone farther than past administrations in its statements concerning Washington's commitment to Taiwan, it has not formally discarded "strategic ambiguity."[26] Senior officials have emphasized Washington's continued adherence to the principles that have guided its China policy for the past three decades. In May 2002, for instance, Deputy Secretary of Defense Wolfowitz stated, "We support a one-China policy. . . . we do not support independence for Taiwan. But the other half of that equation is we oppose strongly any attempt to settle that issue by force."[27] These statements were intended to underscore that Washington has not abandoned the longstanding pillars of U.S. policy toward China and Taiwan.

Meanwhile, developments in Taiwan are influencing Taipei's approach toward U.S.-Taiwan security cooperation.[28] The main challenges are Taiwan's ongoing defense reforms, a steady decline in defense expenditures, and the increasing role of the Legislative Yuan (LY) and opposition politics in defense policy issues (issues addressed in Michael D. Swaine's contribution to this volume). These changes in Taiwan, particularly the increasing assertiveness of the LY on procurement questions, have resulted in prolonged indecision on purchases of arms from the United States. Although President Bush's April 2001 approval of major arms sales—including Kidd-class destroyers, diesel submarines, and anti-submarine warfare (ASW) aircraft—signaled an important change in policy, Taiwan has yet to complete the purchase of most of the main components of the package. The LY finally passed the bill approving funding for the Kidd-class destroyer program—in late May 2003, more than two years after the announcement of the arms sales decision. The protracted debate in the LY— during which a number of legislators voiced opposition to the proposed purchase for reasons ranging from cost concerns to objections about the age of the ships, and which reportedly was only resolved after the Taiwan Navy agreed to cut the budget—illustrates the difficulties that the MND now faces in obtaining legislative approval for arms purchases from the United States.

The main obstacle to the submarine sale is that U.S. companies no longer build diesel submarines, and the German and Dutch governments are reluctant to let their own shipbuilders provide the required design information for fear of antagonizing China. Another cause of the submarine sale delay is a dispute between Taiwan and the United States over a down payment that is required before the U.S. Navy can release a request for proposals to U.S. defense contractors.[29] Cost concerns are the major factor holding up the sale of the ASW aircraft. Since building the P3-C aircraft would require reopening the production line, each aircraft would cost roughly US$300 million. The total price of that deal is thus potentially prohibitive for Taiwan, which reportedly is considering buying and upgrading older P3-B aircraft as a less expensive alternative to the originally approved package of P3-C planes.[30] The pressures of competing priorities, high costs, and the anticipated difficulties of winning LY approval for either option, however, are likely to put the purchase on hold indefinitely, according to some U.S. observers. Delays such as these in weapons procurement have reportedly caused frustration in Washington, which in turn has led to consternation in Taipei, prompting President Chen to acknowledge there are "differences of opinion about the timetable for the delivery of U.S. arms and which weapons should receive priority."[31]

CHANGE AND CONTINUITY

The U.S.–Taiwan security cooperation relationship has undergone a series of dramatic changes throughout the past fifty years, shifting once again since the 1995–96 Taiwan Strait Crisis. What has remained the same, however, is the delicate balance that the United States seeks to strike in dealing with the China-Taiwan issue. On the one hand, Washington is trying to strengthen deterrence by helping to improve Taiwan's defense capabilities and further the island's defense reforms. On the other, the U.S. seeks to reassure Beijing that it does not support independence for Taiwan and continues to adhere to a "one China" policy. President Bush's public declaration in December 2003 that the United States opposes attempts by either side to change the cross-Strait status quo and his rebuke of President Chen's referendum plans underscored this commitment.[32] Moreover, there are still a variety of constraints on U.S. security cooperation with Taiwan, ranging from the potential Chinese reaction to precedent-setting initiatives to the concerns of U.S. allies.

CONTEMPORARY U.S.–TAIWAN SECURITY COOPERATION

This section provides a more detailed overview of contemporary U.S.–Taiwan security cooperation, discussing arms sales, strategic defense dialogues, visits by high-ranking officers and senior civilian officials, educational exchanges, observation of exercises and potential combined exercises, and assessment team visits.

ARMS SALES

Arms sales are perhaps the most controversial aspect of U.S.-Taiwan military-to-military relations. This issue has most regularly aroused outrage and indignation in Beijing, given rise to tension between Washington and Taipei, and prompted domestic political battles in the United States.[33] The 1979 Taiwan Relations Act provides the basis for U.S. arms sales to Taiwan. It states that the United States "will make available to Taiwan such defense articles and defense services in such quantity as may be necessary to enable Taiwan to maintain a sufficient self-defense capability" and stipulates that the President and Congress "shall determine the nature and quantity of such defense articles and services based solely upon their judgment of the needs of Taiwan."[34] As discussed above, from 1979 to 1997, arms sales were the central focus of the U.S.-Taiwan security relationship, and since the late 1980s Taiwan consistently has been the second or third largest purchaser of U.S. arms in the world.[35] From 1990 to 2000, Taiwan purchased $16.2 billion in arms from the U.S. through Foreign Military Sales (FMS) and another $1.5 billion through commercial channels.[36] Despite considerable progress in developing its defense industries, Taiwan's design and production capabilities are still limited and the island remains highly dependent on the United States as its primary supplier of advanced weapons and military equipment.[37]

THE "OLD" PROCESS

The "old" arms sales process, in effect before the Bush administration changed it in April 2001, was highly structured. Annual "pre-talks" were held late in the year, at which time Taiwan would present the United States with a "wish list" detailing its arms requests. Early the next year, working-level U.S. teams would travel to Taiwan to discuss the requests with their counterparts in the Taiwan military. Subsequently, the Pentagon, State Department, and NSC formulated their positions on Taiwan's requests, and U.S. officials worked to resolve any disagreements over which requests should be approved.[38] The process would culminate in the spring with the annual U.S.-Taiwan arms sales talks, at which time Washington would inform Taipei of its decisions to approve, disapprove, or defer specific arms sales requests.

The advantages of this process were that decisions were made at a predictable time every year and that officials on both sides were familiar with the format and procedures. In the words of one U.S. observer, "On the positive side, the process used in determining arms sales to Taiwan has evolved over the last two decades into a routine . . . one where Taiwan's evolving defense needs can be expected to be considered carefully every year by the United States at a high level."[39] For Taiwan, one important advantage of the process was its regularity, which allowed for "predictable planning" by officials responsible for defense budget and procurement issues.[40] It also allowed Taiwan to mobilize Congress and the media to put pressure on U.S. executive branch policymakers to approve the sale of the items Taiwan had requested.

The disadvantages included problems of both process and substance. On the process side, current and former U.S. officials point to the sometimes counterproductive media attention that accompanied the arms talks every spring and the bureaucratic difficulty associated with a set of procedures that was used only with Taiwan. The annual arms sales decision was also a perennial source of discord in U.S.-China relations. The bureaucratic process on each side also caused problems. Each of the armed services in Taiwan attempted to distort the arms procurement process to serve its own interests, with the result that procurement policy was irrational and interservice rivalries tended to "distort the allocation of military resources."[41]

On the substantive side, the mission for some of the weapons systems Taiwan requested was often unclear, according to U.S. experts. The leadership of Taiwan's army, for example, held firm to what a former U.S. military officer once described as a "tank fetish," despite doubts among U.S. analysts about the utility of tanks, relative to other less glamorous weapons systems, for the island's ground forces in many scenarios.[42] Rather than national military strategy determining procurement, they say, in Taiwan it has often been the other way around.[43] For their part, officials and analysts in Taipei argue that the main reason military procurement has driven defense planning is the uncertainty surrounding Taiwan's ability to acquire advanced arms from foreign sources, especially the United States. The result is "procurement directed planning."[44] U.S. analysts argue, however, that Taiwan cannot blame deficiencies in the development of strategy and defense planning solely on U.S. arms sales policy.

Beyond these problems, Taiwan often seemed more interested in symbolism than improving its capabilities. According to U.S. observers, Taiwan viewed arms purchases from the U.S. "as a symbolic indicator of American support, attaching less significance to the ability of their military to absorb diverse weapons systems or to integrate them into a single defense strategy."[45] According to a 1999 RAND report, Taiwan's arms purchase requests under Lee Teng-hui were shaped heavily by political calculations. Lee reportedly viewed the weapons sold to Taiwan by the United States "more as symbols of reassurance and resolve than as key components of a larger force structure designed to attain genuine warfighting objectives."[46] Some strategists in Taiwan continue to assert that the symbolism of U.S. arms sales to Taiwan is more important than the contribution the weapons and equipment purchases make to Taiwan's warfighting capabilities. In a brief published by a Kuomintang-affiliated think tank early in 2003, for example, a researcher stated that the primary function of U.S. arms sales to Taiwan is that they "signify the U.S. determination to help defend Taiwan against any possible attack from the People's Republic of China."[47]

Given the extraordinary political sensitivity surrounding the Taiwan issue—both in U.S.-China relations and in U.S. domestic politics—the United States was also concerned about symbolism. To avoid upsetting U.S.-China relations, Washington "sharply restricted any dealings with Taiwan that might suggest steps toward a renewed military alliance."[48] The United

States also wanted to avoid creating a perception in Taiwan that it was unconditionally committed to defend the island, which some observers feared would embolden leaders in Taipei to take provocative steps that might spark a crisis in cross-strait relations. For these reasons, the U.S. frequently agonized over whether weapons requested by Taiwan were "defensive," and refused to provide Taiwan with items that would require increased interaction between the U.S. military and Taiwan's military.

A NEW PATH

Developments since George W. Bush's election appear to have set U.S. arms sales to Taiwan on a new path, both in terms of substance and process. In April 2001, the Bush administration announced its approval of a major arms sales package for Taiwan, including four Kidd class destroyers, twelve P-3C Orion anti-submarine aircraft, and eight diesel submarines. The package was the largest approved for sale to Taiwan since 1992, when the previous President Bush permitted the sale of 150 F-16 fighters. Many analysts saw the arms sales package as sending a message that some of the longstanding constraints on U.S. arms sales to Taiwan had become outdated. Indeed, a few days after the April 2001 arms sales were announced, the Bush administration declared that it would no longer hold annual arms sales talks with Taiwan each April and would instead deal with future requests for arms purchases from Taiwan on a rolling or "as-needed" basis.[49]

U.S. officials say the "new" Taiwan process is the same process used with arms sales customers worldwide. Moreover, there is substantial continuity between the new process and the traditional approach. The considerations U.S. policymakers weigh in deciding which systems to approve for release to Taiwan, for example, remain the same. Yet the new process involves some important changes. Under the new procedures, "pre-talk" sessions, at which Taiwan officials presented the United States with a list of requirements late in the year in advance of each round of spring arms sales talks, are no longer held. Instead, the U.S. and Taiwan hold annual bilateral defense talks in the November/December timeframe. The changes were intended to reduce delays in the decision-making process, diminish media attention, lessen the irritations in U.S.-China relations, and reflect a new approach to security cooperation with Taiwan. It is perhaps too soon to assess the impact of the change in the arms sales process, but some observers argue that it has been successful in reducing the public profile of the arms sales and lessening criticism from Beijing.[50]

Although preliminary assessments in the U.S. are largely positive, and the modification of the arms sales process was intended to recognize Taiwan as a more normal security partner, there has been a negative reaction to the change among many in Taiwan. Taiwan officials are reportedly nervous about the new arrangements governing the arms sales process and the new arms sales arrangement is unpopular with defense and national security researchers in Taiwan who say that Taiwan would have preferred to keep the annual arms sales dialogue. Taiwan appreciates that the gesture was meant to treat Taiwan like a more normal security partner, according to a well-connected Taipei analyst, but many are worried that the process will become hostage to the vicissitudes of U.S.-PRC relations, especially if Washington judges at some point that it is necessary to delay a sale to achieve an objective in its relationship with Beijing.[51] Recent arms sales decisions suggest that Taipei's worries are at least somewhat overstated. In March 2004, despite improvements in U.S.-China relations resulting from China's crucial role in the negotiations on the North Korean nuclear weapons program, the United States agreed to sell Taiwan two long-range early warning radars worth an estimated $1.8 billion.[52]

STRATEGIC DEFENSE DIALOGUES

The level of communication and interaction between the United States and Taiwan on strategic defense issues has increased significantly in recent years. There are presently several forums for U.S.-Taiwan security dialogue. At the strategic level, U.S. officials from the Office of the Secretary of Defense (OSD), National Security Council (NSC), and Office of the Vice President hold annual discussions with the Taiwan Ministry of National Defense (MND), NSC, Ministry of Foreign Affairs (MOFA), and General Staff personnel in Monterey, California. The Department of Defense has stated publicly that several rounds of meetings have been held since 1997.[53]

The initial purpose of the talks, for the U.S. side, was to diversify and enhance the U.S.-Taiwan defense relationship. Specifically, the talks were intended to address Taiwan's utilization of advanced military equipment it acquired from the U.S., to balance the increase in U.S. engagement with the PRC, and to allow U.S. and Taiwan officials to discuss the implications of Chinese military modernization. The Taiwan delegation to the Monterey talks in years past consisted primarily of MND representatives and military officers, but MAC, MOFA, and NSC officials now lead the delegation, at the insistence of the U.S. side.[54] The addition of these civilian national security and foreign policy officials has broadened the agenda for the talks.

Another venue is provided by the U.S.-Taiwan Defense Review Talks (DRTs), which bring together officials from OSD and their policymaking counterparts from the Taiwan MND to discuss defense policy issues. The

U.S. side is led by an official from the Office of the Under Secretary of Defense for Policy, at the assistant secretary of defense (ASD) or deputy ASD level. In past years, one of the vice-chiefs of the General Staff has headed the Taiwan delegation to the DRTs. As a result of the restructuring of the Taiwan defense establishment mandated by the National Defense Law and Ministry of National Defense Organization Law, however, Taiwan delegations participating in security dialogues with the United States are now led by senior civilian defense officials.[55] Washington reportedly agreed to the change in order to show its support for the reorganization of the Taiwan defense establishment and Taipei's efforts to enhance civilian control over the military.

Although the U.S. and Taiwan maintain dialogue on several levels, as outlined above, the consensus among civilian national security analysts in Taipei is that the most important next steps in the relationship are to make strategic dialogue and communication more routine and institutionalized and to enhance coordination between policymakers in Washington and Taipei. "The U.S. has opened the door already, but needs to open it more widely," according to a Taiwan academic.[56] Analysts in Taiwan also report that Taipei would like to have more consultations with Washington on a broad range of strategic issues and U.S. policy decisions.[57] Other Taiwan researchers lamented what they described as a lack of communication with Taiwan about U.S. national policy and strategy, including plans for basing in East Asia, and Washington's thinking on how best to counter the Chinese threat to Taiwan.

National security analysts and military officers in Taiwan also highlighted what they see as the need for more general discussions that would allow the United States to enhance its understanding of Taiwan's perspectives on its security environment. Another related problem identified by Taiwan analysts is what they say is the lack of an adequate appreciation in Washington of the dimensions of Taiwan's national security problems, which are becoming increasingly complex as a result of rapidly expanding cross-Strait economic integration and social exchanges.[58] In the words of one Taiwan defense analyst, "greater understanding of objectives and intentions on the part of both sides is the foundation of strategic dialogue."[59] Such consultations might alleviate the lingering concerns of some in Taipei about the U.S. approach toward the Taiwan issue.[60]

VISITS BY HIGH-RANKING MILITARY OFFICERS AND CIVILIAN DEFENSE OFFICIALS

Another part of the U.S.-Taiwan security relationship in which significant changes are underway is the traditionally sensitive area of exchanges of visits by high-ranking military officers and civilian officials. Because Taiwan and the United States maintain an unofficial relationship, there have traditionally been limitations on such visits.

If a general officer does visit Taiwan as Taiwan media sources predict, observers in Washington, Taipei, and Beijing will see it as a precedent-setting step.[61] Most Taiwan defense policy researchers strongly favor the revision of this policy to permit flag-rank U.S. officers to visit Taiwan, asserting that such visits would be important symbolically, while providing senior U.S. officers with valuable firsthand experience in Taiwan. One well-connected analyst argued that such visits would give senior officers a clearer understanding of why the pace of military reform in Taiwan is slow and would allow them to learn more about Taiwan and Taiwan's domestic politics.[62]

Although most interlocutors have argued that visits to Taiwan by U.S. general officers would have a substantive impact, one Taipei-based analyst said such visits would be "purely political and symbolic."[63] There is no real substance involved, the analyst said, because U.S. general officers can already meet their Taiwan counterparts at various locations in the United States. "General officer visits to Taiwan would simply be another way to signal to China that Taiwan is upgrading its political ties and military-to-military relationship with the United States," according to the analyst. China, for its part, is concerned that high-ranking officer visits signal an upgrading of U.S.-Taiwan defense relations. Analysts in China have read Taiwan press reports on the supposed "secret visit" of a U.S. general officer to Taiwan and at least some apparently believe that U.S. general officers have already visited Taiwan.[64]

Visits by senior civilian officials are an equally controversial subject, as demonstrated by Beijing's reaction to the recent U.S. visit of Taiwan Defense Minister Tang Yiau-ming (for more on Tang's visit, see below). The U.S., for its part, has long maintained restrictions on visits to Taiwan by senior civilian defense policy officials. Although Cabinet-level officials with responsibilities in the areas of economics and trade have visited Taiwan in recent years, high-ranking defense and foreign policy officials do not travel to the island. Conversations with Taiwan researchers suggest that some Taiwan officials would like to see the U.S. modify this policy so that senior civilian defense officials, like the deputy assistant secretary of defense for Asian and Pacific affairs, could also travel to Taiwan for consultations.

Many Taiwan analysts and policymakers are also eager to see more visits by senior Taiwan civilian officials to the United States. Traditionally, Taiwan's Chief of General Staff (CGS) visits the United States every other year and one of Taiwan's service commanders-in-chief visits the U.S. yearly. The ongoing process of defense reforms in Taiwan, however, has led some researchers in Taiwan to suggest expanding the schedule of visits and incorporating more senior civilian participants. In March 2002, Taiwan Defense Minister Tang Yiau-ming visited St. Petersburg, Florida for a defense industry meeting organized by the U.S.-Taiwan Business Council, during which he met privately with Deputy Secretary of Defense Paul Wolfowitz and Assistant Secretary of State for East Asian and Pacific Affairs James Kelly. China protested, warning that Tang's visit, the first by a Taiwan defense minister for other than a transit stop in more than two decades, would harm U.S.-China relations.[65]

Many observers in Taiwan were pleased by Tang's Florida visit, which they see as the first step in a larger process. "Tang's trip to Florida was a good start," said one Taipei-based analyst, "but the Taiwan Minister of Defense should be permitted to visit Washington, DC in the future."[66] If Washington does not treat the minister of defense as the most important defense policy official, the analyst argued, Taiwan will never have true civilian control over its military. "We're a democracy," the analyst said, "and the Minister of Defense has policy power now, so he should visit Washington and go to the Pentagon instead of the CGS." Taiwan's decision to send Vice Minister of Defense Kang Ning-hsiang to Washington for talks in fall 2002 also underscores Taipei's determination to "civilianize" strategic defense dialogues with Washington by sending civilian defense officials to participate in the discussions.[67] The most recent high-level civilian visit took place in June 2003, when Vice Minister of National Defense Lin Chong-pin met with Deputy Secretary of Defense Paul Wolfowitz and Chairman of the Joint Chiefs of Staff General Richard Myers in Washington. In a significant departure from longstanding practice, Vice Minister Lin reportedly met with Wolfowitz in the Pentagon.[68]

EDUCATIONAL EXCHANGES

Education and training is another important component of the U.S.-Taiwan security relationship. In recent years, a large number of Taiwan officers have come to the United States for study or training. Indeed, each year, more than 1,000 Taiwan military personnel receive military training or attend military educational institutions in the United States, according to a Congressional Research Service report.[69] Taiwan personnel study at the National Defense University, the Army, Navy, and Air Force War Colleges, and the Army, Navy, Air Force, and Marine Corps Command and Staff Colleges. Taiwan officers also attend programs like the one sponsored by the Center for Strategic and International Studies in cooperation with the

Institute for the Study of Diplomacy and the School of Foreign Service at Georgetown University in Washington. By contrast, no U.S. military personnel are enrolled at Taiwan's military educational institutions, though Taiwan reportedly has expressed interest in having U.S. officers visit their staff colleges.

Taiwan military officers see military education and training exchanges as an important way to develop long-term relationships between Taiwan officers and their U.S. counterparts. Taiwan officers hope these relationships will pay dividends as officers on both sides are promoted to higher positions throughout the courses of their careers. "Maybe in 10–20 years some participants in these educational exchanges will have become senior officers or even chief of one of the services in Taiwan and will be able to benefit from long-established personal relationships," a Taiwan military officer said.

The most significant problem in the area of military educational exchanges, in the opinion of many U.S. and Taiwan officials, is that Taiwan military officers who study in the United States are unable to take full advantage of their experiences after they return to Taiwan. Rather than rejoining combat units, the officers usually are assigned to teach at Taiwan's military colleges. To increase the chances that they would be assigned to other positions, one Taiwan academic suggested that after Taiwan military personnel finish command, staff, and war college programs in the U.S., they should have the opportunity to stay in the U.S. for a few more months to get hands-on experience training with U.S. forces. "They need to learn how to transform principles into practice," the scholar said.[70]

Military educational exchanges, though a relatively low profile part of the U.S.-Taiwan relationship, are also subject to protocol restrictions. For example Taiwan students do not wear their uniforms while in the United States. Nonetheless, the exchanges have proven controversial at times. In 2002, for instance, the Asia Pacific Center for Security Studies in Honolulu invited Taiwan to enroll students in an executive seminar for the first time.[71] It was feared that China would refuse to participate in the seminar, and, consequently, PRC students were not invited to participate.

OBSERVATION OF EXERCISES AND COMBINED EXERCISES

U.S. military personnel have observed recent iterations of Taiwan's annual Hankuang military exercises, which highlight the efforts of the island's military to improve its capability to conduct joint operations. It is important to recognize that combined U.S.-Taiwan military exercises would be more sensitive than U.S. observation of Taiwan exercises. Indeed, some Taiwan and U.S. national security analysts worry that combined U.S.-Taiwan exercising is potentially provocative.[72] At least a few LY members, however, have stated publicly that they favor holding combined exercises involving U.S. and Taiwan forces, and, in 2001, a Taiwan military spokesperson said that the possibility of conducting combined exercises with the U.S. had never been ruled out.[73] Similarly, some observers in the United States have argued that holding combined U.S.-Taiwan exercises is the only way to ensure that U.S. and Taiwan forces could cooperate effectively in the event of a cross-Strait crisis or conflict. The U.S. Congress has asked the Bush administration to report on the feasibility of undertaking such exercises. Indeed, with influential supporters in Taiwan and the United States holding that the benefits of combined exercises (improved capabilities to coordinate operations and perhaps strengthened deterrence) would outweigh the potential costs (turbulence in U.S.-China relations and cross-Strait ties), it is certainly possible that the United States and Taiwan will eventually hold combined military exercises. Washington and Taipei should approach this issue with great caution, however, as combined exercises have the potential to result in considerable damage to U.S.-China relations and cross-Strait relations.

ASSESSMENT TEAM VISITS

The United States has over the past several years sent a series of teams to Taiwan to assess the capabilities and limitations of the island's armed forces.[74] DOD assessment teams have evaluated the capabilities and needs of Taiwan's military in a variety of areas, including naval modernization, ground forces, air defense, C4ISR, and port defense.[75] The roots of these assessment visits lie in the realization during the 1995–96 Taiwan Strait crises that Washington lacked information on the Taiwan military and that channels of communication between U.S. forces and the Taiwan military were inadequate. The assessments were intended to serve as vehicles for gathering data to weigh when making decisions on arms sales to Taiwan and learning what needed to be done to help the Taiwan military better to integrate and utilize its equipment. For the United States, the assessment team visits have greatly enhanced U.S. knowledge of the Taiwan military. Taiwan, for its part, sees the assessment visits as a "win-win" proposition and has been very cooperative in attempting to ensure their success. Some elements in the Taiwan military reportedly use the teams as outside pressure on their own system because the U.S. assessments are seen as neutral and credible.

Although both sides are generally positive about the assessments, U.S. and Taiwan officials have also pointed to several problems with the visits. One problem centers on the conceptual approach to the assessment team reports, according to Taiwan researchers. The assessment teams display a tendency to suggest "fixing problems in a Western way" that reflects an inadequate understanding of Taiwan's domestic political problems and the MND bureaucracy, according to one Taiwan analyst.[76] "Pentagon solutions are not necessarily applicable to Taiwan MND problems," the analyst said. Another problem, according to the analyst, is that the assessment teams have in many cases been unable fully to comprehend the underlying bureaucratic, political, and organizational problems that Taiwan faces in carrying out its defense reforms. In all, however, the assessment team visits have proven valuable to both Taiwan and the United States despite their flaws. The assessments should continue over the next several years, with future visits focusing on issues such as critical infrastructure protection.

IMPLICATIONS FOR THE UNITED STATES

As the focus of U.S.-Taiwan security cooperation has broadened in recent years, the need to improve coordination between Washington and Taipei effectively to manage an expanding relationship has become more pronounced. As the U.S.-Taiwan security relationship becomes increasingly multifaceted and the tempo of interaction continues to accelerate, there is a growing need for Washington and Taipei to develop mutually agreed upon goals, and to ensure that specific programs and initiatives support those goals. Interviews with officials and analysts in Washington and Taipei indicate they recognize that the necessity for dialogue mounts as the military relationship expands. "The need for coordination at multiple levels has increased as the military-to-military relationship has become more involved," a well-connected Taiwan researcher said. To manage the ever more active security relationship more effectively, in the Taiwan researcher's view, the United States and Taiwan need "regularized, institutionalized channels of communication" to discuss U.S.-Taiwan security cooperation.

Beyond improving coordination at the level of managing security cooperation, the U.S. and Taiwan also need to enhance communication on larger, strategic issues to reduce growing friction in the U.S.-Taiwan military-to-military relationship.[77] Even as U.S.-Taiwan exchanges have expanded greatly, growing bitterness and frustration have been evident in the relationship. As analysts in Taiwan point out, the same complaints have persisted on both sides for the last couple of years.[78] The irony is that even as the United States and Taiwan are moving closer together in many respects, perceptual gaps are widening. Taipei asserts that the U.S. still doesn't understand the implications of defense reforms, domestic politics, and the increasingly assertive role of the LY. Officials in Taiwan are also losing their patience with what they regard as a "paternalistic" U.S. approach. Washington, for its part, is frustrated with delays in arms purchases and the pace of defense reform in Taiwan.[79]

The U.S. is especially impatient with procurement delays. Many observers in Washington feel that Taipei is proceeding too slowly in purchasing weapons the United States has approved to upgrade the Taiwan military.[80] One area of particular concern is missile defense. The U.S. feels Taiwan is moving too slowly on the expansion and upgrading of its missile defenses, especially given the pace of the short-range ballistic missile (SRBM) buildup on the mainland. Defense Department officials have warned that these ballistic missiles, along with land attack cruise missiles expected to be available by 2005, constitute the "most significant coercive threat to Taiwan."[81] The United States has been strongly encouraging Taipei to purchase PAC-3 missile defense systems to counter this threat. At a defense industry conference held in San Antonio, Texas in 2003, for example, Pentagon officials urged Taiwan to improve its missile defense capabilities, stating that "Without defenses, the PRC's growing arsenal of increasingly accurate and lethal ballistic missiles may have devastating strategic and operational-level effects on Taiwan's critical infrastructure, air defenses, and naval operations. . . . we believe it is imperative that Taiwan build upon its existing assets and acquire an integrated air and missile defense capability."[82] In Taiwan, however, many officials and LY members are worried about the system's costs, and some are not convinced that its effectiveness has been proven. Legislators have questioned the performance of U.S. missile defenses in the most recent Iraqi conflict, and some have argued that the Chungshan Institute of Science and Technology should be given the opportunity to develop Taiwan's missile defense system. In addition, many legislators and officials express resentment over the style of the U.S. sales pitch, which they see as patronizing and imperious.[83] These reservations delayed, but ultimately did not derail Taiwan's plans to procure advanced missile defense systems. In March 2004, Deputy Defense Minister Chen Chao-min announced that the MND intends to purchase six PAC-3 batteries from the United States. The execution of the budget is scheduled to begin in 2005, and the MND expects to complete the deployment of all six PAC-3 batteries by 2019.[84]

In Washington, some researchers have argued that the underlying cause of these procurement delays is indecisiveness on the part of the civilian and military leadership, the legislature, and the Chen administration. For some in Washington, this indecision raises questions regarding the seriousness of Taiwan's commitment to its own defense.[85] Reflecting this frustration, DASD Richard Lawless warned recently that Taiwan "should not view America's resolute commitment to peace and security in the Taiwan Strait as a substitute for investing the necessary resources in its own defense."[86] Meanwhile, MND officials in Taiwan bristle at suggestions that delays in the procurement process reflect a lack of commitment to Taiwan's defense. They also resent what some perceive as the overbearing attitudes of U.S. officials who have urged Taiwan to increase its defense budget and quicken the pace of arms purchases from the United States. Speaking to reporters in August 2002, Defense Minister Tang said, "Taiwan is a sovereign state. We will not buy every weapons system that the US wants to sell to us. We will buy only the ones that really serve our defense needs." Tang argued that Washington should understand that the delays are a consequence of the institutionalization of Taiwan's weapons procurement processes. "It is not fair to criticize us as being uncooperative towards offers of arms sales by the US," Tang said.[87]

The differences over arms sales that have emerged during 2002 and 2003 are a symptom of a more fundamental and potentially more serious underlying problem in U.S.-Taiwan relations: the growing divergence between threat perceptions in Taipei and Washington. Over the past several years, officials and analysts in the United States have expressed increasing concern over the modernization of the PLA, which is seen as giving China a growing capability to threaten, coerce, or even attack Taiwan.[88] U.S. officials assess that PLA modernization is moving forward at a much quicker pace than Taiwan military modernization.[89] They worry that the military balance of power is shifting in favor of the PRC, and that the PLA is preparing to compel Taiwan to capitulate before U.S. forces can intervene in a cross-strait conflict.[90] DASD Richard Lawless highlighted the growing PLA threat in comments at the February 2003 U.S.-Taiwan defense industry meeting: "Taiwan faces a concerted Chinese effort to gain the ability to use force decisively sooner rather than later; China is working toward multiple options for coercion. It is believed that surprise and speed will be used to make any potential U.S. assistance to Taiwan . . . ineffective." Moreover, Lawless continued, "Beijing is focused on reducing warning time and the rapid exploitation of Taiwan's military weaknesses."[91]

On paper, at least, Taiwan's threat assessments also reflect growing concern over modernization of the Chinese military and the increasing threat it poses to the security of the island. The bottom-line judgment about Chinese military modernization in the Taiwan MND's 2002 defense report, for

example, is that "The PRC's threat against the ROC's security is ever increasing."[92] At the same time, however, politicians and analysts in Taiwan
seem predisposed to discount the possibility that China might resort to the
use of force against the island in the near-term. As Denny Roy, senior research fellow at the Asia-Pacific Center for Security Studies, observes,
"Outsiders may be surprised to learn that the danger of a PRC military attack is not at the top of Taiwan's list of short-term threats." On the contrary, "Few in Taiwan . . . expect the PRC to attempt to conquer the island
through an overt military attack in the foreseeable future."[93] Instead, they
view the threat from the mainland largely as a political and economic challenge, at least for the remainder of this decade. Lin Chong-pin, Taiwan's
deputy defense minister in 2003, argued that Beijing would not feel confident enough to use force against Taiwan until 2010 to 2015 even if the cross-
Strait military balance tips in China's favor within the next few years.[94] If
this emerging gap in threat perceptions continues to widen, it may result in
increasing tension in U.S.-Taiwan security relations and the further intensification of frustration in Washington and Taipei.

Both sides must take steps to prevent these emerging problems from becoming serious obstacles to the further enhancement of U.S.-Taiwan security cooperation. Washington must recognize that Taiwan's defense establishment is simultaneously undertaking a series of reforms and modernization
initiatives, including broadening civilian control over the armed forces,
streamlining the military, improving jointness, and modernizing to meet the
challenge of an increasingly capable Chinese military, any one of which
would represent a formidable challenge, and that it is doing all of this while
facing serious budget constraints and adapting to work within the context of
increasingly active legislative oversight.[95] Taipei, for its part, must communicate clearly to the United States that it is determined to develop and maintain the capabilities that would be required to resist a determined Chinese
attack, at least for an amount of time sufficient to allow the U.S. to intervene decisively.

Perhaps an even larger challenge for Washington is helping Taipei improve its defense capabilities without exceeding the boundaries of its understandings with Beijing in a way that could spark the very crisis enhanced
cooperation with Taiwan aims to prevent. Any assessment of security cooperation between the United States and its friends and allies must take
into account the diplomatic and political dynamics that shape defense relationships, and this is especially evident in the case of U.S.-Taiwan security cooperation. Indeed, political considerations and constraints define the
limits of the possible for U.S.-Taiwan defense relations, perhaps more so
than for U.S. security cooperation with any other friend, ally, or security

partner. The centrality and sensitivity of the Taiwan issue in U.S.-China relations imposes unique requirements and limitations on U.S.-Taiwan security cooperation.

The overriding policy objective for the United States is preventing a conflict in the Taiwan Strait that would be very costly for all parties. U.S. analysts point to the dangers that would be faced in the event that China starts a war it cannot easily win, and certainly cannot afford to lose.[96] To avoid such a conflict, the United States must continue a longstanding balancing act, finding a policy equilibrium that will allow it to deter Beijing from using force to resolve the Taiwan issue while at the same time ensuring that Taipei refrains from undertaking actions that are unduly provocative and risk dragging the United States into an otherwise avoidable conflict with China. Political changes underway in Taiwan are making this balancing act more and more difficult for the United States. President Chen's insistence on proceeding with the referendum questions on missile defense and cross-Strait relations in the March 2004 election, despite the public rebuke from President Bush, suggests that the ability of the United States to influence politics in Taiwan is at best highly limited. At the same time, however, China has indicated that it expects the United States to use its leverage to prevent Taiwan from taking actions that would change the status quo. China, however, may very well overestimate U.S. influence on Taiwan. As a result, Beijing may become convinced that despite official protestations to the contrary, Washington at least tacitly supports independence for Taiwan. That would greatly complicate the task of reassuring China that U.S. objectives are not inimical to its interests.

This problem suggests a somewhat cautious approach to U.S. security cooperation with Taiwan. On the one hand, Washington cannot allow Beijing's objections to dominate its decisionmaking on Taiwan policy. At the same time, however, in formulating its policy regarding security cooperation with Taiwan, Washington must consider the potential Chinese reaction to its expanding defense relationship with the island. Exchanges with Taiwan should have clearly defined goals and focus on specific purposes in support of the larger policy of helping Taiwan bolster its ability to defend itself and preserve peace in the Taiwan Strait. Furthering Taiwan's defense reforms is perhaps the most important of the issues at hand, especially in that successful defense reform is a necessary condition for the improvement of Taiwan's military and the enhancement of U.S.-Taiwan security cooperation. The United States should thus take additional steps to assist Taiwan in carrying out its defense reforms.[97] More generally, it is most advantageous from the U.S. point of view to avoid high profile, largely symbolic activities that would yield few substantive benefits but nevertheless would be seen in Beijing as especially provocative. For the United States, the crucial policy challenge is enhancing its defense relationship with Taiwan while remaining within the framework of unofficial relations established by the Taiwan Relations Act and the three U.S.-China communiqués. Bearing these considerations in mind, U.S. officials must centralize the management of U.S.-Taiwan security cooperation and ensure that policy decisions are fully coordinated. This presents a considerable challenge as a large number of organizations and offices have related responsibilities, including the NSC, State Department, the Office of the Secretary of Defense, International Security Affairs, the American Institute in Taiwan, the Defense Security Cooperation Agency, the Joint Staff, the Pacific Command and the services. To ensure that policy is fully coordinated and that all ongoing and proposed initiatives are consistent with the overall policy, a senior U.S. official should be designated to serve as a policy coordinator and point of contact for all issues involving U.S. security cooperation with Taiwan. This approach would help ensure that U.S.-Taiwan security cooperation supports the overarching objectives of enhancing Taiwan's security and reducing the risk of conflict with China.

CHAPTER EIGHT

"Strategic Ambiguity Or Strategic Clarity?"

NANCY BERNKOPF TUCKER

STRATEGIC AMBIGUITY has been attacked as a dangerous and anti-quated policy that no longer serves the national interest and must be replaced as quickly as possible with strategic clarity. The indictment of ambiguity has come from all parts of the U.S. political spectrum and has mounted over recent years, particularly since the mid 1990s and with the greatest practical effect since the election of George W. Bush. Of course, ambiguity has never been welcomed by either Taiwan or China and its demise would not be mourned by leaders who prefer to compete for U.S. support anyway. But, if ambiguity is old and hazardous, the conditions created by a newer environment of growing strategic clarity are still more complex and perilous.

The U.S. policy of strategic ambiguity dealt with the Taiwan Strait standoff between China and Taiwan built upon conflicting imperatives of history, geography, domestic politics, international and regional economic and political relations, as well as security responsibilities. U.S. decision-makers have increasingly doubted the durability of existing arrangements and have sought to imbue U.S. policy with greater precision and palpable warnings of where American action would be triggered or patience would

For their efforts to improve my arguments, I thank Warren I. Cohen, Bonnie Glaser, Michael McDevitt, and David Finkelstein.

run out. In the process they have sought to sharpen understanding among the concerned parties of the risks and consequences for mishandling the situation. Their impulse has arisen in part out of impatience with a posture that over the years has frozen them in place, thwarting innovation and making no apparent progress, and in part out of anxiety that events beyond Washington's control may shatter the half century long impasse and bring on war. The potential for disaster has seemed more likely as drastic changes have transformed conditions across the Taiwan Strait, introducing democracy, prosperity, military modernization, and nationalism into the already volatile mix of interests and emotions.

Crisis in the Strait in 1996 invigorated the desire for strategic clarity and, since the spring of that year, U.S. policy has become more transparent. Both the administrations of Bill Clinton and George W. Bush set out parameters for action that previously could only be guessed at. Following from the same events, Beijing and Taipei came to believe that they could anticipate U.S. decisions, including the whens and whys of American choices. Nevertheless, the search for and the realization of clarity has not been as successful as proponents hoped. In fact, the roots of Washington's approach to the Taiwan Strait problem are firmly planted in the policy of ambiguity and the overpowering reasons for that original choice have neither disappeared nor been significantly altered. Moreover, any expectation that clarity can predict behavior exaggerates what can be known about the future.

An additional complicating factor in the pursuit of a more forthright and, presumably, effective Taiwan policy is the link between ambiguity and outcome. Policymakers arrived at strategic ambiguity because they chose not to become the ultimate arbiters of the unification struggle between Beijing and Taipei. That is, Washington acknowledged the assertion made equally by both sides that only one China existed in the world. Prior to January 1, 1979, Washington treated Taipei as the capital of China and afterwards it dealt with Beijing as enjoying that status. The U.S. government did not take the next step, after derecognizing the Republic of China and establishing formal relations with the People's Republic of China, urged upon it by Beijing, of treating Taiwan as a province of the PRC. Nor did it take any formal notice of the position Taiwan adopted in the 1990s that the Republic of China represented only the territory it actually controlled. Instead, the United States remained vague about the meaning of its own One China policy.

Ambiguity, therefore, has been a flexible approach that allowed Washington both to have a One China policy and assist in the defense of Taiwan. Of course, as with ambiguity, there are those who argue that adherence to a One China policy has outlived its usefulness. Others, simply note that it no longer enjoys the consensus position that it held when Washington first subscribed to it. Finally, a combination of pro-China stalwarts and America-first foreign policy figures contend that the escalating peril and unmanageability of the situation dictates diminished involvement with, if not abandonment of, Taiwan.

To address these issues several questions require consideration: What was the origin and intention of strategic ambiguity and how did the interpretation of the policy change over time? What have been the challenges to perpetuating the policy? Is strategic clarity a better policy and how far have policymakers actually moved in that direction? Can strategic clarity and One China co-exist?

THE ORIGIN AND INTENTION OF STRATEGIC AMBIGUITY

Evaluation of the policy of strategic ambiguity has generally been distorted by the failure to see it as an outgrowth of the whole history of U.S. relations with the People's Republic of China. Those who have examined the issue have been political analysts, not historians, and have been prone to foreshorten the development of the policy, linking it to the Shanghai Communiqué and the Nixon opening to China. Neglecting the actual derivation of strategic ambiguity, however, makes it impossible to appreciate its complexity.

The entanglement of Washington with Taiwan that led to the concept of strategic ambiguity began in 1950. Harry S Truman interrupted and froze the Chinese civil war when he placed the U.S. 7th Fleet in the Taiwan Strait in response to North Korea's attack on the South in June 1950. Truman and his advisers feared the Korean conflict would provide a diversion during which the Communist Chinese would try to conquer the offshore islands that remained in Nationalist Chinese hands and then attack Taiwan to dislodge and defeat Chiang Kai-shek's surviving troops.

But, the president gave the 7th Fleet a larger mission. The Nationalists, who were not trusted in Washington, were also to be prevented from using the fighting in Korea as a pretext to launch what Americans believed to be a hopeless assault on China. Once stranded onshore, the United States would be compelled to rescue them. Truman, Secretary of State Dean Acheson, and the Joint Chiefs of Staff all believed that this was the only way that Chiang could recapture the mainland. Truman acted promptly in interposing the fleet, but inserted it solely to prevent operations that would widen the war beyond the Korean peninsula. He intended the move to be temporary, expiring as soon as the clash in Korea had been brought under control.

Truman had, in fact, already accepted the idea that the Nationalists' regime would not, and probably should not, endure. Its history of corruption and ineptitude on the mainland had alienated Truman and Acheson and, in the early weeks of 1950, they made clear privately and publicly that Washington intended to allow Chiang Kai-shek to fall. The Korean War interfered with that calculus, apparently reifying the monolithic nature of the communist bloc and intensifying animosity toward the Chinese. The White House found that its intended disassociation from Chiang had become impossible to pursue.[1]

Truman, therefore, bequeathed the Taiwan problem to the administration of Dwight D. Eisenhower. Although Ike pretended enthusiastically to support Chiang, making a famous pledge in his first State of the Union address that he would unleash Taiwan's leader to deal with the communist mainland, he proved no more happy in the role than Truman. Secretly, he almost immediately tied Chiang's hands, insisting upon a pledge to consult with the United States before mounting any large-scale raids.[2] Nevertheless, Washington confronted two dangerous crises in the Taiwan Strait.

It was just before the first of these confrontations between the PRC and Taiwan that Chiang proposed negotiation of a mutual defense treaty with Washington. Taiwan wanted guarantees of American assistance and protection, paralleling promises then being made to South Korea, the Philippines, Australia, and New Zealand. Chiang demanded that the assurances cover not only Taiwan and the immediately adjacent Penghu islands, but also smaller islands situated close to the mainland to which he laid claim. Eisenhower's secretary of state, John Foster Dulles, sought to evade the commitment. He prized his operational flexibility and found Chiang's willingness to put the United States in harm's way infuriating. As for the offshore island groups of Jinmen (Quemoy) and Mazu (Matsu), Dulles believed that, although the Chinese Communists had so far been unable to capture their heavily defended garrisons, it was just a matter of time.

But, even as the administration sought to minimize prospects for a conflict with China, Eisenhower and Dulles recognized that, for domestic political reasons and to preserve peace in Asia, they could not simply walk away from the Taiwan Strait. Eventually, as artillery shells flew across the waters between the mainland and the offshore islands, they capitulated and signed a treaty with Taiwan, trading freedom of maneuver for Chiang's acquiescence in a UN role in resolution of the 1954–55 Strait crisis. Nevertheless, the treaty did not signify that either Ike or Dulles were prepared to tell Taipei exactly what the United States would do in the contemporary or future crises.

Washington insisted upon ambiguity when it came to the text of the mutual defense treaty. The treaty asserted unity in the face of aggression, but article V specified that in the event of "an armed attack" each signatory would "meet the common danger in accordance with its constitutional processes." As political scientist John W. Garver notes in his careful study of the alliance "This particular choice of words left the United States with considerable flexibility in choosing whether, when, and how to respond to a clash between PRC and ROC forces."[3] Furthermore, Dulles prevented inclusion of language that specifically covered the offshore islands. Only grudgingly did he allow Foreign Minister George Yeh to insert a reference to "such other territories [beyond Taiwan and Penghu] as may be determined by mutual agreement."[4]

In addition, to Chiang's great annoyance, Dulles refused to provide firm public pledges of support for holding the offshore islands. When Chiang threatened to be explicit himself, the U.S. government warned that he would be repudiated. Dulles observed that "he had told Congress that he felt we could not draw an absolute geographic line, or publicly state what islands were considered important and what islands were not important. If you say a place is not important, a new Communist buildup often makes it important."[5] Ike adamantly insisted that "we must be the judge of the military situation that draws us in whether in Quemoy or elsewhere."[6]

Throughout the crisis, Washington followed a parallel strategy of evasiveness and inconsistency toward Beijing. Eisenhower characterized his policy as "keeping the enemy guessing." Dulles explained to members of Congress that the administration had been "hoping the communists would be deterred by uncertainty. They are probing and will continue to probe to find where we will stop them."[7]

Eventually ambiguity rattled members of the administration, including Dulles. At an NSC meeting in January 1955, he asserted that he thought "this policy of obscuring our intentions had . . . begun to backfire, and the Chinese Communists were apparently confident in the belief that the United States was unwilling to fight."[8] When the PRC successfully assaulted Yijiangshan and threatened the Dachen islands, Dulles proposed evacuation with an explicit, and public, promise to defend Jinmen and Mazu. The NSC authorized U.S. forces to protect them until either the UN or Beijing ended the crisis. At the last moment, however, Eisenhower decided to keep the new guarantee secret.[9]

The president's preference for ambiguity regarding the Taiwan Strait reflected his proclivity for vagueness to keep the Congress and the public off-balance and protect executive branch prerogatives. In March 1955, Ike triggered widespread anxiety by alluding to possible use of tactical nuclear weapons against China's cities. The State Department wanted him to bury the issue, but Eisenhower, who enjoyed manipulating the press with mangled syntax, oversimplification, dullness, and feigned ignorance, preferred to "just confuse them." In fact, Ike's statement on the possible use of the atomic bomb also captured the essence of strategic ambiguity as he understood it:

> the most unpredictable factor in war is human nature . . . but the only unchanging factor in war is human nature. And . . . every war is going to astonish you in the way it occurred, and in the way it is carried out. So that for a man to predict, particularly if he has the responsibility for making the decision, to predict what he is going to use, how he is going to do it, would I think exhibit his ignorance of war; that is what I believe. So I think you just have to wait.[10]

The underlying logic of strategic ambiguity as crafted and practiced by the Eisenhower administration, then, fulfilled discrete but complementary objectives. To Eisenhower, the celebrated World War II general turned president, it seemed an excellent tool of triple deterrence. It protected the United States against demands from and miscalculation by Taiwan and China. China would not seek to capture Taiwan or the offshore islands because it could not know what the United States would do, and Taiwan would not take provocative actions since it could not be certain of US support.

The policy also shielded his administration's foreign policy against encroachment by Congress at a time when the depredations of Senator Joseph McCarthy's anti-communist crusade put a spotlight on Asia decisionmaking. In fact, Eisenhower demanded and got a blank check from Congress in the 1955 Formosa resolution, authorizing him to use force to defend Taiwan, including "protection of such related positions and territories of that area now in friendly hands and the taking of such other measures as he judges to be required."[11] Eisenhower had maneuvered Congress into authorizing an open ended commitment and had reinforced strategic ambiguity.

CHANGES IN AND CHALLENGES TO THE POLICY OF STRATEGIC AMBIGUITY

Erosion of strategic ambiguity set in gradually. To the extent that the heart of the policy consisted of uncertainty regarding what actions the United States would take each instance in which Washington broadcast its plans compromised the core. In 1962, for instance, when famine in China led Taipei to plot to topple the communist authorities, John F. Kennedy followed two paths simultaneously.[12] On the one hand, he decided not to decide whether Washington would defend the offshore islands if Taiwan provoked the PRC, fearing that he could not keep the process secret. Instead, strategic ambiguity coupled with having the requisite U.S. forces available would be the best protection.[13] On the other hand, the president did notify Beijing that he would not permit Taiwan to move, thereby preventing escalation. He also had his ambassador remind Chiang that the Mutual Defense Treaty did not "say we will support [a] GRC counterattack against [the] mainland and it would be a mistake to create [an] impression in the minds of the people that [the] US has any such obligations."[14] So Kennedy utilized ambiguity, but threatened very unambiguous actions to keep the United States out of war.

Far more significant changes came in 1971. Richard Nixon and Henry Kissinger did not do away with strategic ambiguity, but they compromised several of the fundamental elements of the policy. For one, the United States at long last publicly if not officially abandoned the fantasy that the Republic of China governed all Chinese and accepted that normalization of relations with the PRC should proceed. Accompanying that leap, the administration downgraded the status of Taiwan even though it retained formal diplomatic ties. Finally, Nixon and Kissinger accepted the idea of One China, and whereas they voiced an expectation that Beijing would pursue unification peacefully, they stopped 7th Fleet patrols in the Strait and did not demand renunciation of force. Kissinger asserted that the military issue would not be "a principal obstacle between us" and gave up the Mutual Defense Treaty and American troops on the island.[15]

The question of Taiwan's future did not seem central to Henry Kissinger, who imagined that a U.S.-China condominium against the Soviet Union meant more to Beijing than it did to Washington. For the Chinese, however, the situation looked quite different. Zhou Enlai challenged Kissinger to address China's core interests from their first meeting in July 1971. On day two, harking back to 1949, Zhou reminded Kissinger that "the U.S. stated . . . that it had no territorial ambitions regarding Taiwan" and would not "interfere in China's internal affairs." After "the Korean war broke out . . . you surrounded Taiwan and declared the status of Taiwan was still unsettled. Even up to the present day . . . this is your position. That is the crux." Beijing demanded that the Americans repudiate the subsequent twenty years of interference in Chinese affairs. Kissinger and Nixon more or less complied, ruling out pursuit of two Chinas or one-China, one-Taiwan or support for Taiwan independence, and further observed (to some laughter) that the White House had clamped down on errant administration statements that the status of Taiwan remained unsettled.[16]

With these concessions on record, even if they remained secret, the nature of strategic ambiguity was altered in significant ways. Although no more transparent about the details of what it might do in the event of a

Taiwan Strait crisis, the United States viewed the idea of a cross-Strait accommodation with considerably greater sympathy. Moreover, the likelihood of a crisis diminished appreciably given that the administration had adopted Beijing's perception of Taiwan's future status. Kissinger told Zhou, "As a student of history, one's prediction would have to be that the political evolution is likely to be in the direction which Prime Minister Chou Enlai indicated to me."[17] Thus Beijing anticipated that progress toward unification would be reasonably rapid. Armed with Washington's assurances and believing that Taipei had been abandoned, Chinese leaders did not think a separate Taiwan would be able to survive.

In Taiwan, in spite of growing prosperity and continued U.S. arms sales, many feared that Beijing's expectations would prove to be correct. They weren't and Taiwan's continued existence perpetuated the policy of strategic ambiguity. Indeed, when Beijing realized Taiwan was thriving and suspected that the United States was again fostering two-Chinas, even as U.S.-China relations remained stalemated, it orchestrated a brief cross-Strait challenge in 1976 to underline its suspicions.[18]

If ambiguity had moved a bit along a continuum toward clarity during the 1950s, 1960s and 1970s, the basic concept continued to define the parameters of U.S. action in the area. No one questioned the fundamental premise of remaining elusive and preserving uncertainty in a policy designed to keep the United States out of war. When it came to the decision to shift diplomatic ties from Taipei to Beijing, however, politicians and diplomats found themselves spelling out the structure of relations and it became harder to be ambiguous. The Carter White House proved vague about its defense commitments to Taiwan whether because it saw those assurances as obvious, as some officials claimed, or in order to avoid provoking the PRC. Members of Congress, however, refused to permit an indeterminate security guarantee.

In the Taiwan Relations Act, a majority of legislators inserted several crucial injunctions into the bill proffered by the administration, saying that "any effort to determine the future of Taiwan by other than peaceful means, including by boycotts and embargoes" would be of "grave concern" to the United States, that defensive weapons in appropriate quantities would be made available to Taipei, and that Washington would "maintain the capacity of the United States to resist any resort to force or other forms of coercion that would jeopardize the security, or the social or economic system, of the people on Taiwan."[19] Even so, the final version of the law preserved ambiguity regarding the U.S. role in the defense of Taiwan. It dictated no specific U.S. actions and gave Congress no power to initiate a military response. On the crucial question of arms sales, moreover, the president would decide what to sell and all Congress could do would be to block his decision.

The fact that arms sales would continue after recognition, although accepted by Deng Xiaoping, nevertheless angered Beijing. Again, as in the launching of normalization with Nixon, recognition by Carter had not provided the leverage over Taiwan that China's leaders wanted and needed. So long as Washington continued to supply weaponry, Beijing believed that Taipei would not be willing to accept unification. So long as Taiwan continued to maintain a separate existence, U.S. actions in the Strait could not be predicted with assurance. So long as U.S. behavior remained unclear and Chinese forces inferior, Beijing could not resolve the Straits issue and it would challenge Chinese sovereignty. Thus in 1981 and 1982 China pressed the United States to cut off arms sales. Prolonged negotiations yielded an August 17 Communiqué in which the U.S. finally pledged not to improve the quality or increase the quantity of Taiwan's weapons as it gradually reduced sales.

But Ronald Reagan, whose sympathies lay with those he called the Free Chinese, muddied the provisions of the arms sales communiqué even before the two sides formally signed it. In his six assurances to Taiwan, Reagan pledged that regardless of the agreement with Beijing, Washington would stand by a series of commitments to Taiwan. The specific points made through AIT Taipei director James Lilley on July 14, 1982 were that:

1. The United States had not set a date for ending arms sales.
2. The U.S. would not engage in prior consultation with the PRC regarding weapons sales to Taipei.
3. The U.S. would not mediate between Taipei and Beijing.
4. The U.S. would not pressure Taiwan into negotiations with the PRC.
5. The U.S. would not revise the Taiwan Relations Act.
6. The American position regarding the sovereignty of Taiwan would not be changed.

Furthermore, the president assured Chiang Ching-kuo that his willingness to go along with the communiqué rested entirely on the maintenance of peace in the Taiwan Strait. In a subsequent secret communication the White House pledged that "the U.S. will not only pay attention to what the PRC says, but also will use all methods to achieve surveillance of PRC military production and military deployment." If at any time Beijing decided to challenge the peace, CCK could count on the fact that "U.S. commitments would become invalidated."[20]

So once more, U.S. actions in the Strait were made explicitly contingent.

Strategic ambiguity remained in place although its parameters had been expanded and contracted on various occasions. From Washington's point of view its relevance and appropriateness continued to be unquestioned. Then came the events of 1995–1996 and the underlying assumption that ambiguity served U.S. national interests became a matter of contention. In the aftermath of the crisis, even without resolution of the debate about the principle, a definite movement toward greater clarity began to alter the way policymakers framed their words and actions.

The 1995–96 Strait crisis had a profound impact because it happened so suddenly and yet almost as if in slow motion, because it seemed so unexpected and yet entailed so much signaling and warning, and, most importantly, because it could have meant war between the United States and China at a time when relations, although not good, were not so bad as to warrant such a horrific end. The crisis began with an invitation to Taiwan's president Lee Teng-hui to speak at his alma mater Cornell University, although it built on exisiting distress in Beijing over Bush administration F-16 sales to Taipei and the Clinton administration's Taiwan Policy Review.[21] The invitation, packaged as a private request to visit informally, had been secured by Taipei after an earlier transit stop in Hawaii had not suited Lee's political needs or personal dignity. The struggle over granting a visa, which overturned U.S. practice on high level visits following derecognition, required a broad lobbying effort by Lee. Ultimately Congress and Clinton could not rationalize barring a democratically elected head of state. The Chinese leadership lashed out at what it deemed an endorsement of Taiwan separatism, calling home China's ambassador, delaying acceptance of a new U.S. ambassador, cutting off cross-Strait dialogue, and launching a series of escalating military exercises.

During development of the crisis, Beijing sought to make certain the United States understood its position, but it failed. China's diplomats did not lobby effectively and members of Congress never recognized how abhorrent a positive visa decision would be. Too many Americans believed that Beijing's dependence on the U.S. market would not let it risk economic ties over a Lee visa. When the decision went against China's interests and the leadership felt outraged, embarrassed and betrayed, nationalism and self-preservation momentarily trumped modernization.

At the same time, Beijing miscalculated what the United States would do. Again, too many at the top believed Americans to be soft, lacking in principles, unconcerned with foreign affairs, ignorant about Taiwan, and eager to avoid confrontation with China. An image of Americans fleeing Somalia in 1993, after the death of just 18 servicemen, seemed reinforced by Washington's mild reaction to China's initial missile firings. As China analyst Alan Romberg notes Beijing may have concluded that 'strategic ambiguity' reflected an underlying 'strategic ambivalence.' "[22] There were those, of course, who warned that Washington might act. They noted that after months in which the administration had been largely passive, the aircraft carrier *Nimitz* had sailed symbolically through the Taiwan Strait in December 1995. Secretary of State Warren Christopher also alluded to discontent in a Congress influenced by Taiwan's democratization. Unfortunately, he did not emphasize sufficiently that, in the American system, the president's policy could be reshaped by these domestic political dynamics.

China's leaders convinced themselves, therefore, that they could punish Taiwan and nothing beyond a brief demonstration of annoyance would occur. Beijing, they believed, had made clear that China would not try to seize any territory or otherwise escalate the confrontation. When Bill Clinton sent not one but two aircraft carrier battle groups in 1996 to respond to missile firings designed to intimidate Taiwan's electorate during presidential balloting, the extent of the deployment stunned Beijing.

Opponents of the administration charged that ambiguity had contributed to China's aggressive behavior. Joseph Nye, Assistant Secretary of Defense had, after all, told Chinese military officers in Beijing in November 1995 that "nobody knows" what the United States would do in the event of a military clash in the Taiwan Strait. By way of explanation he added that "if you go back to 1950 and you look at what the American government said, which is that Korea is outside our defense perimeter, and then realize that six months later, we were at war to defend South Korea, it shows that you cannot know the answer."[23] Nye's words and administration actions, Republican critics believed, like those of Truman and Acheson in 1950 seemed an invitation to a crisis and a perfect campaign issue. Steven Erlanger suggested in the *New York Times* that the White House ultimately dispatched its "ambiguous show of force to head off more drastic measures in an election-minded Congress." Two aircraft carrier battle groups, he opined, would not "infuriate China . . . [as much as] providing more advanced arms to Taiwan, supporting United Nations membership for Taiwan or issuing invitations to high-ranking Taiwan officials to visit the United States."[24]

Nevertheless, members of the Clinton administration, at the time and after, rejected depiction of their policy as strategic ambiguity, feeling the characterization was patently inaccurate and probably detrimental to resolving the crisis. To them the messages sent to Beijing, Taipei, and Congress plainly defined the limits of what each actor could do and what U.S. responses would be. Christopher explained on the TV news show *Meet the Press* that "We've made it quite clear to the Chinese that if they try to resolve this problem through force rather than through peace, that will be a grave matter with us. We've made it as clear as we possibly can to them, because we don't want any miscalculation on their part."[25] Quiet communication with Taipei also sought to prevent unintended outcomes. As Winston Lord, Assistant Secretary of State for East Asian Affairs, noted subsequently, officials "didn't want Taiwan to think that they had a blank check from us."[26]

Robert Suettinger of the NSC, believed that congressional efforts to stiffen Clinton's position on Taiwan actually obliged China to escalate rather than to seek compromise. According to him, the term strategic ambiguity,

> was never used in official policy documents. [National Security Adviser Tony] Lake declared it anathema in the NSC and Lord went to great lengths to disavow the term in public testimony and speeches. During the brewing crisis in the Taiwan Strait, the administration tried to stress it was seeking clarity of policy, not ambiguity. The term, however, had staying power and was an easy catchphrase for critics to use as a characterization of Clinton's policy. Its incessant use put the administration on the defensive.[27]

Indeed, deployment of warships to the waters near Taiwan did send an unmistakable message regarding U.S. interest in peace even if Washington refused to define the precise mission of those ships. To some observers this appeared to have fundamentally undermined ambiguity, whether for good or ill.[28] To others it seemed a perfect illustration of ambiguity in action.[29] As Lord explained to Congress,

> We have strategic clarity on this question. There is some tactical ambiguity. . . . We are urging restraint on both sides. So I don't think our statements—not to mention the movement of naval assets—is an ambiguous message about our interests and the fact we would react seriously. Now, where the ambiguity comes in—and I would argue you have got to have this—is we cannot spell precisely in advance what we would do if there is a resort to force. . . . It depends on what was happening, what provoked it, what the contact was. The fact that it would be serious is very clear, and there is no ambiguity.[30]

It should be noted, before examining the push toward introducing more clarity into U.S. policy, that in one arena officials quite consciously built ambiguity into policy as it was formulated in the difficult spring of 1996. The United States and Japan were, coincidentally, in the process of negotiating new defense guidelines when the Chinese began to fire missiles toward Taiwan. Disturbed by Chinese aggressiveness, Prime Minister Hashimoto Ryutaro allowed the joint security declaration which emerged from his April summit with Clinton to be far stronger than originally intended. On the Taiwan issue, however, ambiguity prevailed. Rather than delineate specific geographic areas that cooperation between Tokyo and Washington should cover, they simply agreed to refer to situations in areas surrounding Japan. China recognized the purview, of course, but could not know precisely what Tokyo acting alone or in conjunction with the United States would do in the event of a new Strait crisis. Uncertainty persisted thereafter as Tokyo-Taipei contacts multiplied and perpetually erratic Sino-Japanese relations show no sign of sustained improvement.[31]

GROWING CLARITY AND ITS IMPACT

As the United States recovered from the events of 1995–96 a shift toward clarity appeared broadly popular. Republican presidential candidate Robert Dole denounced ambiguity during the fall 1996 campaign, proclaiming that "our policy should be unmistakably resolute. If force is used against Taiwan, America will respond."[32] From Taipei, chairman of the Foreign Relations Committee of the Legislative Yuan, Parris Chang, denounced U.S. policy, evoking a parallel to developments in Iraq. Saddam Hussein, he observed, had construed U.S. Ambassador April "Glaspie's equivocal statements to mean that the United States would not intervene in Iraq's militaristic actions. Such 'strategic ambiguity' indirectly led Iraq to advance into Kuwait."[33] But, members of the administration, seeing increased clarity as an idea whose time had come, considered repairing the damage in U.S.-China relations as more pressing than affirmation of Taiwan's interests. Anthony Lake, the president's national security adviser, had by then taken the China portfolio away from the Department of State, initiating a new dialogue with Beijing. But Lake lacked active support from a habitually distracted president, so success in diminishing the threat level did not lead to problem solving.[34]

As it turned out, efforts to keep the momentum going, rather than enhancing clarity reduced it. Seeking a better way to promote Sino-American relations than the much abused concept of engagement, the administration adapted the Chinese construct of "strategic partnership," hedging the idea by suggesting that this was a condition to be achieved in the twenty-first century. Almost immediately, and unsurprisingly, the nuance disappeared. The label not only dismayed genuine strategic partners such as South Korea and Japan, it also sent an erroneous message to Beijing regarding its significance to Washington and raised false expectations about accommodating China's demands on Taiwan. As Lake would later observe, "it create[d] illusions, and disillusion is very dangerous."[35]

In fact, pursuit of clarity made Washington appear willing to redefine its relations with Taiwan. The initial indication had come as the first missile exercises ended and the U.S. government sought to prevent escalation. President Clinton wrote confidentially to Jiang Zemin with an early version of the so-called Three Nos, hoping that setting out U.S. views would allay Beijing's concerns. In this letter delivered by Secretary of State Warren Christopher to Foreign Minister Qian Qichen, the president reportedly used language which departed from the careful constructs of the past, talking about respecting China's One China policy, being "against" independence and adding an assurance that the United States "does not support Taiwan's admission to the United Nations." Furthermore, he omitted the crucial injunction that any settlement in the Strait must be reached peacefully.[36]

After Clinton's first secret recital of the Three Nos, they were redrafted and reiterated several times. The widely disseminated version adhered closer to existing policy as it dropped the word "against," but it also broadened the third No to say Washington would not endorse Taiwan's entry into any international organization for which statehood would be a requirement. These Three Nos were then affirmed orally in conjunction with Jiang Zemin's visit to the United States in 1997, repeated by Secretary of State Madeleine Albright in China in May 1998 and again that spring by Deputy Assistant Secretary of State Susan Shirk to Congress. The exercise in clarity gained support from influential scholars and retired officials devoted to protecting the relationship with China. Fearing that ambiguity encouraged irresponsible elements in Taiwan, particularly the independence-minded Democratic Progressive Party, these individuals called for the administration openly to warn Taiwan against provocative acts and privately to force Taipei to be more cautious.[37]

In essence, Clinton did just that when he restated the Three Nos on Chinese soil in July 1998. Although the administration had not acceded to a written fourth communiqué pushed by Beijing and anathema to Taipei, the tilt toward China seemed significant to many in Taiwan, China, and the United States. Clinton jettisoned the carefully crafted two-decade-old policy of imprecision designed to preserve the right of Taiwan's people to self-determination and neglected to underline Beijing's responsibility for peace. As scholar and China policy critic Andrew Nathan observed,

What was novel . . . was the manner and context of their articulation—on Chinese soil, clustered together as a package of negatives directed at

Taiwan, framed as a reassurance to China, devoid of the other elements of U.S. policy that were favorable to Taiwan, and given canonical status by public presidential utterance. It was, therefore, correct for politicians on both sides of the Taiwan Strait to interpret the statement as an intentional tilt toward Beijing.[38]

The repercussions exceeded whatever benefits the administration believed illuminating its views had gained.

In Taiwan, after nursing resentment for a year, Lee Teng-hui tried his own hand at clarity on July 9, 2000 during an interview with a German journalist, asserting that relations between China and Taiwan ought to be conducted on a "special state-to-state" basis. Lee's motives surely were mixed. He sought to overcome Taiwan's diplomatic isolation, as Beijing wooed the few remaining states that maintained diplomatic relations with Taipei and blocked Taiwan's accession to international organizations. With resumption of cross-Strait talks possible, he wanted equality at the conference table or, perhaps, preferred simply to undermine them. Lee probably also saw an opportunity to entrench his political ideals as he stepped down from 12 years in office. But, clearly, he and his advisors felt it crucial to put Washington on notice that it had gone too far in placating Beijing.[39]

Taiwan analysts had attacked the Three Nos as a betrayal of a policy that had served relations with the United States well for 50 years. Washington, they believed, had replaced "peaceful resolution" of the cross-Strait issue with "peaceful reunification" as its objective, discarding support for freedom of choice and respect for Taiwan's democratization. The United States had reneged on previous pledges not to mediate by sending thinly disguised emissaries such as former defense secretary William Perry and former national security adviser Brent Scowcroft to urge negotiation. But most tellingly, according to Philip Yang of National Taiwan University, Washington "changed its policy from acknowledging Beijing's position of one China . . . to accepting its claim."[40]

In China, at the same time, satisfaction with the Three Nos did not last long. Early in 2000, Clinton rectified one aspect of administration policy toward Taiwan. Urged by Richard Bush, his AIT Washington director, to respond to changing conditions on the island, Clinton declared that Taiwan's future status must be determined with the "assent" of the people. By underlining the significance of democracy in Taiwan, Clinton stepped back from ground surrendered in the Three Nos, and went further than a simple reaffirmation of the U.S. commitment to peace. For Beijing it erected a high and unwelcome barrier to recovery of the island.[41]

At home, the Congress did not like the Three Nos. It made a point of voting almost unanimous support to Taiwan, believing that the pronouncement by the president had weakened Taipei's negotiating hand vis-à-vis Beijing. More vigorous proponents lined up behind the Taiwan Security Enhancement Act (TSEA) proffered by Senators Jesse Helms (R-NC) and Robert Torricelli (D-NJ) in March 1999, which called for regular military consultations between Taipei and Washington and annual reports to Congress on Taiwan's arms requests. Torricelli lauded the provisions that established direct communications between the U.S. Pacific Command and Taiwan's military forces. Not only would this allow for cooperation in the event of an actual clash but, he told his congressional colleagues, it could guard against "a military confrontation by mistake or misinformation. . . . If we pass this legislation, it makes it less likely that we will become engaged in any future conflict because there will be no ambiguity."[42] Opponents of the TSEA succeeded in preventing its enactment and one, Representative Tom Lantos (D-CA), observed, "Ambiguity is as old as diplomacy itself. To eliminate ambiguity is not a virtue." Indeed he chided his colleagues, "It creates rigidities that the fluid nature of this issue doesn't call for."[43]

The congressional focus on the military arena, although logical, was also ironic since in this area the Clinton administration acknowledged a need for action and proposed doing more than some in the Congress favored. Administration officials who had managed the confrontation in the Strait in 1996 saw the absence of regular communication between the military establishments of the United States and China and the U.S. and Taiwan as making the crisis more unpredictable and dangerous. As Kurt Campbell, who had served as deputy assistant secretary of defense at the time, recalled "Pentagon planners and intelligence specialists did not know how Taiwan would respond to the PRC's provocative missile tests across the strait. This blind spot in a tense situation was a wake-up call to the United States, leading to a substantial increase in military contact with Taiwan during the Clinton years."[44] Washington activated broader contacts with the Taiwan military than had existed since the 1970s, including a software initiative that involved assistance with planning, logistics, and training. At the same time, the Pentagon undertook vigorous efforts to demonstrate to the Chinese People's Liberation Army the vast superiority of U.S. capabilities. But those fearful of the China threat did not necessarily welcome the intensified contacts designed to teach such lessons. Some argued that even though the PLA had witnessed the swift U.S. victory in the 1991 Persian Gulf War it persisted in military modernization programs aimed at a Taiwan contingency.

George W. Bush seized upon the need to bring greater clarity into U.S. policy toward Taiwan and China as a campaign theme and an early first term priority. The conception of China as a strategic competitor and Taiwan as a neglected democracy fueled this push. Clarity here aimed not only to eliminate confusion and vagueness, but also to help Taipei.

Bush moved in this direction at the behest of prominent members of the administration's foreign policy team. In August 1999, Richard L. Armitage, subsequently deputy secretary of state, Paul Wolfowitz, who would become deputy secretary of defense and I. Lewis ("Scooter") Libby, the presumptive national security adviser to Vice President Dick Cheney, signed an open letter sponsored by the Heritage Foundation and The Project for the New American Century that called for an end to strategic ambiguity. Asserting that Clinton had undercut the restraining effects of ambiguity, the letter held that "it has therefore become essential that the United States make every effort to deter any form of Chinese intimidation of [Taiwan] and declare unambiguously that it will come to Taiwan's defense in the event of an attack or a blockade."[45] Wolfowitz expanded upon the theme in a controversial article in *The National Interest* in the spring of 2000. Explaining his compromise on the problem he asserted, "While ambiguity on the definition of 'One China' is desirable and on the subject of arms sales is probably necessary, there are two areas involving American intentions where ambiguity serves no purpose. The first concerns the U.S. attitude toward the use of force to resolve the Taiwan issue, the second our attitude toward Taiwan independence."[46] Bush himself talked about using U.S. military forces against China if it attacked Taiwan when interviewed in the *Washington Times* in July 1999. Later at a Boeing plant in Seattle, in one of several such observations, he declared that the Clinton administration had "been inconsistent on Taiwan. I will be clear."[47]

And, of course, Bush proved to be willing to send some strong messages about Taiwan during the first months of his presidency. He approved an extremely large arms sales package which included weapons systems that had long been denied to Taipei as being offensive in nature and, therefore, too provocative. He agreed to visits of high-level Taiwan officials to the United States, including an elaborate transit stop by President Chen Shui-bian in New York City and Houston. But most notably, he sought to dispel uncertainty regarding Washington's reaction to a use of force in the Taiwan Strait by declaring on national TV that he saw the United States as having a clear obligation to defend Taiwan "and the Chinese must understand that." Moreover, he told the ABC interviewer on *Good Morning America*, we would be willing "to do whatever it took to help Taiwan defend herself."[48] Immediate efforts to weaken his words in other news interviews the same day and by commentators who insisted that the president had muffed his lines actually highlighted the startling departure of his original statement.

In fact, although the most striking evidence of a commitment to clarity came in the first months of the administration, it did not disappear. Vice President Dick Cheney signaled this reality when he refused to back away from the president's words. In his own televised remarks he maintained that "people talk about diplomatic ambiguity, and of course, there has been some ambiguity there over the years, But in this particular case, especially given what appears to be a somewhat more threatening posture of the mainland toward Taiwan over the last few months, ambiguity may be exactly the wrong thing to do."[49] In the 2002 Nuclear Posture Review, the Defense Department envisioned "a military confrontation over the status of Taiwan" as an immediate contingency for which the administration had to develop new categories of "nuclear strike capabilities."[50] Again, in the National Security Strategy, the White House pointed to "areas in which we have profound disagreements" with China among which it cited "our commitment to the self-defense of Taiwan under the Taiwan Relations Act."[51] Moreover, the Bush administration welcomed Taiwan's Defense Minister to a conference in Florida. Wolfowitz and Jim Kelly, assistant secretary of state for East Asia, met him there and confirmed continued adherence to Reagan's six assurances, the TRA, and Bush's promise to do whatever it takes to help defend Taiwan. Bush on his own trip to China spoke of the TRA rather than the Three Nos.[52]

The Bush administration, then, began with bold gestures to redefine U.S. policy toward Taiwan. This entailed granting greater dignity to Taipei. It would do this by liberalizing rules for government to government interaction and providing more visible assistance to its military establishment. But two factors arose along the way that modified policy and slowly obscured the clarity to which the administration had aspired: the war on terrorism and Taiwan domestic politics.

The attacks of September 11, 2001 on New York and Washington distracted the White House from its earlier concerns, such as the China threat and rebalancing relations in the Pacific, and elevated Beijing's significance in the subsequent war on terrorism. Hostility ebbed in the wake of Chinese assistance in gathering intelligence, tracing money, influencing Pakistan to cooperate on the Afghan war, and providing support in the UN.

The government in Taipei either did not notice or did not care that its friend in the United States had become increasingly preoccupied and opposed to instability and uncertainty. Thus, Chen Shui-bian, driven by his own priorities, political calendar, and problems with China, surprised the Bush administration with policy initiatives that the United States labeled provocative. Angered almost as much by lack of consultation as by the substance, Washington rebuffed Chen's August 3, 2002 declaration that there was one country on each side of the Strait (*yibian yiguo*) and later proposals to hold a defensive referendum and alter the ROC constitution. It was further dismayed by Chen's campaign driven assertion that "Taiwan is not a province of one country nor it is a state of another," telling his supporters and the public at large that he would not allow them to be bullied by Beijing or Washington.

Suddenly, the Bush administration found itself scrambling to redress a different version of ambiguity and bring renewed clarity to triangular U.S.-Taiwan-China relations. Fears that mixed messages from the administration, and overly sanguine interpretations of favorable gestures, had encouraged rash behavior in Taipei led Washington to try to rein in DPP exuberance. Washington sought initially to communicate its distress quietly, including through the secret dispatch of NSC Senior Asia Director James Moriarity to Taiwan, all to no avail. Therefore, resorting to what should have been a high degree of clarity about the U.S. position, the president told the press, as he stood beside Chinese premier Wen Jiabao in the Oval Office on December 9, 2003, that "the comments and actions made by the leader of Taiwan indicate that he may be willing to make decisions unilaterally to change the status quo, which we oppose." Further, the president not only failed to correct Wen's statement that Bush had said he opposed Taiwan independence, but actually nodded in agreement.[53]

Chen Shui-bian, however, ignored George Bush's warnings and everyone else's advice. He ran a powerful campaign despite a relatively weak record in office, and, although his margin of victory was razor thin at 0.228 percent, he managed to increase the vote for the DPP from 39 to 50.1 percent in just four years. Polling data strongly suggested that without a botched assassination attempt the night before balloting, he probably would have lost. Having survived near death experiences physically and electorally, Chen appeared to see his renewed presidency and his personal agenda in messianic terms. Although the implications for U.S.-Taiwan and cross-Strait relations could not be predicted with certainty, compromise and accommodation would seem increasingly difficult between Taipei and Beijing. In any case, pressure from both sides for the United States to play a larger role, which had begun before the election, only grew after the balloting.

One further point ought to be noted about the new reality in the Strait. When Bush berated Chen Shui-bian for being "willing to make decisions unilaterally to change the status quo," his complaint was already out of date. Rather than having been static, the status quo has been profoundly altered in recent years so that, as Washington analyst Bonnie Glaser notes, China, Taiwan and the United States define it differently.

Beijing insists that Taiwan is a part of China. The legitimacy of its regime is intertwined with preventing Taiwan from gaining juridical stature as a sovereign country. Taipei views itself as an independent, sovereign nation [sic] and is seeking to make that status irreversible, unless the people on the island vote otherwise in a referendum. The U.S. has a "one China" policy and insists that differences between the two sides of the Strait be worked out peacefully, lest the U.S. be compelled to become involved.[54]

Thus, what each seeks to preserve is distinct and, she maintains, since the status quo is "in dispute and is unstable . . . the danger of military conflict is present and may be increasing."

IS STRATEGIC CLARITY A BETTER POLICY?

Defining clear conditions under which Washington would intercede between China and Taiwan has an appealing simplicity and suggests that it is possible to prevent disaster by warning potential combatants that there are lines which may not be crossed. Nevertheless, some 50 years after strategic ambiguity originated as a policy, it remains safer and smarter, as well as more realistic, than attempts at reaching clarity for many reasons:

1. *All contingencies cannot be predicted.* By definition unforeseen events defy comprehensive planning and unfailing defense. Therefore, drawing lines creates a false sense of security. For 50 years, conditions in the Taiwan Strait have been rife with confusion and deception as well as prone to misunderstanding and mistakes. As seductive as it is to imagine that a new policy of strategic clarity will eliminate such risk, it is also unrealistic.

Furthermore, to judge contingencies there must be agreement on what is happening. For instance, it has been assumed that if Taipei provoked a Chinese attack by declaring independence, it would be on its own in defending itself. But strategic clarity does not say who defines what constitutes provocation or independence. Surely at one time many Americans would have believed election of a pro-independence president, as happened in March 2000, would have qualified. How dangerous are symbolic acts such as putting the name Taiwan on passports? In a White Paper released in February 2000, Beijing specifically addressed this issue when it took account of the fact that Taipei probably would not proclaim itself an independent state. Rather, it remarked, should "a grave turn of events occur . . . leading to the separation of Taiwan from China in any name . . . then the Chinese government will . . . be forced to adopt all drastic measures possible, including the use of force, to safeguard China's sovereignty and territorial integrity."[55]

Obviously not just the nature but the timing of events could have enormous importance. If the U.S. government were to be preoccupied with a crisis elsewhere in the world, the fact that lines had been drawn on the China/Taiwan front might not be of sufficient consequence to warrant the government's attention. Clarity about even a few fixed contingencies, for instance, might prove unavailing during a major showdown in the war on terrorism.

2. *By attempting to define what the United States will do under specific circumstances, policymakers will not eliminate probing of the American position by both sides but, more likely, exacerbate it.* Imaginative, self-confident officials or weak and desperate ones have incentives to try to find gaps in U.S. defenses or influence the United States to alter stated positions. Testing will occur in Washington and Asia simultaneously. On the one hand, each party will spend even more money than it already does seeking to shape American views by buying lobbyists or shaping elections.[56]

On the other hand, exploration of the limits of U.S. tolerance will also occur at sea and in the air where such pressure becomes far more dangerous. Lost in the reporting of the EP-3 confrontation of 2001 was the fact that reconnaissance along the China coast occurs largely to gather information on PLA capabilities and operations in case of a conflict over Taiwan. At the same time, the assignment of the Chinese pilot whose plane crashed was to challenge American interference with Chinese sovereignty and to demonstrate that the Chinese could take action against the unwanted U.S. presence should it elect to do so. Moreover, current PLA modernization takes as one of its objectives amassing sufficient capabilities to deter or delay U.S. forces from intervening in a cross-Strait conflict.[57]

3. *American domestic politics as much as circumstances in the Taiwan Strait will determine Washington's reaction to developments between China and Taiwan.* Regardless of what a policy of strategic clarity has said ahead of time, the play of political forces within the electorate and in the halls of Congress will be of equal or greater significance. The United States may assert in advance that it will not support provocative behavior by Taiwan, but how it evaluates Taiwan's behavior and the Chinese response would be different if: the United States and the PRC were in the midst of a human rights crisis akin to Tiananmen, or a military standoff such as the missile firings of 2000, or enjoying a significant reduction of the U.S. trade deficit with China.

Positions on China and Taiwan have become political tests whether of morality, on human rights and democracy, or acuity, on security issues, even among groups and individuals who know little about the situation in the Taiwan Strait. Until the events of September 11, 2001 intervened, the rise of China and the China threat had become a cause for alarm among many analysts, officials, and pundits. The victimization of Taiwan, in turn, aroused consternation among neoconservatives. They so politicized the very definition of strategic ambiguity that it became difficult to recognize. Thus, as Robert Kagan, a contributing editor to *The Weekly Standard* represented the policy, its history, purpose, and impact took on a new coloration: "after 1979 it was the Taiwanese who needed to be made insecure. Hence the birth of America's 'strategic ambiguity' with its unmistakable message to Taiwan's leaders: Act up, provoke the Chinese, refuse to play ball, and the United States just might let you fry."[58]

4) *The prior commitments enjoined by strategic clarity unnecessarily limit the government's options.* The more open U.S. officials seek to be about their policies, the more they relinquish the flexibility that strategic ambiguity originally sought to bring to the complex problem of cross-Strait relations. In the process, they also risk ceding the initiative to China and/or Taiwan to the detriment of both the U.S. national interest and an administration's political welfare. In 1993, the Clinton White House demonstrated the ill effects when it linked most-favored-nation trade treatment to the improvement of human rights behavior in China. Linkage surrendered the upper hand to Beijing, which humiliated the Clinton administration, forcing it to back down. This weakened the administration, demonstrating to China that being tough with Washington could yield significant benefits.[59] Clarity on military redlines might yield the same dismal result.

Furthermore, China's decisions may have nothing to do with Washington's clarifications, but result from its internal dynamics and its vision of the world. Thus, the PLA may have concluded the United States would intercede in the Strait neither from Clinton's 1996 deployments nor Bush's "whatever it takes" remarks, but earlier from the war in Kosovo. According to some analysts, Washington's intercession where it had so little at stake reinforced the view that intervention on behalf of Taiwan could not be forestalled. Former vice chairman of the Central Military Commission Zhang Wannian reportedly warned his PLA compatriots, sometime in 2000, that the future involved "Three Things That Cannot Be Avoided," meaning Taiwan's grab for independence, China's use of force, and U.S. interference. Reducing flexibility to warn the Chinese of something they already take for granted would appear unproductive.[60]

5. *Clarity carries with it the tendency to broaden U.S. responsibilities.* Once Washington lays down "rules of the road," it acquires an inherent obligation either to enforce the rules or be perceived as weak and unreliable for

allowing them to be violated. America's credibility, not just with China and Taiwan, but also among its allies and friends in the region, takes on a new vulnerability under less than ideal conditions. Ironically, in such circumstances, the amplification of Washington's exposure may occur with countries otherwise uninterested in the cross-Strait issue.

This obvious entanglement is also intrinsic to mediation and a key reason why the United States learned to avoid assuming that responsibility. In the ill-fated Marshall Mission of the 1940s, for instance, war hero and soon-to-be secretary of state George Marshall found that he bore obligations but, in spite of Washington's great power, he lacked the ability to enforce agreements. In general, Taipei and Beijing have each welcomed Washington's mediation only so long as each believed the United States would lean in its direction and press the other side to comply; neither wanting impartiality. Taking any kind of initiative, moreover, requires trust, but Washington did not have the full confidence of either China or Taiwan on this issue—even early in 2003—a time of unprecedentedly good relations with both.

6. *Clarity is not needed and has the potential of forcing unwelcome responses.* A central charge made against the existing policy of strategic ambiguity is that in the wake of Clinton's aircraft carrier deployment to the vicinity of Taiwan both Beijing and Taipei have discounted ambiguity and believe the United States will intervene in the event of a military clash. Subsequent military cooperation between Washington and Taipei has reinforced that image. If that is so, then the United States already enjoys the deterrent benefits of a change in policy.

To do more, particularly to make an oral declaration of a policy change, would just increase the negative impact on leaders who have already been provoked and embarrassed. Lee Teng-hui took exception to Clinton's policy clarifications in the 3 Nos and turned to his state-to-state formula. Chinese officials similarly clarified their views, rendering an old, rarely articulated threat into firm policy in their February 2000 Taiwan White Paper as the so-called "third if." Beijing insisted that should Taipei postpone negotiating unification for too long their behavior would trigger an attack. Surely, under such circumstances, opportunities for individuals in the PRC otherwise inclined toward cooperation with Washington are diminished.

7. *Strategic clarity would require amendment of the Taiwan Relations Act (TRA).* Congress insisted on the provision in the TRA that it must be consulted if circumstances arose that threaten the security, economy, or society of Taiwan and only then, after taking U.S. interests into account, would the U.S. government determine what to do.[61] This language explicitly barred the president from acting alone and, therefore, rendered real strategic clarity impossible. It is possible to argue that Carter and his successors

ignored their obligations to work with Congress under the TRA and that the members often shirked their oversight responsibilities. Nevertheless, sloppy implementation is not the same as circumventing the TRA by declared policy. However, any effort to revise, amend, or supplement the TRA risks opening the floodgates to measures that could destabilize both U.S.-China and U.S.-Taiwan relations. In other words, once the process begins there may be no way to constrain it.

8. *If strategic ambiguity is abandoned a key question is what precisely there is to be clear about and how to get a consensus on that.* Advocates of clarity in almost all cases make the argument that it is in the U.S. national interest, but they do not agree on precisely how to define the American stake in the dilemma. Most particularly they do not concur in the relative value of dealing with China and Taiwan given the huge disparity of size and power the two wield and the conflict between principles of sovereignty and democracy their struggle encapsulates.

Should clarity be about what the United States sees as intolerable behavior by both Beijing and Taipei so that "redlines" regarding unacceptable conduct are drawn on a balanced basis? The answer to that would seem to be a simple yes, but can clarity be evenhanded or does it tend to lean to one side? For some, clarity must be about preserving peace until unification can be accomplished.[62] To others, clarity would set out an absolute commitment to protect Taiwan under all circumstances and for however long is necessary. To a few, such a guarantee would extend not just to, but beyond, independence. Proposals to translate the six assurances into law to prevent future presidents from reneging on Reagan's pledges would be a form of clarity, but not one universally applauded.[63]

Strategic ambiguity, moreover, has been about process, not outcome. In the early days, this did not make it a neutral stance since the weight of political influence and military might rested entirely on the side of the Republic of China. Since the 1970s and normalization, Washington has insisted it would be impartial about results so long as the means remained peaceful. However, in the effort to be clearer about process, the specification of which actions are acceptable and which are not, it becomes more difficult to be vague about what the United States wants to see in the future.[64]

9. *Therefore, and finally, strategic clarity compromises the One China policy as interpreted by the United States.* Washington acknowledged the position of China and Taiwan that a single China existed and that Taiwan was a part of it when normalization began, but did not formally accept the idea. Over time the interpretation of One China changed and those shifting interpretations were disputed between Taipei and Beijing. The United States

avoided adherence to any of the varying formulas, including Beijing's equation of One China with the PRC, Deng Xiaoping's "one country, two systems," the fleeting 1992 consensus between China and Taiwan of "one China, with respective interpretations," Lee Teng-hui's "two-states theory" or Chen Shui-bian's "one country on either side."[65] At no point did the United States officially state that it saw One China as the only option for solving the Straits problem.

In 1950, Dean Acheson argued against deflecting the wrath of thwarted Chinese nationalists from the rapacious Soviet Union, which was then holding Chinese territory in Manchuria and Mongolia, to the United States with an ill-started intervention to save a disreputable, incompetent, and authoritarian Chiang Kai-shek in Taiwan. Fifty years later, Taiwan is a different place politically, economically, and socially and Washington is more involved than Acheson could have imagined. In the interim, strategic ambiguity allowed the United States to remain vague about if, when and how it might protect Taiwan, avoiding, so American officials said, intervention in China's internal affairs.

More clarity, however, highlights the fact that Washington is caught in a paradox where two of its key values—self-determination and national sovereignty—do not mesh. Strategic clarity seeks to alert both Beijing and Taipei to actions beyond which they may not go without suffering consequences. Most basically, it is about how to preserve peace. If it is sufficient to say no force to one and no provocation to the other, then existing policy is enough. Strategic ambiguity has been about peaceful resolution. As policymakers push to define what they would do under specific circumstances, they edge ever closer not just to abandoning ambiguity, but also to taking sides in the standoff in the Strait.

Strategic clarity, then, is not the solution to U.S. policy problems in the Taiwan Strait. Even though it appears to be the direction in which many analysts currently wish to travel, it fails to remedy existing problems and could make them worse.[66] Where Washington has been the most blunt to date, on its insistence upon peace and refusal to support independence, suspicions have not been allayed. Many in Beijing believe, and many in Taipei hope, that the United States secretly favors separation of Taiwan from the PRC and nothing Americans have said or done has fully disabused them of the notion. Moreover, Beijing continues to assemble missiles along the Fujian coast opposite Taiwan, seeking to intimidate Taiwan but, if all else fails, preparing for an attack.

So how can a catastrophe be avoided? The harsh reality is that the Taiwan dilemma will not be resolved any time soon. Short of sinking the island or dragging it out to sea, geography condemns the people in Taiwan to continuing struggle. When the stalemate is broken, the answer must come from Beijing and Taipei, not from Washington. Even democracy in China may not yield any greater willingness in Taiwan to unify or in China to let Taiwan go.

This reality subjects the United States to danger and leads some analysts to argue that Washington must take a larger role in finding a solution. Certainly there is room for the U.S. to encourage dialogue across the Strait and to welcome constructive policies. Americans must not, however, be lured into steps that betray their principles or undermine policies that have protected peace and security for more than 50 years. China's leaders at the dawn of the new century are using economic integration and patience rather than military coercion and deadlines to try to facilitate unification. It could be argued that they have chosen this alternative because they believe that time is on their side. It may also be that in the face of strategic ambiguity, a peaceful policy simply seems the wisest course.

Notes

CHAPTER 1. DANGEROUS STRAIT: AN INTRODUCTION

1. Phillips explores some of these issues at greater depth in his book *Between Assimilation and Independence* (Stanford: Stanford University Press, 2003).
2. For an English transcript of the speech, see the BBC World Edition, August 5, 2002. Available at: http://news.bbc.co.uk/2/hi/asia-pacific/2172970.stm (accessed September 25, 2003).
3. Lee Teng-hui, " 'Rectifying' Taiwan's Name," *Far Eastern Economic Review*, October 16, 2003, (accessed May 11, 2004).
4. Reform of DOD was initiated by General David C. Jones, chairman of the Joint Chiefs of Staff (JCS) in 1982 when he asked the House Armed Services Committee to increase the authority of the JCS at the expense of the chiefs of the individual services and to institutionalize "jointness" within the Pentagon. Finkelstein spoke at a State Department workshop "Tempting Fate," August 2003, Washington, DC.

CHAPTER 2. THE UNFINISHED BUSINESS OF TAIWAN'S DEMOCRATIZATION

1. "Who Will Take the Blame for Taiwan's Economic Vacillation?" *Economic Daily News*, December 23, 2002. Translated by Earl Weiman, China Economic News Service. Available at:
http://teacher.cyivs.cy.edu.tw/~hchung/ecovacillate.htm
(accessed September 24, 2003).

2. American Chamber of Commerce in Taipei, *Taiwan White Paper*, 8. Published in *Topics: The Magazine of International Business in Taiwan* 31, no. 4 (May 2001).

3. For an extended discussion of the background and implications of the power plant debate, see Tony Allison, " 'Taiwan'" more than just a nuclear controversy," *Asia Times Online*, November 1, 2000. Available at
http://www.atimes.com/reports/BK01Ai01.html
(accessed November 13, 2003).
Also, Jonathan Dushoff, "Taiwan's Power Struggle," *Multinational Monitor*, 22, no.3 (March 2001).

4. Allen Cheng, "No More Cheers," *Asiaweek.com*, March 2, 2001. Available at:
http://www.asiaweek.com/asiaweek/magazine/nations/0,8782,100235,00.html
(accessed September 25, 2003).

5. President Chen Shui-bian's inauguration speech, Official Translation provided by the Office of the President. Available at:
http://th.gio.gov.tw/pi2000/
(accessed November 13, 2003).

6. See the New Year's Eve address of December 31, 2001. Available at:
http://www.gio.gov.tw/taiwan-website/4-oa/chen/press891231.htm
(accessed September 25, 2003).

7. Taiwanese leaders hold the view that the true meaning of Beijing's "One China Principle" is the definition offered in international forums, that there is but one China, Taiwan is part of it, and it is the People's Republic of China. Chen has said that the issue of One China must be understood as a topic to be discussed; he will not accept "One China" as a predetermined principle or precondition.

8. For an English transcript of the speech, see the BBC World Edition, August 5, 2002. Available at:
http://news.bbc.co.uk/2/hi/asia-pacific/2172970.stm
(accessed September 25, 2003).

9. Francois Godement, "Chen Shui-bian: Between a ROC and a Hard Place," CSIS Pacific Forum Pacnet Newsletter, August 16, 2002. Available at:
http://www.csis.org/pacfor/pac0231D.htm
(accessed September 25, 2003).
"Whatever it takes" refers to President Bush's statement on April 25, 2001 in an interview with ABC news that the US would do "whatever it takes" to ensure Taiwan's defense.

10. Editorial, "Cross-Strait Ties Key to Election Win," *Taipei Times*, August 15, 2003. Available at:
http://www.taipeitimes.com/News/edit/archives/2003/08/15/2003063828
(accessed November 13, 2003).

11. For more on the referendum debate, see Holmes Liao, "Referendum: Taiwan's Provocation?" *China Brief* (July 1, 2003). Available at:
http://russia.jamestown.org/pubs/view/cwe_003_013_003.htm
(accessed November 13, 2003).

Also David Lai, "A Referendum on Taiwan's Future: No Easy Exit," *Issues and Insights* 3 (2003), 6. Available at:
http://www.csis.org/pacfor/issues/v03n06_lai.htm
(accessed November 13, 2003).
For a PRC statement linking the referendum issue to independence efforts see the PRC government statement "Chinese Mainland Opposes Taiwan's Separatism, Referendum" dated October 29, 2003. Available at:
http://www.chinaembassy-org.be/eng/58647.html
(accessed November 13, 2003).

12. The referendum questions were:

- Should mainland China refuse to withdraw the missiles it has targeted at Taiwan and to openly renounce the use of force against us, would you agree that the government should acquire more advanced anti-missile weapons to strengthen Taiwan's self-defence capabilities?
- Would you agree that our government should engage in negotiation with mainland China on the establishment of a 'peace and stability' framework for cross-strait interactions in order to build consensus and for the welfare of the peoples on both sides?

13. Juan Linz and Alfred Stepan, "Toward Consolidated Democracies," in Larry Diamond, ed., *Consolidating the Third Wave Democracies: Themes and Perspectives* (Baltimore: Johns Hopkins University Press, 1997), 15 (emphasis in original).

14. Larry Diamond. *Developing Democracy: Toward Consolidation* (Baltimore: Johns Hopkins University Press, 1999), 66.

15. Ibid., 75.

16. Ibid., 75.

17. Bi-khim Hsiao, speech to the Brookings Institution, Center for Northeast Asian Policy Studies, June 25,2003. Transcript available at:
http://www.brookings.edu/dybdocroot/fp/cnaps/20030625.pdf
(accessed July 20, 2003).

18. Diamond, *Developing Democracy*, 75.

19. Ibid., 75.

20. "Editorial: Throwing away a good idea," *Taipei Times*, October 6, 2003. Available at:
http://www.taipeitimes.com/News/edit/archives/2003/10/06/2003070632
(accessed October 9, 2003).

21. Joseph Jau-hsieh Wu, "New constitution for a new nation," *Taipei Times*, October 1, 2003. Available at:
http://www.taipeitimes.com/News/edit/archives/20003/10/01/2003069997
(accessed October 9, 2003).

22. Kuo Cheng-tian, "Taiwan's Distorted Democracy in Comparative Perspective," in Wei-Chin Lee (ed.) *Taiwan in Perspective* (Leiden: Brill, 2000), 93.

23. A number of scholars have written on this subject. See, for example, John Fuh-

sheng Hsieh, "The 2000 Presidential Election and Its Implications for Taiwan's Domestic Politics." *Issues & Studies* 37, no. 1 (2001): 1–19.

24. Wu Yu-shan predicted that the vote of no confidence would be a useless instrument, given its high cost and low probability of success. See Wu Yu-Shan, "The ROC's Semi-Presidentialism at Work: Unstable Compromise, Not Cohabitation." *Issues & Studies* 36, no. 5 (2000): 1–40.

25. The following offices are subject to regular, competitive elections: president, Legislative Yuan, county executives, city mayors, county and city councils, town and township executives, town and township councils, village and neighborhood heads. If it is convened, an election must be held for members of the National Assembly.

26. For a discussion of the SNTV electoral system and its effects on voting behavior in Japan, see Thomas Rochon, "Electoral Systems and the Basis of the Vote," in John C. Campbell (ed). *Parties, Candidates, and Voters in Japan: Six Quantitative Studies* (Ann Arbor: University of Michigan Press, 1981), *passim*.

27. Yang Tai-shuenn, "*Woguo xuanju zhidu de tese*" ("The Peculiarities of our Electoral System"), *Zhongguo Xianzheng* 24 (1989): 12; Central Election Commission. *Xuanmin de toupiao xingwei* (*The Voting Behavior of the Electorate*) (Taipei: Central Election Commission. 1987): 156; Lin Jih-wen. *Consequences of the Single Nontransferable Voting Rule: Comparing the Japan and Taiwan Experiences* (PhD dissertation, University of California Los Angeles, 1996), *passim*.

28. According to the Vice President Annette Lu and other officials from the presidential office, Paal did not say the United States opposed referendum, but reminded Chen of the PRC's objections, and conveyed U.S. officials' concern that the campaign for referendum could exacerbate cross-Strait tensions.

29. Diamond, *Developing Democracy*, 75.

30. Sarah Birch, "Electoral Systems, Campaign Strategies, and Vote Choice in the Ukrainian Parliamentary and Presidential Elections of 1994." *Political Studies* 46, no. 1 (March 1998): 104.

31. For an interesting discussion of the Legislative Yuan's transformation, see Liao Da-Chi, "How Does a Rubber Stamp Become a Roaring Lion? The Case Study of the Transformation of the Taiwanese Legislative Yuan's Role during the Process of Democratization (1950–2000)" Paper presented at the annual meeting of the American Political Science Association in Philadelphia, August 27, 2003. Available at
http://archive.allacademic.com/publication/docs/apsa_proceeding/2003–08–26/1663/apsa_proceeding_1663.PDF
(accessed October 3, 2003).

32. Chiu Hei-yuan, "The Deterioration of the Legislature," *Taipei Times*, June 17, 2003. Available at:
http://www.taipeitimes.com/News/edit/archives/2003/06/17/2003055614
(accessed November 13, 2003).

33. Data from 2002 on public views of the political system is available in Vincent Wang and Samuel Ku, "Learning Democracy: Citizen Attitudes Toward Elec-

toral Democracy in Taiwan." Paper presented at the annual meeting of the American Political Science Association Philadelphia, August 31, 2003. Available at:
http://archive.allacademic.com/publication/docs/apsa_proceed-ing/2003–08–31/2786/apsa_proceeding_2786.PDF
(accessed October 3, 2003).

34. Shelley Rigger. *Politics in Taiwan: Voting for Democracy.* (London: Routledge, 1999), 41–42.

35. This preference for a two-vote system is consistent with Birch's predictions in the *Political Studies* article quoted above.

36. "Parliamentary Reform, *ETaiwanNews,* December 5, 2001. Available at:
http://etaiwannews.com/Editorial/2001/12/05/1007514647.htm
(accessed October 6, 2003).

37. Ku Chung-hwa, "Legislative Reform is in the Nation's Interest." *Taipei Times,* March 5, 2003 available at:
http://www.taipeitimes.com/News/edit?pubdate = 2003/03/05
(accessed October 6, 2003).

38. Fiona Lu, "Referendum regarded as boost to legislative reform," *Taipei Times,* July 21, 2003. Available at:
http://www.taipeitimes.com/News/taiwan/archives/2003/07/21/2003060296
(accessed October 6, 2003).

39. Fiona Lu, "DPP wants referendum on assembly," *Taipei Times,* July 17, 2003. Available at:
http://www.taipeitimes.com/News/front/archives/2003/07/17/2003059715
(accessed October 7, 2003).

40. Shelley Rigger. *From Opposition to Power: Taiwan's Democratic Progressive Party.* (Boulder: Lynne Rienner Publishers, 2001), 95.

41. See *China Times (Zhongguo Shibao)* poll published April 15, 2004.

42. According to an exit poll by the cable television news station TVBS, 4 percent of voters identified with the TSU. "*2004 nian zongtong daxuan TVBS toupiaosuo chuko mindiao (Exit Poll) jieguo baogao*" available at:
http://www.tvbs.com.tw/FILE_DB/files/yijung/200404/yijung-20040414111305.pdf
(accessed April 15, 2004).

43. Wang and Ku "Learning Democracy," 25.

44. Lee Chang-kuei, "Taiwan in Quagmire," *Taipei Times,* December 30, 2000. Available at:
http://www.taipeitimes.com/News/edit/archives/2000/12/30/67735
(accessed October 7, 2003).

45. Stephen Haber, "Introduction: The Political Economy of Crony Capitalism," in Haber (ed). *Crony Capitalism and Economic Growth in Latin America: Theory and Evidence* (Palo Alto: Hoover Institution Press, 2002), xii.

46. Kuo, "Taiwan's Distorted Democracy," *passim.*

47. Ibid., 99.

48. Lee, "Taiwan in Quagmire."

49. "Legislators receive poor grades in poll," Central News Agency report dated September 17, 2000. Available at:
http://www.taiwanheadlines.gov.tw/20000918/20000818p5.html

CHAPTER THREE: BUILDING A TAIWANESE REPUBLIC

1. Most Taiwanese came from provinces along the southeast coast of the mainland during the Qing Dynasty (1644–1912) prior to the Japanese occupation in 1895. Traditionally, the Taiwanese have been divided into two main groups, Hokkien and Hakka. The Minnan people from Fujian are often called Hokkien or *Fulao* (Old Fujianese). (Minnan means south of the Min River, which cuts through Fujian.) They constitute about 85 percent of the Taiwanese population. The smaller group is the Hakka, also called *Kejiaren* or *Yuemin* (*Yue* is a traditional term for Guangdong Province). "Mainlanders" (*daluren*) are Chinese who came to the island after 1945, the majority arriving between late 1948 and mid-1950 as the Nationalist government faced defeat at the hands of the Chinese Communists. Aborigines (*yuanzhumin*) comprised about two percent of the population. They are not Han Chinese, but are most closely related to the Austronesian peoples of island Southeast Asia. Due to intermarriage and cultural assimilation, the borders between these groups are often unclear. Self-definition is often the only effective way to categorize the inhabitants of Taiwan.

2. The Republic of China (*Zhonghua minguo*) is also known as Nationalist China. This state was guided by the Kuomintang (the Nationalist Party). The Kuomintang was formed around the ideology of Sun Yat-sen, called Three Principles of the People (*Sanmin zhuyi*): Nationalism, Democracy, and People's Livelihood. Chiang Kai-shek dominated the party after Sun's death in 1925.

3. As detailed by Robert Marsh, the island's population could be divided into four segments: nationalists; unification advocates; "pragmatists," who would support unification with a democratic and prosperous China; and those who feel comfortable only with the status quo. He points out that up to one third of those surveyed provide no response. In short, the independence movement has the support of the first group, no hope with the second, but may be able to influence the pragmatists. See Robert M. Marsh, "Taiwan's Future National Identity: Attitudes and Geopolitical Constraints," *International Journal of Comparative Sociology* 42, no. 3 (July 2001): 299–315.

4. For example, *Separatism, Democracy and Disintegration* includes chapters on the Soviet Union, Yugoslavia, Sri Lanka, Quebec, etc., but no mention of Taiwan even though this volume seeks to investigate "the temporal coincidence between surges of democracy and surges of secessionist movements." Metta Spencer, ed., *Separatism, Democracy, and Disintegration* (New York: Rowman & Littlefield, 1998), 9. Peter Alter's overview of nationalism seems to cover every movement and nation-state except Taiwan. *Nationalism* (London: Edward Arnold, 1985).

Ditto for Louis L. Snyder's exhaustive study, *The New Nationalism* (Ithaca: Cornell University Press, 1968).

5. John Dahlberg-Acton. *Essays in the Liberal Interpretation of History* (Chicago: University of Chicago Press, 1967), 146.

6. "Many of the most uncompromising, fanatical adherents of an independent Khalistan do not live in the Punjab but have prosperous businesses in Melbourne and Chicago." Benedict Anderson. *The Spectre of Comparisons: Nationalism, Southeast Asia, and the World* (London: Verso, 1998), 73.

7. Ibid., 64.

8. Ian Buruma. *Bad Elements: Chinese Rebels from Los Angeles to Beijing* (New York: Random House, 2001), 12.

9. Elie Kedouri, one of the most prominent scholars of nationalism, has noted that "National self-determination is, in the final analysis, a determination of the will; and nationalism is, in the first place, a method of teaching the right determination of the will." Elie Kedouri, "Nationalism and Self-Determination," in John Hutchinson and Anthony D. Smith, eds., *Nationalism* (Oxford: Oxford University Press, 1994), 54.

10. The life and career of Zheng Chenggong (1624–1662) linked Taiwan to the mainland's political history. Zheng was a regional strongman and pirate who gained increasing influence as the Ming collapsed. He is also "claimed" by supporters of unification. His support of the Ming court against the non-Han Manchu invaders made Zheng a permanent icon of Chinese patriotism. Even today he remains a particular source of local pride in Tainan, the city on the site where Zheng's army forced the Dutch to evacuate their small colonial outpost in 1662. Zheng's anti-Qing efforts also became an important symbol for a later regime in exile, the Chinese Nationalists. A combination of effective military strategy and generous peace terms, however, in 1683 enticed Zheng's heirs to surrender.

11. A few prominent islanders formed the Republic of Taiwan when the island's transfer to Japan was announced. The short-lived republic accomplished little, and was more an attempt to interest another foreign power in the island, and thus block Japan's ambitions. For more information on the failed Republic see Harry J. Lamley, "The 1895 Taiwan Republic," *Journal of Asian Studies* 27, no. 4 (August 1968): 739–762.

12. For example, see Hiroo Mukoyama, translated by L.S.F. "Taiwan Independence Movement" *Taidu* 50 (April 28, 1976): 21.

13. A good brief overview of Liao Wen-i's life is found in Zhang Yanxian, Hu Huiling, and Zeng Qiumei. *Taiwan duli yundong de xiansheng: Taiwan gongheguo* (The first voice for the Taiwanese independence movement: The Republic of Taiwan) (Taibei: Wu Sanlian jijinhui, 2000), 1–18. See also Li Xiaofeng, "Ziwo fangzhu de 'da zongtong': Liao Wenyi" (Liao Wen-i: the self-exiled 'great president,'" in Zhang Yanxian, et al, eds. *Taiwan jindai mingrenzhi*, vol. 1 (Taibei: Zili wanbao, 1987), 279–296.

14. Many Taidu groups use the word Formosa (from the Portuguese for "beautiful

island") instead of Taiwan in order to accentuate their rejection of the identity given to them by mainlanders. The use of Formosa has gradually faded.

15. For a biography of Hsieh that tends to portray her as favoring looser ties to the mainland, see Chen Fangming, *Xie Xuehong pingzhuan* (A Critical Biography of Xie Xuehong) (Taibei: Qianwei chubanshe, 1991). On Taiwanese communists and their role in the party and united front efforts on the mainland, see part two of Chen Muxiu, *228 zhenxiang tantao* (A discussion of the real form of February 28) (Taibei: Boyuan chuban, 1990).

16. "Statement of Conference of President Roosevelt, Generalissimo Chiang Kai-shek, and Prime Minister Churchill, Cairo, December 1, 1943," *United States Relations with China: With Special Reference to the Period 1944–1949*, Department of State Publication 3573, (Washington: Government Printing Office, 1949), 519.

17. When President Harry S Truman announced that the United States would neutralize the Taiwan Strait on June 27, 1950, he noted that "The determination of the future status of Formosa must await the restoration of security in the Pacific, a peace settlement with Japan, or consideration by the United Nations." The San Francisco Treaty of 1951 marked the formal end of the state of war between Japan and non-Communist nations, including the United States, France, and Great Britain. The Treaty reiterated Japan's renunciation of its colonial conquests. The Soviet Union, the People's Republic of China, and the nations of Eastern Europe did not sign. The Republic of China on Taiwan signed a separate treaty with Japan. Some scholars have suggested that John Foster Dulles, the chief American negotiator for the San Francisco Treaty, wanted to provide for flexibility on Taiwan's future status. The Treaty states that Japan renounces all claims to the island, but does not explicitly state that the island was part of China—either the ROC or PRC. See Robert Accinelli. *Crisis and Commitment: United States Policy toward Taiwan, 1950–1955* (Chapel Hill: The University of North Carolina Press, 1996), 81.

18. In 1949 and 1950, Taiwan was rife with rumors of plots against Chiang. Nancy Bernkopf Tucker has suggested that American trained General Sun Li-jen (Sun Liren) was preparing a coup attempt with American acquiescence, if not support. Nancy Bernkopf Tucker. *Patterns in the Dust* (New York: Columbia University Press, 1980), 181. However, Robert Accinelli notes that "the odds were long that the Nationalist army commander could depose the cunning Chiang, a master of the art of political survival and intrigue." Robert Accinelli, *Crisis and Commitment*, 21.

19. Xu Dong, "Taiwan dixia zuzhi bibai wuyi" (Taiwan's underground organizations must be defeated without a doubt), *Taiwan chunqiu* 2 (October 1948): 4.

20. *United States Relations with China*, 309.

21. "The Acting Secretary of State to the Consul General in Taipei (Krentz), November 23, 1948," *Foreign Relations of the United States, 1948*, Volume 7, China (Washington: Government Printing Office, 1973), 604. (Hereafter *FRUS*.)

22. The Minister-Counselor of Embassy in China (Clark) to the Director of the Office of Far Eastern Affairs (Butterworth), June 30, 1948, *FRUS, 1948*, 7: 332.

23. Secretary of State Dean Acheson and others in the Truman Administration held out the hope of building diplomatic relations with the Chinese Communist regime until the Korean War. For this reason, they were not eager to see Chiang reestablish his regime on the island, nor did they want to see an independent Taiwan. For example, on March 3, 1949, Acheson stated before the thirty-fifth meeting of the National Security Council that "We are most anxious to avoid raising the specter of an American-created irredentist issue just at the time we shall be seeking to exploit the genuinely Soviet-created irredentist issue in Manchuria and Sinkiang [XinChiang]. We cannot afford to compromise an emerging new U.S. position in China by overtly showing a pronounced interest in Formosa." Thirty-fifth Meeting of the National Security Council, National Archives, Record Group 319, Department of Defense Files, G-3 Decimal Files, 091-Formosa, 1949–1950, Box 154.

24. Central Intelligence Agency, "China Research Report SR-8," August 1948 (Library of Congress, microfilm number 86/212).

25. Acheson's willingness to consider forging a diplomatic relationship with the new Beijing regime is detailed in Warren I. Cohen, "Acheson, His Advisers, and China, 1949–1950," in Dorothy Borg and Waldo Heinrichs, eds. *Uncertain Years: Chinese-American Relations, 1947–1950* (New York: Columbia University Press, 1980). A more thorough examination of American foreign policy toward China at that time can be found in Tucker, *Patterns in the Dust*. Acheson's own account of events comes from *Present at Creation: My Years in the State Department* (New York: Norton, 1969).

26. Kenneth C. Krentz, American Consul in Taipei, to J. L. Stuart, Ambassador in China, January 26, 1948, National Archives, Record Group 59, Department of State Decimal Files, 894A.00/1–2648 (hereafter NARA).

27. William Sebald, American Consul in Tokyo, to John Allison, Deputy Director, Division of Far Eastern Affairs, April 12, 1949, 894A.01/4–1249, NARA.

28. Secretary of State Dean Acheson ordered United States diplomats as follows: "When situation develops to point where we know government groups US will have deal with on Formosa, US should seek develop and support local non-Comm Chi regime which will provide at least modicum decent govt Formosa. We should also use influence wherever possible to discourage further influx mainlanders. US should also discretely maintain contact with potential native Formosan leaders with view future date being able utilize Formosan autonomous movement if it appears in US natl interest." Secretary of State Acheson to American Counsul, Taipei, Livingston Merchant, March 2, 1949, 894A.00/3–2249, NARA.

29. For example, in 1953, one of Liao's supporters reported to American diplomats in Tokyo that the Formosan Democratic Independence Party's vice president had been removed from office because "Lan [the vice president] had been using the Party's name as a means of collecting funds for personal purposes." First Secretary of the Embassy to the Department of State, June 16, 1953, 794A.11/6–1653, NARA.

30. One brief overview of the movement in Japan is in Zhong Cai, "Zhanhou Taiwan liu Ri xuesheng de duli jian'guo yundongshi" (A history of postwar overseas Taiwanese students in Japan's independence movement) *Taiwan shiliao yanjiu* 4 (October 1994): 107–118.

31. Liao's most important work that combined history and manifesto was *Inside Formosa: Formosans vs. Chinese since 1945* (Tokyo: Formosan Press, 1960?).

32. For example, see the collection of petitions and statements from Taidu activists by the Formosan League for Independence. *Memoranda on the Formosan Independence Movement*, (Tokyo, 1949).

33. One good example of Liao's efforts is his September 15, 1955 letter to President Dwight Eisenhower, found in Department of State files, 794A.00/9–2055. See also the memoranda of conversations with independence leaders in Tokyo in November and December 1955. Department of State files, 794A.00/12–2955, NARA.

34. Chen Jiahong. *Haiwai Taidu yundongshi* (History of the overseas Taiwan independence movement) (Taibei: Qianwei chubanshe, 1998), 59.

35. Liao complained of harassment by Nationalist supporters in Japan, including "a bunch of Chinese rascals" who attempted to disrupt meetings and harm independence leaders. Liao toEisenhower, 794A.00/9–2055; Memoranda of conversations with independence leaders, 794A.00/12–2955, NARA.

36. This was probably not the only time the Nationalists used this tactic. It was revealed in 1970 that WUFI's Japan branch chairman had engaged in secret talks with the Nationalists. Song Chongyang. *Taiwan duli yundong siji* (A personal account of the Taiwan independence movement) (Taibei: Qianwei, 1996), 206–207.

37. Longtime Taidu activist, Song Chongyang, noted that Nationalist propaganda claimed that the movement was dead after Liao's return. Song Chongyang. *Taiwan duli yundong siji*, 210.

38. Zhang Yanxian, Hu Huiling, and Zeng Qiumei. *Taiwan duli yundong de xiansheng: Taiwan gongheguo* (The first voice for the Taiwanese independence movement: The Republic of Taiwan) (Taibei: Wu Sanlian jijinhui, 2000), 18.

39. Taidu publications from Japan included articles in Japanese and Chinese.

40. Chen Jiahong, *Haiwai Taidu yundongshi*, 59.

41. On typical protest activities, and the difficulties activists faced from hostile Japanese authorities, see "Chiang Ching-kuo's Visit to Japan and the Anti-Chiang Activities of the Independence Movement," *Independent Formosa* 6, no. 6 (December 1967): 19–22.

42. He would help form yet another organization in 1967, the Independent Formosa Society (*Duli Taiwan hui*), to espouse these views.

43. The memoirs of Wang Xiling, who served as Chief of the ROC Ministry of Defense' Military Intelligence Bureau (*Guofangbu qingbaoju*) from 1983 to 1985 is a valuable record of Nationalist intelligence efforts in the 1970s and early 1980s. He also details efforts to spy on Taiwanese dissidents and independence activists in the United States—creating what were euphemistically called "reference name

lists" (*cankao mingce*). Wang Shichun, *Zhong yu guo: Qingzhi shouzhang Wang Xiling de qiluo* (A matter of honor: the rise and fall of Wang Xiling) (Taibei: Tianxia yuanjian, 1999), 178–180.

44. Chen Jiahong, *Haiwai Taidu yundongshi*, 62.

45. Many articles focused on the fate of individual activists, such as "Let Us Follow the Hsieh Brothers, Our National Heroes!" *Independent Formosa* 5, nos. 3–4 (August 1966): 3–4. See also the lists of hundreds of prisoners: "Taiwan zhengzhifan mingdan, Taiwanren bufen" (Taiwan political prisoners, Taiwanese section) *Taidu* 21 (November 28, 1973): 7–9; and "Taiwan zhengzhifan mingdan, daluren bufen" (Taiwan political prisoners, mainlanders section) *Taidu* 22 (December 28, 1973): 6–8.

46. For example, see the reprint and discussion of Marilyn Blatt Young's article (originally published in *The Nation* in March 1968) in *Independent Formosa* 7, no. 1 (March 1968): 15 18; and her letter to the editors of the Committee of Concerned Asian Scholars in *Independent Formosa* 8, no. 2 (Summer 1969): 6–8.

47. Kerr was a United States government employee on Taiwan after World War II who became a strong advocate for the rights of the Taiwanese. He became a hero to many Taidu activists, and constituted "evidence" of American meddling to the Nationalists. His most famous work is *Formosa Betrayed* (Boston: Houghton Mifflin, 1965).

48. For insight into attempts by some activists to return to Taiwan, see the memoirs of Song Chongyang, a longtime independence leader in Japan. He notes that he returned briefly in 1967 by simply signing up for a group tour of Hong Kong, Macao, and Taiwan. Song Chongyang, *Taiwan duli yundong siji*, 103–110.

49. For example, in 1961 more than 300 Taiwanese, including Yunlin County Council member Su Tung-ch'i (Su Dongqi), were arrested for allegedly plotting an armed uprising inspired by independence sentiment. Su would be released in 1976.

50. For an overview of the careers and beliefs of some Taiwanese independence activists, including Peng, see Li Xiaofeng, "Guojia rentong de zhuanxiang: yi zhanhou Taiwan fandui renshi de shige ge'an wei lei" (The shifting of national identity: ten case studies of postwar Taiwanese dissidents) in *Rentong yu Guojia: Jindai Zhong-Xi lishi de bijiao* (Nangang: Zhongyang yanjiuyuan jindaishi yanjiusuo, 1994), 323–362. Li stresses that Nationalist misrule built support for the independence movement.

51. Peng's sister was president of a Presbyterian college that was considered a hotbed of dissent by Nationalist officials.

52. *A Taste of Freedom: Memoirs of a Formosan Independence Leader* (New York: Holt, Rinehart and Winston, 1972).

53. For an explanation of how the Presbyterian Church has combined Christianity and political dissent, see Chen Nanzhou, *Taiwan Jidu Presbyterian Church de shehui zhengzhi lunli* (The social and political moral principles of the Changlaohui) (Taibei: Yongyuan wenhua, 1991). This work emphasizes that their criticism of the Nationalists was entirely compatible with Christian doctrine.

54. On the Church's political activities, see Christine Louise Lin. *The Presbyterian Church in Taiwan and the Advocacy of Local Autonomy*, Sino-Platonic Papers #92 (Philadelphia: Department of Asian and Middle Eastern Studies, 1999), 69–90.

55. He had been in prison from 1962 to 1977 for sedition, then returned to prison after the Kaohsiung Incident until released in 1990. He would become a key leader of the DPP.

56. Besides the groups involved in publishing *Independent Formosa*, Canadian groups participated. In 1963, Huang I-ming (Huang Yiming) had established the Taiwan Compatriots Society (*Taiwan tongxiang hui*) in Canada.

57. For an overview of his writings, see Zhang Canhong, *Taiwan du li yun dong san shi nian: Zhang Canhong xuan ji* (Thirty years in the Taiwan independence movement: collected writings of Zhang Canhong) (Taibei: Zong dai li jian wei chu ban she, 1991)

58. Chen Jiahong, *Haiwai Taidu yundongshi*, 92–93.

59. Huang would hide in the United States, and returned to Taiwan in 1996, where he became director of the Taiwan Association for Human Rights. His accomplice would eventually found the Taiwan Progressive Society, a leftist independence group, in Sweden.

60. Editorial, *Independent Formosan* 9, no. 1 (Spring 1970): 2.

61. "Taiwanese Picketing Chiang Ching-kuo," Ibid., 5.

62. Qing Tian (pseud.), "Taiwan changshi de ziwo ceyan" (A self-test of common knowledge about Taiwan) *Taidu* 4 (June 28, 1972): 12.

63. "Taiwan renmin duli zijiu shouce" (Taiwan peoples' independence self-preservation handbook) *Taidu* 5 (July 28, 1972): 8–10.

64. Lin Mingshan (pseudonym?), "Chu han cheng xiong: Taiwan benbu di shier xingdongdui baogao" (Eliminating traitors and punishing villains: report of the Taiwan branch's twelfth action corps) *Taidu* 56 (October 28, 1976): 8.

65. Shih Ming credits the Taiwan Independence Revolutionary Army (*Taiwan duli gemingjun*) a small group that engaged in sabotage on the island, with much of this activity. It was probably a WUFI splinter group, and disbanded after a series of arrests in 1974, when the Nationalists uncovered an alleged plot to assassinate Chiang Ching-kuo. Shih Ming detailed the activities of the army in *Taiwan minzu zhuyi yu Taiwan duli geming* (Taiwan nationalism and Taiwan's independence revolution) (Taibei: Qianwei, 2001), 106–112.

66. Chen Jiahong, *Haiwai Taidu yundongshi*, 107.

67. The last major country to switch recognition was South Korea, in 1992.

68. For a fuller discussion of these developments, see Thomas Gold. *State and Society in the Taiwan Miracle* (Armonk: M.E. Sharpe, Inc., 1985) and John Copper. *Taiwan: Nation-State or Province?* (Boulder: Westview Press, 1989). For an overview of various interests groups that emerged in the 1980s, see Hsin-Huang Michael Hsiao, "Emerging Social Movements and the Rise of a Demanding Civil Society on Taiwan," *Australian Journal of Chinese Affairs* 24 (July 1990): 163–179.

69. Two superb overviews of the problems of democratization and Taiwanese iden-

tity are Alan M. Wachman. *Taiwan: National Identity and Democratization* (Armonk: M. E. Sharpe, 1994) and Michael Ying-mao Kau, "Democratization on Taiwan and Its Impact on the Relationship with Mainland China," in J. W. Wheeler, ed.. *Chinese Divide: Evolving Relations between Taiwan and Mainland China* (Indianapolis: Hudson Institute, 1996), pp. 47–72.

70. Lu's statement is contained in a translation of a transcript of the rally, *The Kaohsiung Tapes* (Seattle: International Committee for Human Rights in Taiwan, 1981), 39–45.

71. The Kaohsiung Eight, the most important opposition politicians, received twelve years to life imprisonment. Thirty-three others were given two to six year terms, and ten persons in the Presbyterian Church who helped Shih Ming-te avoid the police received lesser sentences, except for the general-secretary of the Church, who received a seven-year sentence.

72. See *Taidu* 94 (December 29, 1979): 2.

73. Buruma, in his examination of Chinese dissidents in the United States, notes "a common accusation made against political refugees, especially when they prosper abroad. Their foreign success is seen as treachery, their freedom to live as they like an affront to those who have to bear the strictures of life at home. Germans who fled the Third Reich in the 1930s were, on the whole, not made to feel welcome when they returned after the war. They had 'had it easy,' and they didn't 'know what it had been like.' " Buruma, *Bad Elements*, 72.

74. Chen Jiahong, *Haiwai Taidu yundongshi*, 169–171.

75. Buruma claims that *zige* (credentials or qualifications) was the key area of competition among dissidents. It is impossible to measure clearly, but is something one must have to be accepted in the movement. Buruma, *Bad Elements*, 89.

76. Shih Ming. *Taiwan minzu zhuyi yu Taiwan duli geming*, 122.

77. Lin Hao, "Taiwan minzhu yundongshi shang bu xiu de laobing: Guo Yuxin" (Kuo Yu-hsin: the old soldier who will not fade away from the history of Taiwan's democracy movement) in Guo Huinuo and Lin Hengzhe, eds. *Guo Yuxin jinian wenji* (Taibei: Qianwei, 1988), 185.

78. The Coalition for Taiwanese Nationhood, formed by Hsu in December 1979, failed to unite overseas Taiwanese. This group was more radical and criticized WUFI for its lack of militancy. Hsu and Shih Ming allied in 1982 to form the Taiwan Peoples' Democratic Revolutionary League (*Taiwan minzu duli geming tongmeng*), but this organization accomplished little.

79. "1983 nian Meidong Taiwanren xialinghui zhengzhi taolunhui jishi" (A record of 1983 Eastern United States Taiwanese summer political discussion) *Taidu* 7 (Fall 1983): 89.

80. Ibid., 100.

81. Ibid., 88.

82. Ibid., 98.

83. Ibid., 75.

84. Ibid., 72.

85. Ibid., 77.

86. A few of those who left joined Hsu Hsin-liang to form another organization devoted to independence, the Taiwan Revolutionary Party (*Taiwan gemingdang*). This group accomplished little. In 1986, Hsu Hsin-liang would shift his focus from overseas Taiwanese to politics on the island when he helped organize the Committee for the Establishment of a Taiwan Democratic Party (*Taiwan minzhudang jiandang weiyuanhui*), a predecessor to the DPP. Hsu, who transformed from Nationalist politician in the 1970s to opposition firebrand in exile in the 1980s, to DPP chairman in the 1990s, left the party and ran as an independent in the 2000 president election as an advocate for returning to the one China policy. Independence was impossible, he claimed.

87. Lin I-hsiung was one of the Kaohsiung Eight. On February 28, 1980, his mother and two of his daughters were murdered, probably at the behest of the Nationalists. Chiang Nan was a pseudonym for Henry Liu (Liu I-liang), a businessman, writer, and possibly an agent for various intelligence services, who authored a critical biography of President Chiang Ching-kuo. In October 1984, he was murdered outside his California home by members of the Bamboo Gang, a criminal organization with long ties to the Nationalist Party. Several Nationalist officials, including the head of the Military Intelligence Bureau, Wang Hsi-ling, were implicated in the killing, and would be sentenced to prison on Taiwan.

88. "1983 nian Meidong Taiwanren xialinghui zhengzhi taolunhui jishi," 91.

89. Ibid., 97.

90. In July 1988, the Nationalists' 13th Party Congress elected a majority of Taiwanese to the Central Standing Committee, symbolizing the changing of the guard within the regime.

91. The temporary provisions of the constitution, which rendered constitutional guarantees of civil rights meaningless, were repealed in the early 1990s. A subsequent series of elections led to the replacement of legislators and National Assembly members (most of whom had been elected on the mainland in the late 1940s). In late 1994, free elections were held for the provincial governor and mayors of the two largest cities (Taipei and Kaohsiung) and, in 1996 and 2000, for the presidency.

92. Perhaps the most important election was the December 1989 national legislature elections, where the DPP obtained enough seats to propose legislation. The Nationalist Party still dominated, but its aura of invincibility was gone. The 1992 Legislative Yuan elections increased the DPP's share of representatives.

93. Joyce Huang, "Formosa Generation Moving On" *Taipei Times* (December 10, 2000), 1.

94. For example, see the article in *Gongheguo* (The Republic), the name of WUFI's publication since 1997. Song Chongyang, "Minjindang, huigui Taidu jiben linian ba!" (DPP, return to the basic idea of Taiwan's independence!) *Gongheguo* 1 (October 27, 1997): 31–32. Song was part of the Japan chapter of WUFI. See also Huang Chao-t'ang, "Taiwan duli jian'guo lianmeng yao zhichi zhuzhang Taidu de houxuanren" (WUFI must support candidates who advocate independence) *Gongheguo* 9 (July 1999): 3–4.

95. Taiwan duli jianguo lianmeng zhengce gangling (WUFI Platform), adopted in 1996 and revised in 2002. www.wufi.org.tw/wufiplank.htm.

96. Ibid.

97. The Peng-Hsieh Platform, www.taiwandc.org/dpp/019607.htm.

98. Message from Dr. Peng Ming-min, www.taiwandc.org/dpp/109601.htm.

99. The opposition has also been hampered by charges of corruption and complaints that it has become too similar to the Nationalist Party (*Kuomintanghua*).

100. Keith B. Richburg, "Leader Asserts Taiwan is 'Independent, Sovereign,'" *Washington Post* (November 8, 1997): A-1.

101. Sima Wenwu, "Zhe ci mei jiang cuo hua, jiang zhen hua, fan zaocheng zhenhan" (This time he does not say the wrong thing, [but] saying the correct thing creates uproar) *Xin xinwen* 558 (November 15, 1997): 2.

102. Note that *guo* and *guojia* can be translated as nation, state, country, or nation-state. Lee Teng-hui and ROC publications translated these terms as "state."

103. See the translation of the interview with Deutsche Welle as reported by the China Central News Agency, July 9, 1999. "Li zongtong jieshou Deguo zhi sheng zhuanfang quanwen" (The complete text of President Lee's interview with Deutsche Welle), Sina.com, July 10, 1999, twnews.sina.com/ckp/twPolitics/1999/0710/98292.html. See also Seth Faison, "Taiwan President Implies His Island Is Sovereign State," *New York Times* (July 13, 1999): 1; and Michael Laris, "Taiwan Alters Old 'One China' Formula," *Washington Post* (July 13, 1999): A-14.

104. A third party candidate, James Soong, followed a more traditional pro-unification policy. Chen won the election with a plurality of the vote.

105. "Liang'an zhengzhi jiangju zeren wanquan zai Taiwan dangju" (Responsibility for the cross Strait impasse lies entirely with Taiwan authorities) *Renmin ribao*, May 31, 2001, 4. After the most substantive cross Strait talks to date, the PRC's Wang Daohan and ROC representative Koo Chen-fu (Gu Zhenfu) agreed in November 1992 that there was but one China, although both sides stipulated that the meaning (hanyi) of one China differed.

106. As many as 75,000 marched in Taipei in early September 2003 to support the name change, an effort led by the Campaign for Rectifying the Name of Taiwan.

107. For example, see the WUFI American branch statement of January 20, 2000, "Fangqi dui Zhongguo de taohao zhengce, liqing Taiwan renmin duli zizhu de yinian" (Discard the obsequious policy toward China, harness completely the Taiwan people's idea of independence and sovereignty) *Gongheguo* 18 (March 2001): 2.

108. Chen was behind in most polls on the eve of the March 20 election. A botched assassination attempt that wounded Chen and his running mate, Annette Lu, probably swung votes to the DPP. Chen won by about 30,000 votes out of more than 13 million cast. Leaders of the Pan-Blue opposition hinted that the assassination attempt was a DPP trick and claimed that a state of emergency declared after the shooting prevented many soldiers from voting. In the month after the election, Pan Green (the DPP and allied parties) and Pan Blue leaders fought over the scope of the recount.

109. Chang Yun-ping, "Chen Tells BBC of New Constitution," *Taipei Times* (April 1, 2004): 1. See also his interview with the *Washington Post*, Philip P. Pan and David E. Hoffman, "Taiwan's President Maintains Hard Line: Chen Rebukes China in Interview," *Washington Post* (March 30, 2004): A1.

110. "Policy of the United Young Formosans of [sic] Independence," *Independent Formosa* 6, no. 4 (August 1967): 6.

111. Language is another key area. In March 2003, the Council for Cultural Affairs took responsibility for drafting a language law for Taiwan away from the Mandarin Promotion Council of the Ministry of Education. There was great debate over whether or not to revise the constitution to designate an official language. Chen's administration rejected the Mandarin-based romanization system used by the Nationalists and the widely accepted *pinyin* system promoted by the mainland. In July 2002, the Ministry of Education's Language Promotion Committee voted to promote the *tongyong* system, over the objections of Nationalist politicians. *Tongyong pinyin* is designed to allow easy romanization of *Taiyu*, the first language of most islanders. According to the Ministry of Education, this highly controversial decision represented a rejection of the Nationalists' attempts to "Sinify" Taiwanese through language.

112. For example, see Zhang Yanxian's overview of the connection between political developments and the growth of a "Taiwan-centered" history. "Taiwanshi yanjiu de xin jingshen" (The New Spirit of Taiwanese Historical Research), *Taiwan shiliao yanjiu* 1 (February 1993): 76–86.

113. In September 2003, debates heated up over revised guidelines for high school history textbooks between China and Taiwan-centered approaches. The proposed curriculum would focus on Taiwan's history first, then move on to China and world history. Jewel Huang, "Academics Quarrel over Chinese History Lessons," *Taipei Times* (September 22, 2003): 3. See also Chang Yun-ping, "New Curriculum to Stress 'Taiwan-Centered Values,'" *Taipei Times* (January 23, 2003): 2. Mainland sensitivity toward alternative interpretations of the island's history should not be underestimated. For example, entire books have been published that criticize history textbooks on Taiwan which allegedly substitute local loyalty (often called *bentuhua*) for Chinese consciousness. Chen Kongli, et. al. *"Renshi Taiwan" jiaokeshu pingxi* (A critical analysis of the textbook, recognizing Taiwan) (Beijing: Jiuzhou tushu chubanshe, 1999).

CHAPTER 4. LEE TENG-HUI AND "SEPARATISM"

1. "The One-China Principle and the Taiwan Issue," *Beijing Review* (March 6, 2000): 20. A few American China specialists hung the same independence label on Lee; see Chas. W. Freeman, Jr., "Preventing War in the Taiwan Strait: Restraining Taiwan—and Beijing.," *Foreign Affairs* 77 (July-August 1998): 7, 9; Robert S. Ross, "The 1995–96 Taiwan Strait Confrontation: Coercion, Credibility, and the Use of Force," *International Security* 25, no.2 (Fall 2000): 87–123.

2. Specifically, the white paper asserted that the view "the ROC is an independent sovereign state," one that all major Taiwan leaders share, was "splittist."

3. For Ye's nine points, see Stephen P. Gibert and William M. Carpenter. *America and Island China*, (Lanham, MD: University Press of America, 1989), pp. 288–290. This was preceded in January 1979 by the "Message to Taiwan Compatriots" by the Standing Committee of China's National People's Congress; see *Beijing Review*, (January 5, 1979): 16–17. Sheng Lijun suggests that the 1979 and 1981 overtures reiterated in part secret proposals made to Chiang Kai-shek in the 1950s; see Sheng Lijun, "China Eyes Taiwan: Why is a Breakthrough so Difficult?" *Journal of Strategic Studies*, vol. 21, no. 1 (March 1998): 65–69.

4. "An Idea for the Peaceful Reunification of the Chinese Mainland and Taiwan," June 26, 1983, *Selected Works of Deng Xiaoping* (Beijing: Foreign Languages Press, 1994), 40–41.

5. As Deng Xiaoping had made clear a few months before, the "local inhabitants" who ran Hong Kong had to be "patriots"; see "One Country, Two Systems," June 22–23. 1984, *Selected Works of Deng Xiaoping*, 3: 70–71.

6. "International Press Conference," February 22, 1988, in *Yingjie Tiaozhan, Chuangzhao Shengli: Zhonghua minguo 77 nian yuan yue zhi 12 yue Li zongtong Denghui xiansheng yanlun xuanji* (Accepting the challenge, creating victory: Collected speeches of President Lee Teng-hui, January-December 1988) (Taipei: Zhongyang wenwu gongyingshe, 1989), 129–153.

7. Even the PRC does not suggest that the early Lee Teng-hui position is a separatist one. In the 2000 white paper, it acknowledged that during that period he "publicly stated time and again that the basic policy of the Taiwan authorities was that 'there is only one China, not two,' and 'we have always maintained that China should be reunited, and we adhere to the principle of "one China."'" See note 1 above.

8. Hungdah Chiu, ed., *China and the Question of Taiwan: Documents and Analysis* (New York: Praeger, 1973), 345; Gibert and Carpenter, *America and Island China*, 208.

9. Stephen D. Krasner, *Sovereignty: Organized Hypocrisy* (Princeton: Princeton University Press, 1999), 11; Hurst Hannum, *Autonomy, Sovereignty, and Self-Determination: The Accommodation of Conflicting Rights*, rev. ed. (Philadelphia: University of Pennsylvania Press, 1990), 15. It is true that there might have been a political value for Lee to use the term "*duli*," but his primary intent was to make a point about the ROC's legal status.

10. "Opening a New Era for the Chinese People, Inaugural Address by the Eighth-Term President of the Republic of China, May 20, 1990," in Lee Teng-hui, *Creating the Future: Towards a New Era for the Chinese People* (Taipei: Government Information Organization, 1992), 7–9; also in *Li Denghui Zongtong xiansheng qishijiunian Yenlun Xuanaji*, 53–54.

11. From "Relations Across the Taiwan Straits," Mainland Affairs Council, July 1994, reprinted in John F. Copper, *Words Across the Taiwan Strait: A Critique of Beijing's "White Paper" on China's Unification* (Lanham, MD: University Press

of America, 1995), 110; Lee Teng-hui and Tsou Ching-wen, *Lee Teng-hui Zhi-zheng Gaobai Shihlu* (Taipei Co.: Yin-ke, 2001), 183. This work is a retrospective account of Lee's presidency that was written with his cooperation.

12. "Guidelines for National Unification," *Creating the Future*, 159–161.

13. "Termination of the Period of National Mobilization for the Suppression of Communist Rebellion," *Creating the Future*, 37–62; also in *Kaichuang Weilai: Maixiang Zhonghua Minzu di Xinshidai* (Creating the Future; Striding toward a New Era of the Chinese Nation) (Taipei: Government Information Office, 1992), 65, 67, 70.

14. Interview with Lin Bihjaw, February 24, 2003; interview with Chu Yun-han, March 3, 2003; *Lee Teng-hui Gaobai Shihlu*, 182, 194–195.

15. Democratization on the mainland was apparently receding as an essential requirement in Lee's approach to unification.

16. For the rhetorical combat on Taiwan's role in the international community see "The Taiwan Question and the Reunification of China," Taiwan Affairs Office and Information Office, State Council, August 1993; and "Relations Across the Taiwan Straits," both in Copper, *Words Across the Taiwan Strait*. Neither offered new ideas.

17. Steven Goldstein, "The Rest of the Story: The Impact of Domestic Politics on Taiwan's Mainland Policy, *Harvard Studies on Taiwan* 2, no. 2 (1998): 62–90.

18. Interview with Lin Bih-jaw, February 24, 2003.

19. Interview with Chu Yun-han, March 3, 2003; Goldstein, "The Rest of the Story, 72.

20. Interview with Chu Yun-han, March 3, 2003; FBIS, Daily Report China, FBIS-CHI-92–198-S, October 13, 1992, 42–43.

21. Specifically, ARATS said, "Both sides of the Taiwan Strait uphold that One-China principle and strive to seek national unification. However, in routine cross-Strait consultations, the political meaning of "One China" will not be involved." SEF said, "Although the two sides uphold the One-China principle in the process of striving for cross-strait national unification, each side has its own understanding of the meaning of one-China." On Lee's role in the 1992 consensus, the relevant sections of Tsou, *Gaobai Shihlu* (pp. 186–191) suggest that he had no role at all. The skepticism about one China comes from an interview with Chiao Jen-ho, February 26, 2003.

22. "Report on the State of the Nation Given at the Second Extraordinary Session of the Second National Assembly," January 4, 1993, from no-longer-operative website of the Office of the President established during Lee Teng-hui's tenure (hereafter cited as OOP website); "International Press Conference," May 20, 1993; "Transcript of a Press Conference Held After President Lee's visit to the Southeast Asian Countries," February 16, 1994, *Jingying Da Taiwan*, 423–446; "Report on the State of the Nation Given at the Fourth Extraordinary Session of the Second National Assembly," May 19, 1994, OOP website; "Written Responses to Questions Submitted by Mr. K. F. Own, Editor of Sunday Times, Johannesburg," October 10, 1994, OOP website. Note that Lee and his government

were using two different concepts to describe the ROC and the PRC and their relationship to China. On the one hand, he referred to China as divided. On the other hand, there was the insistence that the ROC was a sovereign state, in effect a successor to the Qing dynasty, as was the PRC. But there is either one divided China state, or two successor states. Taiwan officials appeared to resolve the contradiction both by fuzzing it with the assertion that the ROC and the PRC were "political entities," and by saying that "one China" referred not to a state but a "historical, geographical, cultural, and racial entity." See "Relations Across the Taiwan Straits," 110.

23. "The Taiwan Question and the Reunification of China"; Interview with Chu Yun-han, March 3, 2003.

24. See Lee Teng-hui, *The Road to Democracy: Taiwan's Pursuit of Identity* (Tokyo: PHP Institute, 1999), 96–98; "Transcript of a Press Conference Held After President Lee's visit to the Southeast Asian Countries," February 16, 1994, *Jingying Da Taiwan*, 423–446. Note that Lee stated his desire to visit the United States two months before he was angered by the restrictions of a transit through Hawaii, which is usually viewed as the stimulus for his later effort to secure his Cornell visit.

25. *Jingying Da Taiwan*, 469–483; cited passage on 472.

26. Interview with Lee Teng-hui, July 31, 2003. "Continue to Promote the Reunification of the Motherland," Xinhua English, Foreign Broadcast Information Service (FBIS), CH-95–019, January 30, 1995, 84–86.

27. "Text of President's Speech," translated from *Lianhobao* in FBIS, CH-95–068, 77–80. Lee's reference to an 84-year existence of the ROC was apparently the first time that he himself asserted that the ROC had existed since 1912 (as the NUC had done in August 1992).

28. See Ross, "The 1995–96 Taiwan Strait Confrontation."

29. Additional plausible explanations of Lee's trip were a desire to enhance his bargaining power vis-à-vis Beijing; that he was responding to the Taiwan public's demand for an end to international isolation; and that he was angry over his treatment by the U.S. government on his transit of Hawaii in April 1994.

30. See "Message to the Opening Ceremony of the Eighth Session of the First National Assembly," February 19, 1990, *Li Denghui Zongtong xiansheng qishijiunian Yenlun Xuanaji* (Selected Opinions of President Lee Teng-hui, 1990) (Taipei: Government Information Office, 1991), 17; "Interview with Michael Richardson of the International Herald Tribune," March 22, 1990, *Xidu Li Deng-hui* (Reading Lee Teng-hui in Detail)(Taipei: Central Daily News Press, 1996), 251.

31. "Reportage on Li's Visit To Cornell University 'Text' of 9 June Cornell Speech," CNA, July 9, 1995, FBIS, OW1006051095. Lee had first mentioned the theme of popular sovereignty in October 1994; see "Responses to Questions Posed by Holman Jenkins Jr., Editor of the Editorial Section, *Asian Wall Street Journal*, October 3, 1994, OOP website; "Speech by Taiwan President Li Teng-hui at Chungshan Hall in Taipei on 10 October, 1994," FBIS, CHI-94–196, October 11, 1994; "Taiwan's New Role and Image in Asia and the World"—Address to the

1994 Business Week Asia Chief Executive Forum," October 5, 1994, OOP website. In his Cornell speech, Lee spoke in general and routine terms about cross-Strait relations.

32. "Text of President Li Teng-hui's Inaugural Speech," May 20, 1996, FBIS, CH-96–098.

33. Some of the other allusions:

   - "a new beginning"
   - "a new frontier"
   - "This gathering of today does not celebrate the victory of any candidate, or any political party for that matter. It honors a triumph of democracy for the 21.3 million people."
   - "Four years will soon pass; . . . let us get off to a very good start today"

34. "Closing Remarks to the 13th Plenum of the National Unification Council," July 22, 1998, in *President Lee Teng-hui's Selected Addresses and Messages: 1998* (Taipei: Government Information Office, 1999), 113–120. In his *Road to Democracy (Taiwan de Zhuzhang)*, Lee did touch on cross-Strait relations (on pages 50–55 and 117–125), but he only cited passages of his 1998 National Unification Council speech, spoke of the need better to define Taiwan's identity, and asserted that Taiwan was a model for mainland development. Jiang Zemin replayed old themes himself in his political report to the Communist Party's Fifteenth Congress. He also stressed Beijing's opposition to "splittist tendencies" on the island and refused to renounce the use of force or talk to the "handful of people who stubbornly cling to the position of independence of Taiwan." See "Jiang Zemin's Political Report," Beijing Central Television, September 12, 1997, FBIS, OW1209033297.

35. "VOG Interviews Li Teng-hui," *Zhongyang Ribao*, July 10, 1999, FBIS, OW12007135899.

36. Interview with Lee Teng-hui, July 31, 2003.

37. "President Lee's Foreign Policy Address, *Topics* (magazine of the Taipei American Chamber of Commerce), August 1997, 36, 39; "Response to Questions Submitted by Bruce W. Nelan, Senior Editor for *Time Magazine*," in *President Lee Teng-hui's Selected Addresses and Messages: 1998*, 78–101.

38. See, for example, James Crawford, *The Creation of States in International Law* (Oxford: Clarendon Press, 1979), 31–71.

39. The position of the small group was somewhat at odds with the National Unification Guidelines, which said that the jurisdiction of the ROC was confined to Taiwan, Penghu, Jinmen, and Mazu but that its sovereignty extended to all of China.

40. Jacques deLisle, "The Chinese Puzzle of Taiwan's Status," *Orbis* 44 (Winter 2002): 48–51.

41. Washington tended to focus on the increased tensions that followed Lee's statement rather than on substance of what he said.

CHAPTER FIVE: CHINA-TAIWAN ECONOMIC LINKAGE:

1. Joanne Gowa and Edward D. Mansfield, "Power Politics and International Trade," *American Political Science Review* 87, no. 2 (June 1993): 408–420. Gowa and Mansfield contend that trade thrives among political allies but tends to be averted among political adversaries. Trade enhances welfare, creating externalities for security. The richer one's allies are, the easier it is for a defense burden sharing arrangement to work; the poorer one's enemies are, the less pressure there will be for an arms race. This line of reasoning is further elaborated in Joanne Gowa, *Allies, Adversaries, and International Trade* (Princeton: Princeton University Press, 1994).

2. Li Thian-Fok, "Taiwan's Economic Hara Kiri," *China Brief,* May 20, 2003, Jamestown Foundation. Li points out that Taiwan has sumptuously invested in China 4 percent of its GDP annually, while Japan and the the United States have put in 0.04 percent and 0.05 percent, respectively.

3. It is hard to imagine a natural process of integration between two economies without the two governments working assiduously and purposely in creating it. Merchants can trade, investors can sink their capital beyond national borders, but disputes surely will arise, both international and national legal frameworks will be needed to solve the dispute or even simply to smooth the flow of goods and capital; and whenever jurisdiction becomes an issue, the governments will be involved. In his famous book, *The Great Transformation,* Karl Polyani contends that there is nothing natural about a market, and that market as an economic institution is created, permitted, and needs to be maintained. Notice that nearly all proposals for economic integration across the Strait contain, or are regarded as having, noneconomic objectives. Economic interdependence may deepen without economic integration. Transactions cost will be high; and "externalities" (unintended consequences), especially national security, may be unavoidable. Now, will political integration be the ultimate externality of economic interdependence? It is theoretically possible, but empirically not probable. Political integration, as economic integration, is an intentional, goal-driven process, which in the case of China and Taiwan would require a change of heart on the part of the latter. Nations engaged in economic integration (EEC and later on, EU) are a far cry from political integration. Will economic interdependence without integration between the two sides of the Taiwan Strait lead Taiwan residents to embrace the idea of political integration? See Peter Chow, "Economic Integration and Political Sovereignty: Problems and Prospects for an Integrated Chinese Economic Area," in Deborah A. Brown and Tun-jen Cheng, eds., *New Leadership and New Agenda* (Jamaica, NY: Center for Asian Studies, St. John's University, 2002), 161–198.

4. In the wake of President Lee's visit to Cornell University, his alma mater, China staged military maneuvers and fired missiles off Taiwan's coast in the 1995–96 Crisis.

5. On July 9, 1999, President Lee stated that the relationship across the Strait was a special kind of relationship between two states. China responded with intensified military maneuvers.

6. One week before the March 20 election, Taiwan's second presidential election, Premier Zhu of China issued a stern warning that a wrong choice on the part of Taiwan voters would have grave consequences.

7. The SARS crisis began in Canton, China, in late 2002; undisclosed and uncontained, it spread to Hong Kong, Singapore, Vietnam, Canada, and finally to Taiwan in the spring and early summer of 2003. Taiwan's investment slowed down a bit during the SARS crisis, but there was no real impact on exports to China. In May 2003, the growth rate of cross-Strait trade dropped to 8.4 percent, but the total amount of trade for the January–May 2003 period showed a 25.7 percent increase over the corresponding period of the previous year. For press release of the Board of International Trade, Ministry of Economic Affairs, Taiwan, reflecting this see *China Times*, July 31, 2003.

8. Taiwan residents remit more than $1 billion to China, and spend around $1.5 billion in touring China annually.

9. *Taishang* could use trade proceeds to invest abroad, or they could store them in Taiwan. As of today, the private sector has about $30 billion deposited in Taiwan's banks.

10. Koo Cheng-fu from Taiwan and Wang Dao-han from China met in Singapore. Koo and Wang were the heads of two quasi-official organizations dealing with cross-Strait relations.

11. See Tun-jen Cheng and Chi Schive, "What Has Democratization Done to Taiwan's Economy?" *Chinese Political Science Review* (January 1997): 1–24.

12. *United Daily News*, July 17, 2002.

13. *United Daily News*, April 9, 2003. Most Taiwanese firms are involved in OEM or ODM. OEM means original equipment manufacturing, an arrangement under which Taiwan firms produce the model designed by foreign firms. Original design manufacturing (ODM) requires the subcontracted Taiwanese firms to engage in designing products using foreign brand names. In either case, Taiwanese firms manufacture and export, but do not market their outputs to consumers, at least not under their own brand names.

14. For the shift, see Susan Shirk, *How China Opened Its Door: The Political Success of the PRC's Foreign Trade and Investment Reforms* (Washington DC: Brookings Institution Press, 1994).

15. The most widely publicized case was Formosa Plastics' project to build a power plant and a petrochemical complex in Fujian. Both projects were aborted.

16. See Peggy Pei-chen Chang and Tun-jen Cheng, "The Rise of the Information Technology Industry in China: A Formidable Challenge to Taiwan's Economy," *American Asian Review*, 20, no.3 (Fall 2002):125–174, esp. 128–134.

17. See report in *Commercial Times*, July 25, 1998. Minister Zhu was also reportedly praising the information technology sector for keeping Taiwan immune to the Asian financial crisis.

18. Lee later packaged this "bargain" by linking economic mutual benefits to political reconciliation. See his response (dubbed as Lee's Six Points) to Jiang Zeming's call for talks on the Chinese New Year, 1995 (known as Jiang's Eight Points). Note that a senior politician, Chen Li-fu, also called upon Beijing leaders to forsake Deng Xiaoping's four cardinal principles (to follow the socialist path, the dictatorship of the proletariat, the leadership of the Chinese Communist Party, and Marxism-Leninism-Mao Zedong Thought) in exchange for Taiwan's economic aid. See Central News Agency, "Kuomintang xing-xuay jian-zheng-ren" (Eyewitnesses of the rise and decline of the KMT), February 10, 2002.

19. For GSNH policy, see Tun-jen Cheng and Peggy Pei-chen Chang, "Limits of Statecraft: Political Economy of Taiwan under Lee Teng-hui," in Wei-chin Lee and T. Y. Wang, eds., *Sayanara to the Lee Teng-hui Era* (Lanham, MD: University Press of America, 2003).

20. Late President Yang Shang-kun laid down these two guiding principles in December 1990 in his speech to the Working Session on Taiwan Affairs.

21. *United Daily News*, December 30, 2002. Vice President Lu did not explain why the PLA would highlight the year 2010.

22. This is what the "obsolescent bargaining theory" has posited. See Theodore H. Moran, *Multinational Corporations and the Politics of Dependence: Copper in Chile* (Princeton: Princeton University Press, 1974).

23. The last figure was Tung Cheng-yuan's estimate; the rest were from the Chunghua Institute of Economic Research and Ministry of Economic Affairs, see Tung, "The Impact of Taiwanese Businesspeople's Outward Investment in China on Their Competitiveness: A Case Study of the Information Technology Industry," paper presented at the Chinese Economist Society 2003 conference on Chinese Economy After WTO: Opportunities and Challenges of Globalization, August 2–3, 2003, Ann Arbor, Michigan., 48–49.

24. Nicholas Lardy, *Integrating China into the Global Economy* (Washington DC: Brookings Institution Press, 2002), 158ff.

25. Stephen Cohen has mapped the flows of commodity, personnel, messages, and so on among the members of the Pacific Community for the decade of 1990s, with this refreshing finding: the cross-Pacific interaction was as dense as ever. Intra-Pacific Asia flows still paled by comparison. Thus, although China-Hong Kong-Taiwan interaction has intensified, the process has to be understood in the context of continuously dense ties across the Pacific. See Stephen Cohen, "Mapping the Pacific," *American Asian Review* 20, no. 3 (Fall 2002): 1–30.

26. The formula for IIT ratio is $[1 - (X–M)$ or $(M–X) / (X+M)] \times 100$. The IIT ratio ranges from 0 to 100; 0 indicates complete interindustry trade or no intraindustry trade, 100 indicates complete intra-industry trade.

27. Tung, "The Impact of Taiwanese Businesspeople's Outward Investment," 47. The first study is cited on page 42. The manufacturing sector includes Section 6 through 22 of the HS data, see table 5.2 for a full description.

28. The obsolescing bargaining theory is based on a study of MNCs in extractive industries. The logic seems to apply to MNCs' investment in infrastructure.

29. Theodore Moran, "Introduction," in Moran, ed., *Multinational Corporations* (Lexington, MA: D.C. Heath and Co., 1985), 9–16.

30. Budget deficits for the central government have not been redressed since the mid-1990s, when a new fiscal plan was installed. See Szu-chien Hsu, "Central-Local Relations in the PRC under the Tax Assignment System," *Issues and Studies* (March–April 2000): 32–72. State-owned enterprises have been losing money. The debt-equity ratio is 5:1, dragging the financial sector down. The financial sector is kept afloat by the high savings of the public. Once the public loses confidence in the financial institutions, the sector will suffer. See Nicholas Lardy, *China's Unfinished Economic Revolution* (Washington, DC: Brookings Institution Press, 1998); Victor Shih, "Zhu Rongji and the Financial Reform," paper presented to the American Political Science Association convention, 2002; Tung Chen-yuan, "The Impact on Taiwan," in *The Globalization of the Chinese Economy* (London: Elgar, 2002), 295. Indeed, for banks, *Taishang* would be better customers than state owned enterprises.

31. Interview with Chang Jong-feng, June 2002.

32. Brian Job et al., "Assessing the Risks of Conflict in the PRC-ROC Enduring Rivalry," *Pacific Affairs* 72, no.4 (1999–2000): 515–535.

33. The statistics provided by the Office of Taiwan Affairs in Shanghai showed that in late 2002 some 220,000 Taiwan people lived in Shanghai alone. See *United Daily News*, October 30, 2002.

34. Although it is impossible to show that the saga of the Formosa Plastics' proposed Fujian investment project was instrumental to getting the Mai-liao petrochemical project going, it seems logical to assume that the two pursuits were somewhat related.

35. Leng Tse-kang, "High-Tech Talents Flow Across the Straits," paper presented to the Sino-American Conference on Contemporary China, University of California, San Diego, May 2001. Notice that the literature on multinational corporations (MNCs) recently contends that MNCs are more national than cosmopolitan; they are affiliated with the financial institutions from their home countries, display distinct management styles and organizational setups, and their activities are embedded in domestic structures. See Paul N. Doremus et al., *The Myth of the Global Corporation* (Princeton: Princeton University Press, 1998).

36. Wang Gungwu reflects on the psychological saga of overseas Chinese as sojourners in his *The Chinese Overseas* (Cambridge: Harvard University Press, 2000). For the concept of transnationality, see Aihwa Ong, *Flexible Citizenship: The Cultural Logics of Transnationality* (Durham: Duke University Press, 1999). For discussion on *Taishang* as modern nomads, see Tun-jen Cheng, "Taishang wei xian-dai yu-mu ming-zhu," *INPR Biweekly*, September 1997.

37. Given that the issue of political loyalty is a sensitive one, one that is likely to elicit a politically correct answer, our speculation in some of the following paragraphs is probably as interesting as interview-based studies.

38. Tung, "The Impact on Taiwan."

39. Obviously this is due to a lack of interest among *Taishang*, but this also indicates

the limited political space for *Taishang* in China. See *Today's Morning News* (*Jin-re-zau-bao*), November 18, 2002. The Standing Committee of the National People's Congress stipulates that Taiwan's investors can participate in people's congress election at the county and township levels.

40. But even MNCs with this "safety net" were burned: Japanese big business suffer from non-payment all the time as well as from violation of intellectual property rights (IPRs); a survey shows that, in 2002 alone, Japanese firms lost $8 billion IPRs See *Economic Daily*, July 17, 2003.

41. *United Daily News*, July 15, 2003; *China Times*, July 16, 2003; *Epoch Times*, July 16, 2003.

42. Of course, firms may form new enterprises not entirely for tax holidays, and to bypass the onerous approval process for big investment, and at the request of local officials who run industrial estates. See *United Daily News*, July 6, 2003. But the very fact that foreign group companies are the usual suspects of tax authorities probably reveals the Beijing regime's mixed feelings toward capitalism, which is being practiced, but not whole-heartedly legitimated.

43. This would be predominantly those who came to Taiwan in 1949 and remained unmarried who in the pursuit of old age companionship and low living cost went to China. After having trouble adapting, 267 returned to Taiwan. See *China Times*, October 2 and 19, 2002.

44. *United Daily News*, July 16, 2003.

45. Well-to-do U.S. retirees reside in Central America, cast absentee ballots in the U.S. presidential election and go to Miami for important medical care. Although Medicare benefits do not reach Central America, private Blue-Cross and Blue-Shield is moving in. I thank George Grayson for this point.

46. See "AIT Director Issues Economic Advice to Taiwan," *Topics: The Magazine of International Business in Taiwan* 32, no. 8 (October 2002): 12. See also the editorial in this issue. *Topics* is an official publication of the American Chamber of Congress in Taipei.

47. See Tung Chen-yuan, "The Impact on Taiwan," 203, 213. Tung uses this calculation: the balance of payments gain = FDI income + FDI-driven exports (estimated to be around 34 percent of total exports to China) – outflow of FDI. The 34 percent was based on a Chung-hua Institute of Economic Research study that was completed in 1993. It was a conservative estimate; others put the figure at around 50 percent. Tung's study shows that FDI in China led to capital accumulation (not depletion) in Taiwan.

48. These two reports were cited in Tung, "The Impact on Taiwan," 204–205.

49. Higher labor productivity—measured by real GDP divided by total employment—not only means more labor output per input, but also indicates higher quotients of technology, knowhow, and equipment used in production.

50. These are the well-known theses that Stephen Hymer and Raymond Vernon advanced to explain why firms go abroad to invest rather than stay home and export their products. Hymer focused on the industrial organization aspect, while Vernon stressed the product cycle aspect. Raymond Vernon, *Sovereignty at Bay*

(New York: Basic Books, 1971), esp. 46-59 and Stephen H. Hymer, *The International Operations of National Firms: A Study of Direct Foreign Investment* (Cambridge: MIT Press, 1976).

51. Keith Cowling and Philip R. Tomlinson, "The Japanese Crisis: A Case of Strategic Failure?" *Economic Journal* (June 2000): F358-F381.

52. Lin Wu-lang, "Revisiting the Issue of 'the Hollowing out of Taiwan's Industry,' " *Taiwan Economic Forum*, April 2003, 19–41 (in Chinese).

53. This is the main thesis in Stephen Cohen and John Zysman, *Manufacturing Matters: The Myth of the Post-Industrial Economy* (New York: Basic Books, 1987).

54. For a most optimistic analysis on this, see Tung Cheng-yuan, "The Impact of Taiwanese Businesspeople's Outward Investment."The crucial missing element in Tung's analysis is the growing production share of overseas operation of Taiwanese firms.

55. The Bureau of Industrial Development, Ministry of Economic Affairs, established ITRI in 1973. On the divergent strategies for industrial deepening, see Tun-jen Cheng, "Political Regimes and Development Strategies: South Korea versus Taiwan," in Gary Gereffi and Don Wyman, eds., *Manufacturing Miracles* (Princeton: Princeton University Press, 1990), 163–171.

56. For the rise of semiconductor sector, see J. A. Mathews, "Silicon Valley of the East: Creating Taiwan's Semiconductor Industry," *California Management Review* 39, no. 4 (1997): 26–54. See also, Gregory Noble, *Collective Action in East Asia: How Ruling Parties Shape Industrial Policy* (Ithaca: Cornell University Press, 1998).

57. See Peggy Pei-chen Chang and Tun-jen Cheng, "The Rise of the Information Technology Industry in China," 125–174.

58. For the tripartite (IDM, fab-less, and the fab) structure of the semiconductor industry, see "A Survey of the Semiconductor Sector," *Topics* (April 2003): 48–57.

59. On the contribution of "social network" to the rise of the semiconductor industry in Taiwan, see Chen Dong-sheng, *Ji-ti wang-lo* [Integrated networks], Taipei: Qun-hsieu, 2002.

60. Semiconductors are made on round silicon wafers, the size and shape of dinner plates. Circuits as small as a 0.13 micron are etched onto the wafer. Larger wafer sizes allow manufacturers to pack more chips, thereby saving cost; similarly, a finer line width micron technique also allows more chips to be etched onto a wafer.

61. *Taipei Times*, June 26, 2000.

62. *Taipei Times*, June 29, 2000.

63. *Taipei Times*, July 26, 2000.

64. *Taipei Times*, February 21, 2002.

65. James Soong, an insurgent KMT presidential candidate established the People's First Party upon the KMT's electoral debacle in 2000.

66. The Taiwan Solidarity Union is the fourth largest political party, composed primarily of a group of legislators, mostly former KMT members, who strongly opposed the KMT's conciliatory policy toward the mainland.

67. The following is distilled from press reports as well as based on my interviews with a few industry leaders.

68. The rebuttal prepared by Professor Lin and Professor Lo—both associated with the Taiwan Think Tank—was widely regarded as the most coherent and convincing one. For a summary of their presentation, see Chin-hsin Liu and Cheng-fnag Lo, "Long-term effects may have serious implications," *Taipei Times*, March 9, 2002, Internet version.

69. *China Times*, February 22, 2003.

70. *China Times*, February 20, 2003.

71. Established in November 2000 with capital of $ 1.6 billion, Hungli, using the 0.25–0.18 micron welding technique, expected to turn out 27,000 units of 8-inch wafers per month by late 2004. Incorporated in April 2000 with a $3 billion investment, Zhongxin completed its first fab in August 2001, using the 0.25 micron welding technique to produce 8-inch wafers for China's domestic market. In early 2003, its monthly output was 24,000 wafers, but its monthly capacity was expected to reach 80,000 wafers when the other two fabs were completed in mid-2004. In 2003 this company had 3,101 employees, including 600 from Taiwan and 300 from Japan, the U.S., and Europe. See *United Daily News*, February 12, 2003. The CEO of SMIC, Richard Chang, was once a key deputy of Morris Chang. GSC was co-founded by Wen-yang Wang (son of Yung-ching Wang, CEO of the Formosa Plastic Group) and Jiang Man-heng (son of Jiang Zemin), but many of their deputies are former employees of TSMC. A former key person of UMC has just established a new firm in Shanghai in the summer of 2003.

72. *United Daily News*, February 11, 2003.

73. *Economic Daily*, March 31, 2003.

74. These technology transfers that SMIC has received are reported in *United Daily News*, February 9, 2003, *China Times*, February 22, 2003; *Economic Daily*, March 25, 2003; *Commercial Times*, May 20, 2003.

75. *Economic Daily*, March 31, 2003.

76. *Economic Daily*, July 4, 2003.

77. This is an assessment by Solomon Securities, Barings Hong Kong, summarized in *United Daily News*, April 18, 2003.

78. *United Daily News*, April 18, 2003.

79. *Economic Daily*, January 17, 2003.

80. The first case involved two venture capital funds, Cheng-yu and Global Strategy (the former chaired by former vice premier Hsu Li-teh and partially founded by the government-owned development fund, the latter chaired by a former minister without portfolio, both holding office under the KMT government). These two venture capital companies had invested in SM Conductor, and are being fined and required to divest. The second case was Hongli Shanghai Semiconductor, a joint venture between Jiang's son and YC Wang's son. The third case was Dalien Shengli Shopping Mart. Either the companies or their chairs were to pay fines and all were required to divest within a time limit. The two

venture capitalists divested. The other two cases are still pending. No one be-lieves that they will be divested. See *China Times*, January 18, 2003.

81. With 10 percent of TSMC shares in-hand, the Taiwan Government is the second largest shareholder, next to the Dutch Philips group, which holds 21.72 percent of TSMC's common shares. See Taiwan Semiconductor Manufacturing Co., Ltd., *Annual Report 2002*, p.20.

82. For political logic of this alliance, see Tun-jen Cheng and Yunhan Chu, "State-Business Relations in South Korea and Taiwan," in Laurence Whitehead, ed., *Emerging Market Democracies* (Baltimore: Johns Hopkins University Press, 2002), 31–62.

83. See William W. Keller and Louis W. Pauly, "Crisis and Adaptation in Taiwan and South Korea: The Political Economy of Semiconductors," in William W. Keller and Richard J. Samuels, eds., *Crisis and Innovation in Asian Technology* (Cambridge: Cambridge University Press, 2003), 137–159.

84. According to Minister Lin Yi-fu, the goal will be reached. See *China Times*, July 30, 2003.

85. China is active in labor-intensive, downstream production of LCD; but such production, and indeed the whole industry, are the extension of leading Tai-wanese firms, including Chi-Mei.

86. *Taipei Journal*, July 4, 2003.

87. Goldman Sachs predicts that TFT-LCD is replicating the success story of semi-conductors in Taiwan. See *Commercial Times*, August 1, 2003.

88. *China Times* June 17, 2003.

89. Interview with Min-hsian Chen of the Ministry of Economic Affairs, August 14, 2003.

90. *China Times* July 31, 2003.

CHAPTER SIX. TAIWAN'S DEFENSE REFORMS AND MILITARY MODERNIZATION PROGRAM

1. Stability in this situation is also ideally dependent upon the ability of the Unit-ed States and China credibly to reassure one another that in the case of Wash-ington, any unilateral attempt by Taiwan to attain full independence will not be supported, and in the case of Beijing, a priority will be placed on the peace-ful resolution of the problem. However, that said, the existence of strong mu-tual distrust between the two powers results in an increasing reliance on mili-tary deterrence.

2. Many of the issues covered in this article are extremely sensitive to both the U.S. and Taiwan governments and are thus not often discussed in detail in the open media. Hence, much of the information and analysis presented herein was de-rived from personal interviews conducted in the spring and summer of 2003 with both U.S. and Taiwan participants and knowledgeable observers. These in-dividuals requested that their names and organizational affiliations not be cited.

3. For further details on the points raised in this paragraph, see Michael D. Swaine and James C. Mulvenon. *Taiwan's Foreign and Defense Policies: Features and Determinants* (Santa Monica, CA: RAND Center for Asia-Pacific Policy, 2001, MR-1383-SRF), 15, 37, 65.

4. Under this system, the CGS acts, in the military command system (*junling*), as chief of staff to the president for operational matters; while in the administrative system (*junzheng*), he serves as chief of staff to the minister of national defense. Government Information Office. *The Republic of China Yearbook 1997* (Taipei, Taiwan, 1996), 123–124.

5. Michael D. Swaine. *Taiwan's National Security, Defense Policy, and Weapons Procurement Processes* (Santa Monica, CA: RAND, National Defense Research Institute, 1999, MR-1128-OSD), 8.

6. Arthur Ding, "Civil-Military Relations in Taiwan and China: A Comparison," unpublished paper prepared for the CAPS-RAND International Conference on PLA Affairs, August 15–16, 2003, San Diego, California, p. 4.

7. These laws—the National Defense Law (NDL) and the Ministry of National Defense Organization Law (sometimes referred to collectively as the "Two Defense Laws")—after being ratified by the LY were promulgated by the R.O.C. president in January 2000 and subsequently went into effect on March 1, 2002. See *2002 National Defense Report, Republic of China*, published by the Ministry of Defense, Taipei, Taiwan R.O.C., July 2002, 164, 227, 230–232, available at www.mnd.gov.tw/report/index.htm. Also see John Pomfret, "Also on Taipei's Radar: Reform," *Washington Post*, April 25, 2001; Michael Tsai, "Organizational Reinvention and Defense Reform," *Taiwan Defense Affairs* 2, no.3 (Spring 2003).

8. Under this restructuring, the General Staff Headquarters (GSH) would serve as both the military command staff for the defense minister and commanding organ of military operations of the three armed services under the defense minister's supervision. See Hu Zhenya, "Guofangfa yu guofangbu zhuzhi tiaozheng [The National Defense Law and the Organizational Re-structure of the Ministry of National Defense] in
http://www.dsis.org.tw/peaceforum/papers/2000–02/TM0001001.htm,
and Arthur S. Ding, "Bijiao liangan de guofangfa" [The National Defense Laws of Taiwan and China: A Comparison], in
http://www.dsis.org.tw/peaceforum/papers/2000–02/TM0001002.htm.

9. Ding, "Civil-Military Relations," 9; Interviews, Taipei, summer 2003; *2002 National Defense Report*, 231.

10. Ding, "Civil-Military Relations," 9.

11. For further information on the development of civilian control over the military, see M. Taylor Fravel, "Towards Civilian Supremacy: Civil-Military Relations in Taiwan's Democratization," *Armed Forces and Society* 29, no. 1 (Fall 2002): 59–63.

12. For example, the deputy minister responsible for policy and strategic and force planning will ostensibly play a very important role in this new system; Interviews, Taipei, summer 2003.

13. Much of the following discussion of Taiwan's military modernization program has been drawn from interviews conducted in Washington, in the summer of 2003; Swaine and Mulvenon, *Taiwan's Foreign and Defense Policies*, 160–61; Alexander Chieh-cheng Huang, "Taiwan's Defense Modernization for the 21st Century: Challenges and Opportunities," unpublished paper prepared for the Conference on War and Peace in the Taiwan Strait, February 26–28, 1999, Duke University, Durham, North Carolina.

14. Interviews, Taipei and Washington, spring, summer 2003.

15. Interviews, Taipei, summer 2003; Also see "New Defense Minister Tang announces troop reduction," *Taiwan News*, February 3, 2002. The Chinese language version of the *2002 National Defense Report: Zhonghua Minguo Guofang Baogaoshu 2002* (Taipei: Guofangbu, July 2002) refers to the *Jing Jin* program in Section 5: Defense Management, Chapter 3: Defense Resources Management, 196–197. More recent references to *Jing Jin* can also be found in the *Lifayuan Gongbao* (*Legislative Gazette*) 92, no. 44 (October 29, 2003): 298–300.

16. Any significant reduction in force size would also carry a longer term benefit in cost savings, presumably allowing the military to devote larger portions of Taiwan's defense budget to weapons and equipment improvements. See Chen Chao-min, Vice Minister of Armament and Acquisition, Ministry of National Defense, Remarks to the U.S.–Taiwan Defense Industry Conference, San Antonio, Texas, February 13, 2003.

17. See the interview with Chen conducted by Philip P. Pan and David E. Hoffman of the *Washington Post* on March 29, 2004, found on http://www.washington-post.com/wp-dyn/articles/A33322–2004Mar29.html.

18. Given the general unpopularity of military service among the population, terms of service for conscripts have been reduced over the years.

19. The Taiwan military is top-heavy, with a high ratio of officers to soldiers, and it lacks an adequate number of professional NCOs (almost all existing NCOs are conscripts; only the sergeant majors in units are professionals).

20. Interviews, Washington, summer 2003.

21. The development of such a more sophisticated force structure has also led to a perceived need to acquire a wide variety of greater technical skills.

22. For details, see Swaine and Mulvenon, *Taiwan's Foreign and Defense Policies*, 15, 37, 65.

23. Specifically, Taiwan's military forces were given three largely independent missions: (1) air superiority (*zhikong*) for the ROC Air Force; (2) sea denial (*zhihai*) for the ROC Navy; and (3) anti-landing warfare (*fandenglu*) for the ROC Army. For the official definition of Taiwan's national security strategy, military strategy, and supporting policies, see the *2002 National Defense Report*, 59–78. For further details on Taiwan's defense strategy, see Alexander Chieh-cheng Huang, "Taiwan's View of the Military Balance and the Challenge It Presents," in James R. Lilley and Chuck Downs, eds., *Crisis in the Taiwan Strait* (Washington DC: National Defense University Press, 1997), 282–285; and Swaine, *Taiwan's National Security, Defense Policy*, 53–55.

24. The Taiwan General Staff Headquarters has a J-5 office nominally responsible for strategic plans and policy, but it historically focused on narrow aspects of defense planning. Equally important, it did not exercise as much influence as the U.S. military's J-5, given the superior position enjoyed by the individual service headquarters in the Taiwan military.

25. That is, a more sophisticated security strategy and defense plan more effectively attuned to the growing challenge posed by the PLA would give Taiwan a much stronger basis for evaluating and, if necessary, resisting U.S. pressure to acquire certain types of weapons and systems. Interviews, Taipei, spring and summer 2003.

26. On the third point, Taiwan has a total area of 36,000 square kilometers, measuring only 394 km from north to south, and 144 km from east to west. Its long and narrow shape is not conducive to defense. Moreover, about two-thirds of the island is mountainous, and almost all inhabitants and military bases are concentrated on the plains and undulating hills. The great density of the population also makes it difficult for Taiwan to deploy and move its army in times of war. See Yuan Lin, "The Taiwan Strait is No Longer a Natural Barrier—PLA Strategies for Attacking Taiwan," *Kuang Chiao Ching*, April 16, 1996.

27. "Taiwan: Nine Ex-Military Officers Indicted in Arms Scandal," *Los Angeles Times*, July 6, 2001; "Taiwan president orders probe into alleged scandals," *Agence France Press* (AFP), July 31, 2000; "Taiwan military under fire in kickback, murder scandal," *Agence France Press* (AFP), August 3, 2000; "Taiwan and France work together over arms scandal: report," *Agence France Press* (AFP), August 6, 2000.

28. Interviews, Taipei, summer 2003. Public attitudes toward defense spending are discussed further below.

29. Interviews, Washington, spring 2003 suggest all competition with SPD over responsibilities has not been settled. The emphasis on increasing the indigenous production of weapons and support systems is contained in the *2002 National Defense Report*, 65, 74.

30. The political commissar system of the original KMT-created party-army structure still exists. No longer a mechanism for maintaining KMT control and instilling belief in Chinese nationalist views, it now reportedly carries out morale-building and social welfare functions. In the view of some analysts, it is excessively large and thus acts as a drain on much-needed resources.

31. For an excellent overview of the achievements and difficulties of the attempt to establish civilian control over the military, see Fravel, "Towards Civilian Supremacy," 57–84.

32. Article 15 of the amended version of the MND Organization Law states that this goal must be achieved by January 29, 2003, but allows for a one-year extension of the deadline. This extension was activated.

33. Such an examination is required for all government employees.

34. Interviews, Taipei, spring, summer 2003. Also see Lin Mei-chun, "NSC Defends Loyalty Test Plans," *Taipei Times*, June 13, 2002; and Crystal Hsu, "Civil Service Vetting Proposal Raises Opposition Ire," *Taipei Times*, June 12, 2002.

35. Interviews, Taipei, summer 2003; Ding, "Civil-Military Relations," 3. The Chinese version of the *2002 National Defense Report*: *Zhonghua Minguo Guofang Baogaoshu 2002* (Taipei: Guofangbu, July 2002) discusses the *Jing Shi* program in Section 5: Defense Management, Chapter 2: Defense Law Reform, 180 and more recently it is reviewed in the *Lifayuan Gongbao* (*Legislative Gazette*) 92, no. 44 (October 29, 2003): 298–300.

36. Li Wenzhong, He Minhao, Lin Zhuoshui, Duan Yikang, Chen Zhongxin, Tang Huosheng, and Xiao Meiqin (LY members representing the DPP). *Taiwan bingli guimo yanjiu baogao [Research Report on the Scale of Taiwan's Armed Forces]*, DPP Policy Committee Research Report Series, March 2003. The stated purpose of the report is to examine in detail the plans for the scale of manpower of the armed forces in order to ensure the optimization of the use of Taiwan's limited national defense resources by lowering the percentage of the defense budget that is used for personnel costs. Also see "Taipei 'Needs Leaner, Meaner Armed Forces' " *Agence France Presse*, March 31, 2003.

37. The above-cited DPP Report also proposes raising the proportion of volunteers in the armed forces and decreasing the period of compulsory military service to a mere nine months.

38. Interviews, Washington and Taipei, summer 2003.

39. One major exception is the submarine program. The absence of an available supplier, the desire of Taiwan to manufacture at least part of the submarines, and both financial and technical considerations have delayed agreement. See "Sub Impasse Continues," *Taiwan Defense Review*, May 30, 2003.

40. John Pomfret and Philip P. Pan, "U.S. Hits Obstacles in Helping Taiwan Guard Against China," *Washington Post*, October 30, 2003, A1.

41. For a detailed discussion of the C4ISR assistance program between the United States and Taiwan, see "Po Sheng Decision Imminent," *Taiwan Defense Review*, July 17, 2003.

42. For further details on U.S. defense assistance to Taiwan, see the article by Michael S. Chase in this volume, "U.S.–Taiwan Security Cooperation." Also see "Pentagon Reviews Taiwan Ties," *Taiwan Defense Review*, January 18, 2003, and "Taiwan Reviews Defense Ties with Taiwan, Says Report," *Central News Agency*, Taipei, January 20, 2003.

43. The decision to acquire ballistic missile defense systems of any kind remains a highly controversial subject within the ROC military, however. According to one very knowledgeable observer of this issue, "Many ROC Army officers do not view conventional ballistic missiles as a particularly significant threat to its ability to perform its mission of countering a PLA amphibious invasion. While viewing increasingly accurate and lethal ballistic missiles as a significant threat to its ability to sustain operations, many within the Air Force would rather increase the proportion of the budget to 'defensive counterstrike operations' (*fangyuxing fanzhi zuozhan*). The Navy has been perhaps more supportive of missile defense, particularly as part of an AEGIS program." Also, many within the LY and the media (and some military analysts) argue

that missile defenses would be easily exhausted or saturated in a large scale missile strike.

44. For apparent references to the acquisition of such a capability, see *2002 National Defense Report*, 71.

45. Interviews, Washington, 2003.

46. For example, according to a knowledgeable U.S. observer, Taiwan has reportedly established a joint operations structure, at least on paper. U.S. observers of Taiwan's exercises believe such a structure is a significant advancement over previous years.

47. Interviews, Washington and Taipei, spring and summer 2003.

48. Although the United States has urged Taiwan to establish a third, highly mobile, helicopter-equipped army brigade rapidly to plug holes in its defense line, some observers believe that Taiwan should equip such a unit with existing AH-1H Super Cobra attack helicopters and not the more costly Apaches. See, for example, "Taiwan seeks to purchase attack helicopters," *Taipei Times*, February 26, 2002. Also see "MND Studies Effectiveness of Patriot Missiles," *Taiwan News*, March 26, 2003.

49. According to some knowledgeable Taiwan military observers, the acquisition of important C4ISR technologies such as the U.S. Link-16 system are limited to tactical applications, and overall communications networks are largely to be used to strengthen top-down controls, not to increase the awareness of local commanders. For these observers, Taiwan needs to expand its level of battlefield awareness by directly accessing satellite-based C4ISR systems operated by the United States.

50. The special defense budget, presumably to begin in 2005, will primarily fund the acquisition of submarines, ASW platforms, and the PAC-3 missile defense system. Other items approved in recent years, such as long-range early warning radar and C4ISR systems, will eventually be funded through the regular defense budget. See "FY2004 Defense Budget," *Taiwan Defense Review*, September 18, 2003.

51. Interview, Washington, summer 2003. For reference to the MND draft budget, see *Naval News*, Taipei, Taiwan, April 12, 2004.

52. For an assessment of the state of the PRC missile threat and the difficulties involved in developing an adequate response by both Taiwan and the U.S., see Eric A. McVadon, Director, Asian-Pacific Studies, Institute of Foreign Policy Analysis, "Joint Air and Missile Defense for Taiwan: Implications for Deterrence and Defense," paper delivered at the Conference on Taiwan Security and Air Power, organized by the Center for Taiwan Defense and Strategic Studies (Taiwan) and the Institute for Foreign Policy Analysis (USA), held in Taipei, January 9, 2003.

53. See *Lien Ho Pao* (United Daily News), March 11, 2003, and citing *Lien Ho Pao*, "Taiwan Speeds Up Anti-Missile Arms Buy Due to 'U.S. Pressure.'" *Agence France Press* (AFP), March 14, 2003.

54. Moreover, defense analysts and researchers from the United States have provided training and advice in the areas of strategy development, resource allocation,

and defense analysis to SPD and IAO personnel. See Michael S. Chase, "U.S.–Taiwan Security Cooperation," 167–69, 177–80.

55. See Zhanlue guihua si (Outline of the Strategic Planning Department), available on the MND's website at www.mnd.gov.tw/division/~defense/mil/mnd/spd/Index.htm and Zhenghe pinggu shi zixungang (Outline of Integrated Assessment Office) available at www.mnd.gov.tw/division/~defense/mil/mnd/iao/TOCFrame.htm. Interviews, Taipei, summer 2003.

56. *2002 National Defense Report*, 227.

57. Interviews, Washington and Taipei, 2003; *Defense Report of the Republic of China, 2002*, 227.

58. Interviews, Washington, summer 2003. Also see Michael S. Chase's article in this volume for details.

59. For example, it remains unclear whether Taiwan should retain claims to sovereignty made by the former KMT government, such as those regarding territories in the South China Sea. Interviews, Taipei, summer 2003.

60. *2002 National Defense Report*, 73–74. The definitions of "jointness" contained in the National Defense Report are rudimentary and largely focus on integrating operations within, not between, the services. In the absence of such a strategy, it is difficult to determine what level and type of jointness might be best for Taiwan. In the view of some observers, the interests and concerns of Taiwan's ground forces continue to dominate efforts to develop military strategy and doctrine.

61. During the initial years of the talks, Taiwan participants primarily included MND representatives and military officers. In recent years, however, officials from the Mainland Affairs Council, the Ministry of Foreign Affairs, and the National Security Council also attend, largely as a result of U.S. insistence.

62. Interviews, Washington and Taipei, spring and summer 2003.

63. The changing role of the LY in defense reform is discussed in greater detail below.

64. Interviews, Washington, summer 2003.

65. Interviews, Washington and Taipei, spring and summer 2003. Tang announced in March 2004 his intention to retire from the post of minister of defense. He was replaced by Admiral Lee Jye.

66. However, Chen has apparently attempted to weaken such sentiments among the senior officer corps by accelerating the promotion of native-born Taiwanese officers to higher posts in recent years. See Foreign Broadcast Information Service (FBIS) report in Chinese, April 12, 2004, entitled "Highlights: Taiwan Military Issues 6 April 2004."

67. Chen Shui-bian undoubtedly heightened public awareness of the threat posed to Taiwan by Chinese missiles when he pushed for a referendum on missile defense during the March 20, 2004 presidential election. However, the failure of what is regarded by many as a politically—-not militarily—-inspired initiative, and the absence of any subsequent attempt by Chen to heighten public awareness of the need for serious civil defense efforts, suggest that Taiwan's

leaders remain ambivalent over the necessity of alerting the public to the Chinese threat.

68. Less than two years ago, Army control over the national security establishment was very strong. At that time, almost every position responsible for operations and planning was controlled by an Army officer. The Army also controlled all personnel assignments, and most billets in the GSH were also dedicated to the Army. Although the Army leadership does not seem to have the veto power it had in the past, it can still wield enormous influence and can obstruct, if not overcome, efforts by civilians, other services, and the MND to advance defense reform. Interviews, Washington and Taipei, 2003.

69. Pomfret and Pan, "U.S. Hits Obstacles in Helping Taiwan," locate this resistance primarily within the Taiwan army.

70. The author is indebted to Arthur Ding for these observations.

71. For further details, see Swaine, *Taiwan's National Security, Defense Policy,* 45–47 and Swaine and Mulvenon, *Taiwan's Foreign and Defense Policies,* 65, 87–88.

72. For a discussion of public attitudes regarding defense spending, see ibid., 74–75.

73. See "Pentagon Reviews Taiwan Ties," *Taiwan Defense Review,* January 18, 2003. After two years of deliberation and debate, the LY finally passed the bill approving funding for the Kidd-class destroyer program in late May 2003, but only after the Navy agreed to cut the budget for the program. At the same time, the Taiwan military is reportedly learning some valuable lessons from these experiences on how to attain funding from the LY.

74. For example, many LY members, along with much of the public, believe that U.S. business circles (perhaps with collusion from the Taiwan military and business) drive U.S. policy regarding weapons sales, thus resulting in inflated prices or efforts to dump obsolete weapons on Taiwan. Although there is little doubt that U.S. defense corporations and their Taiwan contacts influence the arms sale process, the level of influence they exert is by no means as large or pervasive as some LY members apparently think.

75. And of course this problem is exacerbated by the suspicions discussed in the previous paragraph.

76. For a detailed discussion of the procurement process and the involvement of the LY therein, see Swaine, *Taiwan's National Security, Defense Policy,* 46.

77. For further analysis of the problems involved in legislative supervision of the military, see Fravel, especially, 71–72.

78. See Directorate General of Budget Accounting and Statistics, *Guoqing tongji tongbao,* no. 93, May 16, 2003, at http://www.dgbas.gov.tw/dgbas03/bs3/report/N920516.htm and http://www.moea.gov.tw/english/eindex.html

79. See "Pentagon Reviews Taiwan Ties," *Taiwan Defense Review,* January 18, 2003. For a detailed analysis of the defense budget process and the composition of Taiwan's national defense expenditure, see Teng Yang-hsi, Senior Specialist, LY Budget and Accounts Committee, "A Preliminary Inquiry Into the Defense Budget," *Taiwan Defense Affairs,* no. 1 (October 2000): 165–192.

80. Interviews, Washington, D.C., summer 2003. Also see Ho Po-wen, "Military Purchases Top $NT700 Billion in the Next Ten Years," *Chung-kuo Shih-pao*, May 17, 2003.

81. One very knowledgeable U.S. observer interviewed by the author believes that Taiwan can acquire and fund many major weapons systems approved by the United States (such as the PAC-3, EW radar, enhanced C4ISR, Apache helicopters) if it increases its annual defense acquisition budget to $1 billion over a ten year period. However, programs such as submarines, P-3C ASW aircraft, and a possible future AEGIS-equipped destroyer sale would require special funding unless the annual defense acquisition budget were dramatically increased even further.

82. Interviews, Washington and Taipei, spring and summer 2003.

83. Interviews, Taipei, spring and summer 2003.

84. See, for example, Richard D. Fisher, *China Brief*, Jamestown Foundation, January 28, 2003.

85. "ROC Military Doesn't Rule Out Pre-emptive Attack on Mainland: Tang," *China News Agency*, October 8, 2003, quoting Defense Minister Tang Yiau-ming

86. Interviews, Taipei, summer 2003, and Swaine and Mulvenon, *Taiwan's Foreign and Defense Policies*, 66–67.

87. Chen Shui-bian, *New Century, New Future: Chen Shui-bian's Blueprint for the Nation*—Volume I: *National Security* [*Xinshiji xinchulu: Chen Shui-bian guojia lantu*—diyice: *Guojia anquan*], Taipei: Chen Shui-bian Presidential Campaign Headquarters, 1999), 50–51.

88. Ibid, 50–51. More recently, Chen has attempted to counter the strong impression that he supports the acquisition of offensive weaponry by emphasizing the need for Taiwan to strengthen its "counter-strike capabilities." But strengthening such capabilities could require what most analysts would regard as offensive weapons, such as ballistic and cruise missiles and ground-strike configured attack aircraft. In other words, this shift in terminology could amount to a distinction without a difference. See Chen's interview with the *Washington Post* of March 29, 2004.

89. "Taiwan Defends Long-Range Missile Plans," *Agence France Press* (AFP), December 9, 1999. Lien Chan has reportedly since backed away from that statement, however.

90. Interviews, Taipei, spring and summer 2003.

91. Swaine and Mulvenon, *Taiwan's Foreign and Defense Policies*, 67.

92. "Pentagon Reviews Taiwan Ties," *Taiwan Defense Review*, January 18, 2003 states that U.S. opposition emanates "mainly from the State Department," but the author has heard similar views expressed by senior U.S. military officers.

93. Interviews, Washington and Taipei, spring and summer 2003. For a highly critical take on the restraints placed on Taiwan's NCO corps, see Wendell Minnick, "Taiwan's Military Needs to Use its NCOs," *Taipei Times*, December 23, 2001.

94. In the area of strategic dialogue between Washington and Taipei, for example, inherent limitations exist on the extent to which the United States is willing to

discuss such issues as basing plans in East Asia and military approaches to countering a Chinese assault on Taiwan.

95. Although both Taipei and Washington now generally agree—after considerable wrangling—on the importance of emphasizing C4ISR, TMD/long-range radar, passive defense, and airborne ASW capabilities, differences reportedly remain over the specific sequencing of developments within and between each area, and the amount of funds devoted to each. Taiwan continues to press for the transfer of more critical military technologies than the United States is willing to provide, partly in an effort to make itself less dependent. However, some observers believe that the United States resists such transfers in order to maximize profits over the long run. Clear differences remain over the strategy for acquiring or producing submarines and their cost. Finally, differences also persist over the level and type of coordination that should exist between U.S. and Taiwan forces.

96. "Pentagon Reviews Taiwan Ties," *Taiwan Defense Review*, January 18, 2003.

97. As one senior defense official stated to the author in summer 2003, "Because of the unpredictability of U.S. arms sales, Taiwan had fallen into a pattern of asking for far more weapons systems than it expected would be approved."

98. These could include the ability to strike Taiwan with a significant number of highly accurate, short-range ballistic and cruise missiles, to severely damage Taiwan's off-shore defenses with a larger number of more capable submarines and surface combatants, to severely disrupt Taiwan's communication capabilities with new space-based and information warfare systems, and perhaps even to seize strategic locations on Taiwan with a significant number of special operation forces.

99. "Pentagon Reviews Taiwan Ties," *Taiwan Defense Review*, January 18, 2003.

100. Many politicians and experts in Taiwan seem to downplay the likelihood of a Chinese attack, even if they acknowledge that China's capabilities are growing at a significant rate. As Chase states (page 183), "Instead, they view the threat from the mainland largely as a political and economic challenge." During interviews with senior ROC officials undertaken by the author in summer 2003, only one official of several questioned stated that Taiwan's defense reform effort is "urgent." Most stated that reforms are important but not urgent, and the single official who stated that they are urgent, explained that this is largely because of U.S. pressure.

101. The C4ISR system eventually decided upon by Taipei is a substantially less ambitious system than the one originally proposed by the U.S. government, based on outside studies. The price of the system was reduced from $3.9 to $1.4 billion and is thus viewed by Washington as significantly underfunded. At such reduced levels, the resulting capabilities will be less than desired or optimal. See "Po Sheng Decision Imminent," *Taiwan Defense Review*, July 17, 2003. Moreover, according to interviewees, there is still some concern in Taiwan that the long-range radars to be purchased from the United States (at nearly $2 billion) will not provide the level of warning desired.

102. For example, some U.S. experts (both in and out of government) apparently seem to be encouraging Taiwan to acquire offensive weaponry capable of carrying out strikes deep into China. Others send conflicting messages about the

likelihood that major weapons systems such as the AEGIS-equipped destroyer will be approved in the future. More broadly, many Taiwan observers voice uncertainty over Washington's "true" stance regarding independence versus reunification. Some observers believe that the Bush administration is opposed to eventual reunification, even if it is achieved peacefully, while others believe that Washington will eventually be disposed to make a "deal" with Beijing that promotes reunification. This uncertainty contributes to confusion regarding U.S. intentions in a military crisis or conflict and hence serves to complicate Taiwan's defense planning effort.

CHAPTER 7. U.S.–TAIWAN SECURITY COOPERATION

1. For an account of U.S.-China relations in the 1970s and 1980s see Robert S. Ross, *Negotiating Cooperation: The United States and China, 1969–1989* (Stanford: Stanford University Press, 1995). Ross demonstrates that Washington and Beijing never "agreed to disagree" on the Taiwan issue in the interests of facilitating cooperation against the Soviet Union. On the contrary, Taiwan was a source of conflict in U.S.-China relations throughout this period.
2. Kurt Campbell and Derek Mitchell, "Crisis in the Taiwan Strait?" *Foreign Affairs* (July/August 2001) 14.
3. David M. Lampton and Richard Daniel Ewing. *U.S. China Relations in a Post-September 11th World* (Washington D.C.: Nixon Center, 2002), 70.
4. For more on recent tensions in relations between the United States and Taiwan, see Michael Swaine, "Trouble in Taiwan," *Foreign Affairs*, March/April 2004; and Susan Lawrence, "U.S.–Taiwan Relations: Headstrong Island," *Far Eastern Economic Review*, March 11, 2004.
5. For an article that presents a variety of views on U.S.–Taiwan security cooperation, see John Pomfret, "In Fact and Tone, U.S. Expresses New Fondness for Taiwan," *Washington Post*, April 30, 2002.
6. For a comprehensive, well-researched history of U.S.–Taiwan relations that draws extensively on declassified official documents, see Nancy Bernkopf Tucker, *Uncertain Friendships: Taiwan, Hong Kong, and the United States, 1945–1992* (New York: Macmillan/Twaine, 1994). For more on the history of U.S.–Taiwan security cooperation from the 1950s to the present, see Denny Roy. *Taiwan: A Political History* (Ithaca: Cornell University Press, 2003), 105–137; and Kenneth W. Allen, "Foreign Military Relations: Taiwan and China Look Abroad," *Issues and Studies* 38 (June 2002): 187–199.
7. U.S. arms sales to Taiwan were halved from nearly $600 million in 1979 to a modest $290 million in 1980, which surely intensified Taipei's concerns.
8. For recollections of key American participants in the negotiations that produced the August 17, 1982 U.S.-China Communiqué, see Nancy Bernkopf Tucker, ed. *China Confidential* (New York: Columbia University Press, 2001), 359–370.

9. Michael D. Swaine, *Taiwan's National Security, Defense Policy, and Weapons Procurement Process* (Santa Monica, CA: RAND, National Defense Research Institute, 1999, MR-1128-OSD).

10. Roy, *Taiwan*, 143–144.

11. James Mann, "Congress and Taiwan: Understanding the Bond," in Ramon H. Myers, Michel C. Oksenberg, and David Shambaugh, eds., *Making China Policy: Lessons from the Bush and Clinton Administrations* (New York: Rowman and Littlefield, 2001), 203–206.

12. Roy, *Taiwan*, 144–146. One particularly damaging incident was the 1984 murder in Daly City, California of Henry Liu, a journalist working on a highly critical biography of Chiang Ching-kuo under the penname Chiang Nan. The killing was traced to senior officials from Taiwan's Military Intelligence Bureau, who had hired members of a criminal organization known as the Bamboo Gang to murder Liu.

13. Tucker, *China Confidential*, 339.

14. Steven M. Goldstein and Randall Schriver, "An Uncertain Relationship: The United States, Taiwan, and the Taiwan Relations Act," in Steven M. Goldstein and Richard Louis Edmonds, eds. *Taiwan in the Twentieth Century: A Retrospective View*, China Quarterly Special Issues Series (Cambridge: Cambridge University, Press, 2001), 162.

15. Pomfret, "In Fact and Tone"; Campbell and Mitchell, "Crisis in the Taiwan Strait?" 22. For another participant's account of the decision to deploy two aircraft carrier battle groups to the Taiwan area during the 1996 missile tests, see Tucker, *China Confidential*, 482–490. At the same time, the Clinton administration also wanted to send a message to Taipei to avoid any unnecessary actions that might provoke Beijing. Two senior U.S. officials were dispatched to New York, where they met with a senior Taiwan national security official, warning him that Taipei did not have a "blank check" from Washington.

16. Goldstein and Schriver, "An Uncertain Relationship," 162.

17. Interview, April 2002.

18. Goldstein and Schriver, "An Uncertain Relationship," 162.

19. Ibid., 166.

20. See, for example, Jim Mann, "U.S. Has Secretly Expanded Military Ties with Taiwan," *Los Angeles Times*, July 24, 1999.

21. U.S. Department of Defense, Executive Summary of Report to Congress on Implementation of the Taiwan Relations Act, December 18, 2000, 2.

22. James Mann, "Congress and Taiwan" 201–219.

23. Interviews, U.S. analysts and former U.S. officials, May 2002.

24. Deputy Secretary of Defense Paul Wolfowitz, Remarks to U.S.–Taiwan Business Council, as delivered, March 11, 2002. The transcript of Wolfowitz's remarks was obtained by a reporter through a Freedom of Information Act request.

25. David Lague, "United States-Taiwan: This Is What It Takes," *Far Eastern Economic Review*, April 25, 2002.

26. On a recent trip to Taiwan, several researchers said reports about the death of "strategic ambiguity" were greatly exaggerated. Indeed, it appears that the enhancement of Washington's declaratory commitment to and substantive cooperation with Taiwan has not allayed the anxieties in Taipei.

27. U.S. Department of Defense, News Transcript, Deputy Secretary Wolfowitz at the Foreign Press Center, Washington, D.C., May 29, 2002.

28. On the influence of domestic politics in the foreign and defense policy decision-making process, see Michael Swaine and James Mulvenon, *Taiwan's Foreign and Defense Policies: Features and Determinants* (Santa Monica, CA: RAND, Center for Asia-Pacific Policy, 2001, MR-1383-SRF), 42–92.

29. Kathrin Hille, "Taiwan Arms Package Faces Further Delays," *Financial Times*, April 30, 2003.

30. Wendell Minnick, "Taiwan Looks for Cheaper Aircraft Deal with US," *Jane's Defence Weekly*, May 21, 2003.

31. "Chen Admits to Weapon-Sale Frictions," *Taipei Times*, February 26, 2003.

32. For the complete text of President Bush's remarks, see "Remarks by President Bush and Premier Wen Jiabao in Photo Opportunity," The White House, Office of the Press Secretary, December 9, 2003, http://www.whitehouse.gov/news/releases/2003/12/20031209–2.html, (accessed April 19, 2004).

33. This section of the report is intended to discuss Taiwan's approach to the arms sales issue and its role in U.S. military exchanges with Taiwan. It is not intended to serve as a comprehensive catalogue of past or pending arms sales or Taiwan's requests for specific weapons systems.

34. Taiwan Relations Act, 1979. The full text of the TRA and the three U.S.-China communiqués can be found in Kerry Dumbaugh, "Texts of the Taiwan Relations Act and the U.S.-China Communiques," Congressional Research Service, CRS Report 96–246 F, March 18, 1996.

35. Goldstein and Schriver, 162. It has been the largest customer for U.S. arms sales in Asia, with its purchases from the U.S. exceeding those of U.S. treaty allies Japan, South Korea, and Australia.

36. Shirley Kan, "Taiwan: Major U.S. Arms Sales Since 1990," Congressional Research Service, CRS Report RL30957, October 31, 2001.

37. For more on Taiwan's defense industries and its reliance on the United States, see Richard A. Bitzinger, "The Eclipse of Taiwan's Defense Industry and Growing Dependencies on the United States for Advanced Armaments," *Issues and Studies* 38 (March 2002): 101–129.

38. Shirley Kan, "Taiwan: Annual Arms Sales Process," Congressional Research Service (CRS), CRS Report RS20365, June 5, 2001, 5.

39. Ibid., 2.

40. Ibid., 2.

41. Ching-Jyuhn Luor, Huei-Huang Wang, and Jun-Hsiu Yeh, "Reinventing National Defense Organization in Taiwan," *Taiwan Defense Affairs* 2 (Autumn 2001): 150.

42. John Pomfret, "Also on Taipei's Radar: Reform," *Washington Post*, April 25, 2001.

43. Interviews, July 2002.

44. Alexander Huang Chieh-cheng,, "Taiwan's View of Military Balance and Challenge it Presents," in James R. Lilley and Chuck Downs, eds., *Crisis in the Taiwan Strait* (Washington, DC: National Defense University, 1997), 290.

45. Goldstein and Schriver, 162.

46. Swaine, *Taiwan's National Security, Defense Policy, and Weapons Procurement Process*, xv. For Lee, Swaine argues, U.S. arms sales to the island were "critical indicators of greater U.S. support for Taiwan." In response to the charge that symbolism trumped substance in Taiwan's arms procurement requests, one Taiwan analyst said, "If we didn't take what we could get then we would have had nothing." In the past, the Taiwan analyst complained, the U.S. effectively dictated Taiwan's military strategy through arms sales.

47. Joe Hung, "KIDD-class Destroyers," NPF Commentary, No. 092–035, National Policy Foundation, Taipei, January 28, 2003. Hung asserts that: "The whole notion of a Taiwan-China military balance, which U.S. arms sales are aimed at keeping, is ludicrous or at least not paramount in the calculations of war risks. A determined China could certainly and easily handle a Taiwan independence movement, if there were no direct American involvement . . . Taiwan continues to buy American armament to convince China that the United States remains faithfully committed to the defense of the island."

48. Goldstein and Schriver, 162.

49. Dana Milbank and Mike Allen, "Bush to Drop Annual Review of Weapons Sales to Taiwan," *Washington Post*, April 25, 2001.

50. Jason Sherman, "U.S. Allows Further Arms Sales to Taiwan," *Defense News*, July 8–14, 2002.

51. Interview, April 2002.

52. See "Taipei Economic and Cultural Representative Office in the United States— Ultra High Frequency Long Range Early Warning Radars," Defense Security Cooperation Agency (DSCA) News Release, Transmittal No. 04–04, March 30, 2004, http://www.dsca.osd.mil/PressReleases/36-b/2004/tecro_04–04b.pdf, (accessed April 19, 2004). The acquisition of the early warning radars, which the United States had identified as a key priority for Taiwan's military modernization program, would enhance the ability of Taiwan's armed forces to detect Chinese missile launches.

53. Shirley Kan, "Taiwan: Major U.S. Arms Sales Since 1990," CRS Report. In 2002, the Taiwan delegation reportedly was led by Vice Foreign Minister Kau Yingmao and Vice Chief of the General Staff Ju Kai-san; other Taiwan participants included officials from the Taiwan NSC, MOFA, and MND. U.S. participants reportedly included Assistant Secretary of Defense for International Security Affairs Peter Rodman and Assistant Secretary of State for East Asian and Pacific Affairs James Kelly. Deborah Kuo, "Taiwan, U.S. Strategic Talks Open in Monterey," *Central News Agency*, July 17, 2002.

54. "Presidential Office, US to boost ties," *Taipei Times*, January 4, 2002.

55. Nadia Tsao, "Vice Minister of Defense to Take Washington Trip," *Taipei Times*, June 21, 2002.

56. Interview, April 2002.

57. The Nuclear Posture Review and the reorganization of combatant commands were cited as examples of the types of issues on which Taiwan would like to have more dialogue with the United States.

58. Among the consequences of economic integration and social interaction, for instance, is the uncertain status of the children of PRC-Taiwan couples. "It is a problem that everyone in Taiwan was aware of a long time ago, but the issue is coming to the fore now because some of these children with one Taiwan and one PRC parent are reaching the age where they would be required to enter into mandatory military service," a Taiwan analyst said. No decision has been reached yet on whether or not their service in the military would represent an unacceptable security risk.

59. Interview, April 2002.

60. Discussions with active and retired high-ranking Taiwan military officers indicate that some in Taiwan are still unsure of U.S. intentions. A senior retired officer said many analysts in Taipei wonder if the current administration in Washington is opposed to eventual unification of China and Taiwan even if it is carried out peacefully. According to another retired military officer, it is very difficult for Taiwan to plan "when it doesn't know what the U.S. really wants to do, especially in the event of a crisis."

61. "Defense Official Leads Arms Group to U.S.," *Taipei Times*, April 18, 2002.

62. Interview, April 2002.

63. Interview, October 2002.

64. A *PLA Daily* article on Taiwan's Hankuang 18 military exercises, for example, asserts that the exercise was completed under the "direct guidance" of a flag-rank U.S. military officer. See Wang Weixing, "What New Tricks are there in the Taiwan Military's New 'Hankuang' 18 Exercise?" *Jiefangjun Bao*, June 5, 2002, in FBIS June 5, 2002.

65. John Pomfret, "China Protests U.S.–Taiwan Ties," *Washington Post*, March 15, 2002; and "Chinese Ambassador Protests U.S. Official Contacts with Taiwan," *China Daily*, March 14, 2002. Chinese officials called in the U.S. Ambassador to make "serious representations," the Chinese Ambassador to the U.S. "lodged a strong protest" in Washington, and the MOFA spokesperson said the visit "would bring about negative effects in Sino-U.S. relations."

66. Interview, July 2002.

67. Nadia Tsao, "Vice minister of defense to take Washington trip," *Taipei Times*, June 21, 2002.

68. Jason Blatt, "Pentagon Opens Door to Taiwan Defense Man," *South China Morning Post*, June 7, 2003.

69. Shirley Kan, "Taiwan: Major U.S. Arms Sales Since 1990," CRS Report.

70. Interview, April 2002.

71. See Neil Lu and David Hsu, "Taiwan Reps Invited to Attend Asia-Pacific Center for Security Studies Course," Central News Agency, May 12, 2002; and

"Courses Could Spur 'Hell of a Fight,'" *Far Eastern Economic Review*, April 18, 2002.

72. Interviews, April 2002.

73. "Taiwan Military Remains Open to Possibility of Joint Exercises with U.S.," *Taiwan Central News Agency*, July 17, 2001.

74. Pomfret, "In Fact and Tone."

75. See Shirley A. Kan, "Taiwan: Major U.S. Arms Sales Since 1990," Congressional Research Service, December 12, 2002.

76. Interview, April 2002.

77. John Pomfret and Philip P. Pan, "U.S. Hits Obstacles in Helping Taiwan Guard Against China," *Washington Post*, October 30, 2003, and Jason Dean and Murray Hiebert, "Taiwan-U.S. Relations: Strains Between Close Friends," *Far Eastern Economic Review*, October 30, 2003.

78. Interviews, Taiwan analysts, May 2002.

79. Interviews, U.S. analysts, May 2002.

80. See Brian Hsu, "Weapons Purchases 'Too Slow,' " *Taipei Times*, February 28, 2003.

81. "China's Military is Stepping Up the Building of Short-range Missiles Opposite Taiwan," *Washington Times*, May 16, 2003.

82. Richard Lawless, DASD, Asian and Pacific Affairs, "Remarks to the U.S.–Taiwan Defense Industry Conference," San Antonio, Texas, February 13, 2003.

83. Murray Hiebert, Greg Jaffe, Jason Dean, and Susan V. Lawrence, "Taiwan Shops for Missiles," *Far Eastern Economic Review*, May 15, 2003.

84. Taijing Wu, "Taiwan Plans to Buy PAC-3 Missile Systems from U.S.," *Taiwan News*, March 4, 2004.

85. Chris Cockel, "U.S. Frustrated by ROC's Military Dithering," *China Post*, January 25, 2003.

86. Lawless, "Remarks to the U.S.–Taiwan Defense Industry Conference."

87. Brian Hsu, "Defense Minister Takes Offense at Reports from US," *Taipei Times*, August 30, 2002.

88. For the Washington's analysis of China's ongoing military modernization, see *Annual Report on the Military Power of the People's Republic of China*, United States Department of Defense, 2003.

89. See, for example, Lawless, "Remarks to U.S.–Taiwan Defense Industry Conference." Lawless warned in his speech that "the PRC's force modernization appears to be outpacing Taiwan's."

90. Peter Brookes, "The Challenges and Imperatives in Taiwan's Defense," Heritage Lectures, No. 775, The Heritage Foundation, January 9, 2003. Brookes argues that the PLA is acquiring the capabilities to act decisively before U.S. forces can intervene in a conflict and that China would "make every effort to deter, delay, and deny U.S. intervention and military operations" if it decided to use force against Taiwan.

91. Lawless, "Remarks to U.S.–Taiwan Defense Industry Conference."

92. See Ministry of National Defense, ROC, *Defense Report of the Republic of China, 2002* (Taipei, Taiwan), especially Part 1, Chapter 4, "Military Situation in the PRC." In particular, the report assesses that China's military modernization has enhanced the capabilities of the PLAN and PLAAF, improved the PLA's force projection capabilities, and increased the quantity and quality of ballistic missiles that could strike Taiwan. The report estimates that by 2005 the PLA will deploy some 600 missiles capable of hitting targets on the island, and that the mobility, survivability, precision, lethality, and rapid response capability of the Second Artillery's missile forces are increasing. The report also notes that the PLA has dramatically improved its equipment, both through indigenous development and arms purchases, principally from Russia. China's acquisition of Su-27 and Su-30 fighters and Sovremenny-class destroyers from Russia is depicted as "especially alerting." In addition, the report mentions the PLA's improved training, rapidly developing C4ISR capabilities, and increasing focus on joint operations, which it describes as "another increasing threat that the ROC cannot ignore." The report also echoes the U.S. assessment that Chinese military modernization is focused squarely on developing credible military options to threaten or actually use force in a Taiwan scenario, and to diminish or prevent U.S. intervention in the event of a conflict in the Taiwan Strait.

93. Denny Roy, "Taiwan's Threat Perceptions: The Enemy Within," Honolulu, Hawaii: Asia-Pacific Center for Security Studies, March 2003, 1.

94. Deputy Minister Lin is quoted in Benjamin Kang Lim, "Taiwan Sees Military Balance Tipping to China by Next Year," *Reuters*, January 11, 2003. "The simple fact of a crossover is insufficient to make the leaders in Beijing feel 100 percent confident in winning a war," Lin said. Instead, Lin argued, the years "2010 to 2015 will be when the PLA will have such a supremacy in both qualitative and quantitative comparison of forces that it may feel confident to move."

95. The paradox is that Taiwan's democratization makes it more difficult for the U.S. to deal with Taiwan on security issues, yet it is Taiwan's democratization that has strengthened U.S. concerns about the island's security. The author would like to thank James Mulvenon for raising this point.

96. There have been hints that some Chinese strategists also recognize the problems of escalation control and conflict termination that would likely arise in the event of a serious crisis over the Taiwan issue. See, for instance, Sun Jilian and Wei Wei, "Escalating U.S.–Taiwan Military Cooperation Damages Asia-Pacific Peace and Stability: National Defense University Experts and Scholars Discuss Danger of Strengthened US-Taiwan Military Cooperation," *Jiefangjun Bao*, May 20, 2002, FBIS, May 21, 2002. According to Sun and Wei, "If the United States confronts China over the Taiwan problem, it will be very difficult to find a point of balance between interests, risks, and price."

97. Cultivating a cadre of civilians with the competence to control the military and participate in defense policy debates is critical to the success of the defense reforms. Washington should assist Taipei in developing training and education programs for civilian defense researchers.

CHAPTER 8. STRATEGIC AMBIGUITY

1. For an in-depth discussion of the Truman administration's decisionmaking on the China issue see Nancy Bernkopf Tucker. *Patterns in the Dust: Chinese-American Relations and the Recognition Controversy, 1949–1950* (New York: Columbia University Press, 1983) and David Finkelstein. *Washington's Taiwan Dilemma, 1949–1950* (Fairfax, VA: George Mason University Press, 1993).

2. 794A.5/1653 #848 Dulles to Rankin, April 17, 1953, U.S. Department of State. *Foreign Relations of the United States, 1952–54*, vol 14: *China and Japan* (Washington DC: Government Printing Office, 1985), pt I, 191 (hereafter FRUS) ; 794A.5/4–2353 #1118 Jones, Chargé in the Republic of China to Department of State, April 23, 1953, *ibid.*, 193.

3. John W. Garver. *The Sino-American Alliance* (Armonk, NY: M.E. Sharpe, 1997), 59. Text of the treaty in Stephen P. Gibert and William M. Carpenter, *America and Island China* (Lanham, MD: University Press of America, 1989), 124–25.

4. Memorandum of Conversation between Yeh, Ambassador Wellington Koo, and Walter Robertson, November 4, 1954, Box 192, Papers of V.K. Wellington Koo, Columbia University, New York, NY.

5. Memorandum of Conversation, January 28, 1955, Dulles with Yeh, Koo, Robertson and McConaughy, FRUS 1955–57, vol. 2: China (Washington DC: Government Printing Office, 1986), 156–57.

6. Memorandum of Conversation, January 30, 1955, ibid., 175.

7. Gordon H. Chang and He Di, "The Absence of War in the U.S.-China Confrontation over Quemoy and Matsu in 1954–1955: Contingency, Luck or Deterrence?" *American Historical Review* 98 (December 1993): 1511. Chang and He argue that ambiguity was the wrong policy in 1954–55 because it encouraged Mao Zedong to act more aggressively than he would have otherwise.

8. Memorandum of Discussion, 232nd Meeting NSC, January 20, 1955, FRUS 1955–57, 2: 71.

9. Robert Accinelli. *United States Policy toward Taiwan, 1950–1955* (Chapel Hill: University of North Carolina Press, 1996), 190–191. Eisenhower did so to placate the British.

10. Fred I. Greenstein. *The Hidden-Hand Presidency* (New York: Basic Books, 1982), 68–69.

11. Accinelli, *United States Policy toward Taiwan, 1950–1955*,191–92.

12. Drumright noted in reporting on his farewell call on the Generalissimo "it is utterly clear that Chiang is bent on taking some kind of action this year." 793.00/3–662 # 615 Drumright, Taipei, FRUS 1961–63, 22: *Northeast Asia* (Washington DC: Government Printing Office, 1996), 190. Ralph Clough reported that the GIMO was "deadly serious" and views the "conjunction of circumstances . . . as unique." 793.00/3–3062 #658 Clough, Taipei, FRUS 1961–63, 22: 202. See also Ray S. Cline, *Chiang Ching-kuo Remembered* (Washington, DC: United States Global Strategy Council, 1989), 50–51.

13. Hilsman to Harriman, June 21, 1962, FRUS 1961–63, 22: 260–63.

14. 793.00/7–462 #16 Kirk, Taipei, and 611.93/7–562 #22 Kirk, Taipei, FRUS 1961–63, 22: 285–89 (quote at 288). On Kennedy's policies in 1961 and 1962 see Noam Kochavi. *A Conflict Perpetuated* (Westport, CT: Praeger, 2002).

15. Memcon Kissinger with Zhou, July 9, 1971, 4:35–11:20 PM, with Lord cover memo July 29, 1971, NSC, Box 1033, China HAK Memcons July 1971, Nixon Presidential Materials Project, National Archives, College Park, Maryland (hereafter Nixon materials); Richard H. Solomon, *CIA Chronology, 1971–1985* (Santa Monica, CA: RAND, 1985, R-3299), 14; John H. Holdridge, *Crossing the Divide* (New York: Rowman & Littlefield, 1997), 46. Kissinger's inaccurate version is to be found in Henry Kissinger, *White House Years* (Boston: Little, Brown, 1979), 749.

16. Memcon Kissinger with Zhou, July 9, 1971, and Memcon Kissinger with Zhou, July 10, 1971, Nixon Materials.

17. Memcon Kissinger with Zhou, July 9, 1971, p. 13, Nixon Materials.

18. #180639 Kissinger, July 21, 1976, Box 377: Control List of China Material to Mr. Eagleburger 1976 thru China Sensitive Chron July 1–September 30, 1976, F: WL China Sensitive Chron July 1-September 30, 1976, SPC/SP Director's Files (Winston Lord) 1969–77, RG 59, NARA; "Peking's Hard Line on Taiwan," INR Harold H. Saunders to Kissinger, October 4, 1976, ibid., F: China Sensitive Chron October 1–December 31, 1976.

19. Gibert and Carpenter, *America and Island China*, 222–29, text of the Taiwan Relations Act (quotes from 223).

20. Harvey Feldman, "Taiwan, Arms Sales, and the Reagan Assurances," *American Asian Review* 19 (Fall 2001): 87–88. Elsewhere, Feldman concluded that the nonpaper had been the work of Gaston Sigur. He learned of its existence, not from U.S. archives where it remains classified, but from Fred Chien who rendered it into English for him from a Chinese version of the original.

21. Useful analyses of the crisis include John W. Garver. *Face Off* (Seattle: University of Washington Press, 1997); Robert Ross, "The 1995–96 Taiwan Strait Confrontation: Coercion, Credibility, and the Use of Force, *International Security* 25 (Fall 2000): 87–123. Robert Suettinger, who was at the time at the NSC, discusses it at some length in his thoughtful book. *Beyond Tiananmen* (Washington, D.C.: Brookings Institution Press, 2003), 200–263.

22. Alan D. Romberg. *Rein In at the Brink of the Precipice* (Washington, DC: Henry L. Stimson Center, 2003), 173.

23. "China sounds out U.S. reaction to Taiwan crisis," Kyodo News Service (Japan), December 13, 1995, online. Nye described the event in a speech to the Asia Society in Washington, D.C. Suettinger wrote that the Chinese "predisposed as they were to a view that the United States was a declining superpower, unwilling to engage in combat that might entail heavy casualties," believed that Nye was signaling "weakness or indecision." Suettinger, *Beyond Tiananmen*, 244.

24. Steven Erlanger, "'Ambiguity' On Taiwan," *New York Times* (March 12, 1996), A1.

25. Garver, *Face Off*, 103.

26. Nancy Bernkopf Tucker, ed., *China Confidential* (New York: Columbia University Press, 2001), 490.

27. Suettinger, *Beyond Tiananmen*, 259.

28. James Shinn, senior fellow for Asia at the Council on Foreign Relations condemned Clinton for shattering 20 years of ambiguity in "Clinton's Gunboat Diplomacy," *New York Times* (March 24, 1996), A15.

29. "Baker supports US policy of strategic ambiguity on Taiwan," *The Straits Times*, April 19, 1996.

30. Winston Lord, Assistant Secretary of State for East Asian and Pacific Affairs, Testimony in Hearing "The U.S. China and Taiwan: American Policy in a Zone of Crisis," March 25, 1996, Federal News Service, Federal Information Systems Corporation online (accessed June 2003).

31. Nancy Bernkopf Tucker. *Security Challenges for the United States, China and Taiwan At the Dawn of the New Millennium* (Alexandria, VA: Project Asia, CNA Corporation, 2000), 17–18; Michael J. Green and Benjamin L. Self, "Japan's Changing China Policy: From Commercial Liberalism to Reluctant Realism," *Survival* 38 (Summer 1996): 34–58. Ben Self has argued elsewhere that the United States and Japan must "proceed with difficult discussions on military responses to a Taiwan contingency. Ambiguity regarding the ability of the Alliance to respond—because of a lack of coordination or lack of political will in Tokyo—will only destabilize the situation." Benjamin L. Self, "An Alliance for Engagement: Rationale and Modality," in Benjamin L. Self and Jeffrey W. Thompson, eds. *An Alliance for Engagement: Building Cooperation in Security Relations with China* (Washington, D.C.: Henry L. Stimson Center, 2002), 157.

32. "Dole's Views on U.S. Asia Policy: Lost Credibility and Weak Leadership," *New York Times* (May 10, 1996), A8.

33. Parris H. Chang, "Lessons from the Taiwan Strait Crisis of 1996," American Chamber of Commerce *Topics: The Magazine of International Business in Taiwan* (August 1996), 46.

34. Barton Gelman, "Reappraisal Led to New China Policy," *Washington Post*, June 22, 1998, p. A16; Matt Forney and Nigel Holloway, "Sunny Side Up," *Far Eastern Economic Review*, July 25, 1996, pp. 14–15.

35. Lake repeated the observation twice and made certain I had written it down. Interview with the author, October 27, 1999.

36. Garver, *Face Off*, 79. Suettinger asserted that there is no proof that this was the wording, although he also provided no absolute assurance that it was not even though he was at the NSC at the time. In either case, he argued that the Chinese ignored nuanced prose and exaggerated the U.S. position. Suettinger, *Beyond Tiananmen*, 232.

37. The most often quoted was Joseph Nye, "A Taiwan Deal," *Washington Post* (March 8, 1998), C7. Others suggested similar approaches including Kenneth Lieberthal, who subsequently joined the staff of the National Security Council and Chas W. Freeman, Jr., "Preventing War in the Taiwan Strait: Restraining Taiwan—and Beijing," *Foreign Affairs* (Fall 1998): 6–11.

38. Nathan, "What's Wrong with American Taiwan Policy," *The Washington Quarterly* (Spring 2000), 97–98.

39. Interviews with high level officials and former officials in Taipei, Taiwan, 2000.

40. Philip Y.M. Yang, "From Strategic Ambiguity to Three Noes: The Changing Nature of the U.S. Policy Toward Taiwan," Conference on "U.S. and Its Allies" Tel Aviv, Israel, November 9–11, 1998, online at Taiwan Security Research.

41. Clinton's remarks were part of a speech on economic issues at the University of Pennsylvania. Charles Babington, "Clinton Urges Trade, Shrinking U.S. Debt," *Washington Post* (February 25, 2000), A4. My interpretation on the issue of democracy departs here from that of Alan D. Romberg in his essay, " 'China's Sacred Territory, Taiwan Island': Some Thoughts on American Policy," Occasional Paper #44, Henry L. Stimson Center, online (accessed June 2003). Previously peaceful unification could occur with the agreement just of an authoritarian leadership, but under conditions prevailing in Taiwan in the 1990s and after, the people must have a voice in the decision about Taiwan's future.

42. Robert Torricelli, Senate testimony on "Elections in Taiwan," S 1280, 106th Congress, 2nd Session, *Congressional Record*, 146, No. 25 (March 8, 2000), online at http://web.lexis-nexis.com/congcomp/document (accessed August 2003).

43. Greg Torode, "First steps on a long diplomatic journey," *South China Morning Post* (Hong Kong), October 28, 1999, 21.

44. Kurt M. Campbell and Derek J. Mitchell, "Crisis in the Taiwan Strait?" *Foreign Affairs* 80 (July/August 2001) 22.

45. Jonathan S. Landay, "How far would US go to protect Taiwan?" *Christian Science Monitor* (September 3, 1999), 3. Armitage, nevertheless, spoke positively about strategic ambiguity when he said to the press, "On the question of the use of force, anyone sitting in the presidency is going to have to make the decision at the time," he said. "It's very bad business to answer hypothetical questions on force when you may be there to do it.' Jane Perlez, "Bush Carries Some Baggage In Developing China Stance," *New York Times* (August 29, 1999), A15.

46. Paul Wolfowitz, "Remembering the Future," *The National Interest* (Spring 2000): 45.

47. David Postman and Catherine Tarpley, "Bush at Boeing, backs China trade," *Seattle Times* (May 18, 2000), A1; Charles Babington and Dana Milbank, "Bush Advisers Try to Limit Damage," *Washington Post* (April 27, 2001), A19.

48. Brian Knowlton, "Analysts See Comments as a Toughening of American Position," *International Herald Tribune*, April 25, 2001. On April 23, 2001 the administration announced the largest arms sales package for Taiwan following the 1992 sale of F-16 aircraft, including four Kidd-class destroyers, a dozen P-3 Orion anti-submarine aircraft, torpedoes, minesweeping helicopters and amphibious assault vehicles. The most controversial item on the list was eight diesel submarines.

49. Transcript of CNN Larry King Live, "Dick Cheney Discusses the Beginning of the Bush Administration," April 27, 2001, online.

50. Nuclear Posture Review, 16, Submitted to Congress on December 31, 2001, online at http://www.globalsecurity.org/wmd/library/policy/dod/npr.htm, (accessed July 2003).

51. The National Security Strategy of the United States of America, September 2002, online at http://www.whitehouse.gov/nsc/nss.html, (accessed July 2003).

52. Alan D. Romberg, "Origins of the American Role in Taiwan," Henry L. Stimson Center, online, (accessed June 2003), 10–11; Jay Chen and Sofia Wu, "U.S. Committed to Helping Taiwan Defend Itself" Central News Agency—Taiwan, April 09, 2002, online, (accessed June 2003).

53. John Pomfret, "Taiwanese Leader Condemns Beijing, 'One China' Policy," *Washington Post*, October 7, 2003, A18; Edwin Chen, "Talks Yield a U.S. Warning to Taiwan and Pledge by China to Ease Trade Gap," *Los Angeles Times*, December 10, 2003, lexis-nexis, (accessed April 11, 2004).

54. Bonnie S. Glaser, "Washington's Hands-On Approach to Managing Cross-Strait Tension," PacNet #21, May 13, 2004, CSIS Pacific Forum.

55. Taiwan Affairs Office and the Information Office of the State Council, PRC "The One-China Principle and the Taiwan Issue," February 21, 2000, online at http://english.peopledaily.com.cn/features/taiwanpaper/Taiwan.html, (accessed July 2003).

56. The only way to limit this testing would be so to restrict clarifying redlines as to make new policies almost the same as existing policy. This is the fundamental problem with arguments such as that advanced in John R. Carter (LTC, USAF), Peter A. Costello (LTC, USAF), William D. Kendrick (LTC, USA) and Dana J. H. Pittard (LTC, USA), "Implications of the U.S. War on Terrorism for U.S.-China Policy: A Strategic Window," Policy Analysis Paper Series, National Security Program, John F. Kennedy School of Government, Harvard University, 2002.

57. Thomas J. Christensen makes the compelling argument that "China can pose major problems for American security interests, and especially for Taiwan, without the slightest pretense of catching up with the United States by an overall measure of national military power or technology." "Posing Problems without Catching Up," *International Security* 25 (Spring 2001): 7.

58. Robert Kagan, "At Last, Straight Talk on China," *Washington Post* (April 29, 2001).

59. James Mann. *About Face* (New York: Alfred A. Knopf, 1999), 282–314.

60. The argument in this paragraph comes from the remarks made by Dr. David Finkelstein, Lieutenant Colonel, Ret. of the CNA Corporation delivered at a workshop organized by this author "Tempting Fate: US-Taiwan-China Relations," August 20, 2003, Washington, DC.

61. Public Law 96–8, April 10, 1979, 96th Congress.

62. To Pan Zhongqi, a researcher from the Shanghai Institute for International Studies, not surprisingly, the answer is U.S. advocacy of peaceful unification. Pan Zhongqi, "US Taiwan Policy of Strategic Ambiguity: a dilemma of deterrence," *Journal of Contemporary China* 12 (May 2003): 402–407.

63. Romberg, "Origins of the American Role in Taiwan," 13. Natale Bellocchi the former chairman of the American Institute in Taiwan included the suggestion in remarks to the U.S. congressional Taiwan Caucus in Washington and in a column entitled "Toward Better US-Taiwan Relations," in the *Taipei Times*, April 17, 2002, 8.

64. Nancy Bernkopf Tucker, "If Taiwan Chooses Unification, Should the United States Care?" *The Washington Quarterly* (Summer 2002): 15–28.

65. An excellent summary of the development of these policies is in Harry Harding, "'One China' or 'One Option': The Contending Formulas for Relations Across the Taiwan Strait," *Notes from The National Committee on United States-China Relations* 29 (Fall/Winter 2000): 8–11. See also Su Chi and Cheng An-kuo, eds., *One China, with Respective Interpretations: A Historical Account* (Taipei: National Policy Foundation, 2002).

66. Major think tanks, however, have affirmed their support for strategic ambiguity, see Report of the Asia Foundation Commissioned Task Force. *America's Role in Asia: American Views*, 2001, 29; Council on Foreign Relations, Independent Task Force Report, *Chinese Military Power*, 2003.

Index